# Egyptian Mythology

## A to Z

THIRD EDITION

# MYTHOLOGY A TO Z

African Mythology A to Z

Celtic Mythology A to Z

Chinese Mythology A to Z

Egyptian Mythology A to Z

Greek and Roman Mythology A to Z

Japanese Mythology A to Z

Native American Mythology A to Z

Norse Mythology A to Z

South and Meso-American Mythology A to Z

# Egyptian Mythology
## A to Z

### THIRD EDITION

## Pat Remler

CHELSEA HOUSE
PUBLISHERS
An imprint of Infobase Publishing

Egyptian Mythology A to Z, Third Edition

Copyright © 2000, 2006, 2010 by Pat Remler

Grateful acknowledgment is made for permission to reprint charts of the classical Egyptian alphabet and the first month of Akhet from *Ancient Egyptian Magic* by Bob Brier. Copyright © 1980 by Bob Brier. Reprinted by permission of William Morrow & Co., Inc.

Chelsea House
An imprint of Infobase Publishing
132 West 31st Street
New York NY 10001

**Library of Congress Cataloging-in-Publication Data**
Remler, Pat.
Egyptian mythology A to Z / Pat Remler.—3rd ed.
p. cm.
Includes bibliographical references and index.
ISBN 978-1-60413-926-6 (hc : alk. paper)
1. Mythology, Egyptian—Dictionaries, Juvenile. I. Title.

BL2441.3.R37 2010
299'.3113—dc22        2009037735

Chelsea House books are available at special discounts when purchased in bulk quantities for businesses, associations, institutions or sales promotions. Please call our Special Sales Department in New York at (212) 967-8800 or (800) 322-8755.

You can find Chelsea House on the World Wide Web at http://www.chelseahouse.com

Text design by Lina Farinella
Map by Patricia Meschino
Composition by Mary Susan Ryan-Flynn
Cover printed by Yurchak Printing, Landisville, Pa.
Book printed and bound by Yurchak Printing, Landisville, Pa.

Printed in the United States of America

This book is printed on acid-free paper and contains
30 percent postconsumer recycled content.

# CONTENTS

# ACKNOWLEDGMENTS

There are many people I would like to thank for helping in producing this book. David Moyer served as my unofficial editor, standardizing spelling, catching errors, and always giving helpful suggestions. Dick Hall helped with crucial bits of research whenever needed.

With respect to illustrations, I am especially happy to have been able to work with my sister, Mary Jordan, who provided all of the line drawings in this book. Ian Brier's computer skills were especially welcome when it came to preparing the illustrations.

Special thanks go to my husband, Bob Brier, whose constant encouragement and excellent suggestions saw me through the completion of this manuscript.

# INTRODUCTION

## EGYPTIAN MYTHOLOGY

The history of ancient Egypt is a vast and captivating story. From our biblical fore-fathers to modern scholars, many people have been fascinated by the mythology and religion of Egypt. This third edition of *Egyptian Mythology A to Z* is designed to help the reader enter the fascinating world of ancient Egypt. The most important feature of this new edition is the completely revised art program, including for the first time many full-color images.

As Egypt's civilization arose along the banks of the Nile, a rich mythology was born, emerging from the fables and beliefs of the first Egyptians. More than any other ancient culture, the Egyptians were fascinated by the mystery of death, and they put as much effort into creating a "good life" in the next world as they did in this world. The gods of ancient Egypt were complex deities who merged and evolved during Egypt's long history. Even those gods and goddesses with distinct identities were often combined into one, sharing attributes, signs, and duties. We find the mythology of ancient Egypt filled with inconsistencies, a situation that never seemed to bother the Egyptians. The ancient Egyptians were, except for a brief moment in their history, polytheists, believing in many gods, and when a new god emerged and rose to prominence, it was willingly accepted.

## EGYPT: A BRIEF HISTORY

We know very little about the earliest inhabitants of the Nile Valley because no human remains have been found from this period. We do know that the area was first inhabited around 700,000 B.C. by settlers whose only tool was the hand ax. This marked the beginning of the Paleolithic era, or Old Stone Age. By modern standards the rate of change was slow. When we consider the technological advances of the last hundred years, it is almost inconceivable to think that in the first 650,000 years of Egyptian culture, the only improvement was a better ax. When the Egyptians developed additional tools during the Middle Paleolithic period, the climate must have been more temperate, with much more rain, for we know the Egyptians did not live in the desert, and today that is where these stone tools are found. Neanderthals lived during this time—practicing simple surgery, caring for the injured and old, and burying the dead with rituals.

Around 30,000 B.C., the Late Paleolithic period, *Homo sapiens*, modern humans, replaced the Neanderthals (*Homo neanderthalensis*). The level of the Nile began to decline, and the people lived in or near the swampy areas along the banks of the river. They lived on mollusks and fish, cooked on clay hearths, and fashioned grindstones on which they prepared wild cereal grains. Some time around 15,000 B.C. these early inhabitants began hunting with bows and arrows. When the Nile reached its lowest level between 10,000 and 5,000 B.C. and much of the land had turned to desert, survival was difficult. At this time *Homo sapiens* probably numbered no more than a few thousand. Luckily, at about the same time the Nile was low, a freshwater lake appeared in the Fayoum area (southwest of Cairo), and settlements grew up along its shores. Pottery was developed, and the Egyptians began farming and raising cattle. The history of Egypt is so closely associated with the Nile that to understand the civilization, one must understand something about the river.

The Nile is the longest river in the world. Its main branch, called the White Nile, flows north from Lake Victoria in east-central Africa 3,470 miles to the Mediterranean Sea on Egypt's northern border. Starting in Ethiopia, another river, called the Blue Nile, joins the White Nile at Khartoum, Sudan, where the rivers merge and flow into Egypt.

It was the Blue Nile, swollen by spring monsoons and the runoff of melting snow in Ethiopia, that caused the river to rise. Each year the Nile overflowed its banks, depositing fresh, rich topsoil on the flat plains that spread to either side of the river and enabling Egypt to grow an abundance of crops. Other ancient civilizations had to rely on their unpredictable rainfall to water crops, and often there was too much or too little. Egypt's great fortune was to have a river that renewed the topsoil annually and flowed in sufficient volume to water the fields. Every year Egypt harvested a variety of crops, while other countries thanked their gods when they produced only one. No wonder the ancient Greek traveler Herodotus called Egypt "the gift of the Nile."

The annual inundation amazed the Egyptians, who had no explanation for the river's sudden great swelling, nor the change in its color from red to green. At first the silt suspended in the water caused the Nile to look red, and then the slow moving vegetation floating on top made it look green. It was a natural occurrence, of course, but the Egyptians viewed it as the work of the gods, and they noticed that a certain star (Sothis) rose on the horizon just before the inundation began. The annual spectacle of the rising Nile was surpassed only by the daily performance of the dazzling sun. Each day it rose in the east, traveled across a cloudless, jewel-like sky, and descended into a fireball of colors over the western horizon, as constant and predictable as the Nile. The sun god Re was one of Egypt's most ancient deities.

The Nile was the heart and life of the country, and although Egypt was vast, most of the population lived near the banks of the river. Their lives revolved around the Nile, and the seasons of the year were determined by it. Our 365-day calendar comes from the Egyptians, but they counted only three seasons: 1) *inundation,* when the Nile overflowed its banks and flooded the land; 2) *emergence,* when the waters receded; 3) *summer,* the dry season. Each season had four months of 30 days each. At the end of the year, five extra days, the "epigominal days," were added to make 365 days in the year. These days later became known as the birthdays of the goddess Isis and her siblings. Inundation was Egypt's most unusual season, for it changed the look of the land. It was a time when the fields were under water and little work could be done. Emergence was the season for planting, and the crops were harvested in summer.

The food staples of the Egyptians were bread and beer, a phrase that became synonymous with "food"—similar to our "meat and potatoes." A common funerary prayer begins, "May the king make an offering to Osiris, Lord of the West. May he give bread and beer, cattle, geese, oxen, and all things good and pure on which the gods live." The long growing season allowed the Egyptians to grow a variety of crops, the most important being *emer* (wheat) and onions. Meat was reserved for the upper classes, but everyone had bread, beer, and onions as well as fish from the Nile.

Year after year the Nile rose, the crops were abundant, and the Egyptians believed that this was the way their world was supposed to be. This idea was expressed in the notion of "divine order," the way the gods wanted things to be. This belief was encouraged by Egypt's geographical isolation from its neighbors. To the west are endless miles of desert between Egypt and the Libyan border, to the east a hundred miles of desert and the Red Sea. In the south there were huge boulders in the river, called cataracts, that were all but impassable. The Mediterranean Sea formed a natural border to the north, more of a psychological barrier than a real one. The Egyptians never really developed their sailing skills or ventured out into the open sea if they could avoid it. Their navigational skills developed on the smooth-flowing Nile, where they could sail south with the prevailing wind and north with the current. In later centuries military expeditions took Egyptians to other lands and they returned with great riches, but it was always clear to them that their homeland was a paradise on Earth.

Soon after recorded history began, when the Egyptians began to write in a script called hieroglyphs, their burials became more elaborate. At first the dead were buried in shallow pit graves in the desert, and the hot, dry sand preserved the bodies naturally. But as their mythology and religion continued to develop and become more elaborate, so did their burials. To prevent wild animals from digging up the burials, shallow pit graves were replaced with brick-lined tombs; bodies were covered with animal skins and placed on woven mats. The brick structures became more elaborate and varied with the status of the deceased. Because these bodies were now in tombs, far removed from the natural drying process of the hot sand, they began to rot and decay. While the natural preservation of the hot sand in the desert may have spawned the idea of mummification, Egyptian religion required it, so burials in these tombs forced the Egyptians to devise a means of preserving the dead.

Central to the religious beliefs of the ancient Egyptians was the myth of Isis and Osiris, in which Isis's husband, Osiris, is killed by their evil brother Set, who tricks Osiris into climbing into a box. Osiris is sealed in the box and dies when it is thrown into the Nile. Isis, the bereaved wife, searches for and finds the body of her dead husband and is determined to give him a proper burial on Egyptian soil. It is from this myth that the crucial elements of Egyptian funerary practices derived. Like all myths, this one revealed important truths about nature, the universe, and life after death, and many beliefs of the ancient Egyptian funerary cult can be derived from it. The chest that exactly fit Osiris was the precursor of the anthropoid coffin, which is shaped like the deceased and is intended to protect the body. The importance of a proper burial on Egyptian soil is emphasized by the efforts that Isis made to find the body of her husband, and to make sure that it was complete, so that when she spoke her magic words, Osiris would resurrect in the Netherworld. He kept the same body after death that he had during life, so mummification was essential if the deceased was to resurrect and spend eternity in the Netherworld. Here we see a myth answering important questions about life after death.

Mythology, religion, and to some extent philosophy went hand in hand in the ancient world, but the Egyptians did not make a clear distinction between them. All three kinds of thinking try to answer questions about the universe, the nature of humans, and life after death. Mythology answers these questions with stories about the lives of the gods that are not meant to be taken literally. Myths take place in what is sometimes called "primordial time," the time before time began, before calendars and clocks existed.

Religion, on the other hand, answers the same kinds of questions but takes place in chronological time. The biblical story of Moses and the Exodus, for example, presents Moses as a historical character who actually lived on Earth at a particular time.

Philosophy, like religion and mythology, also attempts to answer questions about the nature of the universe, but unlike religion, which requires only faith, or mythology, which is not to be taken literally, philosophy requires proof. We know the ancient Egyptians had a rich mythology and a complex religion, but there is debate about whether they engaged in philosophical thinking. There are no philosophical papyri and no texts carved on temple walls that present carefully reasoned philosophical arguments. Of the three kinds of thinking that deal with basic questions about humans and the universe, this book is about mythology. As you will see, there is an overlapping between religion and mythology because mythology inevitably deals with the gods.

The reader shouldn't be surprised to read different myths giving different answers to the same questions. In Heliopolis, for example, the priests told one story of how the world was created, and in Memphis they told quite a different story. These myths sometimes competed, but the people didn't believe both versions: They tended to believe the version from their hometown.

## SOURCES OF EGYPTIAN MYTHOLOGY

We know about mythology from several ancient sources. Many papyri still exist, and the mythological texts tell the stories of the gods, such as The Contendings of Horus and Set, a classic struggle between good and evil.

From tomb walls we find instructions to help the deceased survive the dangerous journey to the next world. There were several "books" of instructions, all derived from the Book of the Dead, intended to help the deceased reach the next world and resurrection. Each of the "books" have somewhat different expectations of what the next life will bring. In the Book of Gates, the followers of Osiris believe he is the supreme god, and his judgment determines if a soul will go out of existence or will be allowed to resurrect.

Temple walls tell us about the function of the gods and how they interacted with humans. Sometimes the source is smaller than a tomb or temple. The Metternich Stele, for example, a round-topped, flat carved stone, tells the story of the suffering of Isis when her son, the infant Horus, is stung by a scorpion.

Later Greek writers are important sources of Egyptian mythology. The Greeks were always fascinated with Egypt, and many Greek writers were proud to trace their heritage to the ancient Egyptian culture. Herodotus, who lived in the fifth century B.C., wrote extensively about the Egyptians in his work, *The Histories.* Plutarch has left us the most complete story of the Myth of Isis and Osiris in his work *De Iside et Osiride.*

## HOW TO PRONOUNCE THE NAMES OF THE GODS

Unfortunately, there is no standard way to write or pronounce ancient Egyptian names. Sometimes the pharaoh who built the Great Pyramid will be called "Khufu," the Egyptian name as transliterated from hieroglyphs. At other times he is called "Cheops," which is what the Greeks called him. Even Egyptologists don't agree on how to pronounce the names of some of the kings. For example, some call the Middle Kingdom pharaoh "Senwsret" (the ancient Egyptian word), while others call the same king "Sesostris" (the Greek version of his name).

The same problem exists with the names of the gods. The ancient Egyptians called their god of the dead "Osir." The Greeks added the "is" ending, and the name became Osiris, the name we use today. But the difficulty occurs not simply in the choice between Egyptian or Greek pronunciations. It also arises from the ambiguities in the way the Egyptians wrote their language. Many of their hieroglyphs are phonetic—representing sounds—just like our alphabet. The Egyptians didn't write most of the vowels, however, so it is not clear how to pronounce words and names. It would be as if we wrote a word "nt"—do we mean "net," "not," "nut," or "nit"? Another difficulty in figuring out how to pronounce the names of the gods is that ancient Egyptian was a "dead language" for 1,500 years—no one spoke the language, so we have to reconstruct how it might have sounded.

Before the hieroglyphic code was cracked in 1822, scholars debated the meaning of inscriptions on temple walls and papyri. Many of their speculations were based upon the belief that the inscriptions were mystical or magical in nature, and they were not far wrong. When the Greeks first came to Egypt, they called the writings hieroglyphs, or "sacred carvings," since only the priests could read them. When the last priest who could read hieroglyphs died, so did the language. Numerous attempts were made to decipher hieroglyphs, but they all failed because it was believed that hieroglyphs were based on picture writing—that, for example, a picture of a foot meant foot or that a duck meant that the text was talking about a duck. Medieval scholars continued the tradition. It wasn't until the 18th century that modern linguists began to suggest hieroglyphs were not just pictograms but also represented phonetic sounds.

When Napoleon Bonaparte invaded Egypt in 1798, he took a group of scientists, called the savants, with him to study the country. The most significant discovery was the Rosetta stone, which was covered with writing in three different scripts: Greek, and two Egyptian scripts, hieroglyphs and demotic, a cursive form of hieroglyphs. It was this discovery that led to the deciphering of hieroglyphs by the French linguist Jean-François Champollion.

Because the ancient Egyptians did not write their vowels, our estimate of the pronunciation of the ancient Egyptian language is far from certain. When the Greek version of an ancient Egyptian name is more common, we have used that. Sometimes when both the Egyptian and Greek versions are in use, we mention both. Cross-references to other entries are printed in SMALL CAPITAL LETTERS.

# TIMELINE FOR ANCIENT EGYPT

| | |
|---|---|
| PREDYNASTIC | 5500–3100 B.C. |
| EARLY DYNASTIC PERIOD | 3100–2686 B.C. |
| Dynasties 1, 2 | 3050–2686 B.C. |
| Narmer and unification of Egypt | 3100 B.C. |
| OLD KINGDOM | 2686–2181 B.C. |
| Zoser builds Step Pyramid | 2686–2647 B.C. |
| Sneferu builds first true pyramid | 2613–2589 B.C. |
| Khufu builds the Great Pyramid | 2589–2566 B.C. |
| Pyramid Texts | c. 2345 B.C. |
| FIRST INTERMEDIATE PERIOD | 2181–2055 B.C. |
| MIDDLE KINGDOM | 2055–1650 B.C. |
| Coffin Texts | c. 2055 B.C. |
| SECOND INTERMEDIATE PERIOD | 1650–1550 B.C. |
| Hyksos invaders expelled | c. 1570 B.C. |
| NEW KINGDOM | 1550–1069 B.C. |
| Book of the Dead | c. 1500 B.C. |
| Queen Hatshepsut | 1498–1483 B.C. |
| Amenhotep III, Egypt at its peak | 1386–1349 B.C. |
| Akhenaten, the Amarna revolution | 1350–1334 B.C. |
| Tutankhamen's reign | 1334–1325 B.C. |
| Ramses the Great | 1279–1212 B.C. |
| THIRD INTERMEDIATE PERIOD | 1069–747 B.C. |
| LATE PERIOD | 747–332 B.C. |
| Nubia rules Egypt | 712–657 B.C. |
| Persians rule Egypt | 525–404 B.C. |
| PTOLEMAIC PERIOD | 332–32 B.C. |
| Alexander the Great conquers Egypt | 332–323 B.C. |
| Cleopatra VII | 51–30 B.C. |
| ROMAN PERIOD | 30 B.C.–A.D. 395 |

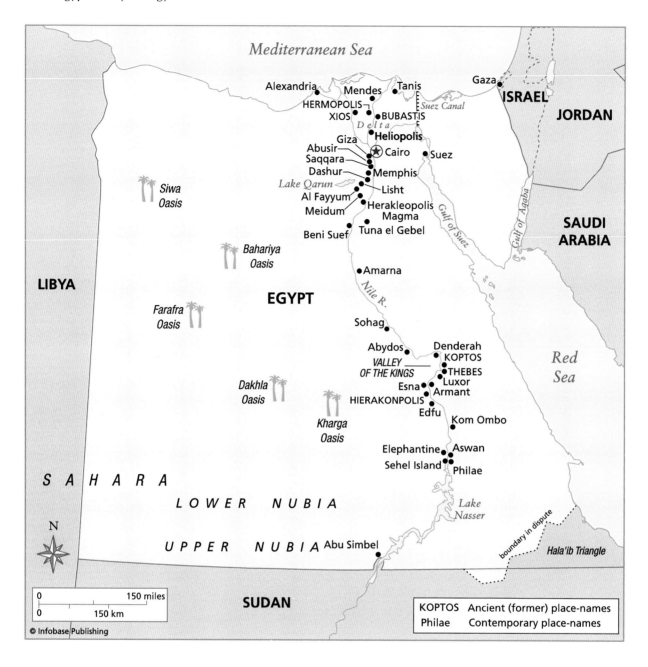

Mediterranean Sea

Alexandria   Mendes   Tanis   Gaza   ISRAEL   JORDAN
HERMOPOLIS   Suez Canal
XIOS   BUBASTIS
Delta
Giza   Heliopolis
Abusir   Cairo   Suez
Saqqara
Dashur   Memphis
Lake Qarun   Lisht
Al Fayyum   Herakleopolis
Meidum   Magma
Beni Suef   Tuna el Gebel

Siwa
Oasis

Bahariya
Oasis

LIBYA   Amarna

EGYPT   Nile R.

Farafra
Oasis   Sohag

Abydos   Denderah
VALLEY   KOPTOS
OF THE KINGS   THEBES
Esna   Luxor
Dakhla   Armant
Oasis   HIERAKONPOLIS
Edfu   Kom Ombo

Kharga
Oasis   Elephantine   Aswan
Sehel Island   Philae

SAUDI
ARABIA

Gulf of Suez

Gulf of Aqaba

Red
Sea

S A H A R A

L O W E R   N U B I A

N   Lake
Nasser

U P P E R   N U B I A   Abu Simbel   boundary in dispute   Hala'ib Triangle

0        150 miles
0        150 km   SUDAN

© Infobase Publishing

| KOPTOS | Ancient (former) place-names |
| Philae | Contemporary place-names |

# A-TO-Z ENTRIES

# A

AAH  A very early form of the moon god, who was sometimes portrayed as a young boy wearing the side lock of youth, a long lock of hair that was not cut until a boy reached puberty. The Egyptians were fascinated with the phases of the moon. When early farming settlements sprang up on the banks of the Nile, farmers used the moon as their planting guide.

In some ways the moon was as important as and far more interesting to the ancient Egyptians than the sun, because over a period of 30 days, the moon changes its shape. This waxing (becoming larger) and waning (becoming smaller) of the moon has four distinct phases.

The first phase or quarter of the moon's cycle is called the new moon. As the moon moves into the

Abu Simbel was built by Ramses II (also known as Ramses the Great) to demonstrate his power and grandeur. One of the four colossal figures was damaged during an earthquake in ancient times and has not been restored. *(Photograph by Pat Remler)*

second quarter, it becomes a half-moon. During the third quarter the half-moon grows into a full moon, and in the fourth quarter it appears as a half-moon again.

As time passed, Aah became Aah-Djuhty, god of the new moon; he later became associated with the god Thoth.

**Aah-Djuhty** God of the new moon, Aah-Djuhty evolved from the moon gods Aah and Thoth.

**Abtu and Ant**  A pair of pilot fish, mentioned in Chapter 9 of the Book of the Dead, that possessed protective powers and swam on each side of the sun god Re's boat to ward off evil spirits as it passed through the Underworld.

**Abu Simbel**  A site in Egypt where Ramses the Great (Ramses II) (1304–1237 B.C.) carved a pair of rock-cut temples. Situated on the west bank of the Nile at Egypt's southern border, Abu Simbel lies 180 miles south of Aswan. The larger of the two temples, the Great Temple, *Hwt Ramesses Meryamun*, called the Temple of Ramses Beloved of Amun, is dedicated to Egypt's principal gods: Amun-Re, Rehorakhty, Ptah, and the deified Ramses. The walls of the Great Temple are decorated with religious scenes, including an array of gods and goddesses, and scenes of Ramses's most important battles—the most well-known being the Battle of Kaddesh, which depicts Ramses's victory over the Hittites.

The most impressive parts of the temple are four 67-foot-tall seated statues of Ramses that occupy the open-air court in front of the entrance to the temple. Each one was carved from the rock face of the mountain. (It has been suggested that Mount Rushmore in South Dakota was based on these figures of Ramses.) One of the statues (on the left as you face the temple) was damaged by an earthquake in antiquity, and the head lies on the ground. Carved on the sides of each throne are Nile gods tying lotus and papyrus plants around the hieroglyph "to unite," symbolizing the unification of Upper and Lower Egypt.

Statues of the royal family are carved between and beside the legs of all four colossal statues of Ramses. Prominently shown around the first southern statue are: Queen Nefertari (the Great Wife), Muttuya (king's mother), and Prince Amen-hir-khep-shef (the firstborn son). From the second southern statue are: Princess Bint-Anat, Princess Nebet-awy-by, and a female figure whose name has been lost, perhaps Esenofre, a minor wife. The family members shown

with the two northern statues are: Queen Nefertari, Princess Beket-mut, Prince Pi-Ramses, Princess Merit-Amun, Queen Muttuya, and Princess Nofretari. Beneath the statues are figures of bound captives, and above the entrance to the Great Temple is a carving of the sun god Rehorakhty. To his right is a jackal-head symbol meaning "power"; to the left is Maat, the goddess of truth. Together the three symbols form an ancient Egyptian pun: they spell one of Ramses's names, *Usr-Maat-Re*, "the Truth of Re is Power." In front of the Great Temple were two stone basins where the priests purified themselves with Nile water before entering the temple.

The Great Temple has four rooms: The first, called the great hall, has eight square pillars each with a statue of Ramses. The four on the right wear the double crown, signifying the unification of Upper and Lower Egypt, and those on the left wear the white crown of Upper Egypt. In the second hall, the four pillars are decorated with religious scenes—the king in the company of the gods: Anubis, Satis, Min, Mut, Wadjet, Amun-Re, Hathor, Montu, and several manifestations of Horus. On the entrance to the vestibule the king makes offerings of wine, incense, bread, and flowers to the gods. The vestibule leads to the sanctuary, where statues of the gods are cut into the rock. From left to right are Ptah, Amun-Re, Ramses II (as a god), and Re-Horakhty. The image of Ramses is the same size as those of the gods, suggesting he is the equal of the gods he is honoring. The holy of holies at Abu Simbel is oriented so that on February 21 (Ramses's birthday) and October 21 (Ramses's coronation date), the rays of the sun shine through the corridor into the sanctuary and illuminate Ramses and the gods.

Just north of Ramses's temple is the Small Temple, built for Queen Nefertari, and dedicated to Hathor as Abshek, an obscure Nubian goddess of love and beauty. The front of Nefertari's temple is shaped like a pylon and faced with six colossal statues: four of Ramses and two of Nefertari, each about 33 feet tall.

An inscription over the door reads:

> Rameses II, he has made a temple, excavated in the mountain, of eternal workmanship, for the chief queen Nefertari, beloved of Mut, in Nubia, forever and ever, Nefertari for whose sake the very sun does shine.

Inside, the great hall is supported by six Hathor-head columns that incorporate the shape of the sistrum, the sacred rattle used in religious ceremonies. In the vestibule, or second room, are religious scenes with Nefertari in the company of goddesses. On the right of the main vestibule door, Hathor-Abshek looks on as Isis places a crown upon Nefertari's head. On the left side of the vestibule door, Nefertari stands with Ramses, who presents a bouquet of flowers to TAURET, the goddess of pregnancy and childbirth. The third room, the Holy of Holies, where the cult statues were kept, is decorated with various goddesses. One wall is carved to show Hathor as a cow goddess emerging from a mountain to protect the king, who stands in front of her. On the side walls, Ramses and Nefertari appear in the company of the gods with Ramses offering incense and libations to himself and his queen, indicating that they are both deified.

The temples at Abu Simbel are unique because they were carved from a mountain, not built of stone blocks. When the Aswan High Dam was being constructed in the 1960s, both temples were saved from the rising water that formed Lake Nasr behind the dam. UNESCO, the United Nations Educational, Scientific and Cultural Organization, and the Egyptian government dismantled the temples, cut the facades into blocks, numbered them, and moved them to higher ground. The reassembled temples were carefully placed so the sun still shines into the holy of holies on February 21 and October 21, just as in ancient times.

**ABYDOS** 🗝🏺 The most sacred city in all of Egypt, located on the West Bank of the Nile near modern Sohag, Abydos was a center for religious activity for centuries, from Egypt's Predynastic period to Christian times. Abydos was the earliest and most important cult center for worship of OSIRIS when the god became popular toward the end of the Old Kingdom. According to the mythology, Osiris's body was cut into pieces and spread over Egypt, and legend had it that Osiris's head (some sources claim it was his phallus) was buried at Abydos.

The earliest buildings at Abydos are the tombs of Egypt's Predynastic and Early Dynastic rulers. The first pharaohs came from a town nearby—its precise location is unknown—and were buried at Abydos. Today the oldest remains are from the temple of Osiris-Khentimentiu, dedicated to an ancient jackal god associated with Osiris. Khentimentiu means "foremost of the westerners" (the west was reserved for the dead) and stresses Osiris's role as a protective funerary god.

Excavations have unearthed Early Dynastic royal tombs and several wooden boats. A mud-brick tomb of the First Dynasty king, Djer, was thought to be the tomb of Osiris in ancient times. This may have

contributed to the growing popularity of the cult of Osiris. The most impressive monument to Osiris at Abydos is the OSIREION, a chapel constructed of huge granite blocks and believed to be his false tomb, or cenotaph. In the Middle Kingdom (2055–1650 B.C.), people made pilgrimages to Abydos and many left STELE, or offering tablets, for Osiris inscribed with their names and prayers.

Abydos was the center for the "mysteries"—passion plays revolving around the life of Osiris. Abydos became a place of pilgrimage, both real and symbolic. A chorus sang prayers, and the audience lit lamps to represent Isis's search for the pieces of her husband's body. Osiris was the first mummy and was believed to be the first one to resurrect. He became the king of the NETHERWORLD: Anyone seeking to enter needed Osiris's permission. Besides being the god of the dead, Osiris also represented the fertility of the land. Tomb paintings often show him with green skin and his arms crossed over his chest in the form of a mummy. The symbol of Osiris at Abydos was a pole covered with an animal skin and two plumes, which was also associated with ANUBIS (see IMIUT).

The Second Dynasty kings Peribsen and Khasekhemwy constructed their tombs at Abydos to be near the burial place of Osiris.

Today, the greatest monument at Abydos is the TEMPLE OF SETI I, the father of Ramses II. No Egyptian temple can match the carvings and the colors in the temple of Seti I, the first ruler of the Nineteenth Dynasty (1295–1186 B.C.). It is so well preserved that visitors can study the ancient religious ceremonies pictured on the walls of the seven chapels.

Pylons that once stood in front of the temple are now gone, so the approach is from the broad stairs leading to the entrance. Inside, seven aisles lead to seven chapels, each dedicated to a different god, one of which is Seti I. At the entrance to each chapel is a carving of Seti I and the god to whom that chapel is dedicated. The Chapel of Osiris is the third from the right, and here one can see the ancient rituals of the Osiris Cult as performed by the king. Seti is shown as the officiating high priest who is being purified with holy oil. Seti approaches the sanctuary dressed in a simple kilt, carrying an incense pipe and an oil lamp to illuminate the sacred darkness of the sanctuary. The king, chanting prayers, approaches the shrine of Osiris; he unbolts the doors of the sacred shrine; the god, in the form of a cult statue, is greeted with morning hymns and offered food and wine, and incense is burned. The statue of the god is anointed with precious oil and dressed in the finest linen. More prayers are offered, and the god is returned to

An aegis, a miniature shield. For the Egyptians, the aegis was a sign of protection, and they often decorated the prows of their boats with it. *(Drawing by Mary Jordan)*

his shrine. The king withdraws, bowing, and sweeps away his footprints. This ritual is repeated in each of the other six chapels that are dedicated to HORUS, Isis (wife of Osiris and mother of Horus), AMUN-RE (the great god of Thebes), RE-HORAKHTY (Horus of the Horizon), PTAH (the creator god), and Seti I. In the chapel of Seti I, the king performs the ceremonies in front of a cult statue of himself.

**ACHET** An AMULET representing the rising Sun on the horizon, the color of the *achet* is always red, usually carved from a red stone or made of red glass or FAIENCE. The achet was a sign of the sun god RE in the early morning; it was believed to protect the wearer.

**ADZE** An instrument shaped like a carpenter's tool used in the "opening of the mouth" ceremony. During the funeral, the adze magically gave the mummy "breath" to live again in the next world. When the adze was touched to the face of the mummy, the priest recited the prayer, "You live again, you breathe again."

**AEGIS** A magical symbol in the shape of a broad collar, often inscribed with an EYE OF HORUS or a SCARAB for protection. *Aegis* is the Greek word for shield. Chapter 158 of the BOOK OF THE DEAD men-

tions a "collar of gold" (aegis) to be placed on the neck of the KA, the spirit of the deceased, on the day of burial. The collar is a symbol for an embrace by the god. An example of this collar can be seen in one of the small chapels in the TEMPLE OF SETI I at ABYDOS. Here, the king presents a collar to RE-HORAKHTY in hope that he will be united with his Ka for eternity.

The aegis sometimes decorated the prow of sacred boats and was usually shown with an animal head at the top. Sometimes the aegis collar was incorporated into jewelry or ritual objects with the head of SEKHMET or ISIS.

**AESCULAPIUS** Greek god of medicine identified with IMHOTEP, the Old Kingdom architect of the STEP PYRAMID, who was deified during the Ptolemaic period (332–32 B.C.) and worshipped as a god of healing and medicine.

**AF** The name given the sun god after it has set on the horizon and moved into the DUAT. Af is the night sun or the dead sun, for it gives no light while it is traveling through the 12 hours of the night in the Sektet boat of the Underworld. Af is shown with the head of a ram and wears the solar disk on his head, a sign representing the sun that is frequently worn on the headdress of Egyptian deities.

**AF-OSIRIS** A composite god derived from the dead sun god, AF, and OSIRIS, the god of the dead. During the festival of SOKAR each year, the ceremonial boat was placed on its sled at sunrise so the first rays of the sun would shine upon the boat and the sacred chest that rested on its deck. The chest supposedly held the bodies of Af and Osiris, who formed the composite sun god.

**AIR, GOD OF** See SHU.

**AKER** One of the early lion gods in Egyptian mythology, Aker, the god of land, is represented by two lions seated back to back or two lions supporting the symbol for the horizon with the sun rising. The two lions symbolize the sun setting in the west and the sun rising in the east. Because of this, Aker is viewed as an ally of RE, when Re makes his nightly journey through the Underworld. Aker is mentioned in the PYRAMID TEXTS as the earth god who guards the gates to the Underworld. In the BOOK OF THE DEAD, he is shown in the solar boat accompanying Re during his nightly journey. In the Fifth Hour, the AMDUAT, which helped the deceased make the journey through the Underworld, Aker appears as the two-headed lion god carrying sand upon his back. In THE BOOK OF CAVERNS, another religious text, the sun god Re travels across Aker as he continues his journey through the caverns.

*AKH*   The *akh* was part of a person's vital force, and when a person died, it was believed that his or her spirit, or *akh*, acquired magical power. The Egyptians thought the *akh* was a radiant light, something like a star. The PYRAMID TEXTS tell us that when a man died, his *akh* went to heaven. From the Pyramid Texts of King UNAS, spell 245, the king joins the stars:

> This Unas comes to you oh Nut [the goddess of
>    the sky]
> This Unas comes to you, oh Nut,
> He has consigned his father to earth,
> He has left Horus behind him . . .
> His magic has equipped him

Nut, the sky goddess, replies:

> Make your seat in heaven,
> Among the stars of heaven,
> For you are the Lone Star. . . .

The *akh* was the resurrected form of the king when he had gained mobility in the Netherworld. The nature of the *akh* changed over time as the intricacies of Egyptian mythology evolved. Much later, when religious beliefs had changed, the BOOK OF THE DEAD viewed the *akh* as an evil force:

> My mouth is strong: and I am equipped against
> the Akhs.
> Let them not have power over me.

**AKHEKH**   A composite animal, something like a griffin, associated with the evil aspects of the god SET. Ancient myths describe the Akhekh as the body of an antelope with wings and the head of a bird, on which sat three cobras.

**AKHENATEN** (1352–1336 B.C.)   Called the "heretic pharaoh" because he changed the religion of ancient Egypt, Akhenaten was the first known monotheist in history. He believed there was only one god, the ATEN. Soon after he was crowned king, he changed his name from Amenhotep IV to Akhenaten, meaning "Aten is on the horizon." He then raised the little-known god, the Aten, meaning "disk of the sun," to supreme god in the religion.

Akhenaten was the son of Amenhotep III, a pleasure-loving king who devoted his life to building

Akhenaten, the "heretic king," changed the religion of Egypt from many gods to one and was the first known monotheist in the world. *(Photo by Pat Remler)*

temples, and Queen Tiye, a strong-minded woman if her portraits tell us anything about her personality. Akhenaten's ideas were revolutionary, and from his statues, we can see that his looks were different as well. Instead of an idealized king with a perfectly proportioned body, images of Akhenaten show a long, thin face, slanted eyes, thick lips, pointed chin, and a scrawny neck. He had breasts, a swollen belly, wide hips, and spindly arms and legs. This highly unusual and perhaps realistic portrayal of the king became an artistic fashion as Egyptian art changed to a more realistic style under his reign.

It is not certain when Akhenaten began worshiping the Aten. There were references to the Aten during his childhood: Akhenaten's mother, Queen Tiye, had a pleasure boat named *The Aten Gleams* that she sailed on her private lake. Right after his coronation, Akhenaten made it clear to everyone how important the new god was. He began building temples to the Aten next to the temple of the traditional god, AMUN, at KARNAK TEMPLE, a group of religious buildings in Thebes.

The Aten was unlike any god the people had ever worshipped. Represented as a sun disk with rays of light reaching down and ending in hands holding an ANKH (the sign of life) and *WAS* SCEPTER (the sign of power), it bestowed light and warmth upon the king and his family. Unlike the traditional gods of Egypt, however, the Aten was an abstract god without personality.

Akhenaten and his followers left Thebes, the capital of Egypt, and traveled north to a remote desert site about halfway between modern Luxor and Cairo to build a new city in the desert, called Akhet-Aten, "the horizon of the Aten." The king erected boundary markers called *stele* that described how the Aten directed him to build the holy city on this site. Akhet-Aten was one of the most beautiful cities in the ancient world, stretching for five miles along the Nile. There were extra-wide streets for the king's chariot procession and planned neighborhoods with houses for the laborers, administrators, and nobles of the court, as well as several palaces for the royal family and temples for the Aten.

The Aten temples were unlike any other temples in Egypt. There were no roofs and no sanctuary, or "holy of holies," for the god. Completely open, their vast courtyards were filled with sunshine and altars for offerings to the Aten.

Akhenaten and his wife, Queen Nefertiti, had six daughters. Akhenaten's happy isolation lasted only a dozen years, as one by one, five of the princesses and Nefertiti died. When Akhenaten himself died after reigning for about 17 years, Tutankhamen, his probable young son by a second wife, became pharaoh. Egypt returned to the old religion, and the city of Akhet-Aten was abandoned when the capital was moved back to Thebes.

It has been said that Akhenaten was a man born before his time, that his ideas were too revolutionary to be accepted in conservative Egypt. He changed his name, the art style, the religion, and the capital. In so doing, Akhenaten's legacy to the world was monotheism, a new art style, and his beautiful prayer praising the Aten (see HYMN TO THE ATEN).

**AKHET** The exact spot on the horizon where NUT, the sky goddess, gives birth to RE the sun god each morning. Egyptian mythology relates that at the end of each day, when the sun set, the sun god traveled through the 12 hours of night, crossing the Underworld. When the sun appeared on the horizon at dawn, it was recognized as a sign of rebirth and renewal and a triumph over darkness. The heretic king AKHENATEN believed the akhet appeared on the horizon to show him where to build Akhet-Aten, his new city in the desert.

Akhet is the hieroglyph for horizon, and the word *akhet* is also the name of one of the three seasons in the ancient Egyptian calendar. It was the first season after the Egyptian new year and corresponds with our month of July. AMULETS in the shape of the akhet represented Re the sun god and provided powerful protection to the wearer. Akhet amulets are almost always red—carved from carnelian or made of red glass or FAIENCE.

**AKHET-ATEN**   See AMARNA.

**ALEXANDER THE GREAT** (352–323 B.C.)   Macedonian ruler who conquered Egypt and was declared a god. When his father, Philip II, died, Alexander became king of the small Greek state, Macedon. Within a few years, he and his army of devoted men united the Greek states and conquered the Levant and a good part of western Asia. When Alexander and his army marched into Egypt and defeated the hated Persians who occupied the land, the Egyptians hailed Alexander as a liberator. Alexander, ever mindful of local customs, made offerings to the Egyptian gods at MEMPHIS, KARNAK, and LUXOR temples and at Siwa Oasis in the western desert near the Libyan border.

This was more than just a goodwill gesture on his part. Alexander believed that he was descended from the legendary Greek hero Heracles (Hercules) and Achilles through his mother and father. To strengthen his claim to the throne of Egypt he needed to be acknowledged as a god by the Egyptian ORACLE at Siwa Oasis in the western desert. Legend has it that on the long march through the desert, when Alexander and his men became lost, a flock of crows appeared in the sky and led them to the safety of the oasis.

When Alexander approached the Oracle of AMUN-RE (called ZEUS-AMUN by the Greeks), he asked one question: "Who is my father?" When the Oracle answered "Amun," Alexander knew he would rule. With the endorsement of the Oracle, Alexander, like all Egyptian kings before him, was recognized as the son of Amun and a god on Earth and was crowned king of Egypt.

Alexander founded his capital city, Alexandria, in 331 B.C. on the site of a small fishing village, Rhakotis (Raqote), on the Egyptian shore of the Mediterranean. The architect Deinocrates, who was

Alexander the Great respected Egyptian religion and culture after he invaded. His image was often commemorated on silver coins called *tetra drachma. (Photo by Marie-Lan Nguyen/Used under a Creative Commons license)*

summoned from the Greek island of Rhodes, drew the plans for the city. Alexandria was based on the Greek city model, complete with a grid design open to the cool breezes from the Mediterranean. The city, completed after Alexander's death, grew to be a thriving international port with a population of more than half a million. The most famous building in ancient Alexandria was the "pharos" lighthouse, designated one of the Seven Wonders of the Ancient World by a Greek librarian. Little of the original structure remains today. Another famous landmark in ancient Alexandria was the library, with its priceless collection of papyrus manuscripts. Legend tells us that the library was burned to the ground when Julius Caesar entered Egypt to settle a quarrel between Cleopatra VII and her brother Ptolemy XIII.

Alexander never saw his city but moved on to continue his conquest of the Persian Empire. For all his dreams of ruling as a living god, Alexander died of a fever in Babylon in 323 B.C. When asked by his generals, upon his deathbed, who should succeed him, he simply said, "The strongest." Eventually Alexander's empire was divided among the generals. General Ptolemy chose Egypt and established the Ptolemaic dynasty there. His was the last dynasty, ending when Cleopatra VII committed suicide and the Roman Empire annexed Egypt.

**AMARNA** (also AKHET-ATEN or "Horizon of the Aten") Amarna was built by AKHENATEN (the heretic king) as a cult city to honor his new god, the ATEN, whose motto was: *ankh m maat,* or "living in truth." Worship of the Aten brought with it a new art style. Emphasis was placed especially on "truth in nature." Artists and craftsmen abandoned the traditional static style of depiction and began painting scenes from nature and carving lifelike natural statues of the royal court.

When Akhenaten (1352–1336 B.C.) changed Egypt's religion from the worship of many gods (polytheism) to the worship of one god (monotheism), he claimed he was guided by the Aten. Akhenaten moved his court from the old capital city THEBES (modern Luxor) to a new desert location some 200 miles north. Akhenaten marked the boundaries of his new city with 15 stelae (stone slabs). Some stelae were carved into the limestone cliffs like shrines; others were actual stone slabs erected along the east and west sides of the NILE. On the stelae, Akhenaten recorded his vow never to leave the holy city of Akhet-Aten:

> The southern stela which is on the eastern mountain on Akhet-Aten ... I shall not pass beyond it southward ever. The middle stela ... [Eastern] I shall not pass beyond it eastward ever. The northeastern stela ... I shall not pass beyond it northward ever. Likewise from the southwest stela of Akhet-Aten to the northwest stela on the western mountain [he will not pass beyond the western stelae] within these four stelae from the eastern mountain to the western mountain is Akhet-Aten itself. It belongs to my father, [the Aten] who gives life forever. I shall not violate this oath which I have made to the Aten my father in all eternity.

Amarna was built on the east bank of the Nile, with three broad streets parallel to the river. Wide enough to accommodate the great chariot processions of Akhenaten and his queen, Nefertiti, the Royal Road was the main street. Because it was a planned city with defined neighborhoods (called the North and the South Suburbs and the Central City), Akhet-Aten grew in an orderly way. Akhenaten's royal palace, official buildings, the Great Aten Temple, and the Small Aten Temple were in the Central City—the hub of all activity. Officials and nobles lived in the North and South Suburbs. The famous Nefertiti bust, now in the Charlottenburg Egyptian Museum in Berlin, was found in the South Suburb house of

Thutmose the sculptor, along with other portraits of the royal family.

Because Amarna is one of the most thoroughly excavated sites along the Nile, Egyptologists know a lot about ancient life there. At the height of Akhenaten's reign, the city had about 20,000 people. All of the buildings were constructed of mud brick with plastered walls, except for the Great Aten Temple called *Gem-Pa-Aten* (the Aten is Found). Its facade was gleaming white limestone. The temple complex included several structures, open courtyards, and 365 altars for offerings from UPPER EGYPT and from LOWER EGYPT (see SUN TEMPLE). The great palace (Mansion of Rejoicing in Akhet-Aten) for receiving foreign dignitaries and conducting palace business was at the end of the Royal Road. A bridge over the Royal Road connected the main palace with the king's living quarters, and the bridge may be the site of the "window of appearances," where Akhenaten and Nefertiti appeared to give necklaces of gold to the Aten's faithful followers. A smaller Aten temple next to the king's living quarters was called *hwt-aten* "Mansion of the Aten" and was probably used exclusively by the royal family.

Houses in Amarna were usually square-shaped, with a large open courtyard in the center. Reception rooms, bedrooms, storage rooms, and a kitchen with a clay bread oven were all built around the open courtyard. Houses of the nobles and wealthy citizens had tall enclosure walls designed with multiple purposes for security, roof terraces, and rooms for bathing. These walls were lined with limestone, and the floors slanted to form a basin. After water was poured over the bather, it drained outside into a large jar. Some houses even had commodes.

After 17 years, Amarna was abandoned when Akhenaten died (1355 B.C.). One of the last remaining royal children was young Tut-ankh-aten, who later changed his name to TUTANKHAMEN and ruled from Thebes.

**AMARNA LETTERS**   In 1887, a local peasant woman walking through AMARNA found a group of clay tablets inscribed in cuneiform script (wedge-shaped writing developed in Babylonia). She had stumbled upon a storehouse of diplomatic letters between Egypt and her Middle Eastern neighbors. More than 350 inscribed tablets were discovered, written mostly in Babylonian cuneiform, the language of diplomats and foreign traders.

The letters were sent from foreign kings with their ambassadors bringing gifts or tribute to AKHENATEN.

Some requested that the king send gold from Egypt. One of the Amarna letters reads:

> . . . Thus spoke the king of Alasia to the king of Egypt my brother
> Know that I am well, and that my land is well. And as to thy good health,
> Even thy good health, the good health of thy house, thy sons, thy wives, thy horses, thy chariots . . .
> Why hast thou not sent thy messenger to me? I have sent my messenger to thee.
> And have I not sent to thee through my messenger one hundred talents of copper?
> Now let thy messenger bring (for me) one ebony bed inlaid with gold, and a chariot with gold, and two horses . . .

The Amarna letters tell us a lot about what luxury goods were prized in the ancient world. They give us a glimpse of how government worked and have helped scholars better understand the language and grammar of cuneiform. But, most important, the letters show the effect of changing Egypt's religion from polytheism (many gods) to monotheism (one god). Akhenaten remained isolated in his holy city, neglected his duties, and ignored his neighbors, and Egypt went from her "golden age" into decline.

**AMDUAT**   "The book of that which is in the Underworld" is an account of the nightly journey of the sun god in his sacred boat through the realm of the Underworld. Unlike earlier FUNERARY TEXTS, the Amduat gives a detailed description of what the god will encounter during the 12-hour journey. The Amduat explains in text and pictures what happens to the sun when it falls below the horizon each night—a phenomenon that must have been debated by Egyptian priests. The Amduat chronicles the perils of the Underworld and the victorious emergence of the sun each dawn.

Amduat, "The book of that which is in the Underworld," first appeared in the tomb of Thutmose III (1504–1492 B.C.) in the VALLEY OF THE KINGS. His walls were painted to resemble papyrus, and the text of the Amduat was in cursive script. The many variations of the Amduat were favorite tomb decorations for Egyptian kings. Most important to the deceased king was the set of directions contained in the Amduat to help him make his way through the 12 dark and dangerous hours of the Underworld.

When priests began to collect and condense assorted myths in the temple libraries, they must have seen the similarity of human life on Earth and the daily life of RE, the sun god. Just as the sun was reborn each day, so, too, could humans be reborn by resurrecting in the next world. If the proper burial rituals were performed, the deceased could join Re in his sacred boat and travel in safety through the 12 hours of the DUAT. In the Amduat, Re and OSIRIS each worked to ensure eternal life for the souls of the deceased, but Re was the more important god. Although his light died each night, Re was still the chief protector and guide for the souls of the deceased as they made their way through the terrors and darkness of the Duat.

The Amduat is divided into chapters representing the 12 hours of the night, each one describing the dangers encountered during each hour.

The **First Hour** of the night is called "Crusher of the forehead of the enemies of Re." Re and the solar (sun) boat are between the sky and the Underworld. The god has lost his vitality and has become a "sun of night," a sun without light.

The **Second Hour** of the night is called "She who knows how to protect her lord." Re and the souls of the deceased enter the Ur-Nes, the land near the Nile of the Underworld. They meet the souls or gods of the Duat and are advised to address them by their names.

In the **Third Hour** of the night, the solar boat enters the realm of "those who slay" and passes over the Stream of Osiris, accompanied by three boats rowed by Osiris, who appears in various forms.

In the **Fourth Hour** of the night, Re and the souls of the deceased travel into the realm of Sokar, a desert guarded by snakes. In order to travel across the sand, the sacred boat turns into a snake and slithers across the desert.

In the **Fifth Hour** of the night, Re and the souls of the deceased, still in their serpent boat, continue through the domain of Sokar. Seven gods and seven goddesses, representing 14 days of a month, tow the sacred boat and accompany the travelers as they approach the secret cave of Sokar.

In the **Sixth Hour** of the night, Re and the souls of the deceased return to the solar boat. They approach the Shrines of Osiris in the Delta. The Shrines of Osiris occupy a large hall with 16 rooms, each holding a mummy. Re commands the 16 mummies to be pleased with his offering, to protect him, and to kill his enemy, the serpent APOPHIS.

The **Seventh Hour** of the night takes the solar boat into the hidden place of Osiris. It describes the terrible battle between Re and his archenemy, the serpent Apophis, who blocks the way of the sacred barque.

In the **Eighth Hour**, Re and his entourage enter the city of Tebat-Neteru, where they come under the protection of the mighty serpent called Mehen. It is here that the gods and souls come to life as Re passes their secret homes, and Re commands them to kill his enemies and all the demons in that domain.

In the **Ninth Hour**, the solar boat reaches the "Hidden Circle of Amentet," where anyone who learns the names of the gods and their places shall be honored in the city. They are accompanied by 12 divine sailors, each carrying an oar so that he might splash water upon the spirits that stand on the banks of the river.

In the **Tenth Hour**, the solar boat continues its journey, with Re holding a snake as his staff. Several boats carrying gods of the Underworld have joined the solar boat, and the gods of the Underworld kill the enemies of Re as they make their way to the eleventh hour.

In the **Eleventh Hour**, Re holds a scepter of authority, and on the bow of the boat a solar disk represents the sun with a serpent around it. The serpent, Pestu, symbolizes time and swallows the stars that represent the hours of the night that have passed.

In the **Twelfth Hour**, Re and the souls of the deceased leave the darkness of the Duat and enter the circle where they will be reborn. Re will enter this world as the rising sun, and the deceased safely enter the NETHERWORLD (heaven).

**AMENHOTEP-SON-OF-HAPU**  A royal scribe in the court of Amenhotep III (1390–1352 B.C.), Amenhotep-son-of-Hapu, was deified during Ptolemaic times (332–32 B.C.) as a man of great wisdom. His cult center was at KARNAK TEMPLE in THEBES (modern LUXOR), where he was worshipped as a healer and benefactor. Petitioners brought their requests and prayers to Amenhotep in the hope that he would serve as an intermediary for their prayers to the great god AMUN.

Amenhotep was a northerner born in the Delta, but he spent most of his 80 years in Thebes in the service of his king. Working his way up through the ranks in the court of Amenhotep III, he impressed superiors with his ability to recruit men for the pharaoh's army and to supervise monumental building projects. He earned the title "chief architect of all the king's building projects." As Amenhotep III's most trusted official, Amenhotep-son-of-Hapu was depicted, along with the king, on the wall of the great temple at Soleb in southern Nubia. A man of many talents, Amenhotep-son-of-Hapu became manager of the vast estates of the royal family and was rewarded with his own mortuary temple on the West Bank at Thebes. He was enormously popular among the people, and his mortuary temple soon became the center for his growing cult. A copy of a royal decree from the Twenty-first Dynasty grants permission for the construction of his temple, the only nonroyal temple to be built among the royal monuments on the West Bank.

Amenhotep-son-of-Hapu, in spite of his fame, seemed to be most pleased with his title as a royal scribe, for his statues often show him sitting with a roll of papyrus across his knee. Many of Amenhotep-son-of-Hapu's statues were found in Karnak temple, and their inscriptions tell us much of what we know about him.

**AMENT** One of the many names for the goddess ISIS. Isis was called Ament, "the Hidden One," when she assisted the souls of the dead as they passed from this world to the NETHERWORLD.

**AMENTET** (also AMENT, AMENTIT, IMENTET) A goddess of the dead, Amentet is the personification of the west, the home of the deceased. Amentet, a compassionate companion, helps the souls of the dead journey to their dwelling place in the NETHERWORLD.

From her home in the branches of a tree at the edge of the desert, Amentet watched for the souls as they approached the entrance to the Netherworld, or next world. Its location was believed to be in the western desert. Amentet offered bread and water to the weary souls, and if they accepted her hospitality, it meant they "walked with the gods" and would peacefully enter the next world. The ancient Egyptian word *amentet* means "the hidden place," the land of the setting sun, where the deceased gathered for their difficult journey through the 12 hours of the DUAT in the sacred boat of the sun god RE.

Another version of the myth tells us that Amentet met the souls of the deceased at the end of their journey to the Netherworld. Here the goddess assisted with the rebirth of their souls and provided them with food and drink.

Amentet often appears in the company of other goddesses associated with fertility and resurrection. Sometimes she is a winged goddess, along with ISIS and NEPHTHYS when they assist with the magical resurrection of a mummy. When Amentet appears with HATHOR (Hathor-Amentet), she becomes a solar goddess of the west. She is often in the company of RE-HORAKHTY (Horus of the Two Horizons). Together they welcomed the souls of the deceased to their new dwelling place in the Netherworld and assisted with their resurrection. Amentet also sometimes appeared with IABET, who, as goddess of the east, was Amentet's counterpart.

Depicted as a young woman, Amentet wears the HIEROGLYPH of the west (𓋹) on her head and carries an ANKH and scepter. The standard of the west is represented by a half circle sitting on two poles of uneven length, with an ostrich plume resting on top of the standard. Sometimes she wears only a falcon as her headdress, showing her association with Re-Horakhty.

**AMENTI** The Egyptian word for "west," Amenti was where the blessed dead lived, and it could only be the NETHERWORLD. The land of the dead was believed to be a beautiful and peaceful place where the deceased would spend eternity.

**AMMUT** A mythical creature of the NETHERWORLD with the head of a crocodile, front legs of a lion, and back legs of a hippopotamus. Ammut was called the "devourer of the dead." In illustrations for Chapter 125 of the BOOK OF THE DEAD, she sits in the Hall of Two Truths, next to the scale of justice, on which the heart of the deceased was weighed against the feather of truth that represents justice or *MAAT*. If the heart was found to be heavy with evil deeds, it fell to Ammut, who devoured it. This was the worst thing that could happen, for then the soul of the deceased could never resurrect in the next world.

**AMULET** An amulet is anything worn or carried by a person for protection or good luck. In ancient Egypt, amulets were often small figures of the gods. Of all the magical objects used by the Egyptians, amulets were by far the most popular. Newborns were adorned with amulets to keep them safe and healthy, and parents placed amulets around their children's necks to ward off evil spirits and protect them from scorpions, snakes, and crocodiles.

Amulets came in many sizes, shapes, and colors. Some were faience like these, but others were carved from stone. *(Photograph by Pat Remler)*

Amulets, made in hundreds of different shapes, were believed to have many different powers. Some amulets were purely protective, and their power came from the gods. If you wore a small cat amulet around your neck, for example, then the cat goddess, Bastet, protected you. The Egyptians believed that some amulets not only kept them safe but also gave the wearer special powers: If you wore a lion amulet, you would be brave, a bull amulet would give you strength, and an ibis or baboon amulet would help you gain wisdom and knowledge.

One of the most popular Egyptian amulets was the EYE OF HORUS, which was worn by the living for good health and also placed on the dead for regeneration. The Eye of Horus is shaped like a stylized falcon's eye, and the Egyptian word for it is *udjat*, or "sound eye."

Amulets were made of almost any material available to the ancient Egyptians, but the finest were carved from stone: lapis lazuli, carnelian, turquoise, feldspar, serpentine, and steatite. Amulets also were made of gold, copper, bronze, iron, and sometimes glass, wood, or bone, but FAIENCE, a self-glazing ceramic paste, was by far the most popular material for making amulets.

Faience amulets were produced in workshops all over Egypt. The first step was to prepare a mold.

A master amulet was carved, usually in stone, and pressed into a lump of soft clay. The clay was baked or fired until it was hard, and that became the mold used to make amulets. Any number of molds could be made from the master amulet, and any number of amulets could be made from each mold. A small lump of faience was rolled into a ball around a string and pressed into the mold. When the mold was fired, the paste hardened and the string burned away, leaving a hole so the amulet could be strung on a cord. Faience amulets came in many colors, but the ancient Egyptians favored shades of turquoise and blue.

Amulets changed over Egypt's 3,000-year history. Those from the Old Kingdom (2686–2181 B.C.) tended to be hawks, hippopotami, or lions. Later, in the First Intermediate period (2181–2055 B.C.), amulets were often in the shape of body parts: arms, hands, feet, hearts, and eyes. The Middle Kingdom produced one of ancient Egypt's most popular amulets, one that is still worn today: the SCARAB beetle.

During the New Kingdom, amulets represented the most popular gods. They were usually worn on a string around the neck or inlaid in other kinds of jewelry. The favorites were of AMUN, ISIS, HATHOR, BES, and TAURET.

**Funerary Amulets** Some amulets were made to ensure that the mummy remained intact and had the power to resurrect in the next world. The MacGregor Papyrus, a version of the BOOK OF THE DEAD, lists 75 funerary amulets and their uses. The list requires that each amulet be made of gold. Since gold doesn't tarnish, it seemed the most enduring material to protect the mummy for eternity.

One of the most important funerary amulets was the *DJED* PILLAR, called the backbone of Osiris, which represents stability for the deceased. Chapter 155 in the Book of the Dead calls for a pillar of gold to be placed on the throat of the mummy, but often a string of faience or bone *djed* amulets was used because gold was too costly.

Another important funerary amulet was the *tet* or the KNOT OF ISIS, sometimes called the "Girdle of Isis" or the "Blood of Isis." During the Greek and Roman periods (332 B.C.–A.D. 395), Isis was identifiable by the distinctive knot on the front of her gown. The *tet* is often carved from a hard red stone like jasper or carnelian or sometimes molded in red glass. The Book of the Dead suggests the *tet* should be made of red jasper and dipped into the sap of the *ankh-imy* plant. This plant is not known today, but the name suggests magical power, for it means

"overseer of life." The ancient Egyptians believed that if the *tet* was inlaid in sycamore wood and placed on the mummy's neck, the power of Isis would protect him or her.

A group of amulets called the FOUR SONS OF HORUS were essential for the mummy. All four deities have the body of a man, but each has a different head. Mesti is human-headed, Hapi is ape-headed, Duamutef is jackal-headed, and Qebesenef is falcon-headed. Amulets of these four gods were usually made of blue faience and had several holes on each side so they could be sewn onto the mummy wrappings. They were almost always placed across the mummy's chest.

Often, a miniature headrest made of hard stone was placed in the mummy wrappings to protect the head of the mummy and to help him or her arise in the next world. Small heart amulets were sometimes wrapped with the mummy to protect the heart and ensure that it did not speak against the deceased when he or she made a plea before the gods.

## Popular Amulets Worn for Good Luck and Protection

**Aegis**  Miniature of a broad collar necklace with the head of a god worn for protection

**Bastet**  The cat-headed household goddess who brought good luck

**Bes**  The grotesque dwarf god who brought good luck to families

**Eye of Horus**  Eye of the falcon god Horus, worn for good health

**Isis**  The greatest Egyptian goddess, who was "Keeper of Secrets"

**Isis Suckling the Infant Horus**  For the protection of mother and child

**Hathor**  Cow-headed goddess of music and dance

**Horus**  Falcon-headed protector god

**Maat**  Goddess of truth and justice, whose attribute was the feather of truth

**Nefertum**  The god of the blue lotus blossom

**Nekhbet**  The vulture goddess who protected the pharaoh

**Nephthys**  The lady of the mansion and sister of Isis

**Ptah**  The god of craftsmen, and a creator god

**Ptah-ek**  Dwarf god protector of children

**scarab**  Beetle whose image means "to exist" for protection and to give long life

**Tauret**  Pregnant hippopotamus, for protection during childbirth

**Thoth**  Ibis-headed god of writing and wisdom

Amun, called "the hidden one," was often shown as a man with two plumes on his crown or as a ram. Sometimes Amun is shown as a goose and called the "great cackler" who laid the cosmic egg and created the world.

**AMUN** The supreme deity of ancient Egypt during the New Kingdom (1550–1069 B.C.), Amun is one of the most ancient gods in the Egyptian pantheon. Amun was the principal god of the city of Thebes, along with his wife, MUT, the lion-headed goddess, and their son, KHONSU, the moon god. Egyptian gods frequently came in threes, or triads. Over Egypt's long history, Amun gained many titles: Amun Kematef; "He Whose Time is Over"; "Lord of the Throne of the Two Lands"; and "Eldest of the Gods of the Eastern Sky," to name a few. Amun's name meant the "hidden one" or "that which is concealed," implying that his nature was unknowable.

A possible origin of his name is the ancient Libyan word *aman*, or "water." In one creation myth, a group of eight gods lived in the Ogdoad, or primordial water, and they were the first gods to come into existence. Amun and his first wife, Amunet, were the gods of the Ogdoad, representing "hiddenness."

In statues and paintings, Amun is personified as a man, either standing or seated on his throne, wearing a kilt and a round, flat crown with a sun disk and two tall ostrich feathers on top. His skin is often blue, perhaps a symbol for water or lapis lazuli, a highly prized stone worthy of the gods.

The animals sacred to Amun were the goose and a special breed of ram with large, curling horns. The ram became the symbol of Amun, as did the ram's horns, and sometimes Amun was depicted as a ram or as a ram-headed man.

Amun probably was first worshipped as an agricultural god who assured abundant crops and fertility in animals. Over time he evolved from a minor local god to the supreme deity in the Egyptian pantheon. Amun is mentioned in the PYRAMID TEXTS, where he is said to "protect the other gods with his shadow." The earliest known temple for Amun was built in the Eleventh Dynasty (2125–2055 B.C.) in Thebes.

In ancient Egypt, religion and politics went hand in hand, and when the Theban princes in the south won a battle with the north, they united the country and started the Twelfth Dynasty (1985–1795 B.C.). The powerful southern kings paid special homage to Amun, in thanks for his divine help, by taking the god's name as their own. King Amenemhet I (Amun-em-het) took the name "Amun is Supreme," as did his immediate successors. Their patron deity became "the king of the gods." As the cult of Amun became powerful, Waset (later called Thebes by the Greeks), grew in power and wealth and was called the City of Amun. During the New Kingdom (1550–1069 B.C.), when Egypt was at the height of its Golden Age, Waset was named the capital of Egypt and the most important religious center in the land.

Amun's most important religious celebration was the Festival of OPET in Thebes. Cult statues of Amun, Mut, and Khonsu were carried from Karnak Temple to Luxor Temple once a year, and the whole city celebrated the joyous event.

Amun was often credited by the queens of Egypt as having fathered their children. When Queen HATSHEPSUT came to power, she inscribed the story of her divine birth, from the union of Amun and her mother, Queen Ahmose, on the wall of her mortuary temple at Deir el Bahri. The queen is visited by Amun in the guise of her husband; the god and the queen sit on a bed, with hands touching. Amun holds an ANKH, the sign of life, to the queen's nose, and in due time she gives birth to Hatshepsut. Carvings on the walls of Luxor Temple show how Amun visited Queen Mutemwiya in the same fashion, and their union produced her son, Amenhotep III. The clear portrayal of this myth helped to strengthen Hatshepsut's and Amenhotep's right to the throne of Egypt, and Hatshepsut boasted that she erected her obelisk at Karnak "for her father Amun."

Thebes (modern Luxor) was the center of the Egyptian universe, and Amun was its most powerful god. By elevating Amun to the position of supreme god, the Egyptian priests came close to the idea of monotheism, a concept that would be fully developed later when Akhenaten came to power (1352–1336 B.C.). Amun's popularity continued even during the Ptolemaic dynasty (332–32 B.C.), for the Greeks saw Amun as a version of their principal god, ZEUS.

**AMUNET**  The wife of Amun in the creation myth of the OGDOAD. Amunet and her husband represented "hiddenness." Mythology tells us that Amunet and Amun resided in the darkness and chaos of the primordial water. Amunet is a symbol of protection and one of the creation goddesses. Her rituals were related to the pharaoh's jubilee festival, and during the later Greek domination of Egypt (332–32 B.C.), she is shown nurturing the king during his coronation ceremony. Amunet is sometimes shown as a goddess wearing a crown of Lower Egypt. Her place of importance was largely taken over by MUT, Amun's wife during the New Kingdom (1550–1069 B.C.). However, there is a statue of Amunet in Karnak Temple.

**AMUN-RE**  In Egyptian mythology, when AMUN of Thebes became associated with the sun god, RE of Heliopolis (modern Cairo), it was a merger of two of the most powerful gods in ancient Egypt. Re was one of the most important deities in the Old Kingdom (2686–2181 B.C.), and it added to Amun's prestige to be identified with such a prominent and venerated deity. Amun of Thebes emerged as a manifestation of the ancient sun god and as such was identified as the "fierce red-eyed lion" (the sun) and "Amun when he rises as Horakhty" (Horus the hawk god on the horizon). Amun-Re is shown with the body of a man and a hawk's head or a human head with a beard. He wears a tall crown with double plumes, a broad collar necklace, and a kilt. He carries an ankh, the symbol of life, and a scepter, a symbol of power. The uniting of these two powerful deities was seen as the symbolic uniting of Upper and Lower Egypt and consolidated power in the priesthood. Amun-Re then became the "king of the gods."

**AMUN-RE-KAMUTEF**  Called the bull of his mother, Amun-Re-Kamutef was the manifestation of Amun-Re and Kamutef. In this instance, Amun-Re was worshipped as a fertility god, represented with an erect phallus. Amun-Re-Kamutef was closely related to the most important fertility god, MIN.

**ANAT** (also ANATH, ANTHAT)  Sometimes linked to HATHOR and viewed as the wife of SET, this foreign warrior goddess originated in Syria and was introduced into Egypt by the HYKSOS when they invaded the DELTA (northern Egypt) around 1650 B.C. The cult of Anat flourished in the Delta during the Nineteenth Dynasty (1295–1186 B.C.). The pharaoh Ramses II (RAMSES THE GREAT) named one of his daughters *Bint-Anat,* "daughter of Anat," and he called one of his hunting dogs "Anat in Strength." He and his dogs are shown on the walls of Beit el Wali (a southern temple) defeating the Libyans.

Although Anat's titles were "mistress of the sky" and "mother of the gods," she was primarily a warrior goddess, known for her ferociousness. For the Egyptians, Anat's greatest virtue was that she protected the pharaoh during battle, and she was often shown holding an ax, lance, and shield above her head in a menacing gesture. She is often shown in a long slim dress or a panther skin, wearing the tall Egyptian crown with two plumes. In Egyptian mythology, Anat and ASTARTE, another foreign goddess, were both seen as daughters of RE the sun god, along with Hathor, who acted as the "vengeful eye" of Re. Anat is sometimes called a "virgin goddess," but in other contexts, she is seen as the wife or consort of BAAL and RESHEF. Similarities between Anat and Astarte sometimes caused their personalities to be combined, but generally they were worshipped as individual goddesses.

**ANHUR**  See ONOURIS.

**ANIMAL GODS**  Animals played a big part in the mythology and religion of ancient Egypt. Some animals were associated with or sacred to the gods, but animals themselves were not worshipped. While the falcon was the symbol of Horus and the cat was the symbol of Bastet, for example, the Egyptians did not worship every falcon and cat or believe these animals were gods. Some animals sacred to the gods were raised on farms specifically to be killed and mummified and sold to people who made pilgrimages to the temples. The faithful could purchase a mummified cat, ibis, or falcon and present it to the god as a votive offering in the hope that their prayers would be answered.

Some animals, however, were designated as the living embodiments of a god. The Egyptians believed a god could inhabit the body of a particular falcon, and that falcon would be considered a living cult

## List of Animals and the Gods to Which They Are Sacred

| | |
|---|---|
| **Baboon** | Thoth, Hapi |
| **Beetle** | Khepri |
| **Bull** | Apis, Buchis, and Mnevis |
| **Cat** | Bastet |
| **Cobra** | Buto (see also snake) |
| **Cow** | Hathor, Isis personified as Hathor, and Bat |
| **Crocodile** | Sobek |
| **Dog/Jackal** | Anubis, Wep-wa-wet, son of Horus, Thoth portrayed as a jackal, Duamutef Son of Horus |
| **Dolphin** | Hat-mehit |
| **Donkey** | Set when he was defeated by Horus |
| **Falcon** | Horus and Horus as Harmachis, Haroeris, Harsaphes, Harsiesis, Hartomes, Horasematawy, Hormerti, Horus-Behdety, Khonsu, Re-Horakhty, Qebesenef son of Horus |
| **Frog** | Nun, Heket, Kek, and Amun in the Ogdoad |
| **Goose** | Geb—the symbol of Amun, and also called great cackler—is said to have laid an egg from which the world came. |
| **Hippopotamus** | Tauret, Set when he is defeated by Horus |
| **Ibis** | Aah, Thoth |
| **Lioness** | Astarte, Sekhmet, Mut, and Tefnut |
| **Lynx** | Maftet |
| **Pig** | Set when he is defeated by Horus |
| **Ram** | Amun, Ba-neb-djet, Bata, Khnum |
| **Scorpion** | Selket |
| **Snake** | Buto/Wadjet, Meretseger, Renenutet |
| **Sow** | Nut |
| **Swallow or Kite** | Isis and Nephthys |
| **Vulture** | Nekhbet |

Animals were sacred to many gods and were often left as offerings in the temples. This mummified falcon was probably a fake sold to an unsuspecting pilgrim. It was impossible to raise enough falcons in captivity to meet the high demand, so often a bundle of rags and sticks was wrapped to look like a falcon. (Photograph by Pat Remler)

image. As the living representation of the god, that falcon would be worshipped as if he were the actual god, Horus. Particularly during the Late and Ptolemaic periods, any animal in which the spirit of the god was believed to dwell was housed in luxury in the temple precincts. The many different manifestations of the gods included the ram of Amun, the ibis of Thoth, the crocodile of Sobek, and the falcon in various forms of Horus, to mention a few.

The faithful had various ways to identify which animal a spirit inhabited. During one ceremony to determine which animal would represent the god, the cult statue, carried by the priests, would seem to dip toward a particular animal. Each year a new living manifestation of the god was chosen and installed in the temple precinct with a great deal of pomp and ceremony. The fate of the deposed animal is not known. Some animals, like the Apis, Buchis, and Mnevis bulls, were chosen for their

Cats were sacred to the goddess Bastet, and cat statues of all sizes were popular offerings in her temple. *(Photo by Oxyman/Used under a Creative Commons license))*

special markings. They were selected after an exhaustive search that began when the previous bull died. Once found, the bull traveled to its new home in the temple to be installed with great ceremony as the living manifestation of Apis, Buchis, or Mnevis, an honor it would hold for the rest of its life. When a bull died, Egypt went into mourning. The bull was mummified and placed in a tomb fit for a head of state.

**ANKH** The sign of eternal life in ancient Egypt, the ankh is something of a mystery, for no one knows what the shape represents. It has been suggested that the ankh symbolizes a key, part of the human anatomy, or, more likely, a sandal strap as seen from above. The hieroglyph means "to live," and the ankh was a powerful and protective force in ancient Egypt. Paintings on tomb walls show the gods offering "eternal life" to the king and again bestowing "eternal life" upon the mummy by holding an ankh to its face and reciting a magical spell. The ankh is the rarest of ancient Egyptian AMULETS and

may have been the property of the gods only, for rarely is a person shown carrying an ankh.

Interestingly, the word *ankh* means "hand mirror" as well as "life." Tutankhamen had a mirror case in the shape of an ankh buried with him in his tomb, a play on words that any Egyptian would have recognized.

**ANKHAT** One of the titles of Isis, meaning "she who gives life."

**ANUBIS** (ANUPU) The jackal god of mummification and the guardian of the cemetery, Anubis played three important roles in the funerary rituals. First, he was the guardian of the cemetery, where he often appears as the jackal wearing a collar decorated with magical inscriptions and holding a flail or whip, a sign of authority.

Second, mythology tells us that Anubis embalmed OSIRIS and was the protector of the god's body during and after the embalming. Anubis's most important role is to prepare the mummy for its journey to the NETHERWORLD.

Third, Anubis is the guardian of the mummy in his or her tomb. Images of Anubis are prominent in the tomb of Tutankhamen. When the British Egyptologist Howard Carter opened Tutankhamen's tomb in 1922, he found the storeroom packed with magical items that the king would need in the next world. Between the paws of a statue of Anubis facing west was a magical reed torch with a brick stand that had a small hole in the middle in which the reed could be placed. Scratched on the brick was the ominous spell:

> It is I who hinder the sand from choking the
> sacred chamber,
> and who repel he would repel him with
> the desert-flames. I have set aflame the desert(?),
>   I
> have caused the path to be mistaken.
> I am for the protection of Osiris.

It was the duty of Anubis to guard this room, which in ancient times was called the "Treasury of the Innermost." Anubis was perched on a shrine that had several compartments, each of which held funerary objects, including four blue faience forelegs of a bovine animal and two wooden amulets in the shape of a mummy.

Different myths claim different gods as the parents of Anubis. One myth says his mother was NEPHTHYS and his father was Osiris; in other myths his father was SET. The Greek writer Plutarch wrote that Anubis was the son of Osiris and ISIS. Plutarch also

Anubis, the god of embalming, has the head of a jackal and the body of a man. He holds an ankh in his right hand to give life and breath to the deceased. *(Drawing by Mary Jordan)*

noted that the dog (Anubis) ". . . is equally watchful by day and by night, making him a good guardian."

Anubis's home was the cemetery, and his most important duty was to preside over embalming and mummification. Anubis is said to have mummified Osiris and wrapped his body in fine linen bandages woven by the sisters Isis and Nephthys. Tomb paintings show him attending the mummy in the tomb, placing his hands on the mummy and saying, "I have come to protect Osiris," for every mummified body was associated with Osiris, the god of the dead. Other scenes show Anubis offering the heart to the mummy in its coffin so the body will be complete when it reaches the Netherworld. In actual mummifications,

a priest wearing a jackal-head mask played the part of Anubis.

Anubis is mentioned in several mythological texts. In the Book of the Dead, he is shown in the vignettes or illustrations attending the weighing of the heart ceremony in the Hall of the Two Truths. Anubis stands next to the scale where the heart of the mummy is weighed to make sure it is as light as the feather of truth; if so, he will prepare the deceased for immortality while Thoth stands ready to record the decision. In the Book of Caverns, Anubis first wraps the head of the deceased king, placing linen strips on the face of the mummy to support and preserve it. It is Anubis who prevents the corpse from decaying by anointing the mummy with sacred oils and fragrant incense. The seven magical unguents used in embalming were also used in daily life. They were called festival perfume, *Hekenu* oil, Syrian balsam, *Nechenem* salve, anointing oil, best cedar oil, and best Libyan oil.

Anubis's several titles acknowledged his varying roles as god of mummification:

*Imy-ut*, "he who is at the place of embalming" (guardian of embalming)
*Tepy-dju-ef*, "he who is upon his hill" (Anubis guarding the necropolis)
*Neb-ta-djser*, "lord of the sacred land" (the actual necropolis)
*Khenty-imentiu*, "foremost of the westerners" (first among the deceased)
*Khenty-seh-netjer*, "lord of the god's pavilion" (a symbol for the tent where mummification took place)

When the Greeks and, later, the Romans ruled Egypt, Anubis was worshipped as a cosmic deity who brought light to the people. Shown on the walls of the catacombs in Alexandria, Anubis appears in the garb of a Roman general while serving as the guardian of Osiris.

In second-century Rome, Anubis was described as he appeared in the Procession of Isis by the author Apuleius:

Immediately after these came the Deities condescending to walk upon human feet, the foremost among them rearing terrifically on high his dog's head and neck—this messenger between heaven and hell displaying alternately a face black as night, and as golden as the day . . .

Golden Ass
Book xi

Anubis remained important as a guardian of the dead until the Christian era, when mummification was outlawed.

**ANUKIS** ⌐ ∼∼∼∼ ◁ ◠ ◷ (ALSO ANQET, ANUKET)  Important in the OLD KINGDOM, Anukis is a water goddess from the south. Her title, "she who embraces," reflects her association with the NILE. Anukis was worshipped in southern Egypt and NUBIA and was honored with an important cult center at Aswan. She was said to be a daughter of RE, the sun god, but Anukis's most important role was her position in the ELEPHANTINE TRIAD. She was the wife of KHNUM, the

Anukis, a water goddess, was worshipped in the south at her cult center on Sehel Island. *(Photograph by Pat Remler)*

ram-headed god who created mankind on the potter's wheel. Egyptian triads traditionally have a father, mother, and son, but curiously, Anukis's child was daughter SATIS, guardian of Egypt's southern frontier. In some versions of the myth, Satis is said to be the consort, or wife, of Khnum. One of Anukis's titles was "Goddess of the CATARACTS [rapids] of the Southern Nile," and her temples were at Sehel Island (south of Aswan) and Elephantine Island (Abu Island). Although her name means "to embrace," Anukis, like many Egyptian goddesses, has a dual nature—both sweet and fierce. It was said that her embrace could also become a chokehold. As "Goddess of the Hunt," her sacred animal is the gazelle. An ostracon (piece of broken pottery) shows Anukis as a gazelle and gives her titles such as "Mistress of the Gods" and "Lady of Heaven." Most often Anukis is portrayed as a woman holding a papyrus scepter and an ANKH and wearing a tall headdress made of ostrich feathers or reeds. Because of her popularity in the south, she was known as "Mistress of Nubia."

**APEDEMAK**  A southern war god whose cult, complete with a temple and cadre of priests, flourished in the eastern desert at Meroe in southern Nubia (modern Sudan). The long and tumultuous relationship between Egypt and Nubia produced an exchange of ideas and religion that was to influence both countries profoundly. When the Egyptians saw Apedemak, the fierce lion, guarding his temple, they equated him with their own fierce gods. Apedemak's Egyptian-style temple in Nubia is covered with perfect Egyptian hieroglyphs praising him as "the splendid god at the forefront of Nubia" and "lion of the south, strong of arm."

**APIS BULL** ◹ ▱ 𓃒 (HAP)  The Apis bull is a rare example of the Egyptians worshipping a living animal as a god. The Apis was a special bull believed to be a god by the ancient Egyptians. He was worshipped during his life and then mummified when he died.

The cult of the Apis was central to Egyptian religion and dates from Egypt's earliest settlements. Because of its strength and virility, the bull was associated with the pharaoh and his divinity. The cult of the Apis, associated with PTAH, the creator god of Memphis, was very popular during the reign of the Ptolemies, Greeks who ruled Egypt from the city of Alexandria (332–32 B.C.).

According to the Greek historian Herodotus, a bolt of lightning came down from heaven and

This 19th-century romantic illustration depicts a joyous procession honoring the sacred Apis bull. *(Drawing by E. Grasset)*

This alabaster embalming table was made especially for the mummification of the Apis bull and is designed so the body fluids can run off during embalming. *(Photograph by Pat Remler)*

impregnated the mother of the Apis. The Apis calf had special markings: It was black with a white diamond on its forehead, an eagle on its back, a scarab under its tongue, and split tail hairs.

There was only one Apis bull alive at any time. When the bull died, all of Egypt mourned, and a search for the new Apis calf began. In general, the Egyptian religion was based on the idea of resurrection: When a person died, he or she could resurrect in the next world. When the Apis bull died, however, the Egyptians seemed to believe in reincarnation, that the bull would be born again in this world in the body of another bull.

During its lifetime, the Apis was pampered, perfumed, and adored each day in luxurious surroundings at the temple complex in Memphis. The cow that gave birth to the Apis was also venerated and associated with Isis as a divine mother; when the cow died, it was buried in a special tomb called the Iseum.

When the Apis bull died, it was mummified on a huge alabaster table, and several of these mummification tables can still be seen at the site of the ancient city of Memphis. After the rites of mummification, the Apis was taken in sacred procession to a special burial place, the SERAPEUM, an extensive underground cavern at SAQQARA that held the granite sarcophagus of each Apis bull. After death the Apis became one with OSIRIS and was called Osirapis (see SERAPIS). The Apis bull was one of three sacred bulls in ancient Egypt (see the BUCHIS and the MNEVIS bulls).

The cult of the Apis bull was so popular and so important to the Egyptians that when the invading Persian king Cambyses (ruled 525–522 B.C.) reached the city of Memphis, he could think of no greater insult than to kill and eat the Apis bull.

## APOPHIS ⌁□□ 〰 (APEP) The serpent god of the Underworld, Apophis represents all that is malicious and evil. As a primeval force of darkness and chaos, Apophis is the opposite of the sun god, RE, and his life-giving rays. The great serpent was the most wicked and eternal adversary of Re, who was forced to battle and defeat him each night. Apophis's greatest threat to the sun god was that if Re was not watchful, Apophis would capsize and destroy the solar boat as it sailed through the hours of the night, making it impossible for the sun to appear on the horizon each day.

Apophis could also take the form of a mammoth crocodile and attack the sun god on land or water. The sound of his voice was so terrifying that even the great god Re shuddered when the serpent roared. One of Apophis's names is "Earth Shaker," and violent storms and earthquakes were attributed to his wrath.

We find Apophis's origin in Egyptian CREATION MYTHS—especially the story from HERMOPOLIS, where he first appears as both serpents and frogs. Here, Apophis represents the first energy, a primeval force thriving in chaos and darkness in a time before *MAAT* and divine order existed.

Help in fighting the forces of the evil serpent could be found in the *Book of Overthrowing Apep* (Apophis), a collection of spells and rituals that could be used against the demon. Originating in the NEW KINGDOM (1550–1069 B.C.), the most complete text is found in the Bremner-Rind Papyrus. Drawings in the PAPYRUS show the "great serpent" subdued with knives and chains in order to diminish his power. Priests in the temple of AMUN-RE at Thebes chanted the spells and called upon the powerful magic of ISIS and THOTH when they listed all the ways that Apophis must be subdued: (1) Spell for spitting on Apep, (2) Spell for crushing Apep with the left foot, (3) Spell for smiting Apep with a lance, (4) Spell for binding Apep with chains, (5) Spell for smiting Apep with a knife, (6) Spell for burning Apep with fire.

Each part of Apophis's body was mentioned with the specific method of destroying him. Sometimes wax figures were fashioned of Apophis and bound with red and black string, then pierced with knives and burned. To further ensure the destruction of Apophis, his secret name was inscribed on a new papyrus and burned over flames.

So detested was the evil Apophis that Chapter 27 of the BOOK OF THE DEAD tells of a local goddess, Henen-su, who turned herself into a cat and killed Apophis, the "Prince of Darkness."

**APULEIUS, LUCIUS** A classical writer from the second century A.D. whose travels took him to Rome where the Egyptian cult of Isis was flourishing. His book *The Golden Ass* has been called the first novel in history. The story tells how the hero was turned into a donkey and then was saved by Isis. His fanciful tale revolves around a man called Lucius who, among his many adventures, was introduced into the "Mysteries of Isis." In Chapter 11, Apuleius describes how Isis appeared to him wearing Roman dress:

> First, she had a great abundance of hair, arranged and scattered about her neck, on the crown of her head she wore many garlands of flowers.... in one hand she held serpents, in the other, blades of corn, her garments were of fine silk in diverse colors, sometimes yellow, sometimes rose....

Apuleius's writing gives a valuable insight into the cult of the Egyptian goddess, who became so popular in the ancient world that she was worshipped throughout the Roman Empire.

**ARES** Greek god of war identified with the Egyptian god Anhur, called ONOURIS by the Greeks.

**ARMANT** (HERMONTHIS) Situated on the west bank of the Nile just south of modern Luxor, Armant rose to prominence as an important religious center during the Eleventh Dynasty when a temple was dedicated to MONTU, the popular Middle Kingdom war god. The temple of Montu flourished until the end of the Roman period (A.D. 205), when all temples were closed during the rise of Christianity in Egypt. Armant is also the home of the BUCHIS bull, the animal sacred to Montu. The Buchis bull was thought to be a physical manifestation of the sun god RE and of OSIRIS, the god of the dead. When the bull died, it was mummified and buried at the Bucheum, a great underground tomb similar to the tomb of the APIS bull, the SERAPEUM. The cult of the Buchis at Armant rose to power during the Late period when King Nectanebo II (360–343 B.C.) presided over the first burial of a Buchis bull. Eventually this tomb grew into an extensive burial place for all Buchis bulls.

When Cleopatra VII (51 B.C.–30 B.C.) visited Armant, she dedicated a MAMMISI, a birth temple for the gods, to her son Caesarion. The temple is in ruins today, but a stone block remains with the cartouche of Cleopatra.

Excavations have shown that during the Predynastic period in Egypt (5500–3100 B.C.), Armant was the site of an extensive settlement and cemetery.

**ARSAPHES** The name Plutarch gave the Egyptian god HERISHEF, a primitive fertility god shown as a ram. His name means "he who is upon his lake." The god's cult center was at Herakleopolis, near modern Beni Suef. At various times he has been associated with RE and with OSIRIS. The Greeks equated him with their hero Heracles.

**ARSENUPIS** Warrior god from Nubia associated with the god SHU. Arsenupis, whose name means "the good companion," is the principal deity of the Ptolemaic Temple of Dakka (south of modern Aswan). He is honored at Kalabsha Temple, the largest free-standing Nubian temple.

**ARTISTS AND CRAFTSMEN, GOD OF** See PTAH.

**ASTARTE** (also ASHTORETH, ASHERAH, ATTORET, ANATH) The great Canaanite mother goddess, Astarte, was the unrivaled goddess of Canaan. As the consort of BAAL, Astarte was also a powerful war goddess, and her reputation as a terrible and destructive force in war earned her the respect and worship of Egyptian kings. Astarte was adopted into the Egyptian pantheon during the New Kingdom, and chapels were built for her in Thebes and Tanis. In Egyptian mythology, she was the wife of SET, who resembled the Canaanite god Baal.

Associated with horses and chariots in Egypt, Ashtoreth/Astarte was often shown driving her chariot or riding her horse and wearing the Egyptian ATEF CROWN with tall plumes and bulls' horns. She was the guardian of the pharaoh's chariot, and during the reign of Ramses the Great (1279–1213 B.C.), Astarte was called "Mistress of the Horse and Chariot." Her cult centers flourished under Ramses's reign.

Worship of Astarte grew rapidly in Egypt, especially in the Delta, where foreign gods were readily associated with Egyptian gods. Astarte was seen as a reflection of ISIS and HATHOR, and like her Egyptian counterparts, the many facets of her personality were understood by the people. Astarte, the mother goddess, was all knowing and understanding, the loving mother of her clan and a leader of her people. In the Delta city of Tanis, Astarte was recognized as a moon goddess and was associated with the moon god Aah as well as with Hathor-Isis, who also had ties to Aah. There are many biblical references to Ashtoreth/ Astarte, and the Bible tells us that even King Saul, the first Hebrew king (1050 B.C.), worshipped Ashtoreth, the Queen of Heaven. In the following Old Testament references to Ashtoreth, we can see that for a time her cult was popular among the Hebrews.

> And they forsook the Lord and worshipped Baal and Ashtoreth.
>
> *Judges 2:13*

> And the People did what was evil in the sight of the Lord, forgetting the Lord their God, and served the Baals and the Ashtoreths.
>
> *Judges 3:7*

> Samuel spake unto the house of Israel, saying if ye do not return unto the Lord with all your hearts, and put away the strange gods and Ashtoreth from among you and prepare your hearts unto the Lord and serve him only, he will deliver you from the hands of the Philistines.
>
> *Samuel 7:3*

So popular and well established was the cult of Astarte/Ashtoreth that it flourished in the Delta well into Christian times.

**ASTRONOMICAL GODS** From earliest times the Egyptians studied the night sky, noting the position of the stars and plotting their courses as the seasons changed. The sky goddess, NUT, who protected mankind from her home in the heavens, was a common tomb decoration; she was often painted with her star-studded body stretching protectively across the ceiling, keeping the mummy safe in the same way that she sheltered the living. During the Old Kingdom (2686–2181 B.C.), two groups of stars were identified in the PYRAMID TEXTS: the *Akhenu seku*, "imperishable stars," which were believed to be the souls of the deceased who had gone to "heaven," and *Akhemu urtchu*, "stars that never rest," known today as the planets.

Later in the Middle Kingdom (2055–1650 B.C.), "star clocks" decorated the wooden coffins of the deceased. The "star clock" was a kind of calendar that identified 36 groups of stars, or decans, and their locations in the sky. By the Middle Kingdom, the Egyptians had identified five planets and called them the stars that "never rested" because they seemed to sail across the sky. The brightest of the decans was Sirius, the Dog Star, whom the Egyptians called the goddess Sopdet. Her appearance around the middle of July signaled the beginning of the season of "inundation," when the Nile rose and flooded

the land, covering it with rich topsoil. The Middle Kingdom "star clocks" seemed more decorative than accurate, because every 40 years a "star clock" was off about 10 days.

During the New Kingdom (1550–1069 B.C.), the decans or stars decorated tomb ceilings, notably the tombs of Senenmut and Ramses IV in the VALLEY OF THE KINGS and in the OSIREION of Seti I at ABYDOS. These astronomical ceilings were inscribed with texts relating the decan's journey through the Underworld. Jupiter was named "Horus Who Limits the Two Lands"; Mars, "Horus of the Horizon," or "Horus the Red"; Mercury, "Sebegu," a god associated with SET; Saturn, "Horus Bull of the Sky"; and Venus, "One Who Crosses" or "God of the Morning." The night sky was divided into "northern sky," which held the big dipper, called "Meskhet," and "southern sky," which held Sirius, called Sopdet and Orion, whom the Egyptians called "the Guardian of the Soul of Horus."

**ATEF CROWN** One of several crowns worn by the Egyptian gods and kings, the atef crown was similar to the tall white crown of UPPER EGYPT. The atef crown had two tall plumes, possibly ostrich feathers, and a disk on the top to distinguish it from the white crown, the symbol of Upper Egypt.

**ATEN** ☥ A sun god worshipped by the pharaoh AKHENATEN when he changed the religion of Egypt. The Aten was symbolized by a sun disk with sunbeams streaming down. The word *aten* means "disk," and when written in hieroglyphs, it refers to the sun as an astronomical body. The origin of the Aten is uncertain, but it may have come from an early sun cult in the city of Heliopolis. Queen Hatshepsut's standing obelisk at Karnak Temple states that the gold and silver cap (electrum) on top of the obelisk would shine on Egypt like the "aten." Hatshepsut's father, Thutmose I, referred to the Aten as a god in an inscription carved during his Nubian campaigns.

The Aten was favored by Akhenaten's father, Amenhotep III, who named a division of his army after the Aten and gave his wife, Queen Tiye, a pleasure boat called *The Aten Gleams* to sail on her private lake. It was not until Akhenaten became king, however, that the Aten became the supreme god in Egypt.

Per-Aten, the first temple dedicated to the Aten, was built at KARNAK next to the temple of Amun, the great god of Thebes. What the priests of Amun thought of the new temple is not known, but after Akhenaten's reign, the temple was torn down. In the 1930s through the 1950s, archaeologists discovered

The Aten, or sun disk, was the only god worshipped when Akhenaten, the "heretic pharaoh," changed the religion of Egypt. The rays of the sun end in hands holding the sign of life, the ankh. *(Drawing by Mary Jordan)*

35,000 blocks from the dismantled Aten temple. The decorations on the blocks and the foundation suggested to Egyptologists that the Aten temple featured open courts with pillars, several sanctuaries, and colossal statues of Akhenaten. One area of the Aten temple called Gem-Pa-Aten, "finding the Aten," was the domain of Queen Nefertiti and her daughters.

Around year five of his reign, Akhenaten moved the royal court from Thebes to his new city dedicated to the Aten in the remote desert. The city was called Akhet-Aten, "the horizon of the Aten," and included two major temples to the Aten: the Per-Aten ("house of the Aten") and the Hwt-Aten ("mansion of the Aten"). Both temples featured the new open-air design with no enclosed rooms and with several offering tables placed around the courtyard. The Per-Aten, which Egyptologists call the Great Temple, was the larger of the two. Its first courtyard was called Per-Hay, "the house of rejoicing," where the first light of the sun was greeted each day. As the sun rose, the worshippers moved into the second court, the Gem-Aten ("finding the Aten") and made offerings. An inner courtyard was reserved for the royal family—Akhenaten, Nefertiti, and their childrento make special offerings and perform the necessary rituals each day. Today nothing except the foundation remains of these temples, for they were demolished when Akhenaten was no longer king.

The essence of the Aten and Akhenaten's beliefs are preserved in the HYMN TO THE ATEN that was carved on the walls of the nobles' tombs at Akhet-Aten. It states that the Aten is the only god, that he manifests himself in the sun's rays, and that nighttime is to be feared. Fierce animals roam the land and danger is present when the Aten's rays are not shining down. Under the beneficent rays of the sun, however, daily life proceeds, and all work is accomplished. All life comes through the Aten, and he protects all forms of life, none too insignificant for his attention. The peoples of the world are created in different colors and are given different speech by the Aten, from whom all the beauty and bounty of nature come. The Aten cannot be understood by man and can be truly known only by his son, Akhenaten. The people cannot worship the Aten directly. Presumably they worshipped Akhenaten, the son of the Aten.

Boundary stelae (carved stone tablets) erected when Akhenaten built his city in the desert tell us about the nature of the Aten.

> The great and living Aten ... ordaining life, vigorously alive, my Father ... , my reminder of Eternity ... who proclaims himself with his two hands, whom no craftsman has devised, who is established in the rising and setting each day ceaselessly ... He fills the land with his rays and makes everyone to live ...

The phrase "whom no craftsman has devised" declared the Aten to be intangible; there could be no statues of him. The Aten was as elusive as the sun's rays. This must have been disturbing to the Egyptian people, who were used to gods with the head of a cat and the body of a woman, or a man with the head of a jackal or an ibis.

The "hymn to the Aten" says that the Aten is the only creator god and that he created not only the Egyptians but also all the peoples of the Earth. This, too, would have been a difficult concept for the Egyptians. If the Aten was the god of all people, then the Egyptians were no longer superior, and the old concept of Divine Order or *MAAT*, "the way the world should be," was clearly askew. Making war on their neighbors was no longer blessed by the gods, and life in the next world did not seem possible, for it was not clear if there was a NETHERWORLD. The teachings of the Aten were a curious mixture of humanitarianism and elitism, for the Aten shone only on the royal family.

**ATHENA** Greek goddess associated with ISIS and Neith. Athena was a goddess of war as well as of peace and compassion and patroness of arts and crafts. When the cult of Isis spread from Egypt to the

Roman Empire, she was readily accepted as a form of Athena.

**ATLAS** In Greek mythology, Atlas was the leader of the Titans, who were defeated in their battle against the gods. Atlas was condemned to carry the world on his shoulders for all eternity. The Greeks associated Atlas with the Egyptian god SHU, the god of air, whose name means "he who holds up." Shu is always shown holding up the sky.

**ATUM** Called the "undifferentiated one," meaning both male and female, Atum was the primeval being and the creator of the world. Recognized as an early form of the sun god, Atum was called the "Lord of Heliopolis," the ancient city that was the center for sun worship. Because of his association with the sun cult, Atum eventually merged with the sun god, Re, to become RE-ATUM. The creation myth from Heliopolis tells us that Atum emerged from NUN, the waters of chaos, onto the PRIMEVAL MOUND before heaven and earth were separated. From his semen Atum created the first gods on land, Shu (air) and Tefnut (moisture). They in turn produced Geb (earth) and Nut (sky), whose children were Osiris and Isis (who were brother and sister and also husband and wife) and Set and Nephthys (who were also brother and sister and husband and wife). These first nine deities formed the Heliopolitan Ennead, a family of gods.

Atum was not only the creator god but also a protector and a guardian of the pharaoh, and one of his titles was "Father of the King of Egypt." In the Old Kingdom (2686–2181 B.C.), it was Atum who embraced the dead king in the burial chamber of the pyramid and lifted him to the heavens, where he became an *Akhenu seku*, an "imperishable star."

During the New Kingdom (1550–1295 B.C.), Atum presided over the coronation of the king, as shown on the walls of the Temple of Amun at KARNAK. In the BOOK OF GATES, Atum subdues the serpent Nekebu-Kau by digging his fingernails into the snake, and he confronts the evil serpent Apophis, condemning him to death. Atum protects the souls of the deceased when they travel through the Underworld.

Atum appears in human form, usually wearing the combined white and red crown of Upper and Lower Egypt. Often he was seated on a throne holding a staff of authority. The bull, lion, lizard, and ICHNEU-MON were sacred to Atum.

**AVARIS** Greek name for the cult center of the god SET, Avaris was built by the HYKSOS kings (1650–1550 B.C.) when they invaded Egypt. Ruling from the north in the DELTA during the Second Intermediate period, the Hyksos fortified their city, built temples with a Canaanite design and accepted Set as a manifestation of their storm god BAAL. Avaris was captured by Ahmose I, first king of the NEW KINGDOM, who defeated the Hyksos and drove them out of Egypt.

Avaris is believed to be the site of the biblical city Pi Ramses, one of two cities built for the pharaoh Ramses II (RAMSES THE GREAT). Excavations have shown the city of Pi Ramses to be one of the largest in the ancient world, covering an area of about six square miles.

*BA* The Egyptians believed that each person came into the world with five separate parts, or facets, that made them a whole being: the physical body, the *KA*, the name, the shadow, and the *ba*. The *ba* is the most difficult to describe. At times it was a part of the soul of the deceased—the person's spirit—and at other times it seemed to be the entire soul or the essence of the deceased. The *ba* is also described as something like the "personality." It was able to fly from place to place and is often shown hovering over the mummy or resting on a shrine. Most commonly it is represented as a bird with a human head and arms. Supposedly it could assume any form it chose, and the BOOK OF THE DEAD has many spells to assist the *ba* in its transformation. One of the most important functions of the *ba* was to unite with the *ka* so the deceased could reach the heavens and become an *AKH* spirit.

Egyptians rarely mentioned the *ba* of a living person, so it seems as if the *ba* came into existence after death. Like the living person, the *ba* had physical needs. Relatives of the deceased were supposed to leave food offerings in front of the tomb to feed the *ba* until it reached the next world. Illustrations in the Book of the Dead show the *ba* flying inside and sometimes outside the tomb. In some ways the *ba* was the alter ego of the deceased. One Middle Kingdom (2055–1650 B.C.) papyrus tells the story of a man who was feeling weary of the world and wanted to kill himself. He had an argument with his *ba*, who told him to "throw his complaints on the woodpile" and threatened to desert the man in the next world. The end of the papyrus is missing, so we don't know if the man followed the advice of his *ba* or not.

Because the *ba* was essential for existence in the next world, a special chapter in the Book of the Dead ensured that the *ba* would be reunited with the deceased. In the following spell for "Causing the Uniting of the Ba and its Body in the Netherworld," the reader is instructed to recite the words over an amulet of the *ba* made of gold, inlaid with the stone that is placed on the deceased's neck.

> . . . Oh great god, cause that my *Ba* may come to me from anyplace where it is. If there is a problem, bring my *Ba* to me from any place where it is . . . If there is a problem, cause my *Ba* to see my body. If you find me Oh Eye of Horus, support me like those in the Netherworld . . . May the *Ba* see the body and may it rest upon its mummy. May it never perish, may it not be separated from the body for ever.

The *ba*, shown with the head of the deceased and the body of a bird, represented the personality or the conscience of the deceased. *(Drawing by Mary Jordan)*

**BAAL**  The principal Canaanite deity and fierce war god associated with the Egyptian god SET. The Egyptians recognized this powerful foreign god as one of their own, and the image of Set was always included when scribes wrote the name of Baal in hieroglyphs. Baal, an all-powerful god, represented the scorching heat of the desert and the destruction of sandstorms; he was master of the sky and lord of violent storms. Baal's cult appeared in Egypt in the Eighteenth Dynasty (1550–1295 B.C.) complete with a temple and priesthood in Memphis, the capital of Egypt, and the cult continued during the Nineteenth Dynasty (1295–1186 B.C.) in Pi-Ramses, the Delta city built by Ramses the Great.

Ramses, in his quest for victorious battles, worshipped Baal, and before his famous Battle of Kadesh in Syria, he assumed the titles Set Great of Strength and Baal, Voice of Thunder. Later Ramesside kings associated themselves with the foreign god as well and referred to themselves as "brave and mighty as Baal in heaven." This close association with a foreign god was not unusual in Egypt, and in Ramses's case, it was no doubt thought to be a good thing to pay homage to such a powerful god.

**BAALAT**  Canaanite word for goddess or mistress. She was the female counterpart of Baal and was identified with HATHOR, the Egyptian goddess of love and music.

**BABA**  A minor god who, in the myth of the CONTENDINGS OF HORUS AND SET, sits on the tribunal of gods. He angers the great sun god RE when he taunts him with the remark, "Your shrine is empty," meaning that neither the gods nor the people have respect for the sun god anymore.

**BABOON**  From the earliest time in Egypt, wild baboons were heard screeching as the first rays of the sun shone on the horizon, and their clamor was interpreted by the priests as adoration of the sun god. In some magical way, baboons were thought to be spirits that greeted the first signs of dawn. When the sun's rays appeared on the horizon, the spirits were transformed into baboons that rejoiced and adored the sun each morning. The baboon and the IBIS both represented THOTH, the god of writing, and were both associated with the EYE OF RE. A frieze of baboons can be seen above the entrance to the Great Temple at Abu Simbel, and the first rays of the sun reach them each morning.

**BA-NEB-DJET** (BA-NEB-DJED)  Sacred ram of the Delta city Mendes, Ba-neb-djet was a fertility god whose name meant "soul of the lord of Mendes." He was called the "soul of Re," but this may have been a play on words, because the "Ba" in his name means "soul." Like so many Egyptian gods, Ba-neb-djet was part of a trinity: His wife, Hat-meh-yt, was the local fish goddess, and their son, Harpocrates, was HORUS, the falcon-headed god as a child. As a god of fertility, Ba-neb-djet was symbolic father of the king. Ramses III claimed Ba-neb-djet as his father, and his mother left an account of her union with Ba-neb-djet carved on a stele in Ramses's mortuary temple at Medinet Habu (located on the west bank at Thebes). The Greeks associated Ba-neb-djet with their fertility gods Priapus and Pan.

In the PAPYRUS Chester Beatty, Ba-neb-djet is called upon to mediate a dispute between the gods Horus and Set. Ba-neb-djet, following the vote of the sun god Re (with whom he was also associated), favored the elder brother Set over Horus.

**BASTET** (BAST)  Beloved cat goddess of the Egyptians, Bastet is goddess of the DELTA, with possible origins in the Libyan Desert. When Bastet is associated with Isis, she becomes "the Soul of Isis," but as a goddess of music and dance, Bastet is linked with HATHOR. Their cult instrument is the SISTRUM, which they carry as one of their attributes.

Bastet's cult city, Per-Bast (modern Bubastis), is located in the Delta and is mentioned in the Bible as *Pibeseth* (Ezekiel 30:17). Bastet's name is written with the *bas* jar (  ) (bs) and a loaf  (t), and means "She of the *bas*-jar"—a special vessel that holds perfume associated with her festivals.

During the OLD KINGDOM, Bastet was called "Goddess of the North," and in the PYRAMID TEXTS of King UNAS, she is "nurse and mother of the king." When SEKHMET the lion goddess was named "Lady of the West," Bastet became her counterpart as "Lady of the East." Early depictions of Bastet show her with the head of a lion and associated with the lion-headed goddess, MUT. She is said to be the mother of MAAHES, a lion-headed deity, and the wife of PTAH.

Like Sekhmet, Bastet has a dual personality, both gentle and fierce. Her association with Sekhmet reveals Bastet's aggressive and vengeful side. In one version of the mythology, Bastet becomes the daughter of the sun god Re, and when she is called upon to protect her father, Bastet becomes the "fury in which were called "Procession of Bastet," "Bastet Protects the Two Lands," "Bastet Goes Forth from Per-Bast" (her city), "Bastet Appears before Re," and the "Festival of Hathor and Bastet." These joyous occasions involved days of music, dancing, and merriment throughout Egypt.

The Greek historian Herodotus provides a lively description of the devotees of the goddess as they made their way to the "Festival of Bastet."

> When the Egyptians travel to Bubastis, [the city] they do so in this manner: men and women sail together, and in each boat there are many persons of both sexes. Some of the women shake sacred rattles, [sistrum, pl. sistra] and some of the men play pipes during the whole journey, while others sing and clap their hands. If they pass a town on the way, some of the women shout and cheer at the local women, while others dance and create a disturbance. They do this at every town on the Nile. When they arrive at Bubastis, they begin the festival with great sacrifices, and on this occasion, more wine is consumed than during any other time of the year.

—Herodotus, *Histories*, Book II, Chapter 60

The worshippers approached the temple singing, beating drums, and playing tambourines. Some carried *sistra* (sacred rattles) as they danced through the streets. Herodotus describes Bastet's lavish temple as standing on raised ground in the center of the city, so it was visible from every quarter. A TEMENOS wall decorated with various animals surrounded the temple. The inner courtyard was planted with a grove of trees.

So popular was Bastet that the Greeks identified her with their goddess Artemis. The third-century Roman poet Ovid refers to the goddess Bastet in his work *Metamorphoses* and said the goddess could turn herself into a cat. Bastet was most often shown with the body of a woman and the head of a cat, wearing a long, narrow, sheath-style dress with wide decorated bands over the shoulders. The goddess holds her sistrum in one hand, and in the other she holds an AEGIS, a talisman representing a broad collar necklace with the head of a cat. Sometimes she is shown with kittens at her feet, a further depiction of her association with hearth and family. The ancient Egyptian word for kitten was *miw*, pronounced "meow"—the sound a cat makes. It became a term of endearment for children, who were called *miw-sheri*, "little cat."

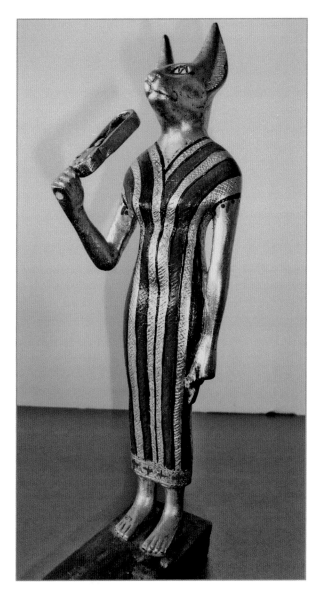

Bastet, the feline goddess, was most often represented as a cat-headed woman carrying a sistrum and an aegis. Because cats were favorite pets in Egypt, Bastet became a popular household goddess. *(Photograph by Pat Remler)*

the eye of Re." As a dutiful daughter, she carried out the orders of Re and was the "means of her father's vengeance."

By the end of the NEW KINGDOM (1550–1069 B.C.), Bastet had become a popular household goddess. Egyptian families welcomed her into their homes as goddess of the hearth and protector of pregnant women. Her festivals were famous, and she was called "goddess of plenty" and "mistress of pleasure." And as her popularity grew, her cult became well-known for its lavish festivals—some of

Pilgrims traveled from all over Egypt to visit Bastet's temple and leave offerings to the goddess. Because the cat was sacred to Bastet, they left bronze statues, amulets, and mummified cats. Thousands of cat mummies have been discovered in underground crypts at the site of Bastet's temple in Bubastis.

**BAT**  Predynastic cow goddess originating in Upper Egypt (southern) whose image appears on the top register of the NARMER PALETTE, the carved stone that commemorates the unification of Upper and Lower Egypt in 3100 B.C. Bat has a human head and the ears and horns of a cow. She was rarely shown in Egyptian art, but when she was, her body was in the shape of the MENAT, the counterpoise for a necklace that was shaped like a keyhole. Egyptian necklaces were often large and heavy, so to keep them in place a counterpoise would hang down the wearer's back for balance. The menat also resembled the shape of the SISTRUM, the sacred rattle, that was one of Bat's ritual objects. One of the names of Bat's cult center was the "House of the Sistrum." The earliest mention of Bat is found in the PYRAMID TEXTS, in which King Unas is said to possess the two faces of Bat. There are few later references, and as was so often the case in Egyptian mythology, the goddess Bat merged with HATHOR, who became the universal cow goddess.

**BATA**  A minor god associated with ANUBIS in the mythological *Tale of Two Brothers*. The story of Bata, the virtuous younger brother, and his brother's wife, who tries to seduce him, is much the same tale as the biblical story of Joseph and Potiphar's wife (Genesis 39:7). Bata's story also parallels the MYTH OF OSIRIS, in which the "good" brother is emasculated because of the evil around him.

**BEER**  The effects of drinking beer so delighted the Egyptians that beer and bread became a basic offering to the gods. Beer is generally believed to be an Egyptian invention, and every temple complex had a brewery and bakery that produced large quantities of bread and beer for the gods. Offerings were presented with great ceremony and were placed before the shrine of each god. After an appropriate length of time, determined by the priests, the bread and beer were removed and consumed by the priests and workers in the temple. The PYRAMID TEXTS include prayers for the good life in the next world: "Let me live upon bread made of white grain and let my beer be made of red grain. . . ." We know that beer was just as important in the afterlife as it was for the living because offerings of beer are frequently painted on tomb walls.

Excavations near the Great Pyramid Complex on the Giza Plateau revealed that bakeries and breweries were placed next to each other because both bread and beer needed yeast as a key ingredient. The workmen who built the pyramids were often paid in bread, beer, and onions. Being a staple of life in ancient Egypt, beer was also given to children. The scribe Ani reminds a son to be kind to his mother for it was she who gave him bread and beer each day when he returned from his lessons.

While the chemistry of beer is complex, the Egyptians followed a simple recipe. Pans of damp, unmilled grain were left in the sun to germinate. The germinated grain was then crushed and became malt. Malt was mixed with crumbled bread made from course flour and soaked in a pot of water. The thickened mixture was then partially baked at a low temperature so the heat of the oven did not destroy the yeast. When the yeast in the half-baked bread fermented, the mixture was strained through a sieve, leaving beer of about 7 percent alcohol. Both barley and wheat were popular for brewing beer, and sometimes the mixture was sweetened with date juice, or red dye was added for a special feast day.

Beer contains nutrients, and the antibacterial action of the alcohol made it safer to drink than water. Egyptian beer must have come in varying strengths, for tomb paintings frequently depict the results of overindulgence. The scribe Ani warned against visiting a house where beer was served by describing its effects:

> Boast not that you can drink . . . a jug of beer. Thou speakest, and an unintelligible utterance issueth from thy mouth. If thou fallest down and thy limbs break there is no one to hold out a hand to thee. Thy companions in drink stand up and say, "Away with the sot." If there cometh one to see thee in order to question thee, thou are found lying on the ground and thou art like a child.

**BEETLE**  See SCARAB BEETLE.

**BENBEN**  Shaped like a short OBELISK, the benben is of ancient origin. It represents RE the sun god, for it was said that the sacred benben stone was the first thing the rays of the sun touched each morning in the sun temple at HELIOPOLIS. The benben symbolizes the PRIMEVAL MOUND, the first bit of earth to emerge from the waters of chaos (creation myth from Heliopolis). The *Hewet-Benben*, the Temple of the Benben, housed the first benben and was closely linked to the Benu bird that landed on the pyramidal top of the benben when it emerged as the first dry land. When sun temples became popular in Dynasty V, the focus of worship in the open-air courtyards was the benben that stood on a raised platform. Fifth Dynasty benbens served as the prototype for later tall obelisks placed in front of temples during the New Kingdom.

**BENU**  The most famous sacred bird, the Benu is a mythological creature that appears in the Heliopolis creation myth. Mentioned in the Pyramid Texts, the Benu is said to be a form of the god Atum who has "risen up, as a benben in the house of the Benu in Heliopolis." Other myths claim that the Benu emerged from a burning Persea tree in Heliopolis or sprang from the heart of Osiris.

The Benu was believed to be the incarnation of Re, for at the dawn of creation, the Benu rested on the first bit of dry land as it emerged from the waters of chaos and, by so doing, symbolized the sun's rays touching the first earth mound (see BENBEN). A Middle Kingdom (2055–2650 B.C.) papyrus refers to the "Benu of Re" and "He who came into being by himself." Seemingly, like Re, the Benu was thought to have created itself.

The name Benu derives from the Egyptian word *weben* "to rise," and the Benu may have been the basis of the Greek phoenix bird that rose from its own ashes. Herodotus, the Greek traveler, visited Egypt in the fifth century B.C. and noted that he had never actually seen a Benu bird (he called it a phoenix), only a painting of one. The priests of Heliopolis told Herodotus that the Benu bird appeared only every 500 years, when its parents died. Then the Benu carried the bodies of its deceased parents, encased in a chunk of myrrh (an aromatic substance used to preserve bodies), to the sun temple at Heliopolis, the final resting place of the deceased Benu.

When Tutankhamen's solid gold coffin was opened, a black scarab with a Benu bird carved on its back was one of the magical objects found on his mummy. A symbol of rebirth in the Netherworld, the image of the Benu was frequently carved on scarabs and buried with the mummy to help with resurrection in the next world.

**BES**  The dwarf god, with a frightening appearance and a kind nature, Bes was a god of the people and his popularity never waned. His grotesque features and the magical knife he brandished were meant only to ward off evil and frighten demons away from the families he protected. Families loved Bes and often painted his image in their houses to

Although he looks grotesque, Bes is a good-natured, friendly god. He protects families and their homes and is the patron god of pregnant women. *(Photograph by Pat Remler)*

bring good luck and well-being. Bes, along with Tauret, the hippopotamus goddess, was a guardian of mothers during childbirth. Bes protected houses from snakes and scorpions that were a constant threat to young children in ancient Egypt. He was always on guard against the problems of daily life. Bes was also a god of music and merrymaking and was often shown with a tambourine.

Bes's strange appearance has caused Egyptologists to speculate on his origin, for he looks nothing like the other slim and elegant Egyptian gods. One of the most significant differences is that he is almost always shown full face and only rarely in profile. Bes looks like a dwarf with a lion's mane on his head, and his tongue is often sticking out. He has short, stubby arms and legs and a lion's tail. At different periods in Egyptian history, Bes has been shown with a large knife; a tambourine; a tall, feathered crown; and a skirt. There are speculations that Bes originated in what is now modern Turkey, since his images have been found in Turkish excavation sites. Bes also might have originated in sub-Saharan Africa, because one of his titles is Lord of Punt, an ancient land on the west African coast. The tall, plumed crown that he sometimes wears is much like the crown of Anukis, a goddess from the southern borders of Egypt. Most Egyptologists now believe that Bes is an Egyptian god with ancient origins. Several different grotesque gods have appeared over time in different communities in ancient Egypt, and whatever their local name was, they eventually evolved into the god Bes.

**BLUE CROWN**   See crowns.

## BOOK OF CAVERNS

A funerary text written in the Nineteenth Dynasty, the Book of Caverns chronicles in gory detail the perils of the sun god's journey through the 12 hours of the night.

Each of the six parts of the Book of Caverns takes place in a cave or cavern where Re is hailed as the "bringer of light and life" and as the executioner of enemies. The Book of Caverns contrasts the rewards of goodness with Re's punishment of his enemies. When the book opens, Re is descending into the Duat, where he encounters various gods and goddesses. Each one is enclosed in an oval shape.

Upon reaching the First Cavern, Re shouts the secret names of the guardian deities so they will let him pass without harm. Now, feeling strong and asserting himself, Re reaches the Second Cavern, where he punishes his enemies by hanging them from their feet or tearing their hearts from their bodies. Upon reaching the Third Cavern, Re greets Aker, a two-headed lion god, and Osiris, god of the dead, who appears with an erect phallus, demonstrating that he is rejuvenated by the light of the sun. The Fourth Cavern repeats the theme of the goodness and light as the sun god's boat travels through.

Punishment is the theme of the Fifth Cavern. Huge cauldrons are filled with decapitated corpses and body parts. Re admonishes, "Look, I destroy my enemies. You will stay in your caverns! Your fires will heat my cauldrons. . . ." As he travels past the Fifth Cavern, Re meets "The Secret One," a manifestation of Nut, the sky goddess. She is surrounded by solar disks and resurrected souls of the dead. Upon entering the Sixth Cavern, the last of Re's enemies are slaughtered. The scene changes and the great god prepares for his rebirth and the first light of the new day. At dawn, Re first appears as Khepri, the scarab beetle, rolling the sun disk toward the eastern horizon. When first light appears upon the horizon, the sun god is reborn and will make his daily journey across the sky.

A complete version of the Book of Caverns can be seen in the tomb of Ramses VI in the Valley of the Kings.

## BOOK OF GATES

One of three major myths about the sun god compiled in the New Kingdom (1550–1069 b.c.), the Book of Gates refers to the 12 gates separating the hours of the night. It is a vast body of writings, spells, and incantations collected from the religious literature stored in temple libraries. The gates divide the 12 hours of the night and separate the enemies that the sun god will encounter. Similar myths tell a slightly different story of Re's perilous journey through the 12 hours of the night and of his joyous rebirth in the eastern sky each morning (see Amduat and Book of the Dead). The Book of Gates is dominated by giant serpents, guardians of the gates, who assist the sun god during his journey, and by an "unquenchable fire" that will consume the enemies of Osiris. Early Christian descriptions of hell may have been derived from this theme.

In the Book of Gates, Re appears with a man's body and a ram's head when he approaches the first gate of the Duat. Each of the 12 hours of the night has a gate that is guarded by a particular serpent. Re must pass through the gate of each hour and overcome the perils of that hour before he can advance to the next gate. The following is a brief description of what is found during each hour of the night.

**First Hour**   The first gate is called "He whose Name is Hidden" and is protected by the serpent known as "The Guardian of the Desert" and is greeted by the souls of the dead who reside in the Mountains of the West.

**Second Hour**   The second gate is called "Intensity of Flame" and is protected by the huge serpent Saa-Set, who opens the entrance so Re, resting in a shrine on his boat, can pass safely through the gods and demons.

**Third Hour**   The gate is named "Mistress of Nurturing" and is protected by the serpent called "the Stinger," who stands on its tail next to nine gods who are wrapped like mummies (mummiform) and are called "the Second Company."

**Fourth Hour**   The gate is called "One of Action," protected by the serpent called "Face of Flames," who stands on his tail in the company of nine mummiform gods called "the Third Company" of the great god.

**Fifth Hour**   The gate is named "Mistress of Continuity," protected by the serpent called "Eye of Fire" and two jackal-headed mummies called Aau and Tekemi.

**Sixth Hour**   The gate is named "Throne of her Lord," protected by the serpent called the "All Seeing Eye" and by 12 mummiform gods.

This tomb painting shows a scene from the Book of Gates. Senedjem approaches the gates of eternity that are set between the hieroglyphs for sky ⌒ on top of the gates and the hieroglyph for horizon ⌣ on the bottom. *(Photograph by Pat Remler)*

**Seventh Hour** The gate is named the "Gleaming One," protected by the serpent called the "Hidden Eye."

**Eighth Hour** The gate is named the "Fiery Heat," protected by the serpent called the "Face of Flames" and nine gods in mummiform shape. Horus calls upon the monstrous serpent with the unquenchable fire to destroy the enemies of his father, Osiris, by burning their corpses and cooking their souls.

**Ninth Hour** The gate is named "Exalted in Veneration," protected by the serpent called "Earth Tusk," and the guardians of each end of the hall are Anhefta and Ermen-ta.

**Tenth Hour** The gate is named the "Sacred Gate," protected by the serpent Setu. The guardians of the hall are the serpents Nemi and Kefi. It is here that the evil serpent, the archenemy of the sun god Apep, is met and subdued in chains.

**Eleventh Hour** The gate is named "Hidden Entrance," protected by the serpent named the "Effluent One," and the hall is guarded by Metes and Shetau. The evil Apep is attacked with knives, and various gods of light and stars appear in preparation for the sun god's return to the sky.

**Twelfth Hour** The gate is named the gate of "Sacred Power" and is protected by the serpent called "Lord of the Dawn and Enveloper." The guardians of the hall are Pai and Akhekhi. Re emerges triumphantly from the last hour of the night and proceeds to the eastern horizon to be reborn.

There are different versions of the Book of Gates. Those written in Thebes are called the THEBAN RECENSION, and those originating in Sais, the capital of the Saite or Twenty-sixth Dynasty (664–525 B.C.), called the SAITE RECENSION, are the most common. In each case, the names of gates and the gods differ somewhat. An example of the text can be found on the alabaster sarcophagus of Seti I, now on display in the Sir John Soane's Museum in Lincoln's Inn Fields in London.

**BOOK OF HIDDEN CHAMBERS**   See AMDUAT.

**BOOK OF NIGHT**   Similar to its counterpart the BOOK OF THE DAY, the Book of Night also appeared in the Nineteenth Dynasty. It is a detailed account of the nightly journey of the sun through the body of NUT, the sky goddess, in order to be reborn at the dawn of each day.

**BOOK OF THE DAY**   Taken from a group of writings composed in the Nineteenth Dynasty, the Book of the Day is an updated version of previous myths dealing with the journey of the sun god. Unlike the books describing the sun's nocturnal journey through the 12 hours of the night, the Book of the Day illustrates the sun god's journey across the daytime sky. Because he is now a daytime god, the sun is represented with a falcon's head instead of the ram's head that represents the sun during his nightly journey. In the Book of the Day, Re sails his SOLAR BARQUE under the sky goddess, NUT, whose arms and legs form the ends of the sky. Although the daytime journey illustrates the solar cycle and lists the names of the gods involved, there are still references to the Underworld, battling APOPHIS, and the FIELD OF REEDS. The Book of the Day can be seen in the tomb of Ramses VI in the VALLEY OF THE KINGS.

**BOOK OF THE DEAD**   An illustrated papyrus scroll placed in the tomb as a guidebook for the deceased during his perilous journey through the NETHERWORLD. The Book of the Dead is a composite of ancient Egypt's oldest and most important religious texts. Some of the writings come from Egypt's Predynastic period and were 4,000 years old during the time of Jesus. The Book of the Dead is not a book as we know it but consists of rolls of papyrus that contain a collection of spells, incantations, prayers, hymns, and rituals that were written by the priests over Egypt's long history. The various copies of the Book of the Dead contain about 200 different spells that have been given chapter numbers so that, for example, any spell dealing with "the heart not opposing the deceased" would be found in Chapter 30.

The Book of the Dead evolved from the PYRAMID TEXTS and COFFIN TEXTS. While the Pyramid Texts were magical spells for the pharaohs only, the Coffin Texts could be used by anyone who could afford to have a coffin carved or painted with magical inscriptions. Eventually there were too many spells to fit on the coffin, and the Book of the Dead was the answer to the problem. Now all of the magical spells could

accompany the deceased, for they could be written on papyrus and placed in the tomb with the mummy.

Scribes filled papyrus rolls with spells for protection as well as instructions on how to behave and how to make the body work again in the next world. Generally, the Book of the Dead had four sections: (1) how to protect the body in the tomb; (2) how to make the journey to the Netherworld; (3) how to pass the judgment of the gods; (4) how to exist in the next world, after having been accepted by the gods.

About 200 different spells or chapters appear in the Book of the Dead, but they appear in no fixed order. Books written in the north or the south of Egypt had a particular style. The actual title of the Book of the Dead is "The going forth by day," which might refer to the deceased going forth to the Netherworld. The Egyptians were fearful of the night, and it would have been considered an advantage to make the journey during the day. Whatever the title actually meant, it undoubtedly was a reference to death. The ancient Egyptians did not mention death directly but instead had many euphemisms or names for death and the deceased. For example, because the west bank of the Nile was associated with death (the sun died there every day, and the dead were buried in cemeteries on the west side), if someone died, it was said that he "went west." The dead were called "Westerners" or "True of Voice."

Many of the Theban versions of the Book of the Dead contain hymns to the gods, especially to OSIRIS, the god of the dead. An abbreviated example of the hymn to Osiris, from the papyrus of Ani (a scribe in the Eighteenth Dynasty), reads:

> Adoration of Re when he appears in the eastern horizon of the Sky.

> Behold, Osiris, the scribe of the divine offerings of all the gods, Ani. He says, praise to thee who has come as Kheperi, the god of existence who is the creator of the gods ... May he give pleasure and power as one who is dead. The living soul [of Ani] goes forth to see Horus of the two horizons, the soul of Osiris, the scribe of Ani, true of voice before Osiris ...

This hymn of praise to Osiris mentions two important features of the deceased: the *BA*, which has been translated as "soul," and the *KA*, which was a kind of spiritual double. The Egyptians believed a person had five different elements: the physical body, the shadow, the name, and, most important, the *ba* and the *ka*. The *ba* was represented as a bird with the head of the deceased, and it seemed to come into separate exis-

An excerpt from the Book of the Dead. *(Photograph by Manfred Wernor)*

tence only after the person died. The *ba* was essential for the deceased's existence in the Netherworld.

The *ka* was a kind of abstract double of the deceased that needed a place to live. Its first choice was the corpse, but in case the body was damaged or destroyed, many Egyptians were buried with one or more *ka* statues carved in their likeness so the *ka* could dwell within the statue.

The Egyptians were almost encyclopedic in their concern with the various parts of the body. The Book of the Dead seems to have been written by priests who drew up a list of every body part that would be needed in the next world and then created a spell to protect it, as in the following examples:

The Chapter of Not Permitting the Head of a Man to Be Cut Off in the Netherworld.

I am the great one, son of the great one. I am fire, son of fire, whose head was given to him after it was cut off. His head shall not be taken away from him . . .

When the Book of the Dead first appeared in the New Kingdom, it was considered essential to anyone seeking immortality by resurrecting in the Netherworld. This belief in the Book of the Dead continued well into the period of Greek occupation of Egypt. The texts themselves remained virtually unchanged for more than a thousand years. No doubt many who purchased copies of the Book of the Dead could not read them, but that was not of great concern. Having the magical words that would guide them safely to the Netherworld was the important thing.

**BOOK OF THE DIVINE COW** A group of spells and incantations intended to protect the body of the king originating during the Amarna period (1352–1336 B.C.). The Book of the Divine Cow is based on the myth that the sun god, in very ancient times, lived on Earth and ruled the people. When he grew old, he found that mankind was plotting against him and he was determined to have his revenge (see DESTRUCTION OF MANKIND, THE MYTH OF). Examples of the Book of the Divine Cow can be found on the inside wall of Tutankhamen's outermost gilt shrine, now in the Egyptian Museum in Cairo. The Book of the Divine Cow is also inscribed on the wall of a side chamber in the tomb of Seti I in the VALLEY OF THE KINGS.

**BOOK OF THE EARTH** A later version of the sun god's journey through the Underworld, the Book of the Earth was created during the Twentieth Dynasty

(1186–1069 B.C.). It has four sections profusely illustrated with scenes of the Underworld. The Book of the Earth appears in the burial chambers of Ramses VI, VII, and IX in the VALLEY OF THE KINGS.

**BOOK OF TWO WAYS** An early version of the BOOK OF THE DEAD painted on the surface of MIDDLE KINGDOM (2055–1650 B.C.) wooden coffins. The Book of Two Ways is a detailed map of the hazards found in the realm of the dead. There are mounds, hills, rivers, and lakes of fire patrolled by terrifying demons wielding knives. As the sun god RE makes his way through the fearsome landscape, he must identify the demons by calling their proper names so they will permit him to pass safely in his SOLAR BARQUE. The Book of Two Ways documents the journey of the sun god both by land and by water and maps the location of the Mansion of THOTH and the Mansions of OSIRIS. By following the instructions carefully, the deceased could join the gods in their heavenly realm. The Book of Two Ways is vividly portrayed on the coffin of Seni, a steward from el Bersha, in middle Egypt (c. 2000 B.C.).

**BOOKS OF THE SKY** (BOOKS OF THE HEAVENS) This group of books on the afterlife appeared in the Nineteenth Dynasty with the journey of the sun god as their central theme and with NUT, the sky goddess, as a dominant character. Three of the best-known compositions from the Books of the Sky are BOOK OF THE DAY, BOOK OF THE NIGHT, BOOK OF THE DIVINE COW.

**BUCHIS BULL** (WHITE BULL) One of three sacred bull cults in ancient Egypt (APIS and MNEVIS being the other two), the Buchis arrived late in Egyptian mythology and is first mentioned in the Thirtieth Dynasty during the reign of Nectanebo II, Egypt's last native ruler. Revered for his strength and belligerence, the Buchis was worshipped as an incarnation of the war god MONTU. He was closely linked to MIN and venerated as a physical manifestation of the sun god RE. Two of his titles were "Living God of Re" and the "Bull of the Mountains of Sunrise and Sunset."

The Buchis was a white bull with a black face, and it was said that his color changed with each hour of the day. This may have given rise to the observation that he was all black and that the outline of a vulture could be seen on his back.

When the Buchis bull died, he was mummified with great ceremony and placed in the Bucheum, the cemetery created for the Buchis bull and his mother, who was also revered during her lifetime. Immediately after the death of a bull, a search began for the new

Buchis bull. Easily identified by the long hairs growing backward on his back, the new Buchis and his mother were installed in the temple complex, where they were perfumed and pampered and lived a life of ease.

A hymn to the Buchis Bull found in the Bucheum:

> Come unto me Buchis my great lord!
> O may he live millions of years
> O may he enjoy the duration of the sun
> I am thy servant my great lord!
> I pray unto thee, I never stop praying. Many are
>    my prayers at night . . .
> If you hear my prayers, come unto me O lord!

Unlike many other Egyptian animal gods, the Buchis does not seem to have been portrayed with a man's body. He is shown as a bull with a sun disk and two tall feather plumes between his horns. The cult center of the Buchis bull, complete with temple, priests, and tomb complex, was visited by CLEOPATRA VII and Julius Caesar when she took him on a tour of Egypt. Located at ARMANT on the west bank of the NILE (south of modern Luxor), today its ruins are one of the few places where the cartouche of Cleopatra VII can be found.

**BUCKLE OF ISIS** See KNOT OF ISIS.

**BULLS, THE SACRED** From the beginning of Egypt's history, the bull was revered for its strength and virility. During Predynastic times, bulls were associated with the king, who wore a bull's tail as part of his royal regalia. Bulls' heads and horns sometimes decorated the MASTABA, the building over a royal tomb. In the PYRAMID TEXTS, the "Bull of Re" assists king Unas when he climbs to heaven on a ladder.

> Hail, four horned bull of Re,
> Your horn in the west, your horn in the east,
> Your southern horn, your northern horn:
> Bend your western horn for Unas, let Unas
>    pass!

"Mighty Bull" and "Bull of Horus" were favorite epithets used to personify the pharaoh, and a favored sport of the pharaohs was wild bull hunting. Amenhotep III, in the New Kingdom (1550–1069 B.C.), issued commemorative scarabs to announce his prowess at hunting wild bulls.

The three sacred bulls in Egyptian religion were the APIS, BUCHIS, and MNEVIS.

**BUTO** See WADJET.

CAIRO CALENDAR   A magical calendar devised by the ancient Egyptians to determine whether each day would be a good day or a bad day to embark on a certain activity. In 1943, the Egyptian Museum in Cairo bought a rolled-up papyrus titled "An Introduction to the start of Everlastingness and the end of Eternity." It was written in hieratic, a cursive script that was often used instead of hieroglyphs, and made predictions about every day of the year. The PAPYRUS was actually three separate books, each relating to the days of the year, but the first and the third books were so badly damaged that they could not be translated. The second book was almost complete, and it was this section that became known as the Cairo Calendar. Each day of the year was divided into three parts. The following translation is from *Ancient Egyptian Magic* (1980) by Bob Brier.

1. The first section tells of the day's auspice or prediction; the days could be "favorable," "mostly favorable," "very favorable," "adverse," "mostly adverse," "very adverse." As it turned out, most days in the Cairo Calendar were either "very favorable" or "very adverse," and only a few days were expected to be partially good or partially bad.
2. The next section determined "very good" and "very bad" days, according to events in the lives of the gods. For example, the day that commemorated the battle between Set and Horus, when Horus lost his eye, was predicted to be a bad day.
3. Section three explained how to behave as a result of the prediction—again based on an event in the lives of the gods. On the day that commemorates the battle when Horus lost his eye in battle, the reader is advised not to leave the house.

For all of its interesting mythological references, the Cairo Calendar is not fully understood. The calendar mentions many minor gods that undoubtedly were known to the ancient Egyptians but are unfamiliar today. Various mythological themes are intertwined, and the mythological references are sometimes incomplete.

CALENDAR   The first Egyptian calendar had only 360 days in the year, and this soon became a problem, because nature's year is 365¼ days long. The Egyptians divided their year into three seasons: inundation, when the Nile flooded; emergence, when the water receded; and summer, the growing season. Each season was four months long, and each month had 30 days. By following a 360-day calendar, in a few years the seasons were not in step with nature and "inundation" occurred when the land was dry. To correct this problem, five days were added at the end of every year. These were called EPAGOMENAL DAYS, and each one was named after the birthday of a god or goddess.

CANNIBAL HYMN   A group of inscriptions inside the pyramid of the Fifth Dynasty king, UNAS (2375–2345 B.C.). The PYRAMID TEXTS suggest the king will have the power of the gods if he devours them. The so-called Cannibal Hymn gained its name in the nineteenth century, when Egyptologists first translated the text and wrongly interpreted it as a sign of cannibalism among the ancient Egyptians. The text shows pharaoh Unas's concern for his safety in the afterlife. One way to attain protection was to steal the power of the gods. On the antechamber east wall of the pyramid, a long inscription states that the king feeds upon the gods in order to gain their power. One of the verses reads:

Unas devours their magic and swallows their
   spirits.
Their big ones are for his morning meal,
Their medium ones are for his evening meal,

Their small ones are for his night meal,
Their old men and their old women are for his
  fuel.
The Great Ones in the north sky, light him fire
For the kettles' contents with the old ones'
  thighs,
For the sky-dweller serves Unas
And the pots are scraped for him . . .

Thus Unas asserted his new power and was equal to the gods. Another portion of the text suggests he became so powerful that even the gods were afraid of him. It was a dramatic solution to the problem of the king's immortality and his continued well-being in the heavens.

Aside from the Cannibal Hymn, which most scholars agree was not to be taken literally, there is no evidence of cannibalism in ancient Egypt. It seems that JUVENAL, a Roman satirist in the first century, started a rumor that surfaced from time to time over the centuries. Juvenal apparently hated the Egyptians; in fact, he detested anything not Roman, and he wrote that the uncouth Egyptians with their strange religion thought it a sin to kill a cat or a ram but thought nothing of eating human flesh (Juvenal, *Satire 15, On the Atrocities of Egypt*).

**CANOPIC JARS**   A set of four stone or ceramic containers made to hold the mummified internal organs of the deceased. Each jar was associated with one of the FOUR SONS OF HORUS, and each held a different organ. The lids of the jars represented the head of the sons. Mesti, the human-headed son, was guardian of the liver; Duamutef, the jackal-headed son, was the guardian of the stomach; Hapi, the baboon-headed son, was guardian of the lungs; Qebesenef, the hawk-headed son, was the guardian of the intestines.

The internal organs were wrapped and placed in the canopic jars with a solution of NATRON and water called the "liquid of the children of Horus." The four sealed jars were placed in a small chest with four compartments, one for each jar, and a magical spell was recited to invoke the protection of the sons of Horus. In addition to this incantation, magical spells were usually written on each jar to doubly ensure the protection of the organs.

Canopic jars took their name from the Greek legend of Canopus, the pilot of Menelaus, the king of

Canopic jars held the mummified internal organs of the deceased. Sometimes the jars were too small to hold the entire liver, kidney, lungs, and intestines, and only a portion of each was preserved. *(Photograph by Pat Remler)*

Sparta, who was buried in Egypt. Canopus was said to have been worshipped in the form of a jar with feet.

**CANOPIC SHRINE** A box carved from stone or made of wood, the canopic shrine housed the set of four CANOPIC JARS that held the internal organs of the deceased. Because of its valuable contents, four different gods protected the shrine.

In Tutankhamen's tomb, the canopic shrine was made of gilded wood, and each of the four sides was protected by a different goddess. Each goddess was associated with one of the FOUR SONS OF HORUS, who protected the internal organs. Mesti was guarded by ISIS, Hapi by NEPHTHYS, Duamutef by NEITH, and Qebesenef by SELKET. Inside the wooden shrine was a smaller alabaster shrine divided into four compartments containing four miniature gold coffins for Tutankhamen's internal organs. A magical spell carved on each coffin invoked the appropriate son of Horus and the protective goddess.

*Words spoken by Isis*: I close my arms over that which is in me. I protect Mesti, who is in me, Mesti Osiris King Neb Kheperu Re, true of voice before the Great God.

*Words spoken by Nephthys*: I embrace with my arms that which is in me. I protect Hapi Osiris King Neb Kheperu Re, true of voice before the Great God.

*Words spoken by Neith*: I encircle with my arms that which is in me. I protect Duamutef who is in me, Duamutef Osiris King Neb Kheperu Re, true of voice before the Great God.

*Words spoken by Selket*: My two arms are on what is in me. I protect Qebesenef who is in me, Qebesenef Osiris King Neb Kheperu Re, true of voice.

It was important that the contents of the canopic shrine be properly oriented to the four cardinal points—true north, south, east, and west—and instructions on the shrine tell which direction each goddess should face. In Tutankhamen's tomb, when the workmen assembled the shrine, they didn't follow directions. Selket should have faced east and Nephthys should have faced south, but the workmen reversed them.

**CARTOUCHE** The magical oval that encircled two of the pharaoh's five names. The cartouche

The cartouche of Thutmose III in Karnak, Egypt *(Photo by Gérard Ducher/Used under a Creative Commons license)*

represented a loop of rope, knotted at one end, and was a symbol for "all that the sun encircles." The name *cartouche* came from the French, following Napoleon's occupation of Egypt in 1798. When French soldiers saw the hieroglyphic inscriptions on all the monuments with the pharaoh's name enclosed in the oval shape, they thought it resembled their cartridge shells or bullets, called *cartouches* in French, and the name has remained.

**CAT** The cat, beloved in ancient Egypt, was a household pet and a feline goddess who could take the form of either a cat or a lioness. Cats are often shown as favored pets in tomb paintings. They must have been domesticated very early in Egypt, for the remains of one was found in a Predynastic burial at Mostagedda (modern Asset).

Cats play an important role in Egyptian mythology. In the Ptolemaic period (332–32 B.C.), BASTET, a daughter of Re, gained great popularity as the pleasure-loving cat goddess. Some cats were raised to be mummified and used as offerings to the gods. Hundreds of mummified cats were discovered in a special cat cemetery at Bubastis, the site of the great temple of BASTET.

**CATARACTS**  A series of treacherous rapids caused by large granite boulders in the NILE, the first cataract is at Aswan, Egypt's southern border. From Aswan to Khartoum in modern Sudan, there are six fields of boulders across the Nile that prevent boats from passing. ANUKIS, the "goddess of the cataracts," protected the first cataract from invasion by "southerners." Her cult center was on Sehel Island at Aswan. Egyptologists have recently excavated an Anukis chapel on Elephantine Island at Aswan. HAPI the Nile god is also associated with the cataracts, as the Egyptians believed he lived below the cataract and controlled the flow of water in the Nile.

**CATTLE**  Prominent in Egyptian mythology, cattle were an important part of the offering rituals. Bulls were a favored offering to the gods. The Greek historian HERODOTUS tells us that for a bull to be deemed suitable for sacrifice, the animal had to be tested in several ways. First a priest inspected the bull to make sure that it had no black hairs on any part of its body. He then examined the animal's tongue to make sure it was clean and inspected the tail to make sure that the hair grew in the proper direction. When a bull passed these rigorous tests, the priest twisted a band of papyrus around the horns and sealed it with wax stamped by his signet ring. When it was time for the sacrifice, the bull was led to an altar, where priests lit a fire, poured a libation of wine, and invoked the god's name before the bull was slaughtered. The head was cut off first. Herodotus said that many curses were placed upon the head before it was taken away, perhaps to ward off any malice harbored in the slaughtered bull. He also wrote that if any Greek traders were in the market that day, the priests would sell the head to them; if not, the head was thrown into the Nile.

**CHAMPOLLION, JEAN-FRANÇOIS**  Little would be known about Egyptian mythology or religion today without the efforts of the great French linguist Jean-François Champollion. The ability to read hieroglyphs had been lost for 1,500 years before Champollion broke the code in 1822. As a youth, Champollion demonstrated an unusual ability to learn language, and because his father was a librarian, he was surrounded by books written in many languages. He studied Latin, Greek, Arabic, Syriac, Chaldean, and Hebrew, but the language most helpful to him in translating hieroglyphs was Coptic, the language spoken in Egypt during the late period. Written in the Greek alphabet with seven special characters added, it is called "Coptic" because the Copts were the Egyptian Christians who used the script.

In 1808, when Champollion was still a teenager, he obtained a copy of the ROSETTA STONE and began his relentless pursuit of its meaning. From his earlier studies he knew there were three separate Egyptian scripts—HIEROGLYPHIC picture writing; DEMOTIC, a later and more cursive form of writing; and HIERATIC, a cursive script used by priests. He deduced this by comparing hieratic papyri with hieroglyphic and demotic inscriptions. Champollion began to compare the hieroglyphic inscription of the Rosetta stone with its Greek counterpart. The key was the name PTOLEMY. It had long been known that the pharaohs wrote their names in ovals called CARTOUCHES. The oval represented a rope showing the pharaoh's dominion over all that the sun encircles. Since the Greek inscription mentioned the named Ptolemy, the name in a corresponding cartouche in the hieroglyphic text had to be Ptolemy. The cartouche read ⬚⬚⬚⬚⬚⬚⬚. Here the ▢ = P, △ = T, ⟑ = O, ⬱ = L, ⌂ = M, ⦀ = I, and ⎮ = S. (Ptolmis was the Greco-Egyptian way of writing the name.) With these letters established, Champollion went on to other names.

From an inscription on an obelisk found on the island of Philae, he had the name Cleopatra. (Champollion knew it was Cleopatra's name because the base of the obelisk had an inscription in Greek mentioning Cleopatra.) Champollion's work on the hieroglyphic alphabet is the basis of what we know today. The Egyptians omitted vowels but did have semi-vowels, sounds close to our vowels. And for most of their 3,000-year history they did not have signs for the sounds "L" and "O," which appear in Ptolemy's and Cleopatra's names.

Throughout his dedicated work on hieroglyphs, Champollion suffered from ill heath, and it was with great difficulty that he traveled to Egypt to continue his studies. When he died in 1832 at the age of 41, a new group of scholars began to translate texts and bring to light the magical nature of hieroglyphs.

**CHAOS, GODS OF**  See CREATION MYTHS.

**CHEMMIS**  A mythical site in the PAPYRUS marshes of the DELTA (said to be near modern BUTO) where

Isis hid her infant son Horus from her evil brother Set, who was intent on destroying the child. A group of myths called the Delta Cycle tell of the trials and tribulations of Isis as she tries to raise her son Horus and mentions Chemmis as their hiding place.

**CHILD, HORUS THE**   See Horus.

**CHILDBIRTH, PATRON DEITIES**   Many different gods and goddesses have acted as the patron deity of childbirth in Egypt's long history. Small statues of these important family deities were kept in household shrines. An expectant mother might wear an amulet of Bes, the lion-headed dwarf, to ensure an easy birth and a healthy child. Most popular among deities who were patrons of childbirth were Bes, Hathor, Heket, meskhenet, Nekhbet, and Tauret.

**CIPPUS** (also Horus stele)   A round-topped stele, carved from a hard black stone, a cippus was inscribed on the base and reverse with magical formulas to guard against the bite of deadly reptiles and scorpions. The image of Horus the child standing on a crocodile and holding snakes and scorpions or other dangerous creatures was carved on the front. This kind of protection, or amuletic device, was popular during the Late period (747 b.c.–a.d. 395). The cippus was believed to have magical powers that could protect children from harm. The largest and most important cippus is called the Metternich stele and is in the Metropolitan Museum of Art in New York.

**CLEOPATRA**   The last ruler of ancient Egypt and the living embodiment of Isis, Cleopatra is one of the most well-known names in history. She was actually the seventh Cleopatra in her family. She was born in Alexandria in the winter of 69–68 b.c. History does not record the name of her mother or the exact date of her birth, but Cleopatra's father was Ptolemy XII, and her family, known as the Ptolemies, had ruled Egypt for 300 years. The Ptolemies were Greek rulers descended from General Ptolemy, who took control of Egypt when Alexander the Great died in 323 b.c. For the most part, the later Ptolemies were corrupt, lazy rulers who cared little for Egypt other than the amount they could collect in taxes.

Cleopatra was different; she loved the land and was determined to restore Egypt to its former glory. As was the custom of Ptolemaic queens, Cleopatra assumed the role of the Living Isis and officiated at ceremonies in the temple of Isis wearing the sacred costume of the goddess. By all accounts, Cleopatra was the brightest and most clever member of her family; ancient sources say she was not beautiful, but she had a captivating personality. She spoke several languages and charmed everyone who met her. Eager to learn and curious about everything, Cleopatra frequently summoned scholars from the museum to answer her questions and often visited the famous Alexandrian library, which held thousands of books written on papyrus.

When Cleopatra was 17, her father, Ptolemy XII, died, and she expected to succeed him on the throne. But her father had written in his will that she was required to marry her 10-year-old brother, Ptolemy XIII (whom she detested), and that they should rule Egypt together. Marriage between brothers and sisters was quite common in Egyptian royal families in order to keep the power in the family, but the union of Cleopatra and her brother was doomed to failure. Cleopatra was drawn into a palace intrigue and had to flee for her life. Shortly afterward, Julius Caesar, the Roman general, arrived in Egypt to settle the differences between Cleopatra and her brother. In order to meet Caesar without being intercepted by forces loyal to her brother, Cleopatra was rolled up inside a carpet that was delivered to Caesar as a gift. When the carpet was unrolled, Cleopatra appeared and pleaded her case to Caesar, who agreed to support her claim to the throne.

By all accounts Cleopatra was intelligent, witty, and determined. It was a winning combination, for she charmed the sophisticated Roman general, and Caesar stayed on in Egypt to be near Cleopatra. Caesar's later murder in the Roman Senate pushed Rome to the brink of civil war and dashed Cleopatra's dreams of power.

Mark Antony, Caesar's loyal friend and general, became Cleopatra's strongest ally. History recorded their love affair and extravagant lifestyle, as Cleopatra again made plans to rule the Roman Empire, this time with Mark Antony. Her dreams of power were never fulfilled, and the fateful sea battle fought at Actium in 31 b.c. between Cleopatra's and Antony's Egyptian ships and the Roman fleet marked the beginning of Cleopatra's decline. As the Roman troops led by Octavian, Caesar's legal heir, entered Alexandria, Antony fell upon his sword and died in Cleopatra's arms. Her two handmaidens, Iras and Charmian, then dressed their queen in her royal regalia. Legend has it that Cleopatra died from the bite of an asp buried in a basket of figs.

Cleopatra's name lived on in history, and her personification as the "Living Isis" gave new life to the

This nineteenth-century illustration of Cleopatra was drawn for H. Rider Haggard's novel *Cleopatra*. *(R. C. Woodville)*

"cult of Isis," which grew and prospered and spread throughout the Middle East and into England and Germany. At its height, the cult had more followers than the new religion, Christianity. The cult of Isis died when the old religions were outlawed by the Christian Roman emperor Constantine in A.D. 382.

**COBRA GODDESS**    See Wadjet.

**COFFIN**    A container to hold a mummified body. Coffins were either anthropoid (in the shape of a human body) or rectangular. Egyptian religion required that the body be intact so it could resurrect in the next world. Early burials in sandpits dried and preserved the body, but wind erosion or wild animals often exposed the corpse. As a protective covering for the body, the first coffins were made of woven reeds and later of wood.

During the Old Kingdom, wood coffins and stone sarcophagi were viewed as a place of rest for the deceased (see sarcophagus). The coffin fit inside the stone sarcophagus. The lids of the sarcophagi were so heavy that they had to he raised and lowered with ropes. The difference between a coffin and a sarcophagus is mainly the material from which each is made. One fits inside the other: The innermost (the coffin) is made of wood, and the outer one (the sarcophagus, Greek for flesh-eater) is made of stone.

In the Middle Kingdom the most popular coffins were rectangular, wooden, and often painted with funerary motifs. These coffins could be highly decorated, both inside and out, with scenes of the deceased sitting in front of a sumptuous offering table. Most Middle Kingdom coffins were decorated with the *udjat* eye. Two Eyes of Horus were painted on the outer panel of the coffin facing east, perhaps so the deceased could still have a view of the world of the living. Anthropoid coffins in the shape of the human body were made in the Twelfth Dynasty (1985–1795 B.C.) and continued to the end of Egyptian civilization. This shape was associated with Osiris, the god of the dead, and the coffins were elaborately painted with religious and mythological scenes.

**COFFIN  TEXTS**    A group of magical spells compiled during the Middle Kingdom (2055–1650 B.C.) to assist the deceased in his or her journey to the Netherworld. With the collapse of the Old Kingdom (2688–2181 B.C.) and the period of lawlessness that followed—the First Intermediate period

(2181–2055 B.C.)—the pyramids were opened by robbers. For the first time, ordinary people could see the magical spells and prayers that helped the king journey safely to the next world. When the magical spells, or Pyramid Texts, became known, they must have inspired the new custom of inscribing prayers and spells on Middle Kingdom coffins.

One of the innovations of the Coffin Texts is that the sun god Re, who previously ruled the Underworld alone, now shared his dominion with Osiris, the god of the dead, who had risen to prominence as the Judge of the Underworld. Another idea to come from the Coffin Texts was that the deceased would be required to labor in the Field of Reeds. The Coffin Texts followed no particular order or structure; they were a group of diverse spells designed to help the deceased reach the Netherworld. Because the spells were written on the surface of the coffin, space was limited, and frequently words or entire passages were omitted, which made the spells difficult to translate. There are more than a thousand coffin spells, but many are repetitious.

Frequently they refer to magic or the magician's power. There are two kinds of magic mentioned in the Coffin Texts: negative and positive. In the negative group, the spells assure the deceased that those who might work malicious magic on him will not harm him. These spells say things like "I will not listen to magic" or "my soul shall not be seized by magic." In addition to worrying about "bad magic," there was also the fear that the deceased's magic would be taken from him by a god disguised as a crocodile. The spell to combat such a catastrophe was:

> Get back! Go away! Get back you dangerous one! Do not come upon me, do not live by magic! May I not have to tell this name of yours to the great god who let you come: "Messenger" is the name of one and *Bedjet* is the name of one.
>
> *The crocodile speaks*: Your face is toward righteousness. The sky enclosed the stars, magic enclosed the settlements, and this mouth of mine enclosed the magic which is in it. My teeth are flint, my tusks are the Cerastes Mountain.
>
> *The deceased replies*: Oh you with a spine, who would work your mouth against this magic of mine, do not take it away, O crocodile, which lives by magic.

Not all spells in the Coffin Texts are negative. Many are intended to assert the deceased's magical abilities,

Coffin Texts were intended to help the deceased reach the Netherworld safely. There were spells for not dying a second death and for not having to do any work in the next world. *(Photograph by Sara Wells)*

and these phrases frequently include, *"I have filled my belly with magic."* Sometimes the deceased could take possession of the power of other magicians: "I eat of their magic, I gulp down their powers. My strength in me is more than theirs. Their powers are with me."

The Egyptians wanted to be sure that once they had the power, they would not lose it, so they included spells to ensure that their magic could not be stolen.

Some of the spells in the Coffin Texts required more than words and included instructions for *how* the incantation was to be spoken. The spell also shows us how the Egyptians thought their magic worked. The spell to overcome foes (Spell 37), for example, ends with *"May you break and overthrow your foes and set them under your sandals."* The accompanying instructions say that the words must be spoken over a wax figure of the enemy and that his name was to be incised on the heart of the figure with the bone of a synodontis fish.

One of the most curious facts about the Coffin Texts is that, while many gods were named and invoked, neither the sun god Re, nor Osiris, the god of the dead, was the most important god. Instead, Shu,

the god of air, is the principal god in the texts. One possible explanation is that the Egyptians believed one had to travel through the sky to reach the Netherworld. In this case Shu's help would be crucial. A common phrase on the coffins was, *"I have gone up to Shu, I have climbed on the sunbeams."* As the god who holds up the sky, Shu was a means by which the deceased reached the Netherworld and a symbol of strength for the deceased to make the difficult journey: "I am strong as Shu is strong, I am hale as Shu is hale, I am beneath the sky, I strengthen its light." The Coffin Texts focus on Shu rather than on Osiris because the priests who wrote them were more concerned with the journey to the Netherworld than with what would happen once the deceased arrived. Very few of the Coffin Texts mention the Netherworld. It was almost as if the Egyptians were merely concerned with avoiding the perils that might end the journey or reduce their powers; once they arrived in the *"west"* they would be safe. The Coffin Texts were most popular in the Middle Kingdom. During the New Kingdom, they were replaced by the more elaborate BOOK OF THE DEAD.

**COLORS, MAGICAL**  In Egyptian mythology, colors were often used as symbols to represent the gods.

**Black**  Black is not a true color but the absence of light and is associated with death, the necropolis, and the mummy. OSIRIS, as ruler of the Netherworld, was called "the black one." Black was the color of the mortuary gods ANUBIS and Khenty-Amentu, and they were shown as jackals with black coats.

**Blue**  Blue was the color of infinity, the cosmos, and the sky. AMUN was sometimes shown as blue, as a reminder of his association with the cosmos. Blue beards, wigs, and crowns adorned the gods, and blue faience amulets were a favorite among the ancient Egyptians.

**Gold**  Gold was "the skin of the gods," the divine metal that never tarnished and symbolized eternal life in the next world.

**Green**  Green was the color of life, renewal, regeneration, and vegetation. OSIRIS, the god of resurrection, bore the title, "The Great Green." Green meant good things. The sacred eye paint that adorned both priests and the statues of the gods was ground from green malachite, and the word meant joy.

**Red**  Red was both a positive and negative color. Red symbolized life, energy, and victory and was often the color chosen for magical amulets such as the TET. A prayer in the PYRAMID TEXTS includes the plea, ". . . let my bread be made of red grain . . ." to ensure that only the finest bread was available to the king in the next world. But red was also the color of the desert, the *barren wasteland* thought to be the domain of evil and the god SET. To do "red things" was bad, the antithesis of doing "green" or good things. Red was an expression of anger, and a person with a "red heart" was enraged.

**White**  White, *the absence of color*, represented purity and sanctity, and it was used in the sacred name "the white wall," the epithet for MEMPHIS. References were made to "white unguents" and "white sandals" used in religious rituals. The priests in the temples wore white linen garments, and the statues of the gods were dressed in fine white linen.

**COLOSSI OF MEMNON**  Two colossal seated statues of the pharaoh Amenhotep III (1390–1352 B.C.), the "Colossi of Memnon," stood in front of Amenhotep III's now vanished mortuary temple.

The Colossi of Memnon are actually statues of the pharaoh Amenhotep III that stood in front of his mortuary temple on the west bank in Thebes. *(Photo by Roweromaniak/Used under a Creative Commons license)*

(He was the father of Akhenaten and the grand-father of Tutankhamen.) During the Ptolemaic period, one of the statues was believed to speak for the gods. The statue to the north (to the right when facing them) was damaged by an earthquake in 27 B.C. The fault created in the stone caused it to make a whistling sound every morning, which was interpreted by the priests as the gods speaking. The Greeks called the statue the "vocal Memnon" and equated it with their Memnon, a character in Homer, who sang to his mother, Eos, goddess of the dawn. The Roman emperor Septimius Severus (A.D. 193–211) ordered that the damage to the colossal statue be repaired, and since then it has not made a sound.

**COMPOSITE DEITIES** The Egyptians never seemed to mind inconsistencies in their religion. Gods who shared similar traits were often merged by the priesthood to create a composite deity. Such was the case with the composite god SERAPIS, who embodied the attributes of APIS and OSIRIS. When the gods of Upper (southern) and Lower (northern) Egypt had similar traits, they often merged into composite deities. AMUN of Thebes in the south and RE of Heliopolis in the north became the composite god AMUN-RE. The goddesses HATHOR and ISIS were sometimes referred to as Isis-Hathor or Hathor-Isis. Foreign deities with traits similar to Egyptian gods were readily accepted by the Egyptians. For example, AESCULAPIUS, the Greek god of healing, and IMHOTEP were seen as one. The Canaanite god BAAL and the Egyptian god SET were worshipped as aspects of each other; they were powerful, if sometimes evil, forces. Composite deities were popular throughout Egypt's history and can be seen as late as the Roman period, when Egyptian gods were associated with the Roman pantheon. The catacombs at KOM EL SHUQAFA in Alexandria show several Egyptian and Roman composite gods, such as ANUBIS, dressed in Roman military garb.

**CONTENDINGS OF HORUS AND SET** A tale from Egyptian mythology of the triumph of good over evil, the Contendings of Horus and Set tells how a quarrel between two gods was settled. During a time when gods ruled on Earth, SET became jealous of his brother OSIRIS and murdered him. The dead Osiris entered the NETHERWORLD, where he became ruler. Osiris's son HORUS, wishing to take his father's place as king on Earth, went before the panel of gods to plead his case, but the evil Set also wanted to become king on Earth.

When Egyptian priests wanted to focus the specific powers of several gods into one, they created a composite god or goddess that held all the positive attributes of each combined god.

For 70 years the gods debated who should rule on Earth, Horus or Set. Some felt Set should rule because he was the stronger, and "might makes right." Others argued that because Set was Horus's uncle, he was the elder and should rule. Some members of the tribunal argued that Horus should rule because the son should inherit the throne of his father. After squabbling for years, the tribunal sent a letter to the goddess Neith for her decision. She declared that the office should go to Horus.

Set objected vehemently, saying he was the strongest, and argued that the trial was unfair because Isis, mother of Horus, was present when the decision was made. The gods, weary of the quarrel, decided to adjourn to the "Island-in-the-Midst" to make their final decision.

The ferryman was instructed not to let any woman on the island, so that Isis could not influence their decision. But Isis changed herself into an old woman by magic and bribed the ferryman with a gold ring to take her to the "Island-in-the-Midst." Once on the island, she changed herself into a beautiful young woman and lured Set to her. She then pleaded with him for help, saying that her husband was a herds-man who had been killed by an evil man who then threatened to beat her son and take his cattle. Set replied that he would defend her: "Shall the stranger take the son's cattle?" At this point Isis turned herself into a bird, flew to the top of an acacia tree, and said, "Your mouth has judged."

Realizing that he had been tricked, Set wept. The god Atum placed the white crown of Egypt on the head of Horus. Angered, Set proclaimed that he would fight Horus and take the crown from his head. He proposed that they change themselves into hippopotami and fight in the sea, and they plunged into the water. Isis, fearful that her son would be defeated, made a harpoon and threw it into the water. It struck Horus, but Isis, using her magic, instructed the harpoon, "Let him go." When she threw the harpoon into the water a second time, it struck Set, who cried out to Isis, "You are my sister. What have you done to your brother?" Feeling sorry for Set, Isis called to the harpoon to release him.

Horus grew angry at his mother and cut off her head. Isis changed herself into a headless statue. When the gods saw this, they wanted to punish Horus, and they searched for him on the mountain where he had retreated. When Set found Horus in the desert, he plucked out his two eyes and buried them on the mountain, and lotus blossoms sprang up from the ground where the eyes of Horus were buried.

Set said to the tribunal searching on the mountain, "I did not find Horus." When Hathor, "Mistress of the Southern Sycamore Tree," found Horus weeping, she poured milk over him and healed his eyes. Hathor then reported to the tribunal that Set had taken both of Horus's eyes but that she had restored them. (In another version of the myth, THOTH restores one of the eyes.) Horus and Set were called before the tribunal to be judged and were told, "Go, and leave us in peace, eat, drink, and stop quarreling."

The story continues with more trickery and battling between the two, for each time the tribunal of gods awarded the earthly kingdom to Horus, Set refused to abide by its decision and through trickery gained power over Horus. Finally the tribunal directed Thoth, the god of writing and knowledge, to send a letter to Osiris in the Underworld asking what to do about Horus and Set. After many days, his letter reached the tribunal, which met at the White Field of XoIS. Osiris chastised the tribunal, saying they had caused *MAAT* (divine order) to sink into the Underworld. He threatened that if the gods did not obey him, he would unleash the demons of the Underworld upon the Earth.

Set, who was brought before the tribunal in fetters, agreed to let Horus rule as king on Earth, and the white crown was placed upon Horus's head. Then Re-Horakhty, master of the sky, saved Set from humiliation by taking him to dwell in the sky, saying, "And he shall be thunder in the sky and be feared." Isis rejoiced that her son had been made king of all on Earth.

## COSMETICS

Of great importance in religious rituals, cosmetics—eye paint, unguents, perfumes, and precious oils—were used in daily life as well. Scenes carved on temple walls show the ritual of honoring the god. At dawn each day, a procession of priests who had been ritually cleansed and anointed with unguents walked through the temple, entered the HOLY OF HOLIES, opened the shrine, and removed the cult statue. The image of the god was adored, cleansed, anointed with green and black eye paint, and clothed in pure linen. Then the cult statue was returned to the shrine, and the doors were sealed. The magical properties of eye paint were written in the PYRAMID TEXTS. Utterance 79 provides UNAS, the deceased king, with eye paint for the next world: "Say four times, Osiris Unas, the sound eye of Horus is being rubbed on the face. [Given to you are] *Two bags of green eye cosmetic.*"

The BOOK OF THE DEAD contained instructions to the deceased about to enter the Hall of Two Truths:

> . . . This is the way to act toward the Hall of the Two Truths. A man says this speech when he is pure, clean, dressed in fresh clothes, shod in white sandals, painted with eye-paint, anointed with the finest oil of myrrh . . .

Egyptians were fond of eye paint and applied it daily as an adornment. A verse from the "Beginning of the Songs of Entertainment" tells us just how important eye paint was.

> "I wish to paint my eyes, so if I see you my eyes will glisten. When I approach you and see your love, you are the richest in my heart."

Both men and women wore eyeliner, applying it to the upper and lower lids, and then drawing a line that trailed onto the temple, enhancing the shape of the eyes. Originally the favored color was green, thought to have health-giving and magical properties, but black gained popularity at the end of the Eighteenth Dynasty. The composition of both colors is known: ground malachite produced green, and ground galena (lead sulfide) produced black to silvery-gray powder that was mixed with fat to form a thin paste and stored in cosmetic jars. Small wands of wood, ivory, or bone were dipped into the jars and used to apply the eyeliner.

Women colored their lips with a brush dipped into a paste of red ochre and fat. Although scholars are not certain, the red lips on some male statues may indicate that men painted their lips as well. Red ochre was also applied to the cheeks. Henna, still used today to color the hands and feet of modern bridal parties, colored the nails of ancient Egyptians. The base of Egyptian cosmetics was fat, and it was thick and difficult to remove, so a cleansing cream was concocted from powdered limestone and a light vegetable oil to remove the cosmetics.

Elaborate inlaid wooden cases held stone or FAIENCE (ceramic paste) cosmetic jars in individual compartments, along with a hand mirror of highly polished metal. Mirrors (called "ankh" in Egyptian) were circular, with wood, metal, ivory, or faience handles, and they were often in the shape of a PAPYRUS column.

Perfume was an essential component of every cosmetic case and was used liberally. By distilling the essence of flowers (or any fragrant substance), the Egyptians had the base for their perfume, which was then added to various oils. Analyses of ancient perfumes shows that iris root or balsam was used as a base. Sometimes cinnamon, cardamom, myrrh, honey, wine, or flowers were used to create fragrances.

Banquet scenes on tomb walls show ladies adorned with cones of perfume. A cone of fat impregnated with perfume was placed on a woman's head, and as the evening progressed, it melted into her wig, releasing a pleasant aroma.

## CRAFTSMEN, GOD OF   See PTAH.

## CREATION MYTHS   During the OLD KINGDOM (2686–2181 B.C.), three different creation myths arose in three different towns in ancient Egypt. Each had its own set of gods promoted by its own group of priests. These were not the only creation stories in Egyptian mythology, but except for the rise of AMUN-RE in THEBES during the Eighteenth Dynasty (1550–1295 B.C.), these myths that began in Hermopolis, Heliopolis, and Memphis were the most well known.

HERMOPOLIS produced the myth of the OGDOAD, or the eight. Based on four pairs of primeval deities, this myth attempted to answer the question, "How did something appear from nothing?" Existing only as a force of power, the first primeval forces appeared as frogs or serpents that later evolved: NUN and Nunette became water, HEK and Heket became space, Kek and Keket became darkness, and AMUN and Amunette became hiddenness.

HELIOPOLIS had another creation myth: the ENNEAD. Its four generations of deities came into existence by the will of their creator. The Ennead asks the question, "How does one become many?"

and is answered by the appearance of a creator god who arises spontaneously from the waters of chaos and magically impregnates himself.

From MEMPHIS came a third view of creation based on the idea that to say it was to do it: The creator-god, PTAH, created everything by saying its name. This was known as the Memphite Theology.

Other creation myths arose in southern religious centers that were inspired by local cults at Esna, Edfu, and Philae, and to some extent they were all based on the three Old Kingdom creation myths.

## CROCODILE GOD   See SOBEK.

## CRONUS   Early Greek harvest god, Cronus was originally a corn god, sometimes associated with GEB, the Egyptian earth god.

## CROOK   Part of the king's royal regalia and a symbol of his power, the shepherd's crook was also carried by the gods.

## CROWNS   Ancient Egypt had several different types of royal crown worn by the gods and by the king. The style and symbols of each crown varied, and no king's crown has ever been found. This has given rise to the theory that there might have been only one of each kind at any time and that it was handed down from king to king. Some scholars have speculated that the crowns were made of leather or woven reeds that were lost over the centuries. Today the only examples of ancient Egyptian crowns we have are those sculpted on statues or painted on tomb or temple walls.

The crowns of the gods often had special attributes that identified the deity. For example, since the ram was sacred to Amun, he wore ram's horns on his crown. Hathor's crown, which included cow's horns and a sun disk, symbolized her sacred animal and her association with the sun. Isis's crown was originally the hieroglyphic sign for "throne," symbolizing her close relationship to the king. Later, when Isis and Hathor were closely associated, Isis wore a crown similar to that of Hathor, with cow's horns and a sun disk. The symbols for the gods changed over time, and by the Ptolemaic period (332–32 B.C.), the gods' crowns incorporated many different elements, indicating that the god or king was associated with several other gods.

The white crown (*hedjet*) of UPPER EGYPT, in the shape of a tall cone with a bulb on the end, was first worn by King Scorpion, and it was depicted on his mace head, a ceremonial weapon. The white crown is also shown on the NARMER PALETTE (c. 3100 B.C.).

The red crown (*deshret*) of LOWER EGYPT looks something like a cylinder that was shorter in the front and stretched up in the back to a peak with a long coil that stuck out from the front.

The double crown was a combination of the white and the red and served as a symbol of the unification of Upper and Lower Egypt. The red crown is depicted on the reverse side of the Narmer Palette.

The *atef*, or feathered crown, was the tall white crown of Upper Egypt with ostrich plumes on either side and a disk attached to the top. It was worn by the gods for religious ceremonies and for funerary rites.

The *nemes* was a head wrap made from striped cloth that was pulled tight across the forehead and secured in the back so that folds of cloth rested on the shoulders. The *uraeus*, the cobra god who protected the king, was fastened to the front of the nemes.

The blue crown (*khepresh*), in the shape of a flanged helmet, appeared in the Eighteenth Dynasty.

**CUBIT, THE EGYPTIAN**  A unit of measurement in ancient Egypt based on the magical number seven, the cubit represents one of the earliest examples of precise measurement in the ancient world. The cubit was critical to PYRAMID building, and the goddess of measurement, Sheshat, presided over all important calculations.

Originally the cubit measured from a man's arm at the bend of the elbow to the tip of the index finger. Because the length of forearms varied, and precise measurement was so important to building projects, the cubit became standardized. A royal or master cubit was carved from granite, and the "master" served as a template for all other cubits used by architects and engineers. The cubit rod (20.6 inches long) is divided into seven palms, each palm is divided into four fingers, and each of the four fingers is divided into 16 sub-digits. Thus a standard cubit has 28 fingers and can measure precisely down to 1.16 mm. Another crucial measurement in ancient Egypt was the seked, devised to measure angles. It was also based on the number seven.

The Egyptian Museum in Turin, Italy, has a granite royal cubit rod divided into 28 units that dates from Dynasty XIX (c. 1300 B.C.). It was presented to Amen-ope, a viceroy to NUBIA. The cubit was developed in the OLD KINGDOM (2686–2181 B.C.) and is mentioned in the TALE OF THE SHIPWRECKED SAILOR.

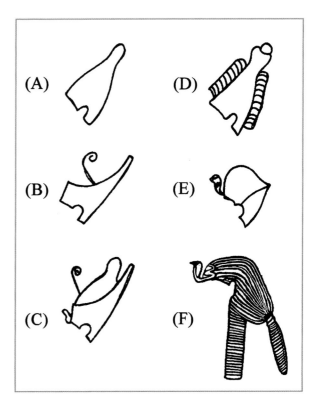

Crowns worn by the kings of Egypt: (A) the white crown of Upper Egypt, (B) the red crown of Lower Egypt, (C) the double crown of Upper and Lower Egypt, (D) the atef crown, (E) the blue crown, (F) the nemes headdress. *(Drawing by Mary Jordan)*

**CULT OF THE KING**  The cult of the king is basic to ancient Egyptian religion. Kings were worshipped as gods during their lives and after death. During a king's coronation, a special ceremony was performed to unite the king's KA (soul) with the "royal *ka*" (a divine double), and in that instant the king magically became a divine being—a *ntr*, or "living god on Earth."

Every year during the OPET FESTIVAL in THEBES, the king's status as a god was renewed. The cult statue of the god AMUN was carried by pious priests from his sanctuary at KARNAK TEMPLE to visit LUXOR Temple. It was during this festival that a symbolic union of Amun and the king's mother took place, and the king renewed and celebrated his divinity as a living god. The story of the Opet Festival is recorded on the walls of Luxor Temple.

Once the king became *ntr*, he was worshipped during his life and after death. As a divine being, the king became a son of RE, associated with AMUN-RE, HORUS, and OSIRIS. Being a god on Earth, it was the king's job to maintain *MAAT* or DIVINE ORDER—to make sure that peace and prosperity continued throughout Egypt.

During the NEW KINGDOM, not only did the king have to be one with the "divine *ka*," but it was important to show that Amun was his father. When Queen HATSHEPSUT crowned herself king, she made her claim to kingship and to becoming a *ntr* by showing that Amun was her father. This magical occurrence, the divine union of her mother and Amun, disguised as her father, is documented along with the scene of her birth on the walls of her mortuary temple at Deir el Bahri.

After a king died, he continued to be worshipped at his mortuary temple. An endowment was made to support priests who would make offerings to his *ka* each day.

**CULTS OF THE GODS** Much of the religious activity in the ancient world revolved around the cults of Egypt's most powerful deities. The most popular—AMUN-RE, HORUS, MIN, HATHOR, and ISIS—had large priesthoods and huge temple complexes, complete with storerooms, living quarters, kitchens, bakeries, and breweries. Large farms were attached to the temples to supply offerings to the gods and food for the priests.

The center of all cult activity was the statue or cult image of the god or goddess, often cast in gold, for it was said that the gods had skin of pure gold and bones of silver. The statues' hair was often made of LAPIS LAZULI. Cult statues were generally small, not more than two feet tall, and they were kept in shrines or NAOS in the HOLY OF HOLIES. Some temples dedicated chapels to other deities, who had shrines and cult statues as well.

Each cult had a number of festival days that were celebrated throughout the year. While some were small and celebrated locally, others lasted for two or three weeks and required the cult statue to travel from one temple to another. Egyptian gods always traveled in boats (sacred barques) that were carried by a group of priests, or else they sailed in a SACRED LAKE or on the NILE.

During the OPET FESTIVAL in Thebes, the god AMUN and statues of his family traveled from KARNAK TEMPLE to LUXOR Temple, a distance of about two miles, and stayed for about three weeks. Other important festivals were the Festival of the New Year, the Festival of OSIRIS at Abydos, the Festival of BASTET at Bubastis, the Festival of HATHOR at Dendera, the Festival of Horus at Edfu, and the Beautiful Festival of the Valley, when AMUN-RE journeyed from Karnak Temple across the Nile to the Temple at Deir el Bahri.

Every deity had secret rituals, special festival days, and sacred animals. By performing the rituals and paying scrupulous attention to details, the faithful could demonstrate their devotion to the god or goddess and hope that their prayers would be answered. Devotion to a cult was a means of expressing one's personal piety. According to JUVENAL, the first-century Roman writer, the women of Rome (who were devoted to Isis) carried their expression of piety to extremes. After CLEOPATRA VII's visit to Rome, many Roman women became addicted to the cult of Isis. Some women made pilgrimages to Egypt to collect water from the Nile to use in their rituals and kept all-night vigils at the shrines of Isis.

**CURSE OF TUTANKHAMEN** The ancient Egyptians never seem to have placed curses on their tombs, but after Tutankhamen's tomb was opened in 1922, a rumor spread that his tomb was cursed. Supposedly a tablet was found in the tomb with the inscription: "Death will slay with his wings whoever disturbs the peace of the pharaoh." It is doubtful that such a tablet ever existed. There are no reliable references to such a curse, and it is not typically Egyptian to speak of death as a winged being or to write on clay tablets.

It was also claimed that several people closely associated with the discovery of Tutankhamen's tomb died soon after the opening, having fallen prey to the ancient curse. The event that caused the most unrest was the death of Lord Carnarvon, the wealthy Englishman who financed the tomb's excavation and died soon after he entered the burial chamber. At approximately the same time Carnarvon died in Cairo, a power failure or blackout plunged the city into darkness. Many took this to be an omen directly related to the curse. While it is true that Carnarvon died soon after he entered Tutankhamen's tomb, it is also true that he was in poor health, and the cause of his death was an infected mosquito bite. Power failures were not uncommon in Cairo in the 1920s.

Some have expressed concern that germs and bacteria in the tomb were the cause of death of those who died later. On the morning after the burial chamber was opened, however, sterile swabs were used to take cultures from the wall, floor, and shrine. Analysis showed that no life of any kind existed in the burial chamber at the time it was first opened, so any illness contracted by members of the excavation did not come from bacteria in the tomb.

# D

**DEAD, GODS OF THE** See ANUBIS, OSIRIS, SOKAR.

**DEAD, ISLAND OF THE** See FIELD OF REEDS.

**DEATH RITUALS** See MUMMIFICATION and OPENING OF THE MOUTH CEREMONY.

**DECANS** The Egyptians divided the night sky into 36 groups of stars, or decans, forming constellations. Each decan was named and associated with a corresponding god or goddess. For the Egyptians, the most impressive constellation in the sky was Orion, and the most important star was Sirius, called the Dog Star by the Greeks. Egyptian mythology equated Sirius with ISIS and saw her as Orion's companion. Together they dominated the southern sky. Sirius was the brightest star in the night sky, and when it appeared on the horizon around July 9, it was a sign that the Nile was about to rise and the season of inundation or flooding was about to begin. The inundation was crucial, because a low Nile would mean less water for irrigation, causing a poor harvest.

Every 10 days, a different decan appeared on the dawn horizon just before the sun rose. Thus the 36 decans could be used for measuring a 360-day year. By noting the positions of decans, the Egyptians also could tell time during the hours of the night. Pictures of the decans, or "star clocks," were sometimes painted on coffin lids or on tomb walls. Eventually "star clocks" were more of a decoration than a timekeeper, for at the end of every year, they were about six hours behind time, and after several years, they were off by weeks. Although the decans and the god and goddesses who represented them were not actually used for telling time, they continued to appear on the walls and ceilings of tombs and as coffin decorations until the Greco-Roman period.

**DEDUN** (also DEDWEN) A Nubian god of wealth, Dedun is generally shown as a man, but he can take the shape of a lion as well. One of his titles is the god of "Four Directions," but he seems to have been best known in NUBIA as the keeper of INCENSE. He appears with incense at the royal births and is mentioned in the PYRAMID TEXTS.

**DEIFICATION** The process by which a person, living or dead, is declared a god. With the possible exception of AKHENATEN, the Egyptians did not deify living people. The king was considered a living god, but he inherited his position; he came into the world as the living manifestation of HORUS, and so he was born a god. Some kings reinforced their position of god on Earth by erecting statues of themselves as gods during their reign. Ramses the Great (1279–1213 B.C.) placed a statue of himself as RE the sun god beside AMUN-RE, RE-HORAKHTY, and PTAH in the sanctuary of his temple at ABU SIMBEL. Another statue of Ramses as Amun was found in his mortuary temple at the RAMESSEUM in Thebes.

A handful of private people, revered for their knowledge, achieved deification after death. Perhaps the most notable was IMHOTEP, vizier (prime minister) and architect to ZOSER (2667–2648 B.C.), the Third Dynasty king for whom the first pyramid was built. Imhotep, a man of many talents, was legendary for his medical skills and wisdom. He was deified 2,000 years after his death. During the New Kingdom (1550–1069 B.C.), Amenhotep-son-of-Hapu, who was the architect for but unrelated to Amenhotep III, was honored for his wisdom and medical skills. Like Imhotep, Amenhotep-son-of-Hapu was deified and worshipped as a god of healing.

During the Late period (747–332 B.C.), drowning in the Nile was sometimes reason enough for deification, as was the case with Pehor and Pehesi, who drowned in the Nile in Nubia at Dendur. Antinous, the companion of the emperor Hadrian, also was deified after he drowned in the Nile, and the town of Antinoopolis, the cult center for the worship of Antinous, was built on the banks of the Nile where he died.

**DELTA** With its lush fertile land and clear lakes, the Delta was a magical place for ancient Egyptians and became the setting for much of Egypt's rich mythology. When the gods roamed the Earth in the time before time began, or "First Time," their home was the Delta. The original gods of the ENNEAD lived on Earth, and during this mythological time, many of the gods' struggles took place in the Delta. It was here that a version of the ISIS AND OSIRIS MYTH called the Delta Cycle evolved. Mythology tells us that after the death of OSIRIS, Isis was held captive by her evil brother SET. When she managed to escape, Isis hid in the PAPYRUS marshes in the Delta, where she gave birth to Osiris's child. Although their son, HORUS (the falcon god), was destined to grow up and defeat his uncle Set, the infant Horus lived in great danger. In spite of the many sympathetic gods who watched over the baby, Horus was bitten by a scorpion. His mother's cries for help brought THOTH from the heavens and help from her sister NEPHTHYS. Because the scorpion was actually the evil Set in disguise and his magic was not as strong as that of Isis, the infant Horus was saved.

The Delta begins north of Cairo, where the NILE splits into the eastern Damietta Branch and the western Rosetta Branch. The modern town Qantar sits at the fork in the river. Many of the ancient sites in the Delta are in ruins or lost completely due to the high water table that causes ancient sites to sink into the ground and topple over. One of the most important cities was Bubastis (modern Zagazig), the flourishing cult center for the goddess BASTET. Farther north (modern San el Hagar) are the ruins of ancient TANIS, believed by many to be the biblical city of Pi-Ramses. The modern town of Tanta is the site of ancient Sais, the capital of Egypt in the Twenty-sixth Dynasty and the cult center for the goddess NEITH. Nearby are the ruins of Nacratus, an ancient Greek city, and Buto, the cult center of Edjo, the cobra goddess of LOWER EGYPT.

**DEMONS** Protecting oneself from demons seemed to be a constant concern of the ancient Egyptians. Of the nearly two dozen amuletic papyri, which were manuals for using amulets and conjuring spells, almost all contain spells for protection from evil demons. One such papyrus in the Egyptian Museum

in Turin, Italy, suggests that demons were found near water.

> We shall keep her safe from any action of a demon and from any interference of a demon. We shall keep her safe from any action of a demon of a canal, from any action of a demon of a well, from any action of a demon of [a pool] left [by the annual Nile flood] from any action of a demon of a cleft [?] and from any action of a demon of swamps.

Another kind of demon was associated with SEKHMET, the lion-headed goddess; when she was in her fierce and corrupt mood, she could unleash demons of all kinds. The Smith Surgical Papyrus (see MEDICINE, GODS OF) mentions Sekhmet and malicious gods and demons as the cause of an epidemic that apparently afflicted the Egyptians every year. One magical spell suggested that these demons of disease rode on the wind.

> Withdraw, ye disease demons. The wind shall not reach me, that those who pass by to work disaster against me. I am Horus who passes by the diseased ones of Sekhmet [even] Horus, Horus, healthy despite Sekhmet. I am the unique one, son of Bastet. I die not through thee.

Demons of water and wind notwithstanding, Egyptian mythology placed all of its most terrible demons in the mythological NETHERWORLD. They resided in the realm of chaos and menaced the souls of the deceased as they made their way through the 12 hours of the night with the sun god Re in his solar boat. While the demons were terrifying, with the correct spells from the BOOK OF THE DEAD and the help of benevolent forces, the demons could be subdued. One of the most popular household gods, BES, had the frightening appearance of a demon but was in fact a benevolent god who was believed to protect families, especially children, from the very real dangers of scorpions, snakes, and crocodiles.

**DEMOTIC** One of the three scripts inscribed on the ROSETTA STONE, demotic is a Late period cursive form of writing hieroglyphs that appeared about 660 B.C. Because demotic was much faster and easier to write, it soon became more popular than HIERATIC, the earlier cursive form of hieroglyphs. Hieratic was then used only for recording religious texts.

An important mythological text from the third century A.D., the Leiden-London Papyrus, is written in demotic, and the magical spells are a mixture of Egyptian and Greek mythology. Occasionally a BOOK

OF THE DEAD was written in demotic, but because of the Greek influence, demotic was eventually replaced by the Greek alphabet. The last known demotic inscription written in A.D. 451 appears on the walls of PHILAE TEMPLES.

*DESHRET* Ancient Egyptian word for "desert" and mythological home of SET, the god of chaos, who ruled over the desert or "red land." Set, as god of the desert, was sometimes called the "red god," emphasizing his adversarial posture toward Osiris, who appeared as a god of vegetation. The seemingly endless desert that stretched beyond the fertile Nile valley was a fearful place to most Egyptians, who avoided the dry wasteland. Depictions of the entrance to the Underworld were often the sandy hills of the Western Desert.

## DESTRUCTION OF MANKIND, MYTH OF THE

An Egyptian myth that tells how the wickedness of the people on Earth aroused the anger of the sun god RE and how Re was determined to punish humankind. The Myth of the Destruction of Mankind is part of a much longer story, the Myth of the Heavenly Cow, found in several Eighteenth Dynasty tombs in the VALLEY OF THE KINGS. Like the biblical tale of the flood, the angry god relents and does not destroy all of humankind. The Destruction of Mankind is found in New Kingdom tombs (1550–1069 B.C.), but scholars think it may have originated in the Middle Kingdom (2055–1650 B.C.). The story is as follows:

It so happened that in ancient times Re the sun god lived on Earth, where he was king of the gods and humankind. One day he discovered that humankind was plotting against him, for it was said that he was growing old and that his bones were of pure silver, his flesh of gold, and his beard of true lapis lazuli. Re became angry with the people of Earth. He summoned all the gods and said, "Oh Nun, eldest god, look, mankind is plotting against me. Tell me what you would do, for I am searching and I will not slay them until I have heard your counsel."

Nun reminded Re that everyone feared Re when his vengeful eye looked upon them. Re looked about and saw humankind fleeing into the desert to avoid his wrath. The gods told Re, "Let your vengeful Eye go and smite those evil people. No Eye is more powerful than yours! May it go down as Hathor!" Then the goddess HATHOR, who represented the terrible power of the Eye of Re, was sent to the desert to destroy humankind, and when she returned, Re welcomed and praised her. Hathor enjoyed her rampage against

humankind, saying, "I have overpowered humankind. It was balm to my heart." Re was pleased that he had regained his power over humankind by diminishing their numbers.

At this point in the story, the Powerful One, SEKHMET, was born. She became the power and the fierce messenger of the Eye of Re against his enemies. Now that Re had regained power over humans, he no longer wanted to kill them, so he devised a plan to stop Sekhmet, who enjoyed acting as his vengeful Eye and who wanted to wade in the blood of humans. Re summoned swift messengers to bring him great quantities of red ochre and maidservants to brew great quantities of beer. When the red ochre and the beer were mixed, the mixture resembled human blood. Seven thousand jars were filled with the mixture and carried to the place were the goddess was to kill humans. It was poured onto the ground and flooded the land. In the morning when the goddess appeared, she was pleased to see what looked like blood flooding the land. She began to drink and consumed so much beer that she became drunk and did not kill humans. Re was pleased that mankind was spared and greeted the goddess, "Welcome in peace, O gracious one."

## DEVOURER, THE   See AMMUT.

## DIONYSUS

Greek god of wine and revelry often associated with the Ptolemaic god SERAPIS, Dionysus's reputation for merrymaking overshadowed his agricultural endeavors. Besides revelry, he was also known for tending the vineyards and producing wine, and it may have been this side of Dionysus that linked him to Serapis, the Ptolemaic god of agricultural abundance. Cleopatra VII and Mark Antony often appeared as Isis and Dionysus in pageants and festivals in Alexandria. Antony, known for his wild living, adopted the title New Dionysus, along with several others, after his resounding victory over the Roman republican forces (led by Cassius and Brutus) in the Macedonian town of Philippi. Hailed as the New God of Wine, Dionysus Redivivus, Antony lived the part as he led his triumphal tour through Greece.

*DJED* PILLAR   A symbol called the backbone of OSIRIS, the *djed* pillar represents stability. One of Egypt's most ancient symbols, the djed's meaning is not fully understood. It has been suggested that originally the *djed* pillar was a standard or totem from which sheaves of grain were hung and that it was used in an early fertility rite. The *djed* pillar became synonymous with power and stability, and

The *djed* pillar represents the backbone of Osiris, the god of the dead. *Djed* amulets represented stability. *(Photo by Pat Remler)*

Ptah, the god of Memphis, was sometimes called the "noble djed." A ceremony called the "raising of the *djed*" took place in Memphis when the king himself elevated a *djed* column by means of ropes with the help of the priesthood. Later in the New Kingdom (1550–1069 B.C.), coffins were often decorated with the *djed* column to give the deceased stability.

The later concept of the *djed* pillar is fully developed in the myth of Osiris. An early fertility god, Osiris represents the spirit of life. From the god of fertility and renewal, he becomes the god of regeneration and life. He is a savior; he renews the deceased, and the *djed* pillar became the symbol of Osiris and stability. When the priests performed the rites of Osiris, one of the last ceremonies was the raising of a wooden *djed* pillar by the king or high priest to symbolize stability and Osiris's triumph over death. Djed pillars were popular AMULETS for both the living and the dead.

## DJEHUTY  See THOTH.

**DOG**  Dogs and jackals were often confused in Egyptian mythology, and part of the confusion may have arisen because dogs and jackals interbreed. What might have looked like dog could have actually been half-jackal. Eventually both animals were recognized as sacred to ANUBIS, the jackal-headed god of the cemetery. Because of the apparent confusion between actual jackals and dogs, both were sometimes called the "Anubis animal."

Several different breeds of dogs are shown on tomb walls with their masters, and dogs as well as cats were favorite household pets. Herodotus, the Greek traveler (c. 450 B.C.) tells us that when the family dog died, the members of the family shaved their bodies, including their heads, as a sign of mourning. It was said that after a dog was mummified, it was placed in a sacred vault in the city and that the city of Cynopolis held dogs in great honor. With the exception of Anubis, however, dogs were not viewed as an incarnation of a god.

**DONKEY**  In mythology, the donkey sometimes represents the god of evil and chaos, SET.

**DOOMED PRINCE, MYTH OF THE**  The story of the doomed prince is found in the Harris Papyrus, written in the Eighteenth Dynasty (1550–1295 B.C.) and now in the British Museum. The papyrus tells the story of a prince of Egypt and his destiny, but, unfortunately, the papyrus is damaged and the end of the story is missing. The story goes as follows:

Once there was a king who longed for a son and prayed fervently to the gods to grant his wish. The gods answered his prayers and a son was born to his wife. Hathor was summoned to decide the young prince's destiny and pronounced: "His death shall be by the crocodile, or by the serpent, or by the dog." Upon hearing the destiny of his son, the king was greatly troubled. To keep the prince safe from harm, he built a palace in the mountains and furnished it with everything that could be desired so that his son would never wish to leave. One day the young prince climbed to the roof of his palace and, looking down, he saw a man walking along the road with a dog. The prince asked his companion, "What is that following the man on the road?" "That is a dog," answered the companion, and the prince said, "Let there be brought to me one like it." When the king was told of the prince's request, he could not deny his son's wish and sent a little dog to the prince.

As the prince grew into manhood, he wanted to leave his palace. He sent a message to his father saying he wished to be free to go his own way: "Though I am fated to three evil fates, let me follow my desires.

Let the gods fulfill their will." The king, who could not deny his son, agreed, and the prince, armed with weapons of many kinds, set out with his dog. First he went north to the desert and lived by hunting game. Then he went to the chief of Naharaina, whose only child was a daughter. The chief had built a great house for her with 70 windows, each 70 cubits from the ground. He then summoned the sons of the chiefs of Khalu, saying, "He who climbs and reaches my daughter's window shall win her for his wife."

When the prince met the sons of the chiefs of Khalu, he was treated with great kindness. They asked the prince where he had come from, and he answered that he came from Egypt: "I am the son of an officer of the land. My mother died and my father has taken another wife, who, when she bore my father other children, grew to hate me. Therefore I have fled." They felt sorry for him and embraced him and told the prince they had come to climb to the windows of the chief's daughter's house. The prince had seen the princess from afar when she stood at her window gazing out, and he was inspired to climb the high wall. When he reached the princess, she kissed him and embraced him and sent a message to her father that a suitor has reached her window.

The chief was pleased until he heard it was the fugitive from Egypt who had reached his daughter. He became angry and ordered that the prince return to Egypt. The messenger rushed to warn the prince, but the chief's daughter refused to let her suitor go, saying, ". . . if he is taken from me, I will neither eat nor drink and in that hour I shall die!" Upon hearing of her vow, the chief sent someone to murder the prince. The princess responded, "By the great god Re, if he be slain, then I shall die ere the set of sun. If I am parted from him, then I will live no longer." When the chief heard his daughter's words, he relented. He gave his daughter and the prince a fine house with servants and land and cattle and many fine gifts.

After some days, the prince confided in his wife that he was "doomed to three fates: a crocodile, a serpent, and a dog." She became afraid and wanted to have his dog killed, but he refused, having had the dog since he was a child. Eventually the time came when the prince wished to travel to Egypt, and his wife, fearing for his safety, went with him. During their travels they came to a town with a crocodile living in the river, but in that town was a strong and mighty man who captured the crocodile and bound it. When the crocodile was bound, the mighty man was at peace and walked abroad.

As the time passed, the prince and his wife were content, and as night fell, the prince slept easily. When her husband was sleeping, his wife poured milk into a bowl and placed it next to him. As she sat waiting, a serpent slipped from its hole and moved toward the prince as if to kill him. The servants of the house quickly poured milk for the serpent and it drank and became drunk and rolled on its back. Drawing her dagger, the wife stabbed the serpent many times, killing it. Awakened by the noise, the prince was astonished to see his wife with a dagger. She said to him, "Behold, thy god hath given one of thy dooms into thy hand. Surely he shall also give thee the others!" The prince sacrificed to the gods of Egypt and praised them.

One day when the prince was walking through his fields, his dog ran away, chasing wild game. The prince, following his dog, plunged into the river, and the crocodile appeared and carried the prince to a place where the mighty man lived. And the crocodile said to the prince, "Behold, I am thy destiny, following after thee."

It is here that the papyrus breaks off; we do not know the fate of the doomed prince.

**DOUBLE CROWN** The double crown worn by the king symbolized the unification of Upper and Lower Egypt. It is a combination of the white crown (*hedjet*) of Upper Egypt, seen on one side of the NARMER PALETTE (c. 3000 B.C.), and the red crown (*deshret*) of Lower Egypt, seen on the other side.

**DREAMS** The Egyptians believed that their dreams were sent by the gods as a means of telling the future. The frequency with which dreams are mentioned in the first two books of the Old Testament indicate just how important dreams were in the ancient world. In Genesis alone there are more than a dozen references to dreams, most of them prophetic.

The Old Testament story of Joseph and his brothers reveals much about ancient beliefs in prophetic dreams. Joseph was sold into slavery partly because he had dreams that foretold he would rule over his brothers (35:5–11). Later, when Joseph was in jail in Egypt with two of the pharaoh's former officials, a cupbearer and a baker, they told him that they had had dreams but that they could not understand them. Joseph correctly interpreted the dreams to mean that in three days the cupbearer would be released and the baker hanged. Joseph was released from prison when he was called upon to interpret the pharaoh's dreams that the royal magicians had failed to decipher. In the first dream the pharaoh had seen seven fat cows devoured by seven lean cows. In the pharaoh's second dream, seven meager ears swallowed seven full ears of corn. Joseph told the pharaoh the dreams meant that Egypt would have seven years of prosperity followed by seven years of famine; the people would have to plan accordingly in order to avoid mass starvation.

Archaeological evidence also provides us with an account of the Egyptians' belief in prophetic dreams. The case of Thutmose IV (1400–1390 B.C.) is perhaps most famous. At the foot of the Great Sphinx is a stele that tells of a dream by the young prince who was to become Thutmose IV. The prince was hunting in the desert one day and stopped at noon for a nap, near where the Great Sphinx lay partially buried in the sand. The prince dreamed that the Sphinx told him if he cleared away the sand that covered it, the young prince would become pharaoh. He cleared the sand from the Sphinx, and he became pharaoh.

The stele supports the impression given in Genesis and Exodus that the ancient Egyptians believed strongly in prophetic dreams. In the Joseph story, the pharaoh had enough confidence in Joseph's interpretation of his dreams to place him in charge of the country's economic future for the next 14 years.

An almost complete *Dream Book* from a hieratic PAPYRUS in the British Museum gives some idea of how the ancient Egyptians interpreted dreams. The book is written on the recto side (front) of a papyrus, but some sections have been lost. The verso (back), the side with the horizontal fibers on top (and the side easier to write on), describes a battle and includes a copy of a letter to the vizier of Egypt. This side was undoubtedly written during the Nineteenth Dynasty (1295–1186 B.C.). Since the verso or back side is always written first, it is certain that the *Dream Book* was written later. This version of the *Dream Book* may have been copied from an earlier papyrus originating in the Twelfth Dynasty (1985–1795 B.C.). As so often happens with papyrus, the beginning and the ending are damaged. What remains is a list of dreams and their interpretations. One wonders for whom the papyrus was intended. Since the common man could not read, one possibility is that, as part of their duties, the priests interpreted dreams. This would be consistent with accounts in the Bible, in which only a select few were able to interpret dreams.

Hieroglyphs suggest that the priests of the HOUSE OF LIFE were the interpreters. Coptic writing, which is ancient Egyptian transcribed in Greek letters with a few characters added, is the strongest connection we have with vocalized ancient Egyptian. In the Coptic (Bohairic) version of the Bible, when the pha-

raoh calls for his dream interpreters, the word used for "interpreters" is *seshperonch*. This is probably a corruption of , *sesh-per-ankh*—scribe of the House of Life. It was common practice for anyone seeking divine guidance to spend a night in the temple, where the priests, for a fee, would interpret the person's dream. In fact, sleeping in a temple to obtain dream oracles was virtually required for any Greek tourist in Egypt, and the Temple of Seti at Abydos was a favorite dream spot. On the walls of the back staircase in the temple are names carved by tourists who slept there. The names are often only a foot or so above the steps, so it seems as if at least some of these travelers passed the hours of the night carving their names. One group recorded, that they "caught a fox here."

The *Dream Book* was written in hieratic, a cursive form of hieroglyphs, and is organized in an orderly fashion, from right to left. Down the right margin are the words, "If a man sees himself in a dream." Each horizontal line gives the description of a dream, followed by the interpretation of the dream. Each interpretation begins with either "Good" or "Bad," followed by an explanation. The following is a partial listing of the *Dream Book* and its interpretations.

| Dream | Prophecy |
|---|---|
| **Killing an ox** | Good. It means the removal of the dreamer's enemies from his presence. |
| **Writing on a palette** | Good. It means the dreamer's status is well established. |
| **Drinking blood** | Good. It means putting an end to his enemies. |
| **Picking dates** | Good. It means finding food given by a god. |
| **Seeing a large cat** | Good. It means a large harvest is coming to the dreamer. |
| **Copulating with a pig** | Bad. It means being deprived of possessions. |
| **Uncovering his backside** | Bad. It means the dreamer will become an orphan later. |
| **Climbing on a mast** | Good. It means being suspended aloft by a god. |
| **Drinking wine righteousness.** | Good. It means living in |
| **Seeing his face as a leopard** | Good. It means gaining authority over his townsfolk. |
| **Capturing a female slave** | Good. It means something from which he will have satisfaction. |

There seems to be no common theme or technique to the interpretation of the dreams. It may have been that the list was compiled over years and the interpretations changed over time.

**DUAMUTEF** One of the four sons of HORUS who guarded the internal organs of the mummy. Duamutef protected the stomach. Duamutef has the head of a jackal.

**DUAT** A place of darkness and home of terrifying demons, the Duat was a mythological location between the world of the living and the world of the dead. The AMDUAT, "The Book of That Which is in the Netherworld," says the Duat is located deep in a valley that separates Earth from the NETHERWORLD. When RE the sun god sinks below the horizon at the end of each day to begin the 12-hour journey he is accompanied by souls of the deceased. Only those souls found to be pure after the WEIGHING OF THE HEART CEREMONY are allowed to accompany the sun god on this perilous journey. At the end of the twelfth hour, after successfully battling and overpowering evil demons that menace the sun god at every hour, Re and the souls emerge safely into the welcoming realm of the sky goddess, NUT. Re appears on the horizon to begin a new day, and the souls prepare for RESURRECTION in the Netherworld.

**DWARF GODS** See BES.

**EILEITHYIA** A Greek goddess of childbirth who was associated with NEKHBET, the vulture goddess of Upper Egypt, who was also a mother goddess. An early reference to this role is found in the PYRAMID TEXTS, where the king's mother is given the title "Great White Cow who Dwells in Nekheb (home of Nekhbet) and Whose Breasts are Hanging." Another reference to Nekhbet as protector and nurse to the king can be found in the mortuary temple of the Fifth Dynasty king, Sahure (2487–2475 B.C.).

**ELEPHANTINE TRIAD** The group of three gods worshipped in Aswan at Elephantine Island: KHNUM, the ram god who created mankind on the potter's wheel; ANUKIS, the goddess who was guardian of Egypt's southern frontier; and SATIS, their daughter, the goddess of the cataracts in Aswan. During some periods in Egyptian history, Satis was considered the wife or consort of Khnum.

**ELOQUENT PEASANT, TALE OF THE** Inscribed on four MIDDLE KINGDOM (2055–1650 B.C.) papyri, the Tale of the Eloquent Peasant is a classic in ancient Egyptian literature. It is the story of Nemtynakht, the corrupt son of a local official who calls upon the gods to give him a "potent vision" so he can steal a peasant's donkey and all the goods it carries, and the good peasant who seeks justice.

As the peasant and his donkey approach, Nemtynakht places a length of linen across the narrow road so the fringe touches the water on one side and the hem touches the field of barley on the other side. Then he shouts at the peasant not to ruin his "clothes." As the donkey moves to avoid the linen, he comes close to the field and takes a mouthful of barley. Nemty-nakht shouts that he will seize the donkey and all the goods it carries in payment for its having eaten one mouthful of grain. He beats the peasant and sends him on his way.

When the peasant approaches the high steward, Remsi, to beg for justice, his words are eloquent. He begins,

Oh high steward, my lord,
Greatest of the great leaders of all! . . .
. . . you are father to the orphan
Husband to the widow
Brother to the rejected woman . . .

He points out that the steward is like a father who looks after his family. So, to make amends, the steward gives the peasant 10 loaves of bread and two jugs of beer, but his donkey and goods are not restored to him. Over the course of time the peasant makes nine petitions to the authorities, each time pleading for the return of his donkey and goods. At first they are delighted with his eloquent words, and even the king hears the peasant's petition. But the officials eventually tire of him and remind the peasant that they have given him bread and beer, and his wife and family have been sent food, and that is his repayment. But still he persists. In the seventh petition, the eloquent peasant says,

My lord be patient, so that a man may invoke
you about his rightful cause.
Don't be angry; it is not for you. The long face
becomes a short temper.
Don't brook on what has not yet come, nor
rejoice at what has not yet happened . . .

Each time the peasant makes a petition, his speech is more eloquent than before. But after the ninth petition when justice is not served, he says, "I have pleaded my case with you and you have not listened. I shall go and plead about you to ANUBIS!" (god of the cemetery and embalming). Since the officials will not grant him justice, the peasant asks a god to intervene on his behalf. As the unhappy peasant walks away, the steward Rensi has a change of heart—perhaps the gods have intervened. Calling for the peasant to come back, he tells him not to be afraid. The steward Rensi calls for the petitions and reads them aloud before the king, who praises the eloquence of the peasant and orders his donkey and goods restored.

**ELYSIAN FIELDS**  The Greek name for the Egyptian mythological site *sekhet-aaru*, or the FIELD OF REEDS. In Greek mythology, Homer describes the Elysian Fields or Elysium as an idyllic spot where the god ZEUS experienced perfect pleasure. Later, in the writings of *Vergil*, the Elysian Fields were said to be found in the Underworld and home to the blessed dead. In the Egyptian BOOK OF THE DAY, the Elysian Fields (Field of Reeds) are described as being the location of the House of OSIRIS and a region with canals and lakes.

**ENNEAD**  A Greek term for the nine gods and goddesses that were the basis of one of ancient Egypt's creation myths. The first creation myth came from Heliopolis and included the nine deities that sprang from the creator god ATUM, who spontaneously arose from the watery abyss called NUN onto the primeval hill, the first mound of Earth. Atum then produced SHU, goddess of air, and TEFNUT, god of moisture. They in turn produced GEB, god of earth, and NUT, the sky goddess. Geb and Nut were the parents of OSIRIS, SET, ISIS, and NEPHTHYS, who populated the land (see CREATION MYTHS). Later enneads had a varying number of gods: Abydos has seven, and Karnak Temple has 15 deities in its ennead.

**EPAGOMENAL DAYS**  The birthdays of five important deities. When the Egyptians realized that their 360-day calendar was out of phase, they added five days at the end of the year to keep the seasons in step with nature. These were called the epagomenal days, and mythology tells us that the goddess NUT gave birth to each of her five children on these special days. On the first day Osiris was born; on the second day, HERU-UR; on the third day, SET; on the fourth day, ISIS; and on the fifth day, NEPHTHYS. Not all the epagomenal days were considered "good days," and the first, third, and fifth days were said to be unlucky. Only the day of Isis's birth, the fourth epagomenal day, was said to be lucky: It was written that on that day was a "beautiful festival of heaven and earth."

**ETERNITY AMULET**  See SHEN.

**EUCRATES**  One of the most famous tales of Egyptian magic comes from the ancient writer Lucian. The story tells of Eucrates, a Greek traveler in Egypt who wants to study magic with the scribes and priests of the temples. Eucrates sailed south to Thebes to see the two COLOSSI OF MEMNON. It was believed that the statues spoke in the early morning, when the wind whistled through cracks in the stone. His trip was successful, for he reported that the statues spoke to him in seven oracle verses. He must have thought the verses important, for he never repeated what the oracle said to him (when the statues were later repaired, the sounds stopped, and they never "spoke" again).

Returning north on the NILE, Eucrates met one of the sacred scribes of MEMPHIS traveling on his boat. The scribe/magician said he had spent 23 years in the underground sanctuaries where ISIS had taught him magic. Eucrates watched the magician work miracles along the Nile—he could ride crocodiles and command every creature in the river. Eucrates was fascinated and asked if he could study with the magician. When they reached Memphis, Eucrates and his servants were invited to stay with the magician. Eucrates could see that the magician had no servants, but clearly he needed none. When there was a chore to be done, he would put clothes on a door bolt, a pestle (a pounder or grinder used to crush ingredients in a bowl), or a broom, recite a magic spell and the objects would come alive and do his bidding. When the chores were finished, the magician said another few words, and his servants returned to inanimate objects.

Eucrates wanted to learn the trick, but the magician was secretive and would not tell him how it was done. One day when the magician was saying the spell over a pestle, Eucrates overheard him and memorized the magic word. (The story specified that the word had three syllables but does not give the word.) When the magician stepped out, Eucrates tested his new power by instructing the pestle to fetch water. After the pestle brought a vessel of water, Eucrates tried to stop him, but he had not learned the word to stop the magic. The pestle kept bringing water. In desperation, Eucrates cut the pestle in two, but then both halves took up vases and continued bringing water. Finally, just as the house was being flooded, the magician returned to restore order.

This story is best known to us through Walt Disney's *Fantasia*, where the sorcerer's apprentice is Mickey Mouse, the pestle is the broom, and the vase a bucket. But the story is basically the tale of the Egyptian magician. This tale demonstrates how much the Greeks believed in Egyptian magic.

**EVIL, GOD OF** See SET.

**EVIL EYE** Because much of the natural world was not understood by ancient cultures, and Egypt was no exception, when something went wrong—someone's fortune changed, he fell ill or died, or his crops failed, for example—it was often attributed to having the evil eye placed upon the person. It was believed that the evil eye was cast upon someone when an envious and evil person looked upon her. To ward off the evil eye, magicians inscribed spells on wooden plaques to help their clients and threatened terrible consequences such as "may the possessor of the evil eye be cursed by ISIS, blinded by HORUS, and pierced by the arrows of SEKHMET."

One of the amulets used to protect against the evil eye was the cowrie shell, perhaps because it resembles an eye. Egyptian tomb paintings often show young women wearing belts of cowrie shells, and amulets in the shape of the cowrie were made from gold and silver. Another protection from the evil eye was a divine decree. When a child was born, a god or goddess might be implored by the family to declare the child's fate, and a priest might write the prediction on PAPYRUS and place it in an amulet holder that was strung on a cord and hung around the child's neck. The decrees always predicted a good life, and they promised to protect the child against harm and especially from the evil eye.

**EXECRATION TEXTS** A group of magical inscriptions, the execration texts list people or places that ancient Egyptians believed to be dangerous. Magical spells or curses that would render an enemy powerless against the Egyptians were inscribed on clay statuettes or bowls. The figures or vessels were specially created to be inscribed, smashed, and buried as part of a ritual to immobilize the enemies of Egypt. The earliest examples of execration texts date from the OLD KINGDOM and are crude images representing an enemy.

During the reign of Sesostris III in the MIDDLE KINGDOM, the names of the enemy were inscribed on terra-cotta bowls. When they were smashed, the curse would take effect. Egypt's traditional enemies were often listed in execration texts (see the NINE BOWS OF EGYPT). Egyptologists have found fragments of execration texts throughout Egypt—at Thebes (modern Luxor) and at SAQQARA.

**EYE OF HORUS** (also *UDJAT, WEDJET*) The Eye of Horus is a stylized representation of the eye of the falcon god, Horus. According to the myth, THE

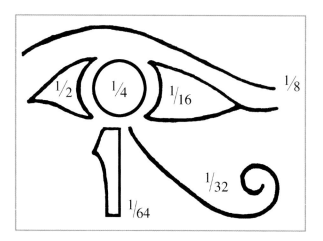

Fractions of Eye of Horus. Each segment of the parts of the falcon's eye was the hieroglyph for a fraction. *(Courtesy of Bob Brier)*

CONTENDINGS OF HORUS AND SET, Horus fought his evil uncle SET to avenge the death of his father, Osiris. In one version of the myth, Horus loses his eyes in the battle, but THOTH, the god of writing, restores one of them. Each element of the Eye of Horus represented a different fraction: the hieroglyph for ½ was ◁, ¼ was ○, and so on. All the parts of the fractions total 63/64, and the missing 1/64 supposedly was supplied magically by Thoth. The amulet representing the Eye of Horus was called *udjat*, or "sound eye." Because it was associated with the regeneration of Horus's eye, the Eye of Horus amulet was worn to ensure good health. The sign of the modern pharmacist, Rx, is a corruption of three proportions of the ancient Egyptian Eye of Horus: 1/4, 1/32, and 1/64.

The Eye of Horus didn't just ensure good health to the living; it was also an important funerary amulet. Chapter 140 of the BOOK OF THE DEAD was to be recited on the last day of the second month of the second season over two Eyes of Horus. One was

These magical Eye of Horus amulets were worn for good health. During a battle with his evil uncle, Horus's eye was plucked out but was restored by magic. *(Photograph by Russell Rudzwick)*

to be made of real lapis lazuli (a rare dark blue stone) or of *hamaget* stone, set in gold; the other was to be of red jasper and worn on "any limb preferred." The reason for the two Eyes of Horus of different colors may come from the belief that one eye of Horus was the moon and the other eye the sun.

**EYE OF RE**  The mythological eye of Re is a symbol that appears in the tale of the DESTRUCTION OF MANKIND. Re's eye turns out to be the goddess HATHOR, who by magic becomes a goddess of terrible destruction and appears as the goddess SEKHMET. Sekhmet served as the avenging eye of the great god Re.

**FAIENCE** The ancient Egyptians called it *tjehnet*, meaning "that which is brilliant." When Egyptian craftsmen discovered how to create faience, they must have thought it was a gift from the gods. Faience (pronounced fay-ahns) is one of the ancient world's most beautiful and prized ceramics. The Egyptians used faience for everything—beads, AMULETS, USHABTIS, SISTRA, cups, vases, bowls, figurines, and decorative inlays for furniture. While the basic ingredients, water and sand, are common materials in Egypt, the final product was pure magic—almost an alchemical process transforming base materials into brilliant colors. The bright blue and green colors were the most popular, for they imitated turquoise and lapis lazuli, semiprecious stones popular from prehistoric times and believed to have magical qualities. One of the earliest examples of faience used on a large scale can be found in the chambers beneath the STEP PYRAMID of ZOSER. The walls are lined with hundreds of pale green faience tiles that measure about two inches by four inches.

Faience is a mixture of ground quartz, or sand with a high quartz content, a little lime or NATRON, and water. A variety of colors can be produced depending on what pigment is added to the paste. Faience is pressed into terra-cotta molds—thousands of molds in different shapes have been found. When the faience is fired in a kiln, the glaze migrates to the surface, leaving a brightly colored, smooth, glassy surface. Faience was inexpensive to produce, and given the number of faience objects found, it seems that most Egyptians had a protective amulet, or good luck charm, or statues of their favorite gods in their homes. Thousands of faience statuettes of the gods were made each year to be left as votive offerings in the temples. Faience amulets were created to be worn by the living and to adorn and protect the deceased.

**FALCON** From Egypt's most ancient history, the falcon, or hawk, has held a place of honor in Egyptian mythology. Soaring through the desert sky, the falcon was believed to be a protector of the king and a manifestation of the sun god RE. HIERAKONPOLIS (hawk city) is the site of one of the earliest cult centers devoted to the falcon god, and many important discoveries have been made at this site. The NARMER PALETTE, an early historical document (c. 3100 B.C.) found at the site, shows the falcon as king, subjugating his enemies.

Hawks have always been sacred in Egyptian religion. They represented the war gods MONTU and SOKAR, and the goddess HATHOR was sometimes portrayed as a female falcon. The Greek historian Herodotus mentions in his *Histories* that the punishment for killing a falcon was death.

In his role as protector of the king, the falcon is frequently shown with outstretched wings. An example of this can be seen on the Fourth Dynasty statue of

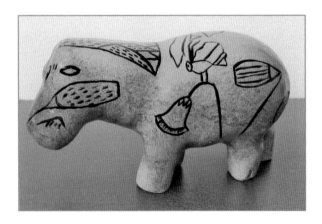

This blue faience hippopotamus is 4½ inches tall and is decorated with aquatic plants that grew in the marshy areas around the Nile. Discovered in the tomb of a nobleman from the Twelfth Dynasty, the hippopotamus is now in the Metropolitan Museum of Art in New York City. *(Photograph by Pat Remler)*

The well-preserved Ptolemaic temple at Edfu is guarded by two monumental falcons carved from black granite. They protect the figure of the king. *(Photograph by Pat Remler)*

King Chephern (*Khafre*), where a falcon figure hovers behind the king's head with outstretched wings. In the PYRAMID TEXTS, the king's soul is equated with the flight of a falcon when it rises to heaven. During the Late period (747–332 B.C.), hawks were mummified and placed in a catacomb at SAQQARA as votive offerings to the falcon god HORUS.

Animal mummification was big business in ancient Egypt, and it seems a large part of it was fraudulent. Ancient Egyptians mummified all kinds of creatures, from bulls to birds, and for different reasons. Some were pets preserved to keep their masters company in the next word, but many were raised to be sacrificed as offerings to the gods.

When an Egyptian wished a favor from a god, he or she might leave an offering of a mummified animal in the god's temple. The largest animal cemeteries in Egypt are the IBIS and falcon galleries at Saqqara—miles of tunnels containing mummified birds. Carved into the walls of each tunnel are thousands of niches, each with a mummified bird inside a clay pot. When the priest ran out of niches, he stacked the pots on the floor. The ibis was sacred

to THOTH and the falcon sacred to HORUS. Along the route to the galleries were stalls where pilgrims could purchase mummified birds, many of which had been raised for that purpose. After a pilgrim selected one, it was placed in a ceramic pot and sealed. Priests of the gallery would place it in a niche and, for a small fee, say a prayer for the pilgrim.

The writings of Hor, a priest in charge of the ibis galleries around 200 B.C., explains that hundreds of people were involved in the animal mummification business at Saqqara. One of the more important jobs was "doorkeeper." *Hor* says the doorkeeper supervised the birds and their young and was probably responsible for raising the ibises. Unlike ibises, falcons cannot be raised in captivity, so there was no way there were enough falcon mummies to meet the demand. So suppliers began to make "dummy mummies." X-rays of falcon mummies show that they are almost always ancient fakes—made with a bundle of rags with beautiful wrappings on the outside. In his writings, *Hor* was concerned that the pilgrims were being cheated when they purchased a falcon mummy for an offering. He wrote, "there must be one god in one vessel"—or a bird in every clay pot.

**FAMILIES OF GODS** (Triads) Gods in ancient Egypt often came in threes, and families of gods were called triads. These trinities of gods, consisting usually of a father, a mother, and their child, could be found in all of the important cult centers in Egypt. Huge temple complexes grew up around the cult centers, and the priests became very powerful and wealthy. The most important cult centers were the following:

| Triad | City |
|---|---|
| Horus; his wife, Hathor; and their son Harsomtus (Harpakhered; Horus the child) | Edfu |
| Khnum; his wife, Anukis; and their daughter Satis | Elephantine |
| Ptah; his wife, Sekhmet; and their son Nefertum | Memphis |
| Amun; his wife, Mut; and their son Khonsu | Thebes |

**The Edfu Triad** Edfu, located just south of Thebes, became an important cult center and home of the Edfu triad during the Ptolemaic dynasty (332–32 B.C.). HORUS, the falcon god, was the principal deity, and inscriptions carved on the temple walls give a complete version of the mythical story of Horus

Ptah, the principal god of Memphis, is often shown in mummiform with a close-fitting cap and holding a staff of authority. *(Photograph by Pat Remler)*

overthrowing his enemy SET. HATHOR was the wife or consort of Horus, and the temple inscriptions also tell the story of her journey from her cult center in Dendera to Edfu, where the marriage of Horus and Hathor took place. Their son Harsomtus, Horus the younger, was through magic born simultaneously at the birth houses in Edfu and Dendera. Hathor is the cow-headed goddess of love and music, and Harsomtus was at the same time a human, a falcon, and a reincarnation of the dead king; one of his titles was "Son of the Earth."

**The Elephantine Triad** Elephantine Island is situated at Aswan. The cult center for the trinity of KHNUM, ANUKIS, and SATIS was in a town called Abdu (modern Syene). The principal god was Khnum, who wore a white crown with ram's horns and a solar disk. Occasionally he was shown with a jug on his head, a symbol for "unite" or "build." His name may originally have had an astronomical reference, uniting the sun and the moon. Khnum is a builder or maker of men. According to his priests, he made the first egg, which produced the sun. Khnum is also believed to have fashioned men on the potter's wheel. His consort or wife, Anukis, was the goddess of the cataracts, the large boulders in the river at Aswan. Their daughter, Satis, was sometimes also shown as the consort or wife of Khnum; she was the goddess of the flood or inundation.

**The Memphis Triad** Memphis, the capital of Egypt during the Old Kingdom (2686–2181 B.C.), was known for its strong fortifications. It was called the city of walls, and shrines to PTAH were sometimes called "his southern wall." Ptah was a craftsman. Following the instructions of THOTH, he created the world, and humankind, on the potter's wheel. He is shown in mummiform shape wearing a skullcap. His wife or consort is the lioness-headed goddess Sekhmet, who was also the avenger of the sun god Re. In her gentler aspect, Sekhmet was a goddess of healing and medicine. Their son, Nefertum, was called the "god of the blue lotus," the blossom with which he was associated.

**The Theban Triad** AMUN was the principal god of THEBES, and his name means the "hidden one." He can appear in many forms but was often portrayed holding a *was* scepter and an ANKH, the signs of power and life, and wearing a double feather crown. When Amun represented one of the primordial gods in the waters of chaos, he had the body of a man with the head of a frog. Amun's chief consort or wife was MUT, whose name means "mother," and she was sometimes called "World Mother," She Who Brings Forth into Existence. Mut was portrayed either as a woman wearing the double crown and holding a papyrus scepter or as a lioness-headed goddess.

In this guise she was associated with Sekhmet and Bastet. The third member of the triad was their son, KHONSU, moon god.

Curiously, the most popular and powerful triad—that of OSIRIS, ISIS, and their son HORUS—did not have a particular cult center where they were worshipped together. Instead, each one had his or her own cult center: Osiris at Abydos, Isis at Philae, and Horus at Edfu.

**FERTILITY, GODS OF**   See MIN and OSIRIS.

**FESTIVALS**  Numerous festivals were scheduled throughout the year in ancient Egypt to honor the gods in their temples—some were local celebrations, and some were celebrated throughout the land. A festival usually began with a procession of the cult statue by the priests, who were accompanied by musicians and dancers. Sometimes the statue traveled in procession from one temple to another, spending a certain number of days in the second temple before returning. Such was the case with the OPET Festival, when a statue of Amun traveled from KARNAK to LUXOR temple.

A "calendar of festivals" inscribed on the southern wall of the temple of Medinet Habu (west bank of the Nile in Luxor) by Ramses III, lists some 60 different festivals. All the festivals of Amum are included with a long list of requirements for each feast and with a note about which treasury will pay for them. The list also includes the 365 daily offerings and the eight "feast of heaven" days. Following are some of the major annual festivals:

> The Festival of the King's Coronation on the twenty-sixth of *pakhons*, the ninth month (originally one day, but lengthened to 20 days).
> The Festival of the New Year, corresponding with the rising of Sirius, the brightest star in the sky.
> The Festival of Opet on the nineteenth day of *paophi*, the second month, for 24 days.
> The Beautiful Festival of the Valley, a procession of Amun, Mut, and Khonsu.

The food offerings for a festival varied greatly: One required 84 loaves of bread, for example, while another required more than 4,000. During the festival, the extra food not used by the priests was distributed to the people.

**FIELD OF REEDS** (also SEHET AARU or ELYSIAN FIELDS)   A mythological realm of the western sky, where crops in the fields grow to enormous heights.

The Field of Reeds was a mythical place where the fields produced crops of enormous height. In this tomb painting, the deceased and his wife are shown harvesting grain. *(Photograph by Pat Remler)*

The goddess associated with the Field of Reeds was called NEHEB-KAU and was often shown as a serpent with wings and the arms and legs of a woman. In her hands she carries two pots of food for the souls of the dead.

Mention of the Field of Reeds first occurs in the PYRAMID TEXTS:

> Cleansed is he who is cleansed in the Field of
>     Reeds
> Cleansed is Re in the Field of Reeds
> Cleansed is he who is cleansed in the Field of
>     Reeds
> Cleansed is this Unas in the Field of Reeds
> Hand of Unas in hand of Re!
> O Nut take his hand!
> O Shu, lift him up!
> O Shu, lift him up!

In the Middle Kingdom (2055–1650 B.C.), the COFFIN TEXTS suggest that the deceased will be required to labor in the Field of Reeds, and at about the same time the Coffin Texts were written, magical figures called *ushabtis* were introduced. Each ushabti was given a magical spell so that when the deceased was called upon to work in the Field of Reeds, the ushabti would answer for the deceased and perform the work. The concept of the Field of Reeds was expanded during the New Kingdom (1550–1069 B.C.), when it was regularly included in the vignettes that decorated the BOOK OF THE DEAD. According to Osirian mythology (see Chapter 145 of the Book of the Dead), the deceased was required as part of his passage into the next world to spend time working in the Field of Reeds. In another version, when the deceased had completed his journey through the Underworld and had undergone his final judgment and acquittal (see WEIGHING OF THE HEART CEREMONY), his ultimate goal was to acquire a plot of land. This symbolized the resuming of his earthly activities in the NETHERWORLD, the Field of Reeds. In the vignettes of the Book of the Dead, the deceased is often shown plowing, sowing, and harvesting, sometimes with his wife, and they are always dressed in their best clothes as if they were on holiday. The location of the Field of Reeds is never specified, but the Book of the Dead seems to place it in the Netherworld. According to myths, the Field of Reeds produced an abundance of wheat and barley that grew to enormous heights. It was said to be the food of the dead, like the nectar and ambrosia of the gods. It was different from the actual food offerings left for the deceased on Earth.

Over the centuries, various texts suggested that there was also an earthly location for the Field of Reeds, perhaps in the eastern Delta, or on an island in the Delta, or in the remote Kharga Oasis. The term "field of reeds" eventually became a euphemism for the Netherworld or for a death.

**FISH** It appears that fish were both taboo and acceptable in ancient Egypt. This taboo seems strange, since fish from the Nile, Mediterranean, and the Red Sea were plentiful staples in the Egyptian diet. In some nomes or provinces, fish were considered sacred, but in others, fish were considered unclean. A fish that was forbidden in one town could be eaten in another. Temple priests were forbidden to eat fish, and the king avoided it as well. Fish is almost never shown on the offering table in tombs or on temple walls. The only exception is a scene on the wall of the tomb of a nobleman named Mena in the Valley of the Nobles in Luxor. The *Lates niloticus*, known as the bolti fish today, appears on his offering table.

The taboo no doubt sprang from the myth of Osiris, which says the Oxyrhynchus fish swallowed the phallus of Osiris after his evil brother Set had hacked Osiris's body to bits and scattered the parts. Because of the popularity of the myth of Osiris, fish were associated with Set, and this led to their prohibition.

Fish seem to have played a part in Egyptian medicine, however, and they were frequently prescribed as a remedy for headaches. Redfish, skull of crayfish, and bone of swordfish were mixed with onions, fruit of the *am* tree, honey, and other ingredients to make a salve which was then rubbed vigorously on the sufferer's head.

HATMEHTY, a fish goddess whose name means, "She Who Is in Front of the Fish," was worshipped at her cult center in the Delta. A pair of pilot fish, Abtu and Ant, mentioned in Chapter 9 of the BOOK OF THE DEAD, swam on each side of the sun god Re's boat to ward off evil spirits as it passed through the Netherworld.

**FIVE ELEMENTS OF BIRTH** Ancient Egyptians believed that the *BA*, the *KA*, the NAME, the shadow, and the physical body were all present when a person was born. Mythology tells us that together these elements comprised the whole person. Egyptologists are not certain of the part each element played in a person's life, but the *ba* seems to have been the soul, and the *ka* was a spiritual double. The name referred to a secret name given to each person at birth that had magical powers of protection.

**FLAIL** (FLABELLUM, *Greek*) (NEKH-AKHA, *Egyptian*) The flail was part of the king's royal regalia carried as a sign of his dominion over the land. It was an instrument of the gods carried by OSIRIS, MIN, and ANUBIS (when he appears as a jackal). The flail, along with the CROOK, symbolized the king's power. The flail originally may have been a shepherd's whip or a fly whisk, to chase flies. Its shape—a wand with several pendants or strings of beads hanging down—suggests both possible uses. Symbolically it was a means of summoning divine power.

**FOOD OF THE GODS** Paintings and inscriptions on tomb and temple walls show all the different foods considered worthy of the gods. The walls of KARNAK TEMPLE indicate that AMUN-RE (when he appeared as a fertility god) preferred offerings of vegetables and fresh flowers. To appease the violent side of her nature, and because she was the goddess of music, love, and dance, HATHOR was given wine. Horus the child was presented with milk. These personalized offerings were accompanied with menus that also might have included roasts of beef and gazelle, ducks, game birds, vegetables and fruits of all kinds, bread, cake, beer, wine, and milk.

The idea of "food of the gods" was an exchange. The pharaoh, by way of the priests, provided specific foods that were thought to please the gods. The food offering was one of many rituals performed each day to ensure that Egypt remained in a state of *MAAT*, or divine order.

Early each morning temple workers began preparations for the daily offering. Every step of the preparation was closely supervised, for no mistakes could be made. The kitchens baked fresh bread and cakes in several different shapes; roasted joints of beef, wild game, and ducks; prepared vegetables and fruits; and brewed the best quality beer. Before the gods could be served, each group of food was purified with water, natron, and burning incense. Food bearers carried platters piled high with every kind of food and set them on offering tables in front of the god's shrine. When the shrine was opened, a selection of food was taken from each tray, placed on a special serving platter, and presented to the cult statue of the god. Later the food was distributed among the priests, except for the loaves of bread; they remained on the offering table until the next morning, when the ceremony would be repeated. The only food item that was never served to the gods was fish. There are two theories about why fish were not deemed a food of the gods. One idea is that fish were sacred to the gods: A pair of fish, Abtu and Ant, swam on either side of the sun god Re's boat to ward off evil spirits when it passed through the Underworld. Another possibility is that when the god OSIRIS was hacked to bits, his phallus was thrown into the Nile and eaten by a fish.

## FOUR SONS OF HORUS

The falcon-headed god Horus was said to have four sons: Duamutef, with the head of a jackal; Qebsenef, with the head of a falcon; Hapi, with the head of an baboon; and Mesti, with a human head. Each of the four sons was responsible for protecting one of the mummy's internal organs (stomach, liver, intestines, and kidneys). The organs were placed in limestone jars, with each lid shaped like the head of one of the sons. These were CANOPIC JARS from the Greek legend of Canopus, the pilot of Menelaus, king of Sparta, who was buried in Egypt. He was said to have been worshipped in the form of a jar with feet.

Once wrapped, the internal organs were placed in the canopic jars. A fluid (probably dissolved NATRON) called the "liquid of the children of Horus" was poured over the organs. The jars were then sealed and placed in a small, decorated chest with four compartments, one for each jar. At this point, a magical spell was recited to invoke the protection of the four sons of Horus:

Mesti says: "I am Mesti, thy son Osiris. I come so that I may protect thee. I cause thy house to

Four sons of Horus were supposed to protect the internal organs of the deceased. These amulets were sewn on the mummy as additional protection. *(Photograph by Russell Rudzwick)*

prosper, to be firm, by the command of Ptah, by the command of Re himself."

Hapi says: "I am Hapi, thy son Osiris. I come so that I may protect thee. I bandage for thee thy head and thy limbs, killing for thee thy enemies under thee. I give to thee thy head, forever."

Duamutef says: "I am thy son Horus, loving thee. I come to avenge my father, Osiris. I do not permit his destruction to thee. I place it under thy feet forever and ever."

Qebsenef says: "I am thy son Osiris. I have come that I may protect thee. I gather together thy bones, I collect thy limbs, I bring for thee they heart. I place it upon its seat in thy body. I cause thy house to prosper."

The PYRAMID TEXTS call the Four Sons of Horus "friends of the king" who "assist him as he rises to the heavens," but in the New Kingdom, they become guardians of the mummy's internal organs.

## FROGS

Long associated with fertility in ancient Egypt, the frog was also a symbol of regeneration. The hieroglyph for 100,000 was the tadpole. HEKET, the most prominent frog deity, was the wife of Khnum, the creator god, and a patron of women during childbirth. Frog amulets have even been found in Amarna, the city founded by AKHENATEN when he banished Egypt's traditional religion. This suggests that Heket continued to be a talisman for women even

Painting from the tomb of Senedjem where the deceased is shown in the company of Anubis, the jackal-headed god. *(Photograph by Pat Remler)*

when every other traditional deity was outlawed. The Egyptian creation myth that originated in Hermopolis suggests that four of the gods of the OGDOAD—HEH, HEK, NUN, and AMUN—appeared with frog's heads. As late as the fourth century A.D., when Christianity became popular in Egypt, the frog retained its association with rebirth.

Another frog goddess, HEKA, is a mistress of magic and she appears as a guardian of the sun god in the BOOK OF GATES.

**FUNERARY BELIEFS** Most of what we know about ancient Egyptian mythology and religion comes from funerary beliefs and burial customs. The Egyptians believed that death was a transition between this life and the next. They also believed that it was possible to achieve eternal life through resurrection. Because of their belief in resurrection, preserving the body was all-important to the Egyptians. Without an intact body, the deceased could not magically travel to the next world where he or she would exist for all eternity. This belief led to complex funerary practices that changed very little over ancient Egypt's 3,000-year history.

The earliest burials were shallow pit graves where the body was placed in flexed or fetal position, with the knees drawn up to the chin. Simple items from daily life—clay pots, beads, and slate palettes—were placed in the burial pit, which seems to indicate some belief in an afterlife. Because of the hot, dry climate, the bodies in these early burials were desiccated, or naturally mummified, but the shallow graves did not protect them from animals or sandstorms. The fact that the bodies were naturally mummified and recognizable, but not protected, must have led to the next step. Burial chambers were dug and lined with bricks, and the bodies were covered with animal skins and placed on woven mats. This provided a much safer resting spot for the deceased. While this method kept the bodies from exposure, because they were no longer resting in hot, dry sand, they began to rot rather than dehydrate. By this time, religious beliefs required that the body be intact, and artificial MUMMIFICATION was necessary. As the art of mummification developed, so did the religious rituals and the importance of the funerary gods (see OSIRIS and ANUBIS).

Although the funerary texts tell us that beliefs changed—the PYRAMID TEXTS refer to the king transforming into a circumpolar star, for example, while the COFFIN TEXTS describe an afterlife toiling in the FIELD OF REEDS—no belief system or god or goddess was ever completely discarded in ancient Egypt. Instead, they were incorporated into a new idea or evolved into an aspect of another deity.

**FUNERARY TEXTS** Funerary texts are prayers, spells, and incantations intended to help the deceased reach the next world. Called PYRAMID TEXTS, the first funerary texts originated in the Old Kingdom (2686–2181 B.C.). Carved on the walls of the burial chamber of the pyramid of the Fifth Dynasty King UNAS (c. 2345 B.C.), the Pyramid Texts are the first large body of written texts in Egypt, and they express a well-developed idea of the afterlife. The Pyramid Texts are concerned primarily with the protection of the body of the king and offer suggestions like "cast the sand from your face." In some texts the king tries to bully the gods into accepting him as one of them. Versions of the Pyramid Texts, comprising some 800 spells in all, are found in eight later pyramids dating from the Sixth to the Eighth Dynasties (2345–2125 B.C.). The spells appear in no particular order, and not every spell was included in every pyramid.

During the Middle Kingdom (2055–1650 B.C.), funerary practices were no longer restricted to royalty and the wealthy. Now ordinary people could also have a proper funeral and an afterlife in the next world. With this development, new religious texts were needed. The Pyramid Texts were expanded and became the COFFIN TEXTS. Called the BOOK OF TWO WAYS, Coffin Texts were guides for the deceased in their quest for the next world. They were inscribed in vertical rows on the wooden coffins popular during the period. One of the innovations of the Coffin Texts was that the sun god was no longer supreme. OSIRIS, god of the Underworld, became the patron of the dead, for they were destined to spend eternity with him. The Coffin Texts also developed the idea of the FIELD OF REEDS, where the deceased would spend an undetermined amount of time plowing, sowing, and harvesting—working in the fields. It was at this time that the idea of a magical substitute worker was initiated. Mummiform statuettes called USHABTIS, complete with magical spells to activate them, would perform the agricultural tasks required of the deceased. When texts became too numerous to inscribe on coffins, they gave way to the BOOK OF THE DEAD, a New Kingdom (1550–1069 B.C.) innovation that continued to assist the deceased on their journey to the next world. The Book of the Dead is a series of magical spells, more than half of which came from the Pyramid Texts and Coffin Texts. They include a series of vignettes illustrating various chapters. The virtue of the Book of the Dead was that it could be written on papyrus and copied easily. Because the Book of the Dead developed from a series of earlier writings, it had no particular organization, and chapters were sometimes repeated or omitted in error when they were copied. Eventually there were several different versions of the Book of the Dead, but the most important chapters were included in each one.

A later group of assorted texts, derived in part from the Book of the Dead, have been grouped together in the modern designation the Book of the Netherworld. These texts, unlike the Book of the Dead, an assortment of magical spells, prayers, and incantations, are religious essays relating, in step-by-step detail, the sun god's journey through the realm of darkness each night. They also describe the World of the Beyond. The Books of the Netherworld included the AMDUAT, the BOOK OF CAVERNS, the BOOK OF THE EARTH, and the BOOK OF GATES.

# G

**GEB** The god of Earth, Geb was one of the nine gods of the ENNEAD, the creation myth that arose in HELIOPOLIS. He was the son of SHU, the god of air, and TEFNUT, the goddess of moisture, who were the children of ATUM, the creator god. Geb's sister and wife was NUT, the sky goddess, and their children were ISIS, OSIRIS, NEPHTHYS, and SET. As the god of earth and vegetation, Geb is sometimes colored green, and with plants sprouting from his back and water spurting from his body. One of his symbols was the goose, which he sometimes wore on his head. His daughter Isis once held the obscure title "Egg of the Goose." At other times Geb was portrayed as a man wearing the red crown of the Delta and reclining on one side or seated on a throne. One myth says that when Geb and his wife, Nut, became the parents of the sun, he was hailed as the "Father of the Gods."

Geb's most important role was that of judge in the CONTENDINGS OF HORUS AND SET. As "Father of the Gods," Geb gave his son Osiris the Earth to rule.

The ancient Egyptians believed Gebel Barkal was a holy mountain and home of the great god Amun. They covered the tall peak in gold because it resembled a rearing cobra. When Egyptologists excavated the ruins around Gebel Barkal, they found the remains of 13 temples and three palaces. *(Photograph by Pat Remler)*

When Osiris was killed by his evil brother Set, Horus avenged his father and was favored by Geb and given the Earth to rule. From this myth came one of the titles of the pharaoh: "Heir of Geb."

**GEBEL BARKAL** A sacred mountain in NUBIA, below Egypt's southern border, Gebel Barkal was home of the great god AMUN. To the ancient Egyptians, the sandstone mountain butte with a freestanding peak looked like a giant rearing cobra (URAEUS) wearing the white crown of UPPER EGYPT, and they took it as a sign of "divine kingship." When the freestanding stone peak was examined by Egyptologist Tim Kendal, he discovered that in ancient times the peak was covered with a sheath of gold (the nail holes are still visible). Egyptian mythology calls Gebel Barkal *djew wab* (the pure mountain), home of the great god Amun, who dwells in the mountain along with other gods. His title "Lord of the Thrones of Two Lands" represents his dominion over Egypt and Nubia. For the Egyptians, the uraeus (or rearing cobra) was a symbol of kingship, of protection of the king, of the divine mother of the king. Images natural or man-made could hold powerful magic, and the Egyptians and the Nubians who followed the Egyptian religion recognized Gebel Barkal as a sacred and magical space.

Because Nubia had gold mines, the pharaoh's armies and trading parties invaded Nubia from the time of the OLD KINGDOM (2686–2181 B.C.). In the Eighteenth Dynasty, King Thutmose III (1504–1452) defeated the local king, erected a STELA (stone slab) at Gebel Barkal, and declared that this was Egypt's new southern boundary. He built a fortress to secure his gold and a large temple to Amun—inscriptions on the temple wall tell us that a statue of Amun "spoke" to the priests. Near the great Temple of Amun were other temples for the goddesses MUT, HATHOR, TEFNUT, and perhaps ISIS—one name has been lost. Later kings enlarged the temple and created new sanctuaries and temple administrative offices of their own.

By the Twentieth Dynasty, Egypt had grown weak, and Gebel Barkal was abandoned. By this time, the Nubians had adopted much of Egyptian culture and religion, and as the Nubian kings grew stronger, they saw themselves as legitimate heirs to the throne of Egypt. Finally they invaded and ruled Egypt for about 60 years. The cult of Amun at Gebel Barkal was continued by the Nubian kings who also worshipped HORUS, OSIRIS, and KHNUM.

The Nubian kings revived the failing religion in Egypt, rebuilt the temples, and built their own pyramids in Nubia, for they wanted to be buried near Gebel Barkal. Within close proximity to Gebel Barkal

One of the decorations on the wall of the Temple of Mut is a picture of Gebel Barkal with the peak shown as a rearing cobra. *(Photograph by Pat Remler)*

are three of the four Nubian pyramid fields—the Gebel Barkal Pyramids, the el Kurru Pyramids, and the Nuri Pyramids. The fourth pyramid site in Nubia is at MEROE, southeast of Gebel Barkal and between the fifth and sixth cataracts.

**GEMSTONES, MAGICAL** (also GNOSTIC or ABRAXAS GEMS) Because of their supposed magical quality, gemstone AMULETS were popular during the Ptolemaic and Roman periods in Egypt (332 B.C.–A.D. 395). Gemstones were basically good luck charms, worn for protection from evil forces; for good health or healing; or to bring the wearer fame, fortune, or love. Three essential elements had to be apparent for the magic to work. Depending on what was wished for, the gemstone had to be a certain color, the proper magical words had to be inscribed on the gem, and the magical figures, often Egyptian gods, had to be in place.

Magical gemstones are best known in the ancient world as Gnostic or Abraxas gems. When the Greeks assigned a number value to the Greek alphabet, the magic became more complex, and the idea evolved into mystical texts.

**GIRDLE OF ISIS** See KNOT OF ISIS.

**GODS OF ANCIENT EGYPT** Egypt's pantheon—group of gods and goddesses—emerged along the banks of the NILE. Wandering the river valley, the first nomadic Egyptians must have feared the unpredictable power of nature—the violent forces of thunder, lightning, and storms. These and the desolate desert became the archetypes for the first gods and goddesses. The early frightening gods of nature changed as Egypt's civilization changed from nomadic groups into farming settlements. Settlements grew into cities, and Egypt prospered. The gods remained powerful, but they became benevolent and kindly and developed human forms with superhuman powers. The gods and goddesses developed personalities: they fell in love, they were jealous, they were angry, and they felt despair. Mythology tells us they lived much like the humans who worshipped them.

Living close to nature, the Egyptians recognized the powerful traits of animals—the strength of the bull, the fierceness of the lion—and wanted to gain the same power for themselves. The powers and essence of an animal seemed to magically transfer to some of the gods, resulting in many ancient Egyptian gods (such as BASTET, ANUBIS, HORUS, and HATHOR) appearing with the heads of animals and the bodies of humans.

More than any other ancient culture, the Egyptians were fascinated by the mystery of death and the prospect of RESURRECTION in the next world. If they were happy in this life, with the help of the gods, they could live an even better life in the next world. If their lives were not so good, there was always the possibility of achieving happiness by resurrecting in the next world.

By any standard, the gods of ancient Egypt are complex—their personalities changing and merging with other deities—and even gods and goddesses with distinct identities often combine and share attributes, signs, and duties with others (see ISIS and HATHOR). Over Egypt's long history, many new, sometimes foreign deities joined the pantheon—there seemed to be room for everyone, and rarely was one discarded.

The one exception to ancient Egypt's religious tolerance was AKHENATEN, the heretic king. He changed Egypt's religion from the worship of many gods (polytheism) to the worship of one god (monotheism), the ATEN. The change lasted only about 17 years, and then the religion reverted back to the worship of many gods. Egyptian tomb and temple paintings show us that power was in the hands of the gods and the king, who was a divine being (a god on Earth) and whose job it was to serve as the messenger between the gods and the people.

**GOD'S WIFE, THE** The title "the god's wife of Amun" was first used in the New Kingdom (1550–1069 B.C.) and was bestowed on Queen Ahmhose Nefertari, wife of Ahmose I (1550–1525 B.C.). A title of great prestige and honor, it meant that in religious ceremonies the queen was viewed as a goddess and played the part of the god's wife on Earth. During the Nineteenth Dynasty (1295–1186 B.C.), the title was passed to the daughter of the pharaoh and was combined with another title, "divine adoratrice." The princess, upon whom this title was bestowed, was expected to devote her life to the god and never marry. Because she could not have children, when the time came for the "god's wife" to leave her post, she chose her successor from one of the current king's daughters. While the position of "god's wife" was a religious one, and the princess who held the title served Amun in the great temple in Thebes, it was also a political position. As the priesthood of Amun grew wealthy and powerful during the New Kingdom, the king needed someone close to him in the temple to keep him informed of the priests' activities, and having a daughter in the powerful position of "god's wife of Amun" served his purpose.

**GOLD** [symbol] The symbol for gold in ancient Egypt was a gold necklace. Gold was called the "flesh of the gods," for it was the metal that never tarnished. One of the five royal titles of the pharaoh, the "Golden Horus" name connected him with the sun god and emphasized the association of gold with the gods. One of the many titles of the goddess HATHOR is "the Golden One." Gold was one of the most precious commodity in ancient Egypt. Gold-mining expeditions were sent to the Wadi Hammamat in the eastern desert and to Nubia. One of the earliest known maps is a drawing of the location of the gold mines in the Wadi Hammamat. The great quantities of gold flowing into the country caused envy among Egypt's neighbors, and King Tushratta of Mitanni wrote to Akhenaten (in what are known as the Amarna Letters), "Gold in your country is dirt. One simply gathers it up. Why are you so sparing of it? I am engaged in building a new palace. Send me as much gold as is needed for its adornment."

Because of its association with the gods, and because it did not tarnish, gold was the perfect funerary adornment. The mummies of kings were fitted with gold masks. Tutankhamen was placed in a solid gold coffin as well. In the tomb, the chamber that held the sarcophagus was called "the chamber of gold," and sometimes the head or the foot of the sarcophagus was decorated with the goddess Nephthys kneeling on the hieroglyph for gold.

**GREAT CACKLER**    Name for the sacred goose who appears in the creation myth of the Ogdoad. One version of the myth tells us that the Great Cackler laid the primeval egg from which the Earth was hatched. In that myth, the Great Cackler is associated with Atum, the creator god who is sometimes depicted as a goose.

The Great Cackler is mentioned in the Coffin Texts (Spell 307):

> I am the soul who created the watery abyss and made a place in god's land: My nest will not be seen nor my egg broken, for I am the lord of those on high, and I have made a nest in the sky.

It is said that the sound of the Great Cackler broke the silence that existed before the world was created:

> . . . He cackled, being the Great Cackler, in the place where he was created, he alone. He began to speak in the midst of silence . . . He commenced to cry when the earth was inert. His cry spread . . . He brought forth all living things which exist. He caused them to live. He made all men understand the way to go and their hearts came alive when they saw him.

The Book of the Dead associates the Great Cackler with the goddess Nut:

> Hail thou sycamore of the goddess Nut!
> Grant me the water which dwells in thee.
> I embrace the throne which is in Unnu
>   (Hermopolis) and
> I watch and guard the egg of the great cackler.
> It groweth, I grow.
> It liveth, I live
> It breathes the air, I breathe the air

Mythology tells us that around the great sycamore tree of Heliopolis grew a variety of plants, and this is where the Great Cackler laid the "egg of the sun," and thus the Great Cackler became associated with the sun god Re.

**GREEK GODS AND EGYPTIAN MYTHOLOGY**
Over its 3,000-year history, Egyptian mythology added and merged gods and goddesses into its ever-growing pantheon. Rather than discard or eliminate any god whose popularity had diminished, the attributes were incorporated into newly evolved deities. When the Greek rulers, the Ptolemies, came to power, they brought two things with them: a pantheon of Greek gods, and a respect for the ancient and enduring religion of the Egyptians. It was clear to the Greek rulers that if their gods were merged with the Egyptian gods, it would promote goodwill among the people. Aesculapius, the Greek god of medicine, and Imhotep, the Egypt god of healing, were called Ptah-Aesculapius, and the healing abilities of the two gods would remain the same.

### Greek Forms of Egyptian Gods

Anubis=*Anupu*
Anukis=*Anuket*
Apollo=*Amun-Re*
Apophis=*Apep*
Ares=*Anhur*
Aset=*Isis*
Athena=*Isis* and *Neith*
Atlas=*Shu*
Buto=*Wadjet*
Cronus=*Geb*
Dionysus=*Osiris*
Eileithyia=*Nekh-bet*
Hades=*Osiris*
Harmachis=*Horus who is on the horizon*
Haroeris=*Horus the elder*
Harpocrates=*Horus the child*
Harsaphes=*Hershef*
Harsiesis=*Hor-sa-ist (Horus son of Isis)*
Hephaestus=*Ptah*
Hermes trismegistus=*Thoth*
Horakhty=*Horus who is on the horizon*
Horus=*Hor*
Iphtimis=*Nefertum*
Khnoumis=*Khnum*
Menes=*Narmer*
Meret-seger=*Mert-sekert*
Mnevis bull=*Wer-mer*
Nephthys=*Neb-thet*
Onouris=*Anhur*
Persephone=*Isis*
Pan and Priapus=*Ba-neb-djed* and *Min*
Satis=*Satet*
Serapis=*Osiris-apis=Osirapis*
Thoueris=*Tauret*
Typhon=*Set*

**HA** God of the western desert and protector of the oasis, Ha is shown as a man with the symbol of the desert on his head. Ha played an important role in temple building, an activity that was overseen by the king but closely supervised by the gods. As a god of the desert, Ha was responsible for transporting the sand that would be used in the ceremony of placing the foundations of the temple. Being a god of the western desert, Ha was also responsible for warding off Egypt's enemies from the west, the Libyans.

**HADES** When the Greeks ruled Egypt during the Ptolemaic dynasty (332–32 B.C.), they associated the Egyptian god OSIRIS with their god of the Underworld, Hades. Unlike Osiris, who was a god of resurrection and hope, Hades was a god of terror and one to be avoided. His name eventually became associated with hell, the place of the lost souls.

**HAIR** In the myth of ISIS and OSIRIS, Isis is said to have cut a lock of her hair to symbolize her grief over the death of her husband, Osiris. When Egyptians mourned their dead, they often cut a lock of hair to express their sorrow over the death of a loved one. The Greek writer Plutarch (A.D. 46–126) believed the tradition of Isis cutting her hair became part of the Isis and Osiris myth when the Ptolemies ruled Egypt. The custom of cutting a lock of hair and wearing black as a sign of mourning is, Plutarch says, more a Greek tradition than Egyptian. The hieroglyphic sign for mourning, however, is three locks of hair, ⌐, and some scholars believe this may be a reference to Isis cutting a lock of her hair. The development of HIEROGLYPHS is, of course, much earlier than the Greek influence in Egypt.

**HALL OF DOUBLE TRUTH** In order to spend a pleasant eternity in the NETHERWORLD, the deceased

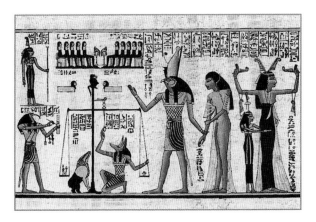

For the soul of the deceased to reach the Netherworld, one of the most important rituals to be performed was the negative confession, which took place in the Hall of Double Truth. The deceased stood before 42 gods and named all the evil deeds that he or she had never committed during life. *(Courtesy of Bob Brier)*

had to be judged by the gods. The first part of the judgment took place in the Hall of Double Truth, where the deceased was confronted by a tribunal of 42 gods. The deceased had to "separate himself from evil doings" by making a NEGATIVE CONFESSION. It listed all of the evil deeds he had *not* committed and convinced the gods of his innocence. Once this test was successfully passed, the deceased moved on to the WEIGHING OF THE HEART CEREMONY.

**HAPI** God of the Nile who lived in the caves under the cataracts or boulders in the Nile. Hapi was actually the god of inundation, the flood, and as such he personified the annual flooding of the Nile. Hapi was a fertility god, for the fate of the crops each year depended on how high the Nile rose and how much rich silt was spread across the flooded fields. Aquatic plants crown Hapi's head, and his

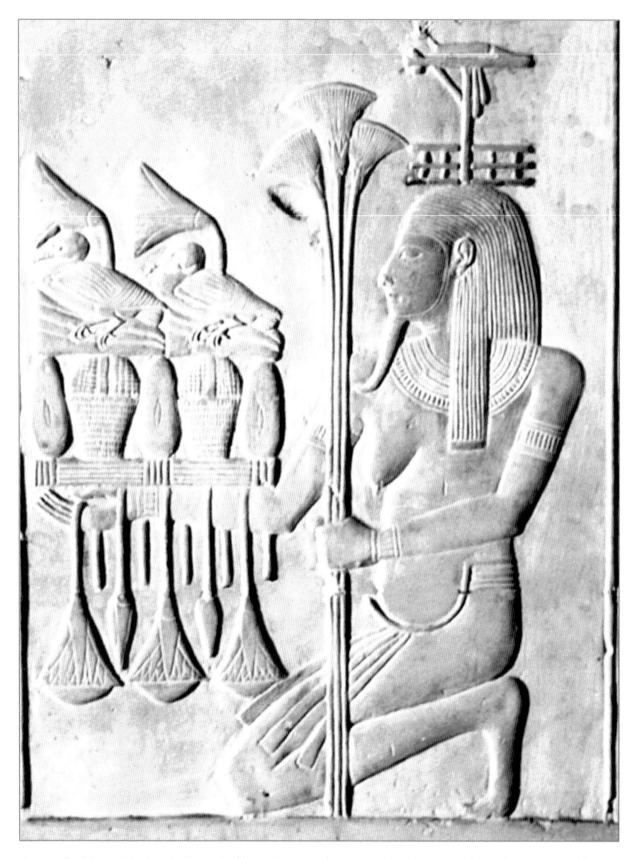

As a god of fecundity, Hapi, the god of the Nile, was shown with both male and female attributes. He was responsible for the flooding of the Nile each year. *(Photograph by Pat Remler)*

pendulous breasts and sagging stomach symbolize abundance and fertility.

Hapi's titles include "Master of the River Bringing Vegetation" and "Lord of Fish and Fowl of the Marshes." In keeping with his aquatic associations, Hapi is attended by frog goddesses and crocodiles. Oddly, no temples were dedicated to Hapi—his statues and reliefs were carved in the temples of other gods. Several versions of a hymn to Hapi have been found that appear to be later copies of an original, perhaps composed in the MIDDLE KINGDOM (2055–1650 B.C.). The hymn tells of the joy experienced in Egypt when Hapi provides a good inundation.

## HARPER'S SONGS, THE   Showing the Egyptians' positive approach to death, the Harper's Songs illustrate an important segment of ancient Egyptian mythology.

Carvings on tomb walls or on a STELA erected for the deceased, the Harper's Songs were composed to help the dead resurrect in the next world and were often accompanied by a harp. Unlike ritual mortuary chants and prayers, the Harper's Songs demonstrated much more creativity in their approaches to death and the next world. The songs' main theme was to sing the praises of the deceased's tomb and the joys of leaving this world and entering the next. One song says "... O tomb you were build for festivity, you were built for happiness!" But because of their freedom to express their own thoughts on death, some harpers took another view and lamented the loss of life and wondered if there really was an afterlife.

The stela of *Neb-Ankh*, in the Egyptian Museum in Cairo, takes the traditional approach and looks forward to eternal life in the next world:

How firm you are in your seat of eternity,
Your monument of everlastingness!
It is filled with offerings of food,
It contains every good thing.
Your *ka* is with you,
It does not leave you,
O Royal Seal-bearer, Great Steward, *Neb-Ankh*!
Yours is the sweet breath of the north wind!
So says his singer who keeps his name alive,
The honorable singer *Teni-o* whom he loved,
Who sings to his *ka* every day.

The musician *Teni-o* assures *Neb-Ankh*, the deceased, that all is well—his KA will not desert him,

his tomb is filled with every good thing, and his name will be kept alive.

## HARSIESE   "HORUS SON OF ISIS," Harsiese appears first in the PYRAMID TEXTS, where he performs the OPENING OF THE MOUTH CEREMONY for the deceased king so that he may "live again and breathe again" in the next world. In this form, Horus is not associated with the ancient god of the sky, but instead he appears as the helpful son of ISIS and OSIRIS. Harsiese assists the souls of the deceased and delivers them to his father, Osiris, in the next world.

## HATHOR   One the oldest and most beloved goddesses in ancient Egypt, Hathor is the universal cow goddess and a symbolic mother of the pharaoh. Her image has been found carved on early flint implements, and her cow head is prominent on the NARMER PALETTE (c. 3100 B.C.), a commemorative slate palette recording a victorious battle of King Narmer.

The goddess Hathor is represented in many different ways. She is the "Great Wild Cow," and her home was the papyrus thicket, where the papyrus plant was sacred to her. When Hathor appeared as a cow-headed woman, she was crowned with the sun disk resting between her cow horns, and in her hands she held a *WAS*, or papyrus scepter. In her temples, Hathor-headed columns with human faces were incorporated into the architecture. So important was Hathor in the Egyptian pantheon that eventually every other goddess, even ISIS, sometimes called Hathor-Isis, was identified with her.

The cow-goddess cult was well established even in Predynastic Egypt (5500–3100 B.C.), and Hathor must have shared attributes with other minor cow goddesses, such as the Predynastic goddess BAT. Hathor is mentioned in the Old Kingdom (2686–2181 B.C.) valley temple of King Chephren as a guardian of the temple. She was so popular with the people that shrines to the great goddess could be found in almost every town. Because of her many attributes, Hathor became the great mother goddess of this world and the next, and her titles and her characteristics grew too numerous to list. In each of the nomes of Upper and Lower Egypt, Hathor was identified with the local goddess and showered with loving epithets. In Memphis she was known as the "Lady of the Sycamore." As "the Lady of Turquoise" she was worshipped at Serabit

Hathor, the goddess of love and music, was called the Lady of Heaven. She wears a metal necklace around her neck. *(Drawing by Mary Jordan)*

the goddess, represented pleasure and joy. During cult ceremonies, the menat, often decorated with the face of Hathor, was carried and shaken as an accompaniment to chanting and singing. One of Hathor's many titles is "Golden One," referring to her special association with gold and precious metals. Highly polished hand mirrors were often made from gold or bronze and were decorated with the image of Hathor, reflecting her association with RE the sun god.

The name Hathor means "House of Horus" and, as a goddess of the sky, she personified the house and sky of HORUS (the hawk) when he is portrayed as the sun god. Horus himself was the oldest form of the sun god, and Hathor is his wife. Since the king was closely identified with Horus (one of his five titles was his golden Horus name), Hathor became the divine mother and protector of the king. This relationship is illustrated in the statue of Amenhotep II (1427–1400 B.C.) being nursed by his divine mother, Hathor, now in the Egyptian Museum in Cairo.

Hathor is also the daughter of the great sun god Re, and mythology tells us that when he called upon her, she became the vengeful eye of her father, Re, bringing violence and destruction wherever she went. When Re wished to destroy humankind, he sent Hathor, as his vengeful eye, to carry out the slaughter. One ceremony in the Hathor cult involved pacifying her dangerous side by playing the SISTRUM, a rattle, something like a tambourine, one of Hathor's ritual objects.

**Love, Music, and Dance**   As the personification of female sexuality, love, music, dance, and drink, Hathor was seen by the Greeks to be the same as their goddess of love, Aphrodite. The cult of Hathor focused on pleasure, and the rituals involved sensual music and dancing. As shown on tomb walls, dancing in honor of Hathor was part of joyous celebrations, of which music was an important part. Ritual music was accompanied by the sistrum and the menat, both of which were shaken with great enthusiasm during processions. The sistrum, a rattle with a long handle, was often decorated with a Hathor head.

As a nurturing goddess, Hathor was sought as a "bringer of fertility" and a protector of women in childbirth. It was believed that Hathor could predict the destiny of a newborn child.

Hathor also was a mortuary goddess, and in Thebes she was known as the "Lady of the Western Mountain." In one myth, each night Hathor protects the evening sun while the deceased offer prayers to

el Khadim in the Sinai, a remote region in the desert. The remains of her temple can still be seen high on the mountaintop, where it was one of the few Egyptian temples built on foreign soil. Hathor was the patron goddess of the miners digging for turquoise, a stone highly prized in ancient Egypt. When Hathor was honored as "the Lady of the Underworld" she wore a MENAT, a counterpoise, or balance, to a large necklace. The menat, a symbol of

The face of Hathor, with her distinctive cow ears. *(Photo by Pat Remler)*

be "in the following of Hathor," or to avoid eternal darkness.

Hathor's main temple was in Dendera, where she was worshipped with Horus of Edfu and their son IHY.

**The Seven Hathors**  Mythology tells us that the Seven Hathors, who predicted the fate of newborns, were often called upon to work their magic for love spells and that the red streamers worn on their heads could bind evil spirits. It is said that because the devotee of Hathor could not worship the goddess in all of her numerous forms, a list of her most important names, called the Seven Hathors, was drawn by the priests. In the temple, seven beautiful young women carrying tambourines and wearing close-fitting dresses with vulture headdresses topped with cow's horns and sun disks represented the Seven Hathors. The Seven Hathors were not always the same seven goddesses: Depending on the location, the list could accommodate a local goddess. The Seven Hathors worshipped at Hathor's main cult center in Dendera are as follows:

1. Hathor of Thebes
2. Hathor of Heliopolis
3. Hathor of Aphroditopolis
4. Hathor of Sinai
5. Hathor of Memphis
6. Hathor of Hierakonpolis
7. Hathor of Keset

Each city could adopt its own selection of Hathors.

HATMEHTY  A fish goddess, worshipped in the Delta, who was at one time prominent enough to have one of the nomes, or states, of Lower Egypt named for her. As the wife of the ram god BA-NEB-DJED and mother of their son Horus the child, Har-pa-khered (or Harsomtus; see HORUS), Hatmehty eventually became part of the triad of Mendes. Hatmehty means "She Who is in Front of Fish," and she is represented as a woman with the head of a fish that looks something like a dolphin. The dolphin was the sacred fish of Hatmehty, and hers is one of the few fish cults in ancient Egypt.

HATSHEPSUT  When Queen Hatshepsut chose to rule Egypt as a king rather than queen, she claimed the right because of her divine birth. Hatshepsut claimed her father was AMUN, the great god of THEBES, and in her mortuary temple at Deir el Bahri, she carved the story of the union of her mother Queen Ahmes and the god. The scene shows the queen and the god sitting next to each other on a couch, and then the queen is shown to be pregnant. Hatshepsut was the first woman to rule as king of Egypt, and she had to legitimize her right to the throne by claiming to be the daughter of a god and by claiming that her earthly father, Thutmose I, chose her to succeed him while he was still alive. Had Hatshepsut been a son, she would have succeeded her father on the throne of Egypt. When, after 20 years of marriage, her husband, Thutmose II, died, Hatshepsut ruled Egypt as queen, for the heir to the throne, her nephew Thutmose III, was a young child. After a few years of ruling as queen, Hatshepsut crowned herself king and ruled Egypt successfully for many years. She brought peace and prosperity to Egypt, avoided wars, and initiated trading expeditions and building projects. For a brief period at the beginning of her reign, Hatshepsut ruled jointly, in co-regency, with her nephew Thutmose III.

## HAWK-HEADED GOD   See HORUS.

**HEART** (Ab, Ib) For the Egyptians, the heart, or *ib*, was the center of all human emotions; love, anger, evil, and courage all came from the heart. The heart was believed to be the source of memory and intelligence, and although the Egyptians did not understand the connection between the heart and the circulation of blood, they believed the heart was the most vital organ in the body. A man's actions were often described in terms of his heart. For example, a Middle Kingdom text says, "Their hearts are the cause of evil . . .", and a COFFIN TEXT says ". . . he whose speech comes from his heart."

It was believed that the heart could reveal the true nature of a person. During mummification, the heart was not removed with the other internal organs but left in the body so that when the deceased resurrected in the next world, his heart would be with him. One of the five chapters of the BOOK OF THE DEAD that give advice on how to protect the heart includes the following: "His heart obeyeth him, he is the lord thereof, it is in his body, and it shall never fall away therefrom" (Chapter 27). Chapter 29 says: "My heart is with me, and it shall never come to pass that it be carried away . . ."

In the Final Judgement chapter in the Book of the Dead, the heart of the mummy was weighed against the feather of truth, or *MAAT*, and if the heart was not heavy with evil deeds, the deceased could enter the next world. Sometimes, however, the heart would speak against its owner, and to prevent this, a Heart Scarab inscribed with prayers was wrapped with the mummy.

Heart amulets were generally make of carnelian, a red, hard stone, although some were made of red glass or other materials and painted red. They were shaped like vases with small handles on either side and often placed on the chest of the mummy during the wrapping procedure.

*HEB-SED* FESTIVAL   Celebrating the rejuvenation of the king's powers every 30 years, the *heb-sed* festival was a demonstration of a king's strength and prowess. During the festival, the king ran around a *heb-sed* court performing feats of strength to demonstrate his ability to continue to rule Egypt. In doing so, he experienced rebirth, maintaining his position as a god on Earth.

The *heb-sed* court of King ZOSER at SAQQARA is a long, rectangular, open court where the king performed the *heb-sed* ritual, part of which was to wrestle with a young man in order to prove he was strong enough to continue ruling Egypt. A limestone relief in a chamber under the Step Pyramid shows King Zoser during his *heb-sed* festival running between the markers representing UPPER and LOWER EGYPT. On the east and west sides of the open courtyard are several symbolic chapels—the interiors were filled with rubble—and only the platforms in front of the chapel were used. Statues of the king and the gods were placed in niches along the wall, and the platforms may have been used for ceremonies during the festival.

*Heb-sed* must have begun in Egypt's Predynastic period with rituals like the "raising of the *DJED* PILLAR" (an ancient sign for OSIRIS) that represented the strength and stability of the king. The earliest reference to a *heb-sed* is shown on the Narmer mace head. Although a king's *heb-sed* was traditionally celebrated every 30 years, often a king chose to celebrate his festival or jubilee much more often. Ramses II (RAMSES THE GREAT) celebrated 14 *heb-sed* festivals or jubilees.

**HEH**   The god of infinity, Heh originally represented the symbol for "millions," but over time he represented the signs for "years" and "eternity." Eventually Heh became associated with the king and his quest for long life. Heh is shown as a man kneeling, sometimes in a basket, which is the sign for "all" or "every." He holds a palm rib, the symbol for "year." On temple walls Heh is shown bestowing millions of years upon the deceased, and frequently he appears on Egyptian jewelry representing eternity. One of the treasures in TUTANKHAMEN's tomb was the lid of a mirror case with the figure of Heh. He holds two scepters, each with a CARTOUCHE of Tutankhamen on top and a *shen*, or sign for eternity, on the bottom.

Heh is crowned with a winged scarab, symbolizing existence, and a sun disk. The message is clear: Heh is giving Tutankhamen millions of years.

**HEK**  One of the eight primeval deities that arose in Hermopolis, Hek was one of the gods of the Ogdoad, or the eight deities of the Egyptian creation myth. The first primeval forces appeared as frogs or serpents that later evolved into the personification of the primeval forces. Hek and Heket represented space.

**HEKA**  A goddess of magic that appears in human form as a woman. Heka and Sia, also a goddess of magic, battled the evil serpent Apophis each night as the sun god made his nightly journey through the Netherworld. One of Heka's most important roles is in the Book of Gates, where she is indispensable as a guardian of the sun god.

**HEKET**  One of the original group of eight deities that form the Ogdoad, the basis of the Hermopolis creation myth. Heket was the female counterpart of Hek, a god of space. She later evolved into a frog goddess who assisted at childbirth. Heket is first mentioned in the Pyramid Texts (c. 2345 b.c.), a group of magical inscriptions, in which she accompanies the spirit of the deceased king to his place in the sky. Her most important association was with childbirth, a distinction she shared with Bes and Tauret, who also protected mothers and children. Heket was especially called upon during the last stages of labor. A Middle Kingdom papyrus (2055–1650 b.c.) tells how Heket assisted the wife of the high priest of Re when she was about to give birth to the future king.

Amulets and scarabs in the shape of a frog were often worn by pregnant women in the hope that Heket would assist them during labor. Magical inscriptions on ivory wands, popular in the Middle Kingdom, refer to Heket as the "defender of the home." A temple dedicated to Heket was found at Qus in Upper Egypt, and there is a reference to her cult in the tomb of Petosiris (fourth century b.c.) at Tuna el Gabel in Middle Egypt. Petosiris was a high priest of the god Thoth, and he recorded on his tomb that Heket led him to a shrine flooded by the yearly inundation of the Nile and asked him to repair her temple. Petosiris says that he summoned his scribe and gave him orders to build a new temple with a wall around it to keep it safe from future floods.

During the Eighteenth Dynasty, representations of Heket, with the body of a woman, are shown in the "divine birth" scenes of the king in Queen Hatshepsut temple at Deir el Bahari. In the Netherworld, Heket was present when the deceased was "reborn." The frog sign in hieroglyphs was a cryptogram for the phrase *wehem ankh* ("repeating life"), a phrase that originated in the Middle Kingdom used to describe the deceased.

**HELIOPOLIS**  The biblical city of On is Heliopolis, one of the most ancient cult centers in Egypt. It is the home of the Heliopolitan Ennead, one of the creation myths in Egyptian mythology. Heliopolis was also the site of the first temple dedicated to Re-Horakhty. The ancient cult combined the worship of Re the sun god and Horakhty, a form of Horus, the falcon god.

**HELIOPOLITAN ENNEAD**  A popular creation myth developed by the priests of Re, the Heliopolitan Ennead was one of three myths that arose during the Old Kingdom (2686–2181 b.c.) in an attempt to explain the universe. The most complete source of information on the ennead is from the Pyramid Texts. They tell us that the Heliopolitan Ennead has two groups of nine gods: the Greater Ennead and the Lesser Ennead, a group of lesser gods ruled by Horus, who was associated with Re. At the beginning of the Greater Ennead, Atum the creator god willed himself into being, or he was created by Nun, the waters of chaos; several versions of the myth have been found. Atum emerged onto the primordial mound, the first bit of land, and since he was associated with the sun god Re, he became Re-Atum and brought light to the darkness. He created Shu, the god of air, and Tefnut, the goddess of moisture. Their children were Geb, the god of Earth, and Nut, the goddess of the sky. These five gods and goddesses were cosmic deities and personified the forces of nature. Geb and Nut were the parents of Osiris, Isis, Nephthys, and Set, who had human characteristics and had important cults of their own.

**HENKHISESUI**  God of the east wind (see also Winds, Gods of the Four).

**HEPHAESTUS**  Called "the divine artificer," Hephaestus, the Greek god of craftsmen, was associated with Ptah and the Roman god Vulcan. The patron gods of craftsmen and smiths were believed to practice magic along with their crafts, and the weapons and tools dedicated to them could have magical powers.

**HERAKLEOPOLIS**  A capital city of the Upper Egypt Nome by the same name, Herakleopolis was a cult center for the ram-headed god Herishef, who was called Harsaphes by the Greeks. They saw him as a version of their god Herakles. The first temple appears to have been built at Herakleopolis during the Middle Kingdom and was in use through Christian times, for several Coptic inscriptions have been found there.

**Herishef** An ancient fertility god whose name means "he who is upon his lake," Herishef had many different traits over Egypt's long history. When Herishef took the form of a ram with a sun disk on his head, he was associated with Re the sun god. When he wore the *atef* crown, the tall crown of Upper Egypt with ostrich plumes, he was affiliated with Osiris, the god of the underworld. One of his titles is "Lord of the Blood," and in this role Herishef is linked to Shesmu, a god with a dual personality.

When Plutarch the Greek historian (first century A.D.) writes about him, Herishef is called Arsaphes.

**Hermes** The winged messenger of the gods in Greek mythology, Hermes was associated with the Egyptian god of knowledge and writing, Thoth.

**Hermonthis** See Armant.

**Hermopolis Magma (Khenmu)** The most important cult center for the worship of Thoth, Hermopolis Magma, renamed by the Greeks, was called Khenmu or "eight town" by the Egyptians. The "eight" referred to the Ogdoad, four pairs of primeval gods who appeared in one of the early creation myths developed in Khenmu. One of Thoth's most important titles was "Lord of the City of Eight." Under the rule of Amenhotep III in the New Kingdom (1550–1069 B.C.), Hermopolis was a thriving city, and the king placed two giant statues of Thoth as a baboon in front of the god's temple; one of them is still standing. In the fourth century B.C., the high priest of Thoth, Petosiris, renovated the temple and created a park full of sacred baboons and ibises. Their mummified bodies were discovered by the thousands in catacombs near Petosiris's tomb in nearby Tuna el Gabel.

**Herodotus (c. 485–425 B.C.)** Greek historian who traveled to Egypt and recorded the customs and religion of the Egyptians. Although some of his observations appear a bit fanciful, his writings were a major source of information on mummification and ancient Egyptian religion. The records of Egypt are found in the second of his nine volumes called *The Histories*.

**Heru-ur** The son of Nut, the sky goddess, born on the third Epagomenal Day, and the twin of the evil god Set, Heru-ur is the Egyptian word for Horus. He was associated with Horus the elder, one of the most ancient gods of Egypt. In the Pyramid Texts, Heru-ur was equal to, but in constant opposition to, his brother Set, owing perhaps to their opposite natures. As a child of Nut, the sky goddess, Heru-ur ruled the sky by day, and his brother Set ruled by night. In the mythology Heru-ur represented light, day, cosmos, life, and good as opposed to Set's darkness, night, chaos, death, and evil.

**Hesat** Cow goddess who nursed the children of the gods and who gave birth to the king in the form of the golden calf. As the goddess of milk, Hesat quenched the thirst of mankind when she provided her divine milk, "the beer of the people." During the Late period (747–332 B.C.), Hesat was understood to be the mother of the Mnevis Bull and was honored in the bull cult.

**Hierakonpolis** An ancient cult center for Horus, the falcon god, dating from Egypt's Predynastic period (3,500 B.C.). Long before the pyramids were built, Hierakonpolis was a bustling trade and religious center stretching more than three miles along the banks of the Nile. It is the site of many important archaeological finds. In 1897, the British Egyptologists James Quibell and Frederick Green discovered a cult statue with a gold head of Horus, the falcon god, and a life-size statue of the Sixth Dynasty king Pepi I cast in copper. A mound the excavators called the "Main Deposit" revealed hundreds of small objects of ivory, stone, and faience and may have been a ritual burial of offerings left for the falcon god.

Best known of the discoveries is the Narmer Palette, perhaps the first political document in the world. It commemorates the unification of Upper and Lower Egypt in 3000 B.C. Also discovered was the Scorpion King mace head, a ceremonial mace on which King Scorpion's name is carved.

Hierakonpolis is the ancient city of Nekhen, today called *Kom el Akhmar*, the "Red Hill," because of the mound of broken red pottery at the entrance. Nekhen is the ancestral home of the Souls of Nekhen and the Souls of Pe, the spirits of ancient ancestors.

**Hieratic** One of the three scripts written in ancient Egypt; hieratic is a cursive form of hieroglyphs. Like hieroglyphs, hieratic was a "sacred writing" but a faster, easier way to copy religious and mythological texts. Hieratic appeared during the Old

Kingdom (2686–2181 B.C.) and was always written from right to left, arranged in columns. Hieroglyphs could be written in any direction. At first, hieratic was used for religious texts written on papyrus. In the Middle Kingdom (2055–1650 B.C.), some COFFIN TEXTS were written in hieratic. During the Middle Kingdom, scribes also began to use hieratic for business and court documents, because they could write much faster in the cursive script. Hieratic eventually became so popular that different forms were developed: a fast shorthand for business, and a more detailed form for literature. Mastering the various forms of hieratic became as important in a scribe's education as learning hieroglyphs.

**HIEROGLYPHS** Script used by the ancient Egyptians. When the Greeks came to Egypt, they called Egyptian writing "hieroglyphs" or "sacred carvings," since only the priests could read them. To the ancient Egyptians, the message conveyed by the hieroglyphs was not the only concern. The aesthetics, the shape and placement of each sign, were of great importance as well. In some instances the hieroglyphs were believed to be magical, and they were rendered with the utmost care. The ancient saying, "magic is everywhere," suggests their belief in the magical nature of hieroglyphs.

Tacitus, the Roman historian, tells us that in the first century A.D., when the Roman emperor Germanicus visited the ruins of Thebes, he was curious about the hieroglyphic inscriptions on the walls of the tombs and temples. He found an old man wandering through the crumbling buildings who claimed he could read the carvings. When the last Egyptian priest died, knowledge of the sacred script was lost, and for almost 1,500 years, scholars wondered what the carvings meant.

Numerous attempts were made to decipher the hieroglyphic inscriptions, but they all failed because it was assumed that the signs were picture writing—that the carving of a foot represented a foot, and so on. Not until the eighteenth century did linguists propose that the ancient Egyptian language was for the most part composed of signs that had a phonetic value—they represented sounds, not objects. However, a select group of hieroglyphs, called determinatives, are pictograms, and they represent what they depict, such as the sun or a figure of a person. Finally, the combination of brilliant scholarship and good fortune revealed the key to understanding hieroglyphs.

When Napoleon invaded Egypt with his army in 1798, he took with him a large group of scholars to study the architecture and art of ancient Egypt. The most significant discovery of the expedition occurred in the summer of 1799, when Napoleon's men were fortifying the northern coast of Egypt. In the course of their digging, they discovered a large black stone, later called the ROSETTA STONE, inscribed with three scripts: hieroglyphs, Greek, and DEMOTIC. This lucky find gave scholars their first clues about how to translate hieroglyphs. After much study, the French linguist Jean-François CHAMPOLLION cracked the code and became the first person in 1,500 years to read the ancient script.

The following is the classical Egyptian alphabet, the alphabet used in Egypt for approximately 3,000 years. While the Egyptians did not write vowels, some of the signs are today used to represent vowels in writing modern names. Thus the Egyptian vulture may be used in place of the sound "a" and the arm in place of "e," etc. To write modern names in hieroglyphs, sound out the name phonetically and use hieroglyphs to represent the sounds. If there is no sign for a sound, such as L, then the L is left out. This use of hieroglyphs to write modern names is not *translating* but *transliterating*, or representing sounds written in one script with the characters of another script. This system of writing has nothing to do with the modern Egyptian language, which is Arabic.

### Classical Egyptian Alphabet

| Hieroglyph | Object Depicted | Sound |
|---|---|---|
| | vulture | a |
| | foot | b |
| | placenta | ch |
| | hand | d |
| | arm | e |
| | horned viper | f |
| | jar stand | g |
| | twisted flax | h |
| | reed leaf | i |
| | snake | j (dj) |
| | basket | k |
| | owl | m |
| | water | n |
| | mat | p |
| | hill | q |
| | mouth | r |
| | folded cloth | s |
| | pool of water | sh |
| | loaf of bread | t |
| | tethering ring | tch |
| | quail chick | u or w |
| | two reed leaves | y |
| | door bolt | z |

Several signs on the Rosetta stone are not found in the basic alphabet, and some of these were later hieroglyphs added by the Egyptians that represented two or three sounds together. Another of Champollion's discoveries was that some of the signs were "determinatives." That is, after a word was spelled out phonetically, there was sometimes a sign at the end of the word that helped clarify the meaning of the word. For example, in ⌒□△⌂, the first three signs spell boat, and the last sign confirms that the word is boat.

## HIPPOPOTAMUS GODDESS  See TAURET.

**HOLY OF HOLIES**  Innermost sanctuary of an Egyptian temple where the statues of the gods were kept. Closed to all visitors except select priests who attended the statues, the holy of holies was a dark and mysterious place. Each morning the priests opened the doors to the holy shrine and cared for the statue as if it were a living god. Food was placed before the statue for its morning meal, cosmetics were painted around the eyes, perfume was poured over the statue, and it was wrapped in white linen. Once these rituals

In the back of every Egyptian temple a small chapel called the holy of holies housed the cult statues and their sacred boats. *(Photo by Pat Remler)*

had been performed, the doors to the shrine were closed until it was time for the next ritual. The only time the average Egyptian ever saw a cult statue was on an important festival day, when the statue was taken out of the temple and placed in a portable shrine made of gilded wood that rested on two long, wooden carrying poles. Priests placed the poles on their shoulders and carried the shrine into the open courtyard of the temple. During these special festivals, the Egyptians would crowd into the yard for a glimpse of the statue that represented their god.

**HOROSCOPE CALENDAR**  Ancient horoscope calendars told the Egyptians what to do on each day of the year. Unlike our modern horoscopes, which are individually based on birth dates and the position of the stars, everyone in ancient Egypt used the same horoscope calendar. If the calendar advised the people not to leave home on a particular day, then they would stay in their houses on that day.

The Egyptian calendar had only three seasons:

1. Inundation, or *akhet*, when the Nile overflowed its banks and farmland was covered with water. This lasted from approximately June 21 to October 21.
2. Emergence, or *proyet*, when the water receded. This season lasted from about October 21 to February 21.
3. Summer, or *shomu*, from February 21 to June 21.

Each of these seasons had four months of 30 days each, so that there were 360 days to the standard year. While the Egyptians did not realize that the Earth rotates around the sun, they did know that a calendar of 360 days would soon be out of phase with nature; eventually inundation would come during the dry season. To correct the discrepancy, the Egyptians added five days at the beginning of the new year, giving the true calendar 365 days.

For the Egyptians, New Year's Day, called "the opening of the year," dawned with an astronomical event that took place every June 21 in about 3000 B.C. The brilliant star Sirius became visible just before sunrise. The event was called "the going up of the goddess Sothis."

In 1943, a rolled-up papyrus was purchased by the Egyptian Museum in Cairo. It was written in hieratic, a cursive form of hieroglyphs, and while portions of it had been eaten away by insects, it was clear that the papyrus dealt with the days of the year and what would happen on each day. The title of the CAIRO CALENDAR, as it has become known, is "An Introduction to the Start of Everlastingness and the End of Eternity." Each day of the year includes a reading in about three sections.

The first part states the day's auspice: "favorable," "mostly favorable," "very favorable," "adverse," "mostly adverse," or "very adverse." Most of the days of the Cairo Calendar are either "very favorable" or "very adverse."

The second part describes the mythological event that occurred on that day. For example, if a day is said to be "very adverse," this part of the reading will tell of a terrible tragedy or violence that happened in the life of the gods, such as Horus fighting with Set and losing his eye.

The third part of the reading advises one how to behave depending on the result of the auspice and the mythological event. On the day Horus's eye is lost, a bad day, readers are told not to go out of the house.

Some portions of the Cairo Calendar are difficult to understand because they mention many minor gods and because the calendar does not tell one sequential mythological story, in part because the papyrus is damaged and portions are missing.

While the Egyptians did not follow our calendar system, an attempt has been made to reconcile the ancient with the modern. See the following page. The one-month calendar begins on August 1 because Sirius no longer rises on June 21, as it did in ancient times, but on August 1.

**HORSE** The horse arrived relatively late in Egypt's history, during the Second Intermediate period (1650–1550 B.C.) with the invasion of the Hyksos. Having no history in Egypt, the animal was associated with a foreign goddess, Astarte. Once the Egyptians adopted the horse and chariot, it revolutionized their military and allowed them to build one of the ancient world's greatest empires. Horses were considered the miracle of the New Kingdom. Ramses spoke with great passion about his two horses, Victory in Thebes and Mut Is Pleased, and praised the part they played in his great victory at Kadesh. No divine horse arose in the Egyptian pantheon to honor the noble beast, however, possibly because the gods and goddesses of ancient Egypt either evolved from ancient prehistoric deities or were composites of gods that over time had merged into one.

**HORUS** "Lord of the Sky" and symbol of divine kingship in ancient Egypt, Horus, the falcon god,

is one of the most important gods in the Egyptian pantheon. He appears on the NARMER PALETTE, the earliest record of a historical event, in celebration of the unification of UPPER and LOWER EGYPT. An ivory comb with the inscription of King Djet from Dynasty I shows Horus prominently above the king's name. When the king died, the phrase used to announce his death was "The Falcon has flown to heaven." This not only announced his death but also emphasized the notion that the king was a manifestation of the god. In his many mythological roles, Horus was portrayed both as a falcon and as a man with a falcon's head, but he is most often shown in his anthropomorphic form, with the body of a man.

Besides being the solar deity, "Lord of the Sky," Horus was active in the Underworld, vanquishing the

Horus, the falcon god, avenged the death of his father, Osiris. *(Drawing by Mary Jordan)*

## First Month of Akhet—INUNDATION

| August 1 Day 1 | August 2 Day 2 | August 3 Day 3 |
|---|---|---|
| First Day of the Year<br><br>Very favorable<br><br>It is the day of the birth of Re-Horakhty. The Nile begins to rise. All the gods and people celebrate. | Very favorable<br><br>It is the day the ennead go before Re.<br><br>If you see anything on this day, it will be good | Mostly favorable<br><br>. . .<br><br>Anyone born on this day will die by a crocodile. |
| August 7 Day 7 | August 8 Day 8 | August 9 Day 9 |
| Very favorable<br><br>It is the day of welcoming the rising of the river and of offering to the gods.<br><br>If you see anything, it will be good. | Mostly favorable<br><br>It is the day Re goes forth . . .<br><br>Do not go out at night on this day. | Very favorable<br><br>It is the day of pacifying the hearts of those in the horizon in front of His Majesty, Re.<br><br>If you see anything, it will be good. |
| August 13 Day 13 | August 14 Day 14 | August 15 Day 15 |
| Mostly adverse<br><br>It is the day of the killing of Meret Shemat [goddess of music].<br><br>Anyone born on this day will die of blindness. | . . .<br><br>. . .<br><br>Make offerings to the gods of your city. | Mostly adverse<br><br>It is the day of the rage of Set battling Horus.<br><br>Do not go in a boat on this day. |
| August 19 Day 19 | August 20 Day 20 | August 21 Day 21 |
| Very favorable<br><br>The ennead is in festivity in front of Re, a happy day in heaven.<br><br>Burn incense. | Very adverse<br><br>It is the day the great ones—the followers of Set and Horus—are in conflict.<br><br>Do not do any work on this day. | Very favorable<br><br>. . .<br><br>Make offerings to the followers of Re. Do not kill a bull or even let it cross your path. It is a day to be cautious of bulls. |
| August 25 Day 25 | August 26 Day 26 | August 27 Day 27 |
| Mostly favorable<br><br>It is the day of the going forth of Sekhmet to the Eastern district and of the repelling of the confederates of Set.<br><br>Do not go out of your home or on any road at night. | Very adverse<br><br>It is the day of Horus fighting with Set.<br><br>Do not do anything today. | Very favorable<br><br>It is the day of peace between Horus and Set.<br><br>Make a holiday today. Do not kill any ankhy-reptile. |

| **August 4** Day 4 | **August 5** Day 5 | **August 6** Day 6 |
|---|---|---|
| Mostly favorable<br><br>The gods go in a contrary wind.<br><br>Do not navigate a boat today. Do not do anything on this day. | Very favorable<br><br>The gods are peaceful in heaven, navigating the great barque.<br><br>If you see anything, it will be good. | Mostly adverse<br><br>Anyone born on this day will die trampled by a bull.<br><br>. . . |
| **August 10** Day 10 | **August 11** Day 11 | **August 12** Day 12 |
| Very favorable<br><br>It is the day of the going forth of Hedj-Hotep [goddess of weaving]. All is festivity.<br><br>Anyone born on this day will die honored in old age. | Very adverse<br><br>It is the day of the going forth of the Great Flame [the fire-spitting cobra goddess].<br><br>Kindle the fire today. Do not look at a bull. Do not copulate today. | Very adverse<br><br>It is the day anyone disobeying Re in his house will fall down at once.<br><br>Do not go out today. Wait till Re sets in his horizon. |
| **August 16** Day 16 | **August 17** Day 17 | **August 18** Day 18 |
| Very adverse<br><br>. . .<br><br>Anyone born on this day will die of a crocodile. | Very adverse<br><br>It is the day the offering to Sobek was taken away.<br><br>Do not eat any mehyet-fish today. | Very favorable<br><br>It is the day Horus was judged greater than his brother Set.<br><br>If you see anything on this day, it will be good. |
| **August 22** Day 22 | **August 23** Day 23 | **August 24** Day 24 |
| Very adverse<br><br>Is is the day Re swallows all the gods. When they move about, he kills them and vomits them out into the water. Their bodies turn to fish and their souls to birds.<br><br>Do not eat fish today. Do not warm oil. Do not eat birds. | Very adverse<br><br>It is the day of causing the heart of the enemy of Re to suffer.<br><br>Anyone born on this day will not live. Do not listen to singing or watch dancing on this day. | Very favorable<br><br>The God [Re] sails peacefully with a favorable wind.<br><br>Anyone born in this day will die honored in old age. |
| **August 28** Day 28 | **August 29** Day 29 | **August 30** Day 30 |
| Very favorable<br><br>The gods are happy when they see the children of Nut [Horus and Set].<br><br>If you see anything, it will be good. | Mostly favorable<br><br>. . .<br><br>Do not kindle fire in the house today. Do not burn incense. Do not go out at night. | Last Day of the Month<br>Very favorable<br><br>House of Re, House of Osiris, House of Horus.<br><br>If you see anything on this day, it will be good. |

Horus as a child was called Harpocrates, a corruption of the Egyptian words meaning "Horus the child." *(Drawing by Mary Jordan)*

enemies of his father, OSIRIS. In the BOOK OF GATES, he calls upon the many serpents that spew fire upon bound prisoners to "spit fire upon the enemies of my father! Burn their corpses and cook their souls." In the AMDUAT, Horus acts as the judge and holds court before the souls of the damned, saying "The blade of vengeance is for your bodies, Death for your souls . . . You never lived . . ."

Horus acquired many titles that emphasized his connection to various temples and mythological events. Following are some of his most important titles:

**Harendotes** This is the Greek name for the Egyptian "Har-nedj-itet," which means "Horus the Savior of his Father." It refers to his vanquishing Set and reclaiming the earthly throne of his father, OSIRIS.

**Harmachis** A Greek form of the title "Horus of the Horizon" refers to Horus rising at dawn each day with the sun.

**Haroeris** "Horus, son of Re" was the title given to Horus when he was worshipped in the temple of SOBEK at Kom Ombo.

**Harpocrates** Harpocrates is the Greek form of the Egyptian "Har-pa-khered," which means "Horus the Child." In this state Horus is a vulnerable young god, a child sitting on his mother's lap. He wears the side lock of youth (one long curl of hair on the right side of his head) and sometimes sucks his forefinger or is shown with ISIS offering him her breast to suckle. In this form, Harpocrates acts as a protector of children and wards off dangerous animals.

**Harsiese** Harsiese, meaning "Horus, Son of Isis," appears first in the PYRAMID TEXTS, associating Horus not as the ancient god of the sky but instead as the helpful son of Isis and Osiris. Harsiese is also seen as the helper and guardian of the deceased as he delivers them to his father, Osiris.

**Harsomtus** This name, meaning "Horus the Uniter," comes from the name "Har-mau" in the Pyramid Texts. "Har-mau" guarded over the unification of Upper and Lower Egypt. During the Ptolemaic period (332–32 B.C.), Harsomtus becomes the son of "Horus the Elder" and Hathor at Edfu Temple.

**Horakhty** Meaning "Horus of the Horizon," this name refers to his rising at dawn each day in the east to survey his domain and to splash in the FIELD OF REEDS. Re-Horakhty is the title bestowed by the priests of HELIOPOLIS, where Horus was worshipped as the son of the sun god Re.

**Horematawy** Mythology tells us that Horus as Horematawy, "Horus, Uniter of Two Lands," is the son of Hathor.

**Horus of Baki** Horus as guardian of Quban, a Nubian fort through which passed the gold being sent from Nubia to the Egyptian treasury.

**Horus of Behdet** Symbolized by the hawk-winged sun disk, Horus of Behdet is the title of Horus as he presides over the marshy northern

Delta area, Behdet. The name may refer to his infancy, when his mother Isis hid the child in the marshes to protect Horus from his evil uncle Set. By the Ptolemaic period (332–32 B.C.), the hawk-winged sun disk was displayed everywhere, and its original meaning was lost.

**Horus of Buhen** During the New Kingdom (1550–1069 B.C.), a southern temple erected at the second cataract was dedicated to Horus of Buhen.

**Horus the Elder** (also Heru-ur) The son of NEPHTHYS, he was born on the third EPAGOMENAL DAY and was said to be the twin of the evil god Set. Horus the Elder was one of the most ancient gods of Egypt and seems to have existed long before his appearance in the Pyramid Texts, where he is equal but in constant opposition to his brother Set. Horus the Elder as Heru-ur ruled the sky by day and his brother Set ruled by night.

**Horus of Mesen** An ancient version of the myth of Horus, the harpooner, when he attacks Set, who appears as a hippopotamus. Horus of Mesen was one of the titles of Horus at the temple of Edfu, which was dedicated to him. On the walls of this temple, the carvings reveal the sacred drama of Set's defeat that worshippers reenacted each year.

**Horus of Miam** The first temple to Horus, built at the Nubian city Aniba, was erected in the Middle Kingdom (2055–1650 B.C.). Horus was eventually associated with the local cult god Miam and was known throughout Nubia as Horus of Miam, the one who opposed his evil uncle Set.

**Horus's Eye** See EYE OF HORUS.

**Horus's Four Sons** See FOUR SONS OF HORUS.

The cult of Horus was universal throughout Egypt from 3000 B.C. to A.D. 400, but the particular cult centers were Edfu, in Upper Egypt; Behdet, in the Delta; Hierakonpolis, in Upper Egypt; and Buhen in the south, at the second cataract of the Nile and Aniba in Nubia.

**HOUSE OF LIFE** ⌐⌐♀ A small temple or building in a larger temple complex, the House of Life was a library, scriptorium (where manuscripts were copied), and a school all in one. Here, priest-MAGICIANS studied magical texts, physicians studied medicine, and they all practiced their arts. They were custodians of all the knowledge of the temple and

guarded their secrets carefully. People would come to the House of Life to have a dream interpreted or to purchase a MAGIC spell, a charm, or a love potion. Lector priests were in charge of the books (written on PAPYRUS scrolls) and specialized in interpreting dreams from standard dream books. Because of their special talents, lector priests did not participate in the daily temple ritual but concentrated on performing magic. They were called "Scribes of the House of Life." The coptic (Christian) word for "magician" is *sheshperonch*. This is derived from the hieroglyphs 𓏞𓐍𓉐𓋹 *sesh per ankh*, which means "scribe in the House of Life."

**HUMAN SACRIFICE** Since the late 1800s, Egyptologists suspected that human sacrifice may have been practiced in ancient Egypt as part of the religion, but they had little evidence to prove it.

Recent excavations of First Dynasty King Aha's (2950–2775 B.C.) royal mortuary complex (large courtyard) at ABYDOS revealed graves of other people buried near the king. It is believed they were servants ritually killed when the king died so they could magically accompany the deceased king to the next world. King Aha has the earliest-known mortuary enclosure (see TEMENOS), with six separate graves around the courtyard. Nearby in King Djer's (Aha's successor) royal mortuary complex, archaeologists found more subsidiary graves, this time lined up in a row, and these seem to be sacrificial burials as well. The practice of human sacrifice appears to have ended early in Egyptian history. But the idea was ritually continued when USHABTI statues were placed inside tombs so they would magically come alive and serve the deceased in the next world. Thus the little statues took the place of living servants.

**HUTCHAIUI** God of the West Wind (see also WINDS, GODS OF THE FOUR).

**HYKSOS** Foreign invaders who ruled in Egypt's northern DELTA after the MIDDLE KINGDOM during the Second Intermediate period (1650–1550 B.C.) and introduced their mythology and religion to the area. Many references to the foreign god SET show that his cult was well established in the Delta and that Set was the patron god of the Hyksos capital, AVARIS. The cult of Set seems to have been a blend of an early god in HELIOPOLIS and the Syrian storm god Baal. Because Egyptian religion was polytheistic, accepting many gods, it was not a problem for the Hyksos gods Set and ASTARTE to be accepted into the Egyptian pantheon.

Because of his violent nature Set was viewed as a god of chaos, but there were devoted followers of Set, and the pharaoh Seti I was one of them.

The identity of the Hyksos foreign kings remains a mystery today. The name Hyksos is the Greek version of the Egyptian *hekau khasut*, meaning "rulers of foreign countries." They were sometimes called *aamu* or Asiatic—the name Egyptians gave anyone from western Asia—and the Christian historian Sextus Julius Africanus (A.D. 160–240) called them Shepard Kings. Whatever the origin of the Hyksos, it is clear from modern excavations that there was a thriving, large, international community in the Delta when the Hyksos ruled. The Hyksos capital, Avaris, is modern Tell el Daba in the eastern Delta. Excavators have found Minoan-style frescoes (wall paintings) in the royal palace, Canaanite style temples, pottery from Syria and Palestine, and Egyptian-style SCARABS decorated with scroll designs. While the Egyptians resented having foreign kings ruling in the Delta, the Hyksos were in many ways innovators. They not only brought their gods, but they also introduced the horse and chariot to Egypt and an improved bow, all of which were readily adopted by the Egyptians when the Hyksos were expelled.

**HYMN TO AMUN**   Taken from the Nineteenth Dynasty Papyrus Anastasi, named for the Swedish Consul of Alexandria who owned it, the following is a short hymn to Amun petitioning the great god to be a patron of the poor.

> Amun, lend your ear to the lonely in court,
> He is poor, he is not rich;
> For the court extorts from him:
> "Silver and gold for the clerks,
> Clothes for the attendants!"
> Might Amun appear as the vizier,
> To let the poor go free;
> Might the poor appear as the justified,
> And want surpass wealth!

**HYMN TO ISIS**   As the universal mother goddess, Isis's virtues are extolled in the hymns to Isis. Priest-poets continued to find new ways to confirm her position as a supreme goddess and to praise her virtues. She was called the Divine Mother, the Lady of the Palace, the Goddess of Nature, and the Lady of Heaven, Earth, and the NETHERWORLD. The best preserved of the hymns to Isis are found in the Temple of Isis on Philae island near Aswan. The following portion is found in room X and shows the king reciting to Isis:

> O Isis, the Great, God's mother, Lady of Philae
> God's Wife, God's Adorer, and God's Hand
> God's mother and Great Spouse,
> Adornment and Lady of Ornaments of the
>     Palace
> Lady and desire of the green fields,
> Nursling who fills the palace with her beauty,
> Fragrance of the palace, mistress of joy,
> Who completes her course in the Divine Palace.
> Rain-cloud that makes the green in the fields
>     when it descends,
> Lady sweet of love, Lady of Upper and Lower
>     Egypt,
>
> Who issues orders among the divine Ennead,
> According to whose command one rules.
> Lady great of praise, lady of charm,
> Who enjoys the trickling of fresh myrrh on
>     her face.

The inscription next to the hymn indicates that Isis was pleased with the hymn dedicated to her. She says:

> How beautiful is this which you have done
> for me my son, Horus, my beloved, Lord of
> Diadems, (king) Ptolemy; I have given you this
> land, joy to your *Ba* forever.

**HYMN TO OSIRIS**   The hymn to Osiris is the account of the OSIRIS MYTH in which Osiris is murdered by his evil brother Set. The hymn is inscribed on the limestone stele of Amenmose, who lived during the Eighteenth Dynasty. (The stele is now is the Louvre Museum in Paris.) The following excerpt from the beginning of the hymn greets Osiris and praises him, recalling how Osiris is honored and remembered throughout the land and the heavens.

> Hail to you, Osiris
> Lord of Eternity, king of gods,
> Of many names, of holy forms,
> Of secret rites in temples! . . .
> Lord of remembrance in the Hall of Justice,
> Secret *ba* of the lord of the cavern . . .
> *Ba* of Re, his very body.
> Lord of acclaim in the southern sky,
> Sanctified by the northern sky,
> The imperishable stars are under his rule,
> The unwearying stars are his abode . . .
> The ancestors rejoice to see him.
> Those yonder are in awe of him . . .

## Hymn to the Aten

When you set in western lightland,
Earth is in darkness as if in death,
One sleeps in chambers, heads covered,
One eye does not see the other.
Were they robbed of their goods,
That are under their heads?
People would not remark [know] it
Every lion comes from its den,
All the serpents bite;
Darkness hovers, earth is silent,
As the maker rests in lightland.
Earth brightens when you dawn in
Lightland,
When you shine as Aten of daytime . . .
The entire land sets out to work,
All beasts browse on their herbs;
Trees, herbs are sprouting,
Birds fly from their nests . . .

## Psalm 104

You bring darkness on, night falls,
All the forest animals come out.
Savage lions roaring for their prey,
Claiming their food from God.

The sun rises, they retire, going back to
Their lairs,
And man goes out to work,
And to labor until dusk.

Yahweh, what variety you have created.

**HYMN TO PTAH** The hymn to Ptah was written in the New Kingdom (1550–1069 B.C.) and is inscribed on the funerary stele of Nefer-Re-Bu, who confesses that, because he told a lie, the gods made him blind. Nefer-Re-Bu is shown at the top of the stele kneeling before Ptah, who sits inside his shrine.

Give praise to Ptah, Lord of Maat,
King of the Two Lands,
Fair of face upon his great seat,
The one God among the Ennead,
Beloved as king of the Two Lands.
May he give life, prosperity, health. . . .

On the reverse of the stele he continues:

I am a man who swore falsely by Ptah, Lord of
   Maat,
And he made me see darkness by day.
I will declare his might to the fool and the wise.
To the small and the great:
Beware of Ptah, Lord of Maat!
Behold, he does not overlook anyone's deed!
Refrain from uttering Ptah's name falsely,
Lo, he who utters it falsely, lo he falls . . .

**HYMN TO RE** During the Eighteenth Dynasty, when the local god Amun rose to prominence, he was assimilated with the sun god Re and became the supreme god of Thebes, AMUN-RE. There are many variations of the hymn to Re, but generally the first part mentions the sun god by several of his 75 names. The second part is a series of incantations associating the king with various gods and the sun god in particular. A passage from the first part of the hymn to Re carved on the stele of the brothers Suti and Hor (now in the British Museum) follows.

Hail to you, Re, perfect each day,
Who rises at dawn without failing,
Khepri who wearies himself with toil!
Your rays are on the face, yet unknown,
Fine gold does not match your splendor;
Self-made you fashioned your body,
Creator uncreated.
Sole one, unique one, who traverses eternity,
[remote one] with millions under his care;
Your splendor is like heaven's splendor,
Your color is brighter than its hues.
When you cross the sky all faces see you,
When you set you are hidden from their sight;
Daily you give yourself at dawn,
Safe is your sailing under your majesty . . .

**HYMN TO THE ATEN** Prayer written by AKHENATEN in praise of the ATEN, the single god that he worshipped when he became pharaoh.

### The Hymn to the Aten

Splendid you rise in heaven's lightland,
O living Aten, creator of life!
When you have dawned in eastern lightland,
You fill every land with your beauty.
You are beauteous, great, radiant, high over
  every land.
Your rays embrace the lands,
To the limits of all that you have made:
Being Ra, you reach their limits,
You bend them [for] the son whom you love;
Though you are far, your rays are on earth;
Though one sees you, your strides are unseen . . .
How many are your deeds,
Though hidden from sight
O sole God beside whom there is none!
You made the earth as you wished, you alone,
All peoples, herds, and flocks:
All upon earth that walk on legs,
All on high that fly on wings,
The lands of Khor and Kush,
The land of Egypt.
You set every man in his place,
You supply their needs; everyone had his food,
His life is counted.
Their tongues differ in speech
Their characters likewise;
Their skins are distinct,
For you distinguish the peoples . . .
You are in my heart,
There is no other who knows you,

Only your son, Nefer-khepru-Re, Sole one of
  Re,
Whom you have taught your ways and might
· · ·

> From *Ancient Egyptian Literature*.
> Vol. 1. Translated by Miriam Lichtheim
> (Berkeley: University of California Press, 1975)

This selection from the hymn to the Aten gives a sense of its power and beauty. Scholars have often noted its resemblance to Psalm 104 in the Bible. Although the two works are similar in feeling, however, it is unlikely that Psalm 104, written centuries after the hymn to the Aten (circa 1380 B.C.), was directly influenced by Akhenaten's prayer. Perhaps strong beliefs created similar thoughts.

**HYMN TO THOTH** Taken from the Papyrus Anastasi, the following is a portion of the hymn to Thoth:

Come to me, Thoth, O noble Ibis,
O god who loves Khmun;
O letter-writer of the Ennead,
Great one who dwells in Un!
Come to me and give me counsel,
Make me skillful in your calling;
Better is you calling than all callings,
It makes (men) great.
He who masters it is found fit to hold office,
I have seen many whom you have helped.
They are (now) among the Thirty. . . .

**IABET** ⸱⸱⸱ (also IABTET, ABET) A goddess of the vast eastern desert and personification of the land of the East, Iabet was associated with the rising sun and with fertility and rebirth. It was said that she washed the sun god RE each morning when he was reborn. Because of this association she was sometimes linked with KEBECHT, a goddess of pure water.

The Egyptians personified the four cardinal points (north, south, east, and west) by giving each one the name of a goddess. Iabet is the goddess of the East, and her counterpart is her sister AMEMTET, goddess of the west. Mythology tells us that Iabet was thought to be both the mother and wife of the god MIN. A princess in the court of KHUFU in the OLD KINGDOM was given the name *Nefer-Iabet*, "beauty of the east," or "beautiful Iabet."

Unlike her sister goddess Amentet, who appears in the Fifth Dynasty tomb of King Sahure and in the PYRAMID TEXTS, Iabet is not shown in a tomb until the NEW KINGDOM. Images of Iabet appear on the walls of some private tombs along with the sun god Re.

**IB** ⸱ See HEART.

**IBIS** ⸱⸱⸱ There were several species of ibis in ancient Egypt, but the one considered sacred to the god THOTH was distinctive because of its long curved beak, black neck, and white feathers on its body. The tips of its wings, end of its tail and its legs were also black. HERODOTUS, the Greek traveler, wrote that no one was permitted to kill an ibis, for the bird was believed to be an incarnation of the god Thoth. However, the cult of Thoth was especially popular during the Ptolemaic period, and thousands of ibises were raised on ibis farms to be killed and mummified and used as votive offerings. Elaborately wrapped mummified ibises were offered at the cult centers of Saqqara and Tuna el Gabel. The ibis was frequently portrayed on tomb walls. Ibis amulets and statuettes were produced by the thousands for pilgrims to the cult centers. The ibis was also important to the cult of Isis, and wall paintings from Pompeii show them wandering freely in the Isis temples.

**ICHNEUMON** An African mongoose about the size of a large house cat, the ichneumon was celebrated for its skill in killing snakes. Several Old Kingdom tombs at SAQQARA show an ichneumon in their wall

This nineteenth-century romanticized illustration shows the sacred ibises being fed in the temple. *(E. J. Poynter)*

decorations. The animal gained status in the Middle Kingdom (2055–1650 B.C.), when it was included among the many sacred animals of Egypt. Because of its skill in killing snakes, the ichneumon became a symbol of the Underworld, where legend has it that RE once turned himself into an ichneumon in order to defeat his enemy, the evil serpent APOPHIS. The ichneumon was shown with a sun disk on its head, symbolizing its association with Re. Small bronze statues of the animal were plentiful during the Ptolemaic period (332–32 B.C.), when they were left as votive offerings in the temples.

**IHY** A minor god worshipped in Upper Egypt, Ihy was the son of HATHOR and HORUS of Edfu. Ihy was a god of music who personified the sound made by the sacred SISTRUM rattle. He is shown as a child, with the child's side lock of hair and a finger to his mouth.

**IMHOTEP** (2667–2648 B.C.) Imhotep was vizier (prime minister) to the Third Dynasty king Zoser and architect of his magnificent funerary complex at SAQQARA. Zoser's funerary complex included the first stone building in the ancient world, the STEP PYRAMID.

Imhotep was not only recognized for his talents as an architect, but he also was revered as a scribe, counselor, physician, and astronomer. After his death, he was awarded the title "Son of Ptah." Eventually Imhotep joined the triad of gods worshipped at Memphis (the ancient capital of Egypt), replacing the god Nefer-Tem. One of the few nonroyal persons to be deified, over the centuries Imhotep was worshipped as a god of wisdom and medicine. During Egypt's Late period, the Ptolemies associated Imhotep with Asclepius, the Greek god of medicine, and pilgrims flocked to Saqqara, the supposed burial site of Imhotep. His tomb has never been found. Votive offerings were left by the thousands for Imhotep, usually ornately wrapped mummified ibises, for the ibis was associated both with THOTH, the god of wisdom and learning, and with Imhotep. Sometimes pilgrims left clay models of arms, legs, or body parts, hoping to be healed. Bronze figures of Imhotep holding a papyrus scroll were popular offerings in the Late and Ptolemaic periods. His cult center was at Saqqara, but he also had shrines at the Karnak and Philae temples.

Imhotep is mentioned in the Eleventh Dynasty HARPER'S SONG from the tomb of King Intef: "I have heard the words of Imhotep and Hardedef, whose sayings are recited whole . . ."

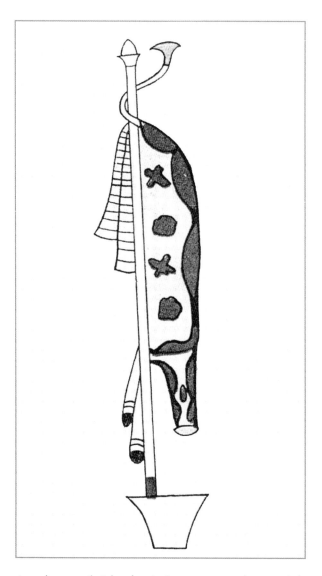

An obscure fetish, the imiut seems to have originated in Egypt's most ancient past. Associated with Anubis and Osiris, the imiut is also connected to resurrection and the Netherworld.

**IMIUT** (anubis fetish) A mysterious fetish or ritual object, the imiut seems to have its origin in Egypt's Predynastic period (5500–3100 B.C.). An Imiut was believed to have special or supernatural powers, and since it was linked with ANUBIS and OSIRIS, it may have assisted with rebirth and resurrection. To create the fetish, a headless stuffed animal skin was tied to a post, and one end of the post was set in a pot, presumably for stability, so it could stand upright. Often the blood of the animal was shown dripping into the pot. One of the many objects found in TUTANKHAMEN's tomb was an imiut. Standing about six feet tall, the imiut's wooden pole is covered with gold gilt and has a lotus shape on top, and the base stands in an alabaster pot. It had been placed at the west end of the burial chamber, along with several magical paddles for rowing the king's funerary boat to the next world.

**IMKIHIU** The Imkihiu were called "the Venerated Ones." They were the deceased who, by virtue of having the proper prayers, spells, and rituals performed, were able to obtain passage in the solar boat of the sun god RE as it passed through the 12 hours of the night.

**IMMORTALITY** The belief in immortality, the idea that you will live forever in the next world, is central to ancient Egyptian religion, and Egyptians spent much of their lifetime preparing for it. Mythology tells us that even the gods were not secure in their exalted positions, and the myth of ISIS and OSIRIS tells of Osiris's murder by his brother SET. In the myth, Osiris becomes the first Egyptian to gain immortality by RESURRECTION in the next world. We do not know when the Egyptians first began to hope for immortality, but it must have been early in the religion. A belief in immortality is clearly stated in the PYRAMID TEXTS.

As gods on Earth, Egyptian kings began preparing for their resurrection and immortality as soon as they came to the throne. Kings fitted their tombs with all the things they liked in this world, so they could enjoy them for eternity in the next world. At first it was only the king who was assured of immortality; his family could only hope that when he ascended to the next world, he would take them with him. Everyone wished to live forever, and by the NEW KINGDOM (1550–1069 B.C.), it seemed possible. If the family of the deceased could afford the several steps required to reach immortality (such as mummification, funeral rituals and ceremonies, and a tomb), then the deceased could resurrect in the next world. Immortality became such an appealing concept that Egyptian funerary customs and rituals were incorporated into the later Greek and Roman religions.

In ancient Egypt the deceased had to pass a test in order to gain immortality. During the WEIGHING OF THE HEART CEREMONY, the deceased's heart was weighed to ensure that it was not heavy with evil deeds. If the heart was heavier than *MAAT*, the feather of truth, then it fell off the scale into the jaws of AMMUT, a terrifying mythical creature who devoured the heart, causing the deceased to go out of existence. The Egyptians had a saying, "To speak the name of the dead is to make him live again." If this saying is true, then TUTANKHAMEN has gained immortality, for he is a household name today, and his treasures in the Egyptian Museum attract a multitude of people from around the world.

**INCENSE** So important was incense to the Egyptians as an offering to the gods that they imported great quantities of the aromatic resins, frankincense, and myrrh from southern Arabia and the Sudan. It is recorded on the walls of Queen Hatshepsut's mortuary temple at Deir el Bahri that her expedition to the land of Punt (possibly modern Eritrea or Somaliland on the east coast of Africa) returned with "incense trees." It was a great accomplishment for the Queen's expedition to acquire the actual myrrh trees, for then the Egyptians could provide their own incense. The Middle Kingdom (2055–1650 B.C.) tale of the SHIPWRECKED SAILOR tells the story of a lost sailor, whose host taunts, "I am the prince of Punt; myrrh belongs to me!"

Incense essential for religious ceremonies was offered as a preliminary, or opening, of a ceremony. Hot coals were placed in one end of a bronze censer in the shape of a hand holding a small open box. The pharaoh, or his stand-in, held the censer in his left hand and dropped pellets of incense onto the embers with his right hand.

The offering of incense was part of every important ritual and was specifically required when making offerings to the gods, performing the rites of mummification or magical spells, and perfuming the body during mummification. While priests chanted, they burned frankincense and myrrh in the temple sanctuary in hope that the smoke would carry their prayers to the gods, who would be pleased with the fine aroma. At festival time, shaven-headed priests carried braziers of burning incense in the processions, and incense was always included on the lists of offerings made to the gods. In the PYRAMID TEXTS, King Unas is said to rise to the heavens on the smoke of the great incense.

During the mummification process, once the internal organs had been removed, frankincense and myrrh were placed inside the body cavity to help with the dehydration of the body and to lend a pleasant odor. Before the mummy was wrapped in linen bandages, the body was anointed with oil and perfumed with frankincense and myrrh. During the "Opening of the Mouth" ceremony performed in front of the tomb on the day of burial, the priests purified the mummy with water, lit four incense burners, one for each of the four corners of the Earth, and invoked the gods.

Frankincense was sometimes used in casting spells, and the magician might burn the substance at specific times while conjuring a spell. To ensure that a bad dream would not come true, a priest magician could recite a spell and then give the dreamer a bit of bread moistened with beer and covered with myrrh, which he was directed to smear on his face. To have a vision from the god Bes, the dreamer was directed, among other things, to obtain ink made from the blood of a cow, the blood of a white dove, frankincense, myrrh, black writing ink, cinnabar, mulberry juice, rainwater, and the juice of wormwood and vetch. With this mixture the petitioner was to write his request before the setting sun. Chapter 140 in the BOOK OF THE DEAD included a spell to be recited on the last day of the second month of the second season to ensure that Re the sun god would ferry the deceased to the NETHERWORLD.

Cones shown on the heads of banquet guests in tomb paintings have been a source of debate among Egyptologists. It is believed that, during the banquet, these cones, made of wax mixed with incense, would melt into the wig and drip onto the shoulders of the guests, creating a pleasant aroma. Other scholars believe that the tomb depictions are not literal and that cones merely illustrate the idea of fragrance wafting around the heads of the guests. Cones of incense have never been found, so it is impossible to say if they existed or if they were simply an artistic device.

**Isis** (IST) The great Egyptian mother goddess and the manifestation of all that is feminine, Isis embodies all the virtues and goodness of the divine wife and mother. She was said to be the feminine power who created and nurtured every living thing. The Egyptians believed she could influence the heavens, the Earth, and the realm of the dead. As the Great Enchantress, Isis held immense magical powers and knew all secrets. Isis's celestial symbol is the star Sirius, and her husband, OSIRIS, was Orion. In the LAMENTATIONS OF ISIS, the goddess cries, "Thy sacred image, Orion in heaven, rises and sets every day. I am Sothis (Sirius), following him, and I will not leave him. . . ." Because the star Sirius appeared at the beginning of the New Year and announced the beginning of the inundation, the flooding of the Nile, Isis is also associated with the fertility of the land. Isis was the symbolic mother of the king and the benefactress of the people, and her universal appeal arose from her devotion to her husband, Osiris, and her son HORUS.

Isis, the great Egyptian mother goddess and goddess of great magical power. One of her attributes is the throne of Egypt that she wears on her head. *(Drawing by Mary Jordan)*

**The Birth of Isis** The cult of Isis is among the most ancient, and her first cult center arose in the Delta, where she was worshipped at Sebennytos. The priests of HELIOPOLIS included Isis in their creation myth (HELIOPOLITAN ENNEAD) as one of the four children of GEB, god of Earth, and NUT, goddess of the sky. Isis's mother Nut, the sky goddess, was originally the wife of Re the sun god but she was much loved by Geb, whose love she returned. When Re heard of Nut's infidelity, he placed a curse upon her, saying that she could not bear children in any month or in any year. The curse of the mighty god Re could not be ignored, and Nut begged THOTH, who also loved her, for his help. Thoth made a bet with the moon goddess, and won some of her light, with which he was able to create five EPAGOMENAL DAYS at the end of each year. On each of these days, Nut gave birth to a child, and Isis was born on the fourth day. Isis and her husband, Osiris, were also brother and sister, and their son was Horus the hawk-headed god. Their sister NEPHTHYS and their brother SET were also husband and wife. One myth says that Nephthys had a child, the jackal-headed god, ANUBIS, with Isis's husband, Osiris, but the event seems not to have caused a rift in her close relationship with her sister Isis.

**Isis and Hathor**  During the NEW KINGDOM (1550–1069 B.C.), Isis and HATHOR were closely linked because of their many similarities. Isis began to wear the Hathor crown—cow's horns with a sun disk resting between them—instead of her traditional throne crown. The attributes of the two goddesses became intertwined, and they shared the titles "Lady of the Heavens" and "Sovereign of the Gods." Isis first appears in the VALLEY OF THE KINGS in the burial chamber of TUTANKHAMEN.

Isis, wearing the traditional throne on her head, and the goddesses Nephthys, NEITH, and SELKET all spread their wings in protection around the four sides of Tutankhamen's sarcophagus. The same four goddesses also appear on the canopic shrine that holds the king's mummified organs.

A figure of Isis standing behind the king was destroyed when a portion of the tomb's wall was dismantled during excavation to remove the large shrines covering the sarcophagus. In the scene, Isis and Anubis welcomed Tutankhamen to the NETHERWORLD, and Hathor, the principal goddess of the west, offered the king eternal life by holding an ANKH to his nose.

Isis, who plays an important role in the myth of Isis and Osiris by gathering the dismembered parts of her husband's body, reassembling his limbs, and breathing life into his body, does not accompany him when he resurrects in the realm of the dead. Isis remains among the living, and it is Hathor who is associated with the "west"—the land of the dead. Often it is hard to tell the difference between images of Isis and Hathor in the royal tombs because Isis sometimes exchanges her "throne" headdress for the headdress of sun disk and cow's horns more commonly associated with Hathor. The only way to tell them apart is to read the hieroglyphs that identify the figures. When their personalities began to merge they were sometimes called Isis-Hathor.

**Isis and Nephthys**  Isis and her sister Nephthys mourned the death of Osiris (see LAMENTATIONS OF ISIS), and while they expressed their grief, the sisters carefully prepared the body of Osiris for divine mummification. As protectors of Osiris, they became the protectors of all mummies. Their images appear on coffins and on CANOPIC JAR boxes, where they guard the mummified organs of the deceased. Sometimes the sisters are represented as hawks wearing their respective symbols on their heads: ⌐ Isis and ⫯ Nephthys, their outstretched wings protecting the deceased. In the BOOK OF THE DEAD, Isis and Nephthys appear with the sun god Re when he prepares for his nightly journey through the Netherworld.

**Isis and the Seven Scorpions**  After the death of Osiris, Isis was faced with many hardships. Her evil brother Set held Isis and the infant Horus captive in a house. Thoth, the great god of wisdom and magic, came to Isis and urged her to escape from Set and to hide her child in a papyrus thicket in the marshes of the Delta. Seven scorpions, who were a manifestation of Selket the scorpion goddess, guided Isis as she fled her evil brother Set. As she traveled to the Delta, Isis sought shelter one night with the wife of the town official, but when the woman saw the seven scorpions accompanying Isis, she shut her door and refused them sanctuary. Angered because Isis had been treated so badly, six scorpions emptied their poison on the tip of the tail of the seventh scorpion, and the seventh entered the house of the inhospitable woman and stung her son. The distraught woman ran through the town crying and lamenting, for she did not know if her child would live or die. Upon hearing the cries of the mother, Isis felt sad, for the child had done nothing wrong, and she called to the woman, "Come to me, for my speech has the power to protect, and it possesses life." Isis placed her hand upon the child and spoke, "O poison of Tefen, come forth, and appear on the ground! For I am Isis the goddess, and I am the lady of words of power, and I know how to work with words of power, and mighty are my words!" The poison left the child and he lived.

Then Isis said to the seven scorpions, "I speak to you, for I am alone and my sorrow is greater than that of anyone in all the Nomes of Egypt. . . . Turn your

Isis hides the infant Horus in a papyrus thicket while fleeing from her evil brother.

faces down to the ground and lead me to the swamps and the hidden places."

This tale is inscribed on a statue base in the Museum of Antiquities at Leiden in the Netherlands and on the METTERNICH STELE.

**The Infant Horus in the Papyrus Thicket** The Metternich Stele also relates the myth of Isis leaving the infant Horus hidden in a papyrus thicket when she is called away. Thoth had advised Isis to keep her son hidden until he grew tall and strong and could claim his father's throne. So Isis kept Horus hidden to prevent her evil brother Set from harming the child. One day Isis was called to a nearby town and an evil scorpion (perhaps a messenger from Set) crept among the papyrus stalks and stung the infant Horus. Upon hearing of this terrible catastrophe, the gods cried out,

"Isis, Isis, come to thy child Horus. . . ." Isis rushed to the infant Horus, crying, "I will protect thee, O my son Horus. Fear not, fear not, O my son, my glorious one." When she saw her lifeless child, she lamented:

I, Isis conceived a man child, and I was heavy with Horus. I, the goddess, bore Horus, the son of Isis, within a nest of papyrus plants. I rejoiced over him . . . I saw him as one who would avenge his father. I hid him. I concealed him, for I was afraid lest he be bitten. Now I went to the city of Am, and the people saluted me, and I passed the time seeking food and provision for the boy; but when I returned to embrace Horus, I found him, the beautiful one of gold, the boy, the child, inert and helpless. The ground was wet with his tears and foam was upon his lips; his body was motionless, and his heart was still, his muscles moved not, and I sent forth a cry . . .

Isis put her nose to Horus's mouth and she found the poison. She embraced his limp body and cried out in anguish, "Horus is stung, O Re thy son is stung. Horus, thy very heir, and the lord of Shu is stung. . . ." Isis's cries were so loud that they were heard in heaven. The sun god Re stopped his solar boat that was sailing across the sky and sent his passenger Thoth, the god of wisdom, to comfort the distraught mother. Isis's sister Nephthys appeared at her side, and when she saw the lifeless Horus, she went running through the papyrus thicket crying and weeping. Thoth calmed the sisters with his soothing words: "I have come from heaven to save the child for his mother." And he spoke magical words, and he restored Horus to life, and the words protected him in heaven and on Earth and in the next world.

**Symbols of Isis** Isis's earliest symbol is a throne worn as a crown, and it is thought to represent her association with the royal throne and protection of the king. It also may represent her role as guardian of the throne of Osiris. In addition to the throne, Isis also wears the Hathor crown, the cow's horns and sun disk. Another symbol of Isis is the *tet*, or KNOT OF ISIS. Mentioned in the Book of the Dead, the tet was an important funerary amulet, lending protection to the mummy. When the Greek Ptolemies ruled Egypt, the knot on the front of Isis's dress represented the tet, and when Isis was shown in Greek and Roman costume, sometimes the tet was the only way to identify the goddess. Isis was the goddess of hundreds of titles: She was the Goddess of the Wind, the Great Enchantress, Great of Magic, Mistress of the Heavens. Her cult centers flourished throughout Egypt at Giza, Behbeit el-Hagar, Dendera, Abydos, Esna, Edfu, and Philae.

**Isis in the Classical World** During the Greek and Roman occupation of Egypt, the cult of Isis grew and flourished, and she was identified with the Greek goddesses Persephone, Tethys, and Athena. Eventually, worship of Isis evolved into one of the "mystery religions." When PTOLEMY I ruled, he introduced the worship of SERAPIS, a composite Greek and Egyptian god, and Isis was seen as his wife. Serapis was popular with the people, but he could not compete with Isis and her mass appeal, and her cult spread throughout the ancient world. These mystery religions (cults) fascinated rich and poor alike, because they were full of exotic rituals, and they gave their followers hope for a happy life in the next world. The cult rituals were austere, requiring initiates to make pilgrimages, fast, and abstain from sexual pleasures so they might enter a state of mystical contemplation. Mystery plays celebrating the life of Isis with pantomimes and music were very popular.

The Roman writer APULEIUS, in his book *Metamorphoses*, describes the ceremony of initiation into the cult of Isis, who was called "Queen of Heaven." On her festival day, the priests entered the temple of Isis at dawn, opening all the doors of the sacred shrine so that only a linen curtain hid the statue of Isis. When the faithful arrived, the curtain was opened to reveal the cult statue. The people began to chant and pray and the women shook a rattle called a SISTRUM. Silent prayer and contemplation followed the opening prayers, and when the sun had risen, prayers were offered to the sun god and the crowds went home. In the afternoon the ceremonies included sacrifices, the shaking of the sistrum, the burning of incense, and a sacred ritual using holy water from the Nile.

Isis became so popular in Rome that a school for the Pastophori, priests of Isis, was opened around 80 B.C. The main temple of Isis in Rome was called the "Isis Campensiis." The only Roman temple of Isis standing today is at Pompeii, preserved by the ash that covered the town in A.D. 79 when Mount Vesuvius erupted. Isis's popularity was so great that in addition to those in Italy, remains of her temples and shrines have been found in Greece, Lebanon, Syria, and England. When Christianity was adopted by the Roman Emperor Constantine the Great in the fourth century A.D., the cult of Isis died out.

**ISIS AND OSIRIS, MYTH OF** The myth of Isis and Osiris, a story of death and resurrection, was central to Egyptian religious beliefs and embodied all the crucial elements of Egyptian funerary rites. No complete Egyptian copy of the myth of Isis and Osiris exists, but the best ancient version comes from PLUTARCH, a Greek priest at Delphi, who wrote *De Iside Et Osiride* about A.D. 100. The two principal gods, Isis and Osiris, were brother and sister and husband and wife. Their brother, SET, and their sister, NEPHTHYS, were also husband and wife. Osiris brought civilization to Egypt by introducing farming and cattle raising to the early inhabitants of the Nile Valley, and Isis taught the people the art of spinning and weaving. So successful was Osiris in his mission that he set out to bring farming and cattle raising to neighboring countries. He left Isis, the goddess of magic, to watch over the people of Egypt and to keep their evil brother Set in check. While her husband was gone, Isis ruled the land wisely and controlled Set, who was secretly plotting against his brother.

When Isis was worshipped by the Greeks and Romans, she was shown in classical dress. *(Photo by Wolfgang Sauber/Used under a Creative Commons license)*

When Osiris returned to Egypt, Set, by trickery, obtained the exact body measurements of his brother Osiris and built a beautiful wooden chest to his proportions. Set then invited Osiris to a lavish banquet and offered the beautiful chest to any guest who could fit inside. Guest after guest tried and failed. Osiris climbed into the chest that fit him perfectly. Set immediately sealed it shut, poured molten lead over it, and threw the chest into the Nile. When Isis heard of her husband's death, she wept and began searching for the chest that held Osiris's body. During a violent storm at sea, the chest washed up on the shores of Byblos in Phoenicia (modern Lebanon) and came to rest in the branches of a tamarisk tree. In time the tree grew to extraordinary size, and the trunk encompassed the chest with the dead Osiris inside. While she was searching for Osiris, Isis had a vision and saw the chest in Byblos.

Malacander, the king of Byblos, was building a palace and needed a large tree for one of the pillars, so the tree was cut down. When Isis learned that the tree had been carved into a pillar in the palace, she befriended the handmaidens of Queen Astarte, who had just given birth to a son. The queen noticed the heavenly scent of the goddess that accompanied the handmaidens and asked that Isis be brought to her. The goddess was made nursemaid to the queen's newborn son. One day, while Isis was performing magic to make the child immortal, the queen was startled to see her nursemaid turn into a bird, and her cries of alarm broke the spell. Isis then enlisted the aid of the queen to help her recover the body of her husband, Osiris. The king cut open the pillar and gave the chest to Isis, who brought the body of Osiris back to Egypt for proper burial. During the journey, Isis magically conceived a child with her dead husband. Once in Egypt, Isis hid in the marshes in the Delta so the evil brother Set would not discover that she was pregnant (with her son Horus). Set discovered the body of Osiris while hunting in the marshes and hacked his brother into 14 pieces, which he scattered throughout the land. Isis once again began searching for her husband and gradually found all the parts of his body except one, the phallus, which had been eaten by fish in the Nile. Isis held a funeral and erected a stele for each part of Osiris's body in the place where it was found, hoping that Set would think each piece was buried separately. Then Isis assembled the pieces of her deceased husband, anointed his body with precious oils, and fashioned an artificial phallus for him. Isis magically assumed the form of a bird, hovered over the body of Osiris, and brought him back to life by reciting magical spells. Because of Isis's powerful magic, Osiris resurrected and became the ruler of the Netherworld.

Almost all the beliefs of the ancient funerary cult can be traced to this myth: The chest that exactly fit Osiris is the precursor of the anthropoid coffin that resembles the human shape and is designed to protect the body. The importance of a proper burial in Egyptian soil is emphasized by the efforts of Isis to recover the body of Osiris. The importance of an intact corpse for resurrection in the next world is demonstrated by Isis's search for all the parts of her deceased husband's body. Finally, and most important, when Isis recites the necessary magical words, Osiris resurrects in the same body he inhabited while alive. Mummification thus becomes essential to immortality: The body must be preserved for the afterlife.

**ITUM** Wife of Reshef, the Syrian war god adopted by the Egyptians, Itum was worshipped along with her husband. She was considered a healer and was particularly called upon to help relieve stomachaches.

**JACKAL** In Egyptian mythology, one animal could represent several different gods, and that is what happened with the jackal. A member of the canine family, jackals eat carrion or decayed meat, and in Egypt they often prowled around cemeteries where not every corpse was protected by a tomb. ANUBIS, the jackal-headed god of embalming and guardian of the cemetery, is always shown with a black coat—perhaps because of his association with mummification, a process that causes the body to turn a dark color. Another funerary god, closely associated with Anubis, is the jackal-headed god WEPWAWET, "Opener of the Ways," who has a white or gray head. He seems to take over for Anubis after the mummification process. Wepwawet protects the souls of the deceased as they travel through the Underworld to the next world. A third jackal-headed god, DUAMETEF, is one of the FOUR SONS OF HORUS and attends every mummification ceremony, for he is a guardian of the stomach that is placed in a CANOPIC JAR with a jackal head carved on the lid.

**JUDGMENT DAY** The ancient Egyptians believed that judgment was a crucial test for admittance into the next world. Actually, there were two judgments: one impartial and objective, and the other somewhat subjective and dependent upon the theatrical and speech-making abilities of the deceased. In the first, the objective test, the Egyptians believed the heart of the deceased was weighed on a balance scale against a feather. The hieroglyph represents the ancient Egyptian word *MAAT*, or "truth." If the heart was as light as the feather of truth, not heavy with evil deeds, the deceased passed the test. This ancient concept is the origin of the balance scale as the modern symbol of justice. To further ensure a fair judgment, OSIRIS, the patron god of the dead, is usually shown presiding over the judgment while the ibis-headed god, THOTH, records the results. If the deceased did not pass the test, his or her heart was thrown to a creature with the body of a hippopotamus and the head of a crocodile. Once the heart was eaten, the deceased ceased to exist. Egyptian mythology had no concept of hell.

If the deceased passed the test with the balance scale, he or she was ushered into the Hall of the Double Truth to undergo a second judging by a tribunal of 42 gods. The deceased was required to "separate himself from evil doings" by making a negative plea, in which he or she denied having done specific wrongs. One of the purposes of the BOOK OF THE DEAD was to reveal the names of the 42 gods, giving the deceased power over them. The following are examples of the mysterious names and the denials follow:

Hail Strider, coming forth from Heliopolis. I have done no wrong.
Hail Eater-of-Shadows, coming forth from the caverns. I have not slain men.
Hail He-Whose-Two-Eyes-Are-on-Fire, coming forth from Sais. I have not defiled the things of the gods.
Hail Breaker-of-Bones, coming forth from darkness. I have not transgressed.
Hail Doubly-Wicked, coming forth from Ati. I have not defiled the wife of a man.
Hail Disposer-of-Speech, coming forth from Weryt. I have not inflamed myself with rage.
Hail, Provider-of-Mankind, coming forth from Sais. I have not cursed God.
Hail White Teeth, coming forth from Ta-She. I have not slaughtered the divine cattle.

If the deceased convinced the gods that he or she was a person worthy of entering the NETHERWORLD, he or she was declared "True of Voice." He or she was now a "westerner," ready to be welcomed by Osiris.

**JUPITER-AMUN** Jupiter, the mightiest god in Roman mythology, was associated with the Egyptian supreme deity, AMUN. After the Romans gained control of Egypt in 30 B.C., many of Egypt's important gods were taken over by the Romans. Lacking a rich mythology of their own, Roman gods often assumed the character of the Greek and Egyptian deities. That was the case with Jupiter-Amun, the Roman name for the ORACLE at Siwa Oasis, which provided answers given by the gods by means of a priest or cult statue. The oracle at Jupiter-Amun gained fame when ALEXANDER THE GREAT traveled across the desert to ask his important question: "Who was my father?" He was told that he was the son of Amun. The oracle at Siwa Oasis was known to the Egyptians as Amun-Re, to the Greeks as Zeus-Amun, and to the Romans as Jupiter-Amun.

**JUSTICE, GODDESS OF**   See MAAT.

**JUVENAL** (DECIMUS JUNIUS JUVENALIS, C. A.D. 65–128)   The Roman poet whose biting satires on the religion of ancient Egypt often focused on the cult of ISIS. When CLEOPATRA VII, known as the "Living Isis," entered Rome, the women of the city became infatuated with her and the cult of Isis. Juvenal's intense dislike for all things Egyptian may stem from his exile from Rome, possibly to Egypt, when he fell out of favor with the Roman emperor Domition. Juvenal saw the Roman upper classes' devotion to Egyptian religion as a silly waste of time, and he ridiculed them in his satires.

> If Isis shall order her, a woman will journey to Egypt to fetch water from the Nile with which to sprinkle at the Temple of Isis . . . [The Temple of Isis in Rome was in the Campus Martius near the polling-booth]. For she believes that the command was given by the Goddess herself—The highest place of honor is awarded to Anubis [the jackal-headed god who serves Isis], who, with his linen-clad and bald crew [of priests], mocks at the weeping of the people lamenting for Osiris as he runs along. He obtains pardon for wives who break the law of purity on days that should be kept holy, and exacts huge penalties . . . His tears and carefully-studied mutterings make sure that Osiris will not refuse a pardon for the fault, bribed, no doubt, by a fat goose and a slice of sacrificial cake.

> *—Satire VI*

*KA* ⊔ The Egyptians believed that a person was born with five elements: (1) the physical body, (2) the shadow, (3) the name, (4) the *BA*, and (5) the *ka*. The *ka* was a kind of astral double or spiritual duplicate of the deceased that was necessary for existence in the next world. When a person died, the *ka* continued to dwell in the body, and one reason for mummification was to ensure the *ka* a dwelling place. In case the mummy was damaged or destroyed, many Egyptians were buried with a *ka* statue. The statue was a portrait of the deceased that the *ka* could recognize and was meant to be an alternative dwelling for the *ka* if the mummy was not suitable.

It was believed that a person's *ka* continued to need nourishment, so priests or family members of the deceased visited the mortuary temple and left food offerings. They didn't believe the *ka* actually consumed the food but that it magically derived benefits from the offering. Sometimes pictures of offerings on the tomb walls replaced the actual food offering. After the priests or family member recited a special prayer, the *ka* could derive the benefit of either offering.

The *ka* represented by the hieroglyph ⊔, a pair of upraised arms, is in Hatshepsut's funerary temple at Deir el Bahri, shown created on the potter's wheel of the creator god KHNUM.

**KAMUTEF** One of the titles of AMUN and MIN when they were worshipped together as a fertility god. Kamutef means "bull of his mother," an epithet given the two gods in the New Kingdom (1550–1069 B.C.). The combined god that embodied all the attributes of Amun and Min was called Amun-Min-Kamutef.

**KARNAK TEMPLE** A large religious complex at THEBES (modern Luxor) with sacred precincts dedicated to the Karnak Triad, the three most important

gods worshipped in the temple: AMUN-RE, MUT, and KHONSU. Karnak Temple is a series of buildings and monuments rising up around two sacred lakes and sprawling over 40 acres. Created over a period of several hundred years, the temple was the

The hypostyle hall at Karnak Temple is one of the architectural wonders of the ancient world. Pharoah Seti I and his son Ramses II had the columns decorated with scenes of the pharaohs in the company of the gods. *(Photograph by Pat Remler)*

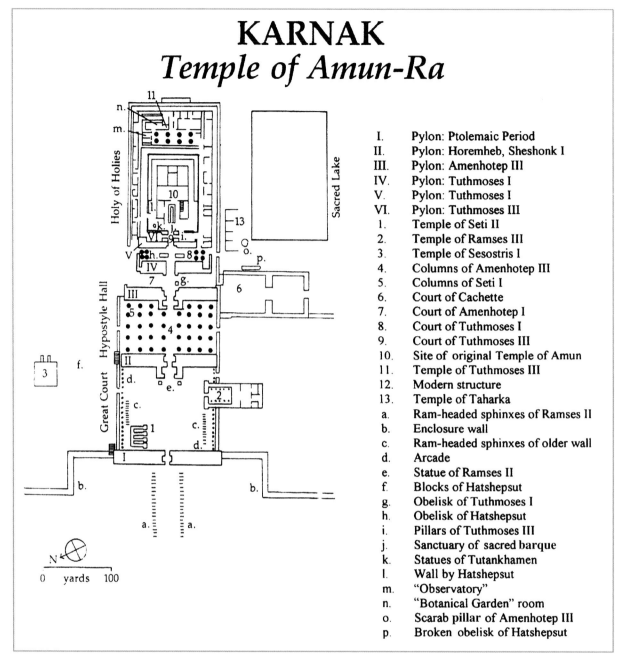

# KARNAK
## *Temple of Amun-Ra*

I. Pylon: Ptolemaic Period
II. Pylon: Horemheb, Sheshonk I
III. Pylon: Amenhotep III
IV. Pylon: Tuthmoses I
V. Pylon: Tuthmoses I
VI. Pylon: Tuthmoses III
1. Temple of Seti II
2. Temple of Ramses III
3. Temple of Sesostris I
4. Columns of Amenhotep III
5. Columns of Seti I
6. Court of Cachette
7. Court of Amenhotep I
8. Court of Tuthmoses I
9. Court of Tuthmoses III
10. Site of original Temple of Amun
11. Temple of Tuthmoses III
12. Modern structure
13. Temple of Taharka
a. Ram-headed sphinxes of Ramses II
b. Enclosure wall
c. Ram-headed sphinxes of older wall
d. Arcade
e. Statue of Ramses II
f. Blocks of Hatshepsut
g. Obelisk of Tuthmoses I
h. Obelisk of Hatshepsut
i. Pillars of Tuthmoses III
j. Sanctuary of sacred barque
k. Statues of Tutankhamen
l. Wall by Hatshepsut
m. "Observatory"
n. "Botanical Garden" room
o. Scarab pillar of Amenhotep III
p. Broken obelisk of Hatshepsut

Plan of Karnak Temple  *(Courtesy of Hoyt Hobbs)*

most important religious center in all of Egypt. The first temple to Amun was built in the MIDDLE KING-DOM, and it was expanded and decorated by later NEW KINGDOM rulers as the city of Thebes gained wealth and prominence as a religious center.

Religion played an important role in ancient warfare, and no temple represented the connection between the gods and the military as well as Karnak Temple. Making war on one's neighbors was standard practice in Egypt, and the king and the military looked to the gods to ensure their victory. A large portion of the spoils of war would be presented to the temple as gifts to AMUN. On the second pylon in the Temple of Amun are scenes of Sheshonk I (Twenty-second Dynasty, 945–924 B.C.) commemorating his victory over Rehoboam, son of Solomon, the king of Judah. When Solomon's temple was robbed of its treasure, it was the Egyptian King Sheshonk I, known as Shishak in the Bible, who defeated him. The relief shows Sheshonk in front of Amun, who offers him a scimitar. Above their heads are the list of cities that Sheshonk claims to have conquered in Israel. Following are the biblical passages that refer to this campaign:

> And it came to pass in the fifth year of king Rehoboam, that Shishak king of Egypt came up against Jerusalem: and he took away the treasures of the house of the Lord, and the treasures of the king's house: he even took away all: and he took away all the shields of gold which Solomon had made. (Kings 14:25–6)

> . . . And it came to pass, that in the fifth year of king Rehoboam, Shishak king of Egypt came up against Jerusalem, because they had transgressed against the Lord, with twelve hundred chariots, and threescore thousand horsemen: and the people were without number that came with him out of Egypt . . . (2nd Chro. 12:2–3)

As the city of Thebes grew wealthy from the pillage of foreign counties, so did Karnak Temple. Every king in the New Kingdom added something to Karnak Temple to show his devotion to the gods, sometimes destroying earlier structures to make room for his building. The site includes temples for Khonsu, the son of Amun and Mut, and numerous dedications to other gods.

Several festivals were celebrated at Karnak Temple, but none was more important than the Great New Year Festival of OPET, when Amun visited his southern harem at LUXOR Temple. The annual rise in the Nile signaled the opening of the festival that lasted for 24 days. Karnak Temple today remains one of Egypt's most impressive sites.

**KEBECHT** (KABECHET, KEBECHET, KEBHUT) An obscure goddess, Kebecht is the daughter of ANUBIS, and a goddess of freshwater and purification. Her attribute is a container of sacred NILE water. She assists her father, Anubis, while he prepares the deceased by providing pure water for the souls of the dead while they await MUMMIFICATION.

The goddess Kebecht first appears in the Fifth Dynasty and is mentioned in the PYRAMID TEXTS of Pepi I: "Kebecht, the daughter of Anubis, goes forth to meet Pepi, with four *nemset* vases. She refreshes the breast of the Great God on the day of his watch, and she refreshes the breast of Pepi with life. She washes Pepi, she censes Pepi." Kebecht is often portrayed as a serpent or an ostrich.

**KEMET** "The black land" was the name the ancient Egyptians gave Egypt. The name resulted from the annual flooding or inundation of the Nile. The fertile black soil from which the Egyptians derived their livelihood stood in stark contrast to the hostile desert—the "red land," or *deshret* . For the Egyptians, the contrast of the black and the red land was another example of duality in their lives, along with the designations of Upper and Lower Egypt, represented by the two goddesses NEKHBET and WADJET and the LOTUS and PAPYRUS plants.

*KHAIBIT* The Egyptians believed that a person was born with five elements: (1) the physical body, (2), the name, (3) the BA, (4) the KA, and (5) the shadow, or *khaibit*. It was believed that the *khaibit* could free itself from the body and move around as a separate entity. It is difficult to understand the purpose of the *khaibit*, but it is clearly associated with the *ba* and seems always to be near it. The BOOK OF THE DEAD provides us with several references: (Chapter 89) "May I look upon my soul and my shadow," and (Chapter 92) "Let my soul (*ba*) not be shut in, let my shadow (*khaibit*) not be fettered, let the way be opened for my soul and my shadow, may it see the great god."

*KHAT* The *khat* is the physical body of the deceased. On the day of a funeral, special prayers were recited over the mummy to aid in its transformation into a spiritual body, AKH, that could rise to heaven to dwell with the gods. The *khat* is mentioned briefly in the BOOK OF THE DEAD regarding the preservation of the mummy.

**KHEPRI** One of the manifestations of the sun god in the form of a SCARAB BEETLE (*scarabaeus sacer*), Khepri means "he who came into being by himself." Always keen observers of nature, the ancient Egyptians noticed that scarab beetles rolled a ball of dung on the ground, from which their offspring emerged. This gave rise to the notion that beetles reproduced without benefit of a mate. Khepri, the scarab god, having been born from the womb of his mother, NUT, onto the eastern horizon, pushes the sun disk across the sky as he emerges from a night in the Underworld.

Also important to the notion of resurrection, Khepri appears in the BOOK OF THE DEAD, Chapter 83: "I have soared as the primeval one soars: I have become Khepri. I have grown as plants grow . . . I am

The ram-headed god Khnum fashions a man upon his potter's wheel, while the god Thoth stands behind him and records the number of years allotted to the man.

the fruit of every god." Early inscriptions for Khepri appear in the PYRAMID TEXTS, calling for Khepri to come into being as a manifestation of RE, the sun god. In HELIOPOLIS, Khepri is called Atum-Khepri, arising from the primordial mound in the mansion of the BENU (bird).

During the MIDDLE KINGDOM (2055–1650 B.C.), the image of the beetle became the scarab amulet that magically imparted the sun god's protection. They appeared in many sizes, and the underside could be inscribed with the owner's name and titles. Some were produced to commemorate specific events, such as Amenhotep III's lion hunts, or his marriage to Queen Tiye.

During the early 1900s, a huge stone carving of the scarab Khepri was excavated at Karnak Temple at the northwest corner of the Sacred Lake, where it still stands. The British Museum has an even larger

green granite scarab some five feet long and three feet wide. Huge scarab statues seem to have been common in ancient Egyptian temples as a symbol of the sun's first appearance on the horizon.

**KHNUM** A ram-headed god who created man on the potter's wheel, Khnum controlled the annual flooding of the NILE from the river's hidden caverns. Khnum's cult center was on Elephantine Island in Aswan, where he ruled with his wife, ANUKIS, and his daughter SATIS. Because of his strong affiliation with the Nile, he is sometimes called "the Lord of the Crocodiles." During the Greek and Roman periods of domination in Egypt (332 B.C.–A.D. 395), rams sacred to Khnum were mummified at Elephantine Island, elaborately wrapped and decorated with gilded masks, and placed in stone sarcophagi. A Ptolemaic copy of an early inscription by King ZOSER (Third Dynasty,

2686–2613 B.C.) on the rocks at Sehel Island, near Elephantine, records a seven-year famine and states that Khnum would let the Nile flood once again if his temple were renovated. The work was done, the Nile flooded, and Egypt was prosperous once again.

**KHONSU** (KHONS) An ancient moon god whose name means "the wanderer," Khonsu was associated with the young or new moon. His cult was well established in Thebes by the MIDDLE KINGDOM (2055–1650 B.C.). When the Theban Triad came into prominence in the New Kingdom (1550–1069 B.C.), Khonsu became the child of Amun and Mut. As the son of the great god Amun, Khonsu became increasingly popular throughout Egypt. Over time Khonsu and THOTH, the personification of the moon, were identified with each other. By the late New Kingdom, Khonsu assumed many of the attributes of Thoth. He was hailed as the lord of writing and literature and as a divine judge.

**KINGSHIP AND THE GODS** The idea of divine kingship was so imbedded in Egyptian society that for 3,000 years the pharaoh was the icon of Egypt. The king was portrayed on temple walls and in colossal statues on a scale nearly equal to the gods. From earliest times, the king of Egypt was viewed as divine—he was a mortal who was also a god. At first, the kings were associated only with HORUS, the falcon god, and they inscribed their royal name in a *SEREKH*, a rectangle representing a schematic diagram of a palace. As early as the First Dynasty, Horus was shown perched on top of the *serekh*. When Horus, the son of OSIRIS, avenged his father's death, he gained justice in heaven. By association, the pharaoh, who was identified with Horus, was responsible for justice on Earth.

As the mythology became more complex, pharaohs took more names. In the Fifth Dynasty, when Egyptian religion focused on worshipping the sun god RE, the pharaoh Nefer-ir-ka-Re ("Beautiful is the soul of Re") took another name, called a *sa Re* ("son of Re") name, and his successor soon followed his lead. By the MIDDLE KINGDOM (2055–1650 B.C.), the pharaoh had five names, each associated with a god.

### The King's Five Titles

1. **The Horus Name.** Written in a *serekh* with a falcon perched on top. An example is "Horus, Divine of Forms."
2. **The Two Ladies (or two goddesses) Name.** Called the *nebty*, ancient Egyptian for "two ladies," this name associated the pharaoh with

The *serekh*, a schematic drawing of the front of the palace, represented the power of the king. *(Drawing by Jeremy Eagle)*

the vulture goddess NEKHBET of Upper Egypt and the cobra goddess Udjat of Buto in Lower Egypt. The pharaoh thus had the protection of two of the oldest and most powerful goddesses in Egypt, confirming his position as king of Upper and Lower Egypt. An example from the Middle Kingdom is "Two Ladies, Divine of Births."

3. **Golden Horus Name.** Gold was often referred to as the "flesh of the gods," and because it never tarnishes, it was the metal of eternity. The idea of a golden falcon goes back to Egypt's Predynastic period, and Thutmose

III says, "Amun made me as a falcon of gold." The association with gold suggests the never-changing, divine nature of the king. A typical Golden Horus name is "Golden Horus, Victor over Set."

4. **The Prenomen.** The first of the two royal names written in a CARTOUCHE, the oval shape that encircles the pharaoh's name. It is called the "prenomen" because it comes just before the king's most common name, or "nomen." The prenomen is always preceded by the title "King of Upper and Lower Egypt." For example, "King of Upper and Lower Egypt, The Lord Re Exists."

5. **The Nomen.** The last of the king's five names and the second name written in a cartouche, it is always preceded by the title "Son of Re," thus presenting the king as the son of the most powerful of all the sun gods. A famous example of this name is, "Son of Re, Tutankhamen."

The five names of the pharaoh demonstrate a crucial link between his earthly realm and the realm of the gods. On the day of his coronation, the king was proclaimed to be "on the throne of Horus like Re." Two crowns—a white one for Upper Egypt (south) and a red one for Lower Egypt (north)—were placed on the new pharaoh's head in two different shrines, one for Udjat of Lower Egypt and one for Nekhbet of Upper Egypt. Thus the gods gave their assent to the king's rule and admitted him to their realm.

**KINGS' LIST** In ancient Egypt there were two kinds of time: mythological (before historic time) and chronological (measured time). Historic dates were recorded by the number of years a king reigned. An important date, such as a festival, was recorded as the year, month, and day of the reign of the current king. For example, it might be recorded that on the second day of the third month of the fourth year of the reign of Tutankhamen, the festival of OPET was celebrated.

Mythology tells us that legendary kings ruled in mythological time. The earliest-known kings' list is the PALERMO STONE carved in the Fifth Dynasty. It names mythological rulers who ruled in the time before historic time was recorded.

The *Turin Canon of Kings* from Dynasty XIX is written on the back of a PAPYRUS that recorded Egyptian tax records. Beginning in mythological times, the *Turin Canon of Kings* lists the reigns of the gods, divine beings, and mythological kings and gives a view of how the Egyptians saw their prehistory. It tells us that PTAH, RE, and SHU were the first three gods to rule and then goes on to list Egypt's historic kings. The *Turin Canon of Kings* ends with the Second Intermediate Period, where the PAPYRUS is fragmented.

A thousand years later, the Egyptian priest Manetho (290–230 B.C.) compiled a kings' list in his *History of Egypt.* Manetho left out the mythical kings but divided the historic kings into ruling families called "dynasties," and it is his dynastic list that Egyptologists use today. Other kings' lists were recorded in temples, but today many of them are fragmented or incomplete. On the walls of the temple of Seti I at Abydos is the best-preserved list. Seventy-six kings are named, and Seti and his young son Ramses II, who would become RAMSES THE GREAT, are shown making offering to the ancestors. This list ends with Seti's name and omits certain kings who could not be named as rulers of Egypt. Queen HATSHEPSUT, who crowned herself king, was not named because she was a woman. AKHENATEN was not named because he was branded a heretic who changed the ancient religion. TUTANKHAMEN was not named because he was the son of Akhenaten and associated with the AMARNA heresy. And the last two kings of Dynasty Eighteen—Aye and Horemheb—were not named because they were minor kings who ruled for only a short time. It was not just a slight that the names were left off the list. Each year a ritual was performed in the "Hall of the Ancestors" by the king, who recited the names of the ancestors so they would have "bread, beer, cattle, geese, oxen and all things good and pure." If your name was not read, you could not exist in the next world.

**KNOT OF ISIS** (BLOOD OF ISIS, *TET*) Called *tet* by the Egyptians, the knot of Isis is similar to the *ankh* in shape but with what appear to be arms folded downward. It also closely resembles the knot worn by the gods at the top of their kilts. The sign is associated with the blood of Isis in the BOOK OF THE DEAD. Popular as a funerary AMULET, the knot of Isis was carved from red carnelian or jasper or sometimes made of red glass, all of which represented the blood, magic, and power of Isis. When TUTANKHAMEN's mummy was unwrapped, a red jasper knot of Isis was found among the many magical amulets. According to the Book of the Dead, whoever wears such a knot will gain the protection of Isis and her son Horus, and they will be welcomed into the next world. In one version of the Book of the Dead, called the Theban Recension, the magical powers of Isis were granted to the deceased if the *tet* amulet was dipped in the sap of the *ankh-imy* plant, placed in sycamore wood, and then placed on the mummy. An incantation completed the spell: "Let the blood of Isis and the magical words of Isis be mighty and protect and keep safely this great god [the deceased] and to guard him from that which is harmful." With this special protection from Isis and the *tet* amulet, the deceased could travel anywhere he or she wished in the Underworld. The *tet* was often combined with the Djed pillar, a symbol for Osiris, as decorative elements on jewelry and temple walls, beds, and sarcophagi.

**Kom el Shuqafa**  A catacomb used for burials during the Roman period. Even after Egypt had been declared a Roman province by Octavian in 30 B.C., there remained a fascination with the gods and religion of Egypt. Attesting to this fascination is the curious mixture of Egyptian mythology as understood by the Romans that appears in the Kom el Shuqafa catacombs, built in Alexandria in the first and second centuries A.D. A descending passageway from the top of a hill allowed the deceased to be lowered by ropes into the catacomb, which has several levels. A vestibule on the first level provided cut rock benches where mourners could gather. The Romans, adopting the Egyptian custom of having a last meal with the deceased and feasting in their honor each year, created an underground banquet room with low benches so they could dine Roman style, reclining on cushions while the meal was served. The bodies of mummified Romans were buried on the lower levels in niches carved into the stone. In an attempt to recognize both Roman and Egyptian gods, the rotunda is decorated with Egyptian papyrus capitals, a winged sun disk, and a falcon soaring overhead. One niche shows a man and woman in Roman dress, serpents wearing Egyptian royal crowns and holding the baton of the Greek god Hermes, and Medusa's head on a shield. Kom el Shuqafa is unique in its curious mixture of Egyptian and Greek and Roman mythology.

**Kom Ombo**  The temple at Kom Ombo, about 25 miles north of Aswan, is dedicated to two gods at once, Horus and Sobek. The temple was divided into two sections with a separate door and aisle for each god. Half was dedicated to Horus as Haroeris (Horus son of Re) and the other half to Sobek, the crocodile. Crocodiles sacred to Sobek were mummified when they died, and many of their mummies have been discovered in the temple. Because Kom Ombo, built by the Ptolemies, lacks a roof, the carvings on the walls are illuminated by the bright sunlight, and it is easy to detect the Greek influence on the art in this temple. All of the gods and goddesses appear with fuller figures than those created in earlier times.

**Koptos**  The cult center of the fertility god, Min, Koptos is about 25 miles north of Thebes (modern Luxor) and in ancient times was the last stop for caravans before entering the Wadi Hammamat, a hostile desert route between Thebes and the Red Sea. Koptos is one of Egypt's earliest settlements, dating from about 3000 B.C., when colossal statues of the god Min adorned the temple complex. Part of a ruined temple from the New Kingdom (1550–1066 B.C.) still remains, and a small temple to Isis was built during the Ptolemaic period (332–32 B.C.).

**Kuk and Kuket**  In the creation story that originated in Hermopolis, Kuk and Kuket were part of the Ogdoad, or original eight gods who created the world. Kuk had a frog's head, and Kuket had the head of a serpent. Together they represented darkness.

**LAMENTATIONS OF ISIS** (LAMENTATIONS OF ISIS AND NEPHTHYS) The Lamentations of Isis are the rituals and prayers performed during a vigil for OSIRIS. Three separate texts have been given modern names: Lamentations of Isis and Nephthys, Songs of Isis and Nephthys, and Hour Watches. Each lamentation has specific instructions on how and when to perform the ritual and who should recite the lamentation. The Songs of Isis and Nephthys were meant to be sung only in Osiris Temples on special designated days, probably because they were part of a larger ceremony performed on those days. The Lamentations of Isis and Nephthys were to be reenacted with chanting and dramatic readings only on the 26th day and were performed only in certain temples. The Hour Watches required special prayers at specified hours during the day.

Mythology tells us that after Isis had gathered all the scattered pieces of her husband's body and reassembled them, she buried Osiris on the island of Biga, near Philae. The faithful Isis visited her husband's tomb each day, bringing milk to rejuvenate his body while she sang songs to soothe him. Because of Isis's devotion to Osiris, she was seen as the eternal mourner. The story of Isis's grief was a favorite theme, told over and over, with temple singers playing the parts of Isis and NEPHTHYS as they lamented the death of Osiris. The story of his life and death was reenacted in great detail and ended with the resurrection and worship of Osiris in the NETHERWORLD.

The directions for the ritual called for two women with beautiful bodies, attended by two priests, to kneel before the door of the Hall of Appearances. The names Isis and Nephthys are written on their arms. They hold FAIENCE jars filled with Nile water in their right hands and loaves of bread baked in Memphis in their left hands. The women chant the prayers for the deceased, in complete seclusion, at the third and eighth hour of the day.

A Ptolemaic papyrus records that the hymn was recited by Isis and Nephthys for Osiris-Khentamenti, the great god, lord of Abydos:

Isis recites:
Come to your house, come to your house!

You of On [referring to Osiris' association with the sun god in Heliopolis], come
to your house,
Your foes are not . . .

While I can see you I call to you, Weeping to the height of heaven!
But you do not hear my voice, though I am your sister (and wife) whom you
loved on Earth,
You loved none but me, the sister, the sister!

Nephthys recites:
O good King, come to your house!
Please your heart, all your foes are not!
Your two sisters beside you guard your bier,
  call for
you in tears . . .

Isis recites:
Oh my lord! There is no god like you!
Heaven has your *ba*, earth has your body,
Netherworld is filled with your secrets.
Your wife is your guard, your son Horus rules
  the lands . . .

**LAPIS LAZULI** The semiprecious stone lapis lazuli was believed to have magical properties. Its rich dark blue color, often flecked with gold, was considered a symbol of heaven by the ancient Egyptians. The ancient word for lapis lazuli is *khesbed*. The stone was as valuable as silver or gold, for it was not found in Egypt, and trading expeditions traveled east to find the best quality lapis lazuli. In the story of the DESTRUCTION OF MANKIND, Re is said to have hair of lapis lazuli. In Tales of Magic, a child born to the wife of a priest has signs of divinity that include limbs of gold and a headdress of lapis lazuli.

The great god AMUN is often shown with skin the color of lapis lazuli, and the BOOK OF THE DEAD calls for the heart amulet to be made from lapis lazuli. A love charm in the Leiden-London magical papyrus begins with: "Thou art this scarab of real lapis lazuli . . ." When the mummy of TUTANKHAMEN was discovered, a lapis lazuli amulet of HORUS was found among the bandages.

**LAW, GODDESS OF** See MAAT, THE GODDESS OF TRUTH AND JUSTICE.

**LETTERS TO THE DEAD** The Egyptians believed that when the deceased entered the NETHERWORLD, life would continue much as it had on Earth, with a couple of exceptions. First, since the deceased had become one with OSIRIS, he or she would have some of the power of the gods. The deceased also was all knowing and, if favorably, inclined could help the living. Sometime before the Middle Kingdom, the Egyptians instituted the practice of writing letters to the dead to enlist their help.

Unlike most ancient letters, these were almost always written on bowls that held offerings. A bowl was placed at the tomb of the deceased to whom an appeal was made. Because the entire text had to fit on the bowl, the letters were often brief and lacked details, such as the reason for the request. It was assumed that since the deceased was all knowing, he or she would understand the plea. The following letter to the dead was written in HIERATIC script on a clay bowl (now in the Louvre Museum in Paris). The message starts at the rim and winds around and around until it reaches the bottom of the bowl. Like most letters to the dead, this letter from a mother to her son consists of five parts:

*Address:* O Mereri, born to Merti

*Greeting:* The god Osiris-Khentamenti assures that you shall live for millions of years, by providing for the breath in your nose and by placing bread and beer by the side of Hathor, lady of the horizon. Your condition is like [one who] lives millions of times by order of the gods who are in the sky and on the Earth.

*Praises:* You make obstacles to enemies who have evil characters [and who are] against your house, against your brother, and against your mother [who loves] her excellent son Mereri. You were excellent on Earth and thou art beneficent in the land of the dead. Invocations and offerings are made to you. The Haker Festival is celebrated for you. Bread and beer are placed upon the altar of the god Khentamenti . . . Make yourself my favorite dead person!

*Wrong:* You know that he said to me, "I shall report against you and your children."

*Appeal:* You report against it; you are in the place of justification.

Clearly Merti believes her son Mereri understands the wrong that is being done and asks her son to testify in her favor in the divine court before the god.

**LITANY OF RE** A celebration of the sun god's association with the NETHERWORLD, the Litany of Re appears on the walls of the New Kingdom royal tombs of Thutmose III, Seti I, and Ramses IV in the VALLEY OF THE KINGS. The text consists of nine litanies, rather than the 12 hours of the night usually mentioned in funerary texts (see AMDUAT). Each litany includes a description of the sun god, the petition of the deceased (his request for entry into the Netherworld), and the characters met on his journey. Re takes the form of a bird that flies to the Netherworld each night, and like the beings of the underworld, he dwells in a cavern.

**First Litany** The deceased king claims he knows the forms of Re and their names, and he petitions Re to open the Netherworld to him.

**Second Litany** The inhabitants of the Netherworld prepare for the arrival of the deceased king.

**Third Litany** The deceased king petitions, "May you lead me to the west," expressing the Egyptian universal desire for resurrection.

**Fourth Litany** Re dispels the darkness and allows those in the Netherworld to see his light, and the deceased king asks for the renewal of his sight and his heart.

**Fifth Litany** A prayer for the care of the god and for the release of those suffering in the Netherworld.

**Sixth Litany** The deceased king petitions, "O Re, come to me, o guide."

**Seventh Litany**   The deceased king recites, "Truly you have caused me to ascend." His limbs are deified and he becomes a god.

**Eighth Litany**   The text ends with prayers to the "west," the realm of the dead.

**Ninth Litany**   The deceased king is associated with Re.

**LOTUS**   A symbol of creation in ancient Egypt, the lotus is a symbol for NEFERTUM, who emerged from a blossom. Another myth tells of the sun coming forth from a lotus blossom floating on the waters of NUN. The association may have arisen naturally, for the petals of the lotus blossom open each morning and close each evening. Tomb paintings show banquet guests holding blue lotus blossoms to their noses to enjoy the fragrance. The Greek traveler Herodotus mentions that the Egyptians sometimes ate part of the lotus plant.

The lotus served as the emblem for Upper Egypt, while the papyrus plant was the emblem for Lower Egypt. Their graceful shapes were translated into the lotus and papyrus capitals seen on temple pillars all over Egypt.

**LOWER EGYPT**   Because the Nile flows from south to north, northern Egypt, or the Delta, is called Lower Egypt, and UPPER EGYPT is in the south. Lower Egypt's crown is the RED CROWN, the plant is the PAPYRUS, and its protective goddess is WADJET. During Egypt's Predynastic period, Upper and Lower Egypt were two separate kingdoms. The NARMER PALETTE commemorates the southern King Narmer's victory over Lower Egypt and subsequent uniting of the two lands. Many of the foreign gods worshipped in Egypt originated in Lower Egypt, having been imported from Syria.

**LUXOR**   Modern name for the site of the ancient city called Waset by the Egyptians and THEBES by the Greeks.

# M

**MAAHES** (MIHOS, MAHES, MIYSIS) A lion god who gained popularity during the NEW KINGDOM (1550–1069 B.C.), Maahes is the son of RE the sun god and BASTET, the cat-headed goddess. Maahes has a lion's head and a man's body and sometimes wears the double crown of UPPER and LOWER EGYPT or the double feather atef crown. He may be seen devouring a captive or wielding a knife in keeping with his fierce nature. A bouquet of lotus flowers beside Maahes reminds us of his gentler side. The first HIEROGLYPH in his name (ma) appears in the word *MAAT*, meaning truth and justice, and Maahes has a reputation for devouring the guilty and protecting the innocent. Maahes is also linked with HORUS the Younger and NEFERTUM.

One of Maahes's titles is "Lord of the Massacre," but he is also called "Lord of Slaughter," "Wielder of the Knife," and "The Scarlet Land." This title double-associates him with the lioness of Upper Egypt, SEKHMET, and the MYTH OF THE DESTRUCTION OF MANKIND.

By Egypt's Ptolemaic period (331–30 B.C.), the Greek city of Leontopolis (in Egypt) was a popular cult center with a large temple dedicated to Maahes. Claudius Aelianus, a Roman historian, wrote about the lion cults in Egypt:

> . . . In Egypt they worship lions, and there is a city called after them [Leontopolis] . . . the lions have temples and numerous spaces in which to roam; the flesh of oxen is supplied to them daily . . . and the lions eat to the accompaniment of song in the Egyptian language.

**MAAT** A concept associated with the goddess Maat, who represented truth, justice, moral law, and divine order. Divine order included natural phenomena, such as the Nile overflowing its banks each year, and political events, such as the Egyptian army conquering its enemies. To the Egyptians, *maat* was an unchanging, unquestioned force. This deep-seated belief in an unchanging, definite order of the universe led to the Egyptians' extreme conservativeness. Change was to be avoided, and innovation was not desired. This is partly the reason for the unchanging nature of Egyptian art. Egypt's art changed less over the centuries than that of any other culture.

When a statue of a god was needed for a temple, an old one was taken out and copied. Strict rules or canons controlled the proportions of tomb paintings. In preparing a tomb wall for a painting, an artist would draw a grid in red to make sure proportions of the god was as it should be: The head was two squares, shoulders seven squares, and so on. In a sense, tomb painting was reduced to paint-by-numbers so it would be in accordance with divine order.

In politics also, the Egyptians resisted change. From the earliest recorded history, around 3150 B.C., Egypt was ruled by a king, considered a divine ruler; there was no other political structure. The most important job of the king was to maintain divine order. Thus, if he made the proper offerings in the temples, the gods would be pleased and repay Egypt with prosperity and stability. Even in warfare, the concept of *maat* was essential. Because divine order decreed that Egypt should rule the Near East, war was considered part of divine order. Divine order dictated that Egypt should make war on its neighbors, and because the gods looked favorably on Egypt, Egypt would be victorious. The Egyptians saw nothing unusual about placing gruesome battle scenes on their temple walls. They believed it was what the gods wanted and was all part of divine order.

Maat, the goddess of truth, personified divine order. *(Drawing by Mary Jordan)*

Disasters were viewed as temporary upsets of divine order. If the Nile did not overflow to its expected level to irrigate the land, Egypt might suffer a famine. This was not viewed as a natural occurrence but instead as a sign that the gods were displeased with Egyptian behavior: Perhaps the proper offerings had not been made at the temples, or the correct prayers had not been recited. The solution was to turn to the gods and beg them to return the order that Egypt had enjoyed.

*Maat* also played a central role in determining whether the deceased was admitted to the NETH-ERWORLD. In order to reach the Netherworld, the deceased was required to make a NEGATIVE CONFESSION before an assembly of gods, listing all the evil deeds he or she had avoided in life, such as not killing anyone, or not diverting the irrigation ditch from its course. It was necessary to convince the gods that he or she had lived in accordance with *maat*. If the gods were convinced, the deceased was declared *"Maat kheru"*—"true of voice"—and was admitted to the next hall.

A second judging of the deceased also involved *maat*. Illustrations from Chapter 125 of the BOOK OF THE DEAD show a balance scale holding the deceased's heart on one side and a feather on the other. The heart represented the person's thoughts or emotions, and the feather was the hieroglyph for truth. Thus a person had to have been truthful, living in accordance with *maat*. If the scale balanced, then the deceased could enter the Netherworld. If his or her heart proved to be heavier than the feather of truth, it fell off the balance scale into the jaws of Am-

mit, the "Devourer of Amenti," who was a creature with the body of a hippopotamus and the head of a crocodile. If Am-mit devoured the heart, then the deceased ceased to exist.

When the heretic pharaoh AKHENATEN tried to change the religion of Egypt to monotheism, he appealed to the concept of truth, *maat*. In addition to changing the religion, he rejected centuries of artistic convention and permitted himself to be shown in statues and paintings as physically deformed. All these changes he covered with the motto for his reign: *ankh em maat*, "Living in Truth." After his death, the conservative Egyptian society erased all traces of his reign and returned to what they considered the true divine order.

**MAAT, THE GODDESS OF TRUTH AND JUSTICE** Closely associated with truth and order, the goddess Maat appears on temple walls in one of the most important religious ceremonies in ancient Egypt. The "presenting of Maat" shows the pharaoh offering "truth" to the gods of Egypt. Maat is usually shown with a feather—the hieroglyph for "truth"—on her head. Spell 80 of the COFFIN TEXTS calls her the daughter of ATUM, the creator god, but in later texts she is called the daughter of RE. Hymns to Maat inscribed on temple walls invoke Maat to be with the King always.

Because of their belief in the goddess Maat, the Egyptians could be optimistic about the future. If a man lived in accordance with MAAT, or divine order, he could expect to do well, both in this life and in the next. In the ancient Egyptian papyrus "The Eloquent Peasant," the main character suggests: "Speak *maat*, do *maat*; for it is mighty, it is great, it endures." This is an early version of the modern proverb "Honesty is the best policy." The Egyptians had such a firm belief that the goddess Maat would impose her order on the world that they had no written laws. With *maat*, there was no need for laws to be created by humans.

In periods of anarchy and political turmoil, Maat was temporarily deposed from her rightful place, and the priests prayed. "Maat will return to her throne; Evil will be driven away."

Maat is different from most other Egyptian goddesses in that we have few mythological stories about her interactions with the other gods and goddesses. She seems to be more abstract, more like the concept of order itself than a goddess.

**MACE** A round-headed stone weapon attached to a handle, the mace became a sign of royal authority and magical power. One of the most ancient and traditional poses of Egyptian kings shows the king smiting the enemies of Egypt with his royal mace. The smiting scene became a metaphor for Egypt's domination over her enemies. The falcon-headed god Horus was called "Lord of the Mace," and the weapon became a symbol for the "sound eye" of Horus (his other eye had been ripped out by Set during battle). The mace also was one of the objects associated with Wepwawet, a jackal-headed god.

**Mafdet** Originally a goddess of justice, Mafdet was also an executioner, and her curious symbol is a pole with a rounded top, a sharp blade, and a coil of rope. Mafdet is usually shown with a feline head—either a cat, lion, or panther—and the body of a woman, although some depictions show Mafdet with the head of a woman and the body of a feline.

Like Egypt's other feline goddesses, Mafdet protected the king. She was the guardian of the palace and the king's private chambers and was given the title "Slayer of Serpents." It was said that Mafdet ripped out the hearts of evildoers and dropped them at the pharaoh's feet. Her cult center was at Bubastis, in the Delta, where she was worshipped with another local feline goddess, Bastet. Because of her ferocious nature, Mafdet is also linked with Anhur, Menhit, and Tefnut. In the Book of the Dead Mafdet is a feline predator that repels serpents. Each night when Re's solar boat enters the Underworld, Mafdet defeats the evil serpent Apep. But she has a kinder side as well, and one of Mafdet's duties is to help the souls of the deceased on their journey to the Netherworld.

**Magic** The Egyptians were famous for their magic throughout the ancient world, and the priest-magicians practiced magic for more than 4,000 years. Magic was part of daily life in ancient Egypt, and it had the same goal as religion—to have some power over supernatural forces—but magic had a more immediate quality and could be used for both good and evil. Magic was different from religion, because when the magician worked his or her magic, it was the magician who made the magic happen. Religious ceremonies required the priest to ask the god for a particular favor, so it was the god, not the priest, who made it happen. Magic could bring good luck, cause a person to fall in love, ward off demons,

keep children safe, cure illness, and help a person get to the next world.

## Symbols of Power and Protection in Ancient Egypt

| | |
|---|---|
| **Aegis** | A sign of protection in the shape of a broad-collar necklace |
| **Ankh** | The ankh was the sign of life in ancient Egypt |
| **Crook** | A symbol of the authority of the king |
| **Djed** | A funerary amulet, the *djed* column symbolized the backbone of Osiris |
| **Eye of An Horus** | amulet for protection and health |
| **Flail** | A sign of the king's power |
| **Lotus** | The sign of Upper Egypt (southern Egypt) |
| **Mace** | An early weapon and sign of the power of the king |
| **Nekhbet** | Vulture goddess and symbol for Upper Egypt |
| **Papyrus** | Plant symbolizing Lower Egypt (northern Egypt) |
| **Shen** | Ring symbolizing eternity |
| **Scarab** | Symbol meaning to exist or life |
| **Sistrum** | Musical instrument sacred to Hathor, Isis, and Bastet |
| **Tet** | Symbol for Isis also called the Knot of Isis |
| **Was Scepter** | Symbol of the gods and scepter for the city of Thebes. |

Magic appears in many forms throughout Egyptian history. The earliest magical objects are stone amulets carved in the Predynastic period (5500–3100 B.C.). They protected the wearer from danger in this life and the next. Magical Pyramid Texts appear on the walls of King Unas's Fifth Dynasty pyramid at Saqqara to keep the king safe and help him resurrect in the next world. In the Middle Kingdom, magical spells were carved on the sides and top of wooden coffins (Coffin Texts) to protect the mummy and help the deceased enter the next world. Books of the Dead were popular in the New Kingdom because they were written on long papyrus scrolls. New magical spells were created to help the deceased resurrect in the next world. One of the versions of the Book of the Dead, called the Book of the Divine Cow, gives specific instructions as to when and how a spell should be uttered.

If a man pronounces this spell over himself he should be anointed with oil and unguent, the censer being in his hand with incense. Natron must be behind his ears, *Bed*—natron must be in his mouth, dressed in two new garments, having washed himself in inundation water, shod in white sandals, and the figure of the Truth goddess being painted on his tongue in green painter's color.

The book also says who should recite the spells.

A magician his head being purified, should make a female figure standing by his south side. He should make her a goddess and in the middle of her a snake standing erect on its tail, her head being placed on its body while its tail is on the ground Thoth should adore him [the magician], all the dignitaries of heaven being on him while Shu stretches his arm toward it. [He should recite:] I am safe from the great and mighty gods who sit in the eastern part of heaven, who guard the sky, who guard the earth . . .

*Heka*, the most common word for magic, is also the name of the god of magic who held specific power over writing and speech. Another important word for magic is *akhu*, from an Egyptian word for soul, and it seems to refer to magic after death. Armed with *heka*, the Egyptians and their gods could make wishes come true.

For Egyptian magic to work there were three important elements—the spell, the ritual, and the magician. Most magicians in ancient Egypt were priests in a temple, and often, before any request to perform magic was considered, it was necessary to consult a HOROSCOPE CALENDAR. This would tell them if it was a lucky or auspicious day. Before they began the ritual the magician-priests purified themselves—usually by bathing in a sacred lake, shaving all their body hair, and rinsing their mouths with a solution of NATRON and water. A typical spell could be to get rid of a headache or indigestion, to give a lame person power in his or her legs, to heal burns, or to make someone fall in love. One spell that could be used in modern times is to drive off cockroaches: "Keep away from me, lips of crookedness. I am Khonsu, lord of the circuit who brings words of the Gods to Re; I report the message to its lord."

**MAGIC, GODS AND GODDESSES OF**   See ISIS, HEKA, and THOTH.

**MAGICAL BRICKS** One of the many rituals observed in the New Kingdom (1550–1069 B.C.) was to place magical bricks inside the tomb to help safeguard the mummy from the enemies of OSIRIS. Four bricks were inscribed with texts from Chapter 151 of the BOOK OF THE DEAD, describing how they protected the mummy. Each magical brick had its own amulet and was placed against one of the four tomb walls to guard against evil approaching from any direction. The brick placed against the west wall had a DJED PILLAR, the symbol of stability; the east wall had an ANUBIS statue; the south wall had a torch; and the north wall had a statuette similar to USHABTI, a servant statue. Magical bricks have been found in the VALLEY OF THE KINGS in the tombs of Thutmose III, Tutankhamen, and Ramses II.

**MAGICAL OBJECTS IN TUTANKHAMEN'S TOMB** When Howard Carter opened Tutankhamen's tomb in November 1922, he found a number of magical objects buried with the boy king. One item reported found was a clay tablet with a curse carved on it: *"Death will slay with his wings whoever disturbs the peace of the pharaoh"* (see CURSE OF TUTANKHAMEN). It is doubtful that the tablet ever existed, but magic played a big part in sending the boy king to the next world. In the first room, the antechamber, two life-size statues of Tutankhamen with black skin and gold kilt (skirt) represented the royal KA—they served as the home or dwelling place of the royal soul during mummification.

Magical objects were found on the floor of Tutankhamen's burial chamber. Next to the shrines that enclosed the coffin were 10 magical oars intended to row the pharaoh's solar boat to the next world. A double wooden chest painted black held two FAIENCE cups—one filled with NATRON and the other with resin, essential ingredients for mummification. Between the cups was a stone amulet shaped like ϒ —perhaps used in the OPENING OF THE MOUTH CEREMONY. Surrounding the shrines in the burial chamber were magical emblems of ANUBIS, the god of embalming—six-foot-tall gilded wooden poles draped with a carved wooden animal skin were set into alabaster pots painted with the royal cartouche. Four wooden staffs, covered with golden leaf shapes (whose religious import is unknown), were propped against another wall. Alan Gardiner, who translated inscriptions for Carter, suggested that the staffs resembled the HIEROGLYPH "to awake," and that they may have been placed there to awaken Tutankhamen

Among the many treasures discovered in Tutankhamen's tomb were magical objects to help the boy king resurrect in the next world. *(Photograph by Pat Remler)*

in the next world. Four small, trough-shaped clay vessels, found next to the staffs, no doubt had a magical function as well. A wooden *djed* column amulet, representing the backbone of OSIRIS and providing stability for the pharaoh, was discovered when the burial chamber was cleared.

More magical protection is offered to the pharaoh by the goddesses ISIS, NEPHTHYS, SELKET, and NEITH, as they spread their protective wings at each corner of the sarcophagus. When the sarcophagus was opened it revealed a gilded wooden anthropoid (body-shaped) coffin with the likeness of Tutankhamen, and inside that was a second anthropoid coffin, and inside that was the famous solid gold coffin containing the mummy of Tutankhamen. The greatest number of magical objects was found within the golden coffin and around the mummy. When the coffin was opened, Tutankhamen's mummy was found to be damaged by the gallons of sacred oil poured over the bandages during the embalming ritual. But it was determined that within the wrappings were more than 100 magical objects, mostly amulets to protect the body.

A black resin scarab inscribed with a BENU bird lay at the mummy's neck and on his chest, protecting his soul, was an inlaid golden *BA* bird. Hanging from the *ba* bird were golden plaques inscribed with magical inscriptions to ensure that Tutankhamen would be welcomed by the gods.

> NUT the sky goddess says, "I reckon thy beauties, O Osiris, King Neb Kheperu Re, thy soul livest, thy veins are firm. Thou smellest the air that goest out as a god . . ."
>
> SET the storm god welcomes Tutankhamen as his son: "My beloved son, inheritor of the throne of Osiris, the king Neb Kheperu Re; thy nobility is perfect; the royal palace is powerful . . ."

**MAGICAL SPELLS** Magic was used by the Egyptians for almost any occasion. If something bad happened or was predicted, magic might be used to change or avoid the situation. If an object or occurrence was desired, magic could make it happen. The following magical spells call upon particular gods for assistance:

HEADACHE—Take this remedy which Isis prepared for Re's headache: Take equal parts of the following: berry of the coriander, berry of the poppy plant, wormwood, berry of the *sames*-plant, berry of the juniper plant, honey. Mix the ingredients together and a paste will form. Smear the afflicted person with the paste and he will immediately become well.

> Papyrus Ebers

BURNS—Make a mixture of milk of a woman
  who has borne a male child, gum, and ram's hair.
While administering to the patient, say:
Thy son Horus is burnt in the desert.
Is there any water there?
There is no water.
I have water in my mouth and a Nile between
  my thighs. I have come to extinguish the fire.

> Papyrus Ebers

A LOVE SPELL—Hail to thee, O Re-Harakhte,
Father of the Gods!
Hail to you, O ye seven Hathors who are adored
  with strings of red thread!
Hail to you, Gods lords of heaven and earth!
Come make (insert name) born of (insert name)
  come after me,
Like an ox after grass,
Like a servant after her children,
Like a drover after his herd!
If you do not make her come after me,
Then I will set [fire to] Brusiris and burn up
[Osiris]

> From a Twentieth Dynasty pottery fragment

TO BECOME A LOTUS FLOWER—I am this pure lotus that has ascended by the sunlight and is at Re's nose. I spend my [time] shedding it [i.e., the sunlight] on Horus. I am the pure [lotus] that ascended from the field.

> Book of the Dead, spell 81

**MAGICIANS**  There were two kinds of magicians in ancient Egypt. First were trained priest-magicians who served in large temples and were part of the religious hierarchy. They kept their knowledge of the occult secret, and they were looked upon with wonderment by the common people. Most magicians belonged to this group—priests who studied and practiced magic. The priest-magicians had a special place in the temple—they worked at the House of Life (⌓ ☥). The ⌓ sign is pronounced *per* and meant "house." The ☥ sign is pronounced *ankh* and here means "life" (*ankh* also means "mirror"). The House of Life was a building or perhaps group of buildings that housed the temple library that contained all the papyrus scrolls with all the knowledge of ancient Egypt. For a fee these magicians would perform vital services for people who came to them for help. First the magician would listen to the problem and then consult one of the sacred texts to decide the best way to help. Magicians could interpret dreams, recite spells to help people recover from illness, cause people to fall in love, or supply magical amulets to keep children safe from scorpions and snakes. With the proper combination of three essential elements—the spell, the ritual, and the magician—Egyptians believed virtually anything was possible. The spell was crucial because, in ancient Egypt, to say something was to make it so. The ritual was the action the magician performed while reciting the spell. Frequently the ritual was elaborate, as in the *HEB-SED* festival, in which the pharaoh had to run, jump, fight, and dance so that his body would be magically rejuvenated. Sometimes the ritual involved making effigies or holding magical amulets. During the ritual, the magician used tools essential to his work: a magic wand, a waxen image, burning incense, or a mysterious potion to be drunk.

The second kind of magicians were what we might call "lay" magicians. They were untrained men or women who practiced magic but were not attached to any temple. They were similar to modern faith healers or occultists, and they served people in the local villages where they lived.

**MAGIC WANDS**  Also called *apotropaic* (meaning "to escape bad luck"), magic wands were meant to turn away or avert evil spirits. They seem to have been most often carved of ivory and were inscribed with magical figures to protect their owners. The oldest wands from the Old Kingdom had little decoration other than animal heads on the ends. During the first Intermediate period (c. 2181 B.C.) magic wands were covered with myriad animals who offered magical protection, such as baboons, bulls, cats, crocodiles, frogs, lions, scarab beetles, snakes, and turtles. Some wands invoked the magic of the Set animal and a two-headed sphinx.

Wands were often used for drawing magical circles on the ground to create a "safe spot" that would repel

Magic wands were often carved from ivory and decorated with figures of the gods and goddesses who were called upon to perform magic and keep the wand's owner safe from harm. *(Photograph by Pat Remler)*

A small temple built to commemorate the birth of a god, the mammisi became an important addition to Late Period temple complexes. *(Photograph by Pat Remler)*

evil spirits or poisonous snakes, especially to protect children. To ensure that one would not be bitten by a scorpion while sleeping, a magical spell had to be uttered and a circle drawn around the person's bed with a magic wand.

**MAMMISI** Special chapels called mammisi were constructed next to the most important Egyptian temples to celebrate the birth of the "divine son the first son of the ruling pharaoh." The rituals of the marriages of Isis and Hathor were also celebrated in the mammisi, but the main function was to illustrate the "divine birth." The walls of the temple were decorated with scenes of the king and queen making offering to the gods in the name of their newborn son, the gods preparing to crown the "new ruler" with the crowns of Egypt while various goddesses are suckling the infant. The name *mammisi*, Coptic for "birthplace," was given to these small temples by Jean-François CHAMPOLLION, the 19th-century Egyptologist who broke the code for hieroglyphs.

Although it is a misnomer, for the actual birth did not take place there, the temples still are known by that name. Mammisis were built at Dendera, Edfu, and PHILAE temples.

**MANDJET BOAT** One of two boats or solar barques that carried the sun god RE across the sky each day. The Mandjet was the morning boat. In the morning, when Re was tired from his nightly ordeal in the NETHERWORLD, he was ferried across the sky in his Mandjet boat, whose name means "growing strong." When Re was growing weak after having shone all day, he traveled in the Mesektet, or the "growing weak" boat, as he approached the Netherworld for his nightly journey. It is said that MAAT, the goddess of truth and order, planned the sun's route at the beginning of creation, and Re followed it ever after. Unlike his evening voyage, when hostile enemies surrounded Re, during the day the sun god was accompanied by friendly gods, Maat, HORUS, and THOTH, who set his course and steered the boat.

**MANDRAKE** (MANDRAGORA) One of the magical plants in the ancient Egyptian pharmacopoeia, mandrake was essential in healing rituals. It was also sometimes associated with death and mourning. Shakespeare made this connection in his play *Antony and Cleopatra* when he wrote these lines for Cleopatra: "Give me to drink mandragora . . . that I may sleep out this great gap of time/My Antony is away."

Mandulis is a Ptolemaic-period god worshipped in Nubia and is often shown with the head of a man and the body of a falcon. *(Photograph by Pat Remler)*

Mandrake was clearly not a plant to be taken lightly. Paul Ghalioungui describes how mandrake was harvested in antiquity:

> Mandrake could be picked only on certain nights, by moonlight, or with the morning dew. The picker stopped his ears with wax, tied the plant to a dog, and ran away; the dog running after its master uprooted it and then dropped dead, for the mandrake was said to utter out, when torn away, such a horrible cry that anyone who heard it or touched it ran mad or died on the spot.

In addition, the Egyptians considered mandrake an aphrodisiac and believed it could promote fertility, because some of the species seemed to resemble male genitals. An Arabic name for the mandrake plant is "devil's testicles."

**MANDULIS** (MERWEL) A Ptolemaic god worshipped in NUBIA, Mandulis originated in southern Egypt. He is prominently featured on the walls of Kalabsha Temple with the Ptolemies and the Roman emperor Augustus. Kalabsha is one of the monuments

that was moved to high ground to save it from being flooded when the Aswan Dam was built. (See ABU SIMBEL). The temple walls show Mandulis with ISIS and important gods of the period receiving offerings from the kings. Mandulis is shown with a falcon's body and the head of a man wearing an *atef* crown with ostrich plumes, a sun disk, and *uraei* (cobra's heads).

**MANETHO** (C. 305–285 B.C.) An Egyptian priest who lived during the Ptolemaic period in Egypt, Manetho may have been instrumental in establishing the cult of SERAPIS, a composite Egyptian and Greek god. Manetho is most well known for his history of Egypt, called *Aegyptiaca*. Although he could read and write Egyptian scripts, Manetho wrote his history in Greek so King Ptolemy I could read of Egypt's past. No copies of his writing have survived intact, but later writers, including the Jewish historian Josephus (first century A.D.) and the Christian historians Africanus (c. A.D. 220) and Eusebius (c. A.D. 320), all recorded fragments of Manetho's writing. *Aegyptiaca* chronicled the history of Egyptian kingship, dividing the rulers into 31 dynasties. Modern scholars continue to refer to Manetho's chronology of kings as they study the succession of kings in ancient Egypt. Although no copies exist, Manetho is said to have written the following other works: *The Sacred Book, An Epitome of Physical Doctrines, On Festivals, On Ancient Ritual and Religion, On the Making of Kyphi* (a kind of incense), *Criticisms of Herodotus*, and *The Book of Sothis*.

**MANSION OF THE *KA*** One of the five aspects of human existence, the *KA*, or "soul," of the deceased continued to exist after his or her death. In order to maintain its existence, the *ka* had to be nourished. The tomb was the house or mansion of the *ka* where, if it received the proper rituals and offerings, it would remain healthy and active. The tomb and the mummified body were essential to the continued existence of the *ka* as well as the deceased. The tomb was part of a funerary complex that included an underground burial chamber and aboveground funerary temple and offering chapels. Usually the family of the deceased replenished the offerings, but in some cases a priest was employed to attend to the needs of the *ka*. He and his family were supported by crops from a plot of land designated by the deceased for this purpose.

**MANSIONS OF THE GODS** See TEMPLES.

**MASTABA** A bench-like structure built over Old Kingdom tombs, the mastaba was the earliest funerary temple, where the family of the deceased could make food offerings for the *ka*. (Mastaba is a modern Arabic word for the mud brick benches outside many Egyptian homes.) The first mastabas were simple shaft tombs cut into the bedrock with a small "bench-like" building over the shaft. As they became more elaborate, mastabas acquired enclosure walls and funerary chapels at ground level so the family and priests could make offerings for the deceased. The chapels were decorated with scenes of the deceased presenting offerings to various gods, and the chapel walls were inscribed with a magical offering formula that would provide food for the deceased if no actual offerings were made by the family.

**MAU-TAI** When THOTH plays the role of the guardian of the HALL OF DOUBLE TRUTH, he is known as Mau-Tai. After the deceased has been judged in the Hall of Double Truth, he is called upon to reveal the secret names of the various parts of the door that opens into the next world. Once the deceased calls out the secret names, Mau-Tai begins his questions: "What is my name?" The deceased answers, "Sa-abu-tchar-khat." Mau-Tai asks, "Who is the god that dwells in his hour?" The deceased answers, "Mau-Tai." Mau-Tai asks, "Who is this?" When the deceased answers, "Mau-Tai is Thoth," he is allowed to pass through the door to his eternal life.

**MEDICINE, GODS OF** The gods of medicine were THOTH, HORUS, IMHOTEP, and ISIS, and one or all could be consulted, depending on the ailment. Egyptian medicine was a combination of magical spells, religious rituals, and the skills of the ancient physician. There was no clear distinction between magic and the remedy prescribed. The physician had a range of medicines to choose from—opium, myrrh, honey, and hundreds of plants and herbs—and he enhanced their healing power with magical spells. Sometimes, in the case of snake and scorpion bites, the physician turned to the gods. The following from the papyrus of Ani was to be recited while applying a remedy to the body of a person:

> I have come from Heliopolis with the great ones of the great house, the
> lords of protection the rulers of eternity . . .
> I belong to Re. Thus spoke he:
> "It is I who shall guard the sick man from his enemies. His guide shall be
> Thoth (patron of physicians) who lets writing speak, who creates the

Books, who passes on useful knowledge to those who know, the physician
and his followers,
That they may deliver the disease . . . that the physicians may keep him
alive.

The following magical spell was recited while applying remedies to a sick person:

> Loosened [free] is he who is loosened by Isis.
> Loosened was Horus by Isis of the evil he felt when his brother Set
> Killed his father Osiris.
> O Isis, great in sorcery,
> Mayest thou loosen me
> Mayest thou deliver me from everything evil and vicious and
> red . . . [perhaps in the hope that the bandaged wound was healing]

**MEHURT** ⸻ (MEHET-WERET) The great celestial cow who gave birth

Mehurt, the great cow goddess of the sky, is said to be the mother of the sun god Re and mistress of the "ocean of the sky." Her name means "the great flood." *(Photograph by Pat Remler)*

to the "ocean of the sky," Mehurt was said to be the birth mother of the sun god RE. Because of this, she is associated with NUT, the sky goddess who gives birth to the sun at the dawn of each day. When Re was born, Mehurt carried him between her horns as a sun disk, and she became associated with HATHOR, whose crown is a sun disk between her horns. Later this became the crown of ISIS.

Mehurt is almost always shown as a cow, and her name means "the great flood." Her representations are easily confused with Hathor, because each is often shown as a recumbent cow resting on a reed mat, a sun disk between the horns.

In the OLD KINGDOM (2686–2181 B.C.), Mehurt appears in the PYRAMID TEXTS of Unas: "Unas has come to his pools which are on the banks of the canal of Mehurt, at the place where offerings flourish, and fields on the horizon, and he has made his garden flourish on the banks of the horizon."

By the NEW KINGDOM (1550–1069 B.C.), Mehurt had become a goddess of rebirth, especially for those souls hoping to resurrect in the NETHERWORLD.

The BOOK OF THE DEAD (Chapter 27) tells us, "I behold Re who was born yesterday from the goddess Mehurt . . . it is the watery abyss of heaven . . . it is the image of the eye of Re in the morning at his daily birth. Mehurt is the eye of Re."

In another myth Re claims to have created Mehurt with the help of Isis and her MAGICAL SPELLS.

When TUTANKHAMEN'S tomb was opened in 1922, a funerary couch was found in his tomb in the shape of the celestial cow. Mehurt was there to assist him when he entered the Netherworld. As a goddess of rebirth and resurrection, Mehurt evolved into a patron or guardian of the necropolis on the west bank of the NILE at Thebes.

**MEMPHIS (MEN-NEFER)** Ancient capital city of Egypt, called "white walls" in the Old Kingdom (2686–2181 B.C.) and home of the Memphite Triad: PTAH, SEKMET, and their son NEFERTUM. Memphis was established shortly after the unification of Upper and Lower Egypt by NARMER and remained the administrative center for most of Egypt's long history, during which time temples, chapels, and shrines were dedicated to most of the major gods at Memphis.

**MEMPHITE TRIAD** See FAMILIES OF THE GODS.

**MENAT** A necklace or broad collar with several rows of beads joined in the back by a counterpoise, which helped to hold the necklace in place. Originally the menat was a symbolic necklace sacred to HATHOR

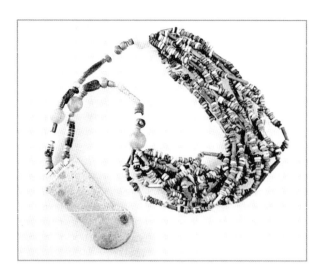

The menat necklace was not worn but was carried by Egyptian women as a sign of their devotion to Hathor. *(Photo by Russell Rudzwick)*

and her son IHY, who were often shown holding the menat and a SISTRUM. As a divine symbol of Hathor the menat was believed to have healing powers, and Hathor, is often shown on tomb walls presenting a menat to the king. One of Hathor's many titles was the "Divine Menat." During the Nineteenth Dynasty (1295–1186 B.C.), amulets were made in the shape of the menat and placed in the tomb with the deceased.

**MENES** See NARMER.

**MENHIT** A foreign war goddess, Menhit is the wife of ONOURIS (Anhur), both of whom may have originated in Nubia. Her name identifies her as a goddess of violence; it means "she who massacres." Associated with SEKHMET, Menhit was seen as a feline goddess and often represented as a lioness. The Egyptian army believed that Menhit rode in front of them to vanquish Egypt's enemies with fiery arrows. She was worshipped in Upper Egypt as the wife of KHNUM and the mother of HEKA.

**MENYU** An ancient god of the desert, Menyu was said to be the son of ISIS. Worshipped at Coptos, Menyu is mentioned on the PALERMO STONE.

**MERET-SEGER (MERT-SEKERT)** The snake-headed goddess of solitude, Meret-Seger's name means "she who loves silence." She was associated with OSIRIS, god of the dead. Meret-Seger, the serpent whose domain was the Theban desert, was said to be the incarnation and guardian of the peaks above the village of the workers who built the royal tombs in the VALLEY OF THE KINGS. The workers in the village of Deir el Medina were devoted to Meret-Seger and took her as their patron deity. Where she appears on the walls of the tombs of Ramses VI and Ramses IX, she wears the AMENTET headdress, signifying the "west"—a feather resting on a standard.

A votive stele dedicated to Meret-Seger, now in the Egyptian Museum in Turin, Italy, calls her Lady of Heaven and Mistress of the Two Lands and portrays her as being both sweet and ferocious. All on earth are warned to "Beware of the Peak of the West," the name by which she was known.

**MEROE** (MEROITIC PERIOD 270 B.C.–A.D. 350) The last city in Africa (in modern Sudan) where ancient Egyptian religion was practiced. As Egypt grew weak in Dynasty XXV (747–568 B.C.), Nubia grew strong and took control of Egypt. Its rulers were called the Kushite kings in the ancient world, and the "pious kings of Kush" are mentioned in the Bible. When the Kushite kings were defeated some 60 years later, their army retreated south to GEBEL BARKAL. Eventually the Kushite royal court moved even farther south to Meroe, near the sixth CATARACT (130 miles north of modern Khartoum). Isolated from Egypt, which was successively invaded by the Persians, Greeks, and Romans, the Kushite royal court at Meroe continued to practice the religion of ancient Egypt, adding a few gods of its own (see APEDEMAK and DEDUN).

Meroe grew into a vast trading center for exotic goods from central Africa, and Meroitic society became a blend of ancient Egyptian and African culture. Kushite queens were powerful figures in the court and played an important role in determining who the next king or queen would be. They could rule the kingdom and have their own pyramids. As the city of Meroe grew and prospered, Kushite royalty built palaces, temples, and pyramids and worshipped Egyptian gods for the next 500 years.

Over time, the Kushite kingdom replaced Egyptian HIEROGLYPHS with a Meroitic script that has never been fully translated. Meroitic script had 23 symbols, and, like Egyptians hieroglyphs, Meroitic is written in both hieroglyphs and a cursive script. Some of the Meroitic alphabet is similar to Egyptian hieroglyphs, but the spoken language was quite different. Meroitic inscriptions have puzzled Egyptologists for more than 100 years, for although they know the sound of each letter, the grammar and vocabulary remain a mystery.

Another Kushite mystery was the location of the burial chamber in the Nubian pyramids. Smaller and closer together than Egyptian pyramids, Nubian pyramids were found to be solid, filled with rubble, and without rooms that could serve as a burial chamber. Eventually burial chambers were discovered in shafts dug in front of the pyramids. Three groups of pyramids were constructed as the burial site for Kushite royalty. The last and fourth pyramid site in Africa was built at Meroe sometime around A.D. 350. Shortly after that, the army of Axum, a rival city (located in what is present-day Ethiopia), invaded and destroyed the city.

**MESENTY** Meaning "Lord of all Creation," Mesenty was one of the titles of the god PTAH.

**MESKHENET** The overseer of childbirth, the goddess Meskhenet determined the destiny of a child when it was born. She had the unusual distinction of being portrayed with her head emerging from two bricks. Women in ancient Egypt gave birth sitting on a birthing stool or squatting on birthing bricks, so the bricks represented the goddess of childbirth. Meskhenet, mentioned in the Westcar Papyrus, a magical papyrus with tales about the Old Kingdom, is one of five deities who assist the expectant mother Rudjedet when she is about to deliver triplets. The goddesses Meskhenet, ISIS, NEPHTHYS, and Heket carried a SISTRUM and MENAT and attended the mother. The fifth god was KHNUM, the ram-headed god.

Magical spells link the four goddesses with the four birthing bricks. Isis stands in front of the mother, while her sister Nephthys stands behind. Heket hastens the birth, and Meskhenet transforms herself into the birthing stool or bricks when the child is born. During some periods of history, Meskhenet was identified with HATHOR.

**MESTI** (IMSETY, IMESTY) One of the FOUR SONS OF HORUS and protector of the internal organs of the mummy, Mesti was guardian of the liver and was portrayed with a human head.

**METTERNICH STELE** A magical carved stone tablet (stele) commissioned during the reign of Nectanebo II (360–343 B.C.), the last native Egyptian king of Egypt, the Metternich stele is inscribed with myriad gods, mythological beings, and spells to prevent or cure poisonous bites and stings. The Metternich Stele tells the story of Isis after the death of OSIRIS and of her magical intervention when a

Metternich Stele: Water poured over the magic carvings was believed to have healing powers.

scorpion bites the infant Horus. Although a papyrus now in the Brooklyn Museum in New York deals specifically with the symptoms and remedies for snakebites, Egyptian medical papyri generally do not list extensive medical treatments for scorpion stings or snakebites. Judging from the number of magical spells discovered to ward off or to cure venomous bites, it seems that magic was the preferred method of treatment, and it demonstrates how fearful the Egyptians were of venomous bites. Children were especially vulnerable, and small wooden plaques inscribed with magical spells were kept in the homes to protect the family. In mythology the sun god RE nearly died from the bite of a snake created by ISIS, and the infant HORUS was stung by a scorpion when he was hidden in a papyrus thicket. THOTH provided Isis with a magical formula to restore her son.

The Egyptians inscribed magical formulas on stone stelae called cippus or "Cippus of Horus," which were placed in front of tombs and temples to protect the deceased and their families from evil spirits manifested as snakes, scorpions, and venomous reptiles. Water poured over the cippus ran into a basin and was drunk for its magical properties. The largest "Cippus of Horus" is the Metternich Stele, named for Prince Metternich, who received it as a gift from the ruler of Egypt, Muhammad Ali Pasha, in the early 1800s. The stele, a hard black stone with a rounded top, is inscribed on both sides. On the front (obverse) is a sculpted figure of Harpocrates, Horus the child, who stands on a crocodile and grasps serpents, scorpions, and hippopotami in his hands. The stele was made for Ankh-Psamtek, the son of lady Tent-Het-Nub, prophet of Nebun, overseer of Temt and scribe of Het. Inscriptions on the stele tell us that it was commissioned to protect the people who worked in a particular building, perhaps a temple, from scorpion stings. The front, back and sides of the stele are covered with the images of more than 300 different gods. The five separate spells carved on the stele are to be recited to counteract a venomous bite. The spells call upon Apep the giant serpent to vomit venom so the victim will also vomit the venom from his bite. Spells call upon Isis, in her many guises, for she was reputed to know the antidote for every poison. The Metternich Stele is now in the Metropolitan Museum of Art in New York.

**MIDDLE KINGDOM** The third major historic period of six in Egyptian history (Predynastic, OLD KINGDOM, Middle Kingdom, NEW KINGDOM, Late,

and Ptolemaic), the Middle Kingdom (2055–1650 B.C.) was a time of recovery and transformation.

After the collapse of the Old Kingdom, the pyramids were opened and robbed, and the PYRAMID TEXTS were no longer a secret. This caused a change in the funerary practices of the Middle Kingdom. Based on the Pyramid Texts, a series of magical spells and prayers called COFFIN TEXTS were inscribed on Middle Kingdom wooden coffins. A coffin from el-Bersha (c. 2000 B.C.) prepared for the steward Seni is decorated with a text called the BOOK OF TWO WAYS. It describes the realm of the dead and the sun god's journey as he travels in his solar boat by water and by land. Middle Kingdom royalty and nobility inscribed texts on their coffins to help them in their journey to the next world.

The god AMUN was worshipped prominently during the Middle Kingdom (and would continue to be the primary god throughout the New Kingdom) and inspired the construction of the KARNAK TEMPLES. The temples for PTAH in MEMPHIS, MIN in KOPTOS, and OSIRIS in ABYDOS were also built or expanded. Several successful military campaigns were launched to occupy NUBIA and Libya. These conquered populations further enriched Egyptian mythology, as their own gods, goddesses, and beliefs were blended into Egypt's religious culture.

Invasion by the HYKSOS brought the prosperous Middle Kingdom–era to an end, with years of civil unrest and strife before the "golden age" of the New Kingdom began.

**MIN** An early fertility god, Min was responsible for the fecundity of the fields and animals in ancient Egypt. The earliest sign for Min was a fetish, an object believed to have magical properties and that resembled a door bolt. But later Min was represented as a partially mummiform figure who holds his erect phallus, a symbol of fertility, with his left hand while his right hand holds a raised FLAIL to smite his enemies. Min wears a flat crown with two tall plumes and streamers hanging down. From the Old Kingdom (2686–2181 B.C.) on, he was associated with long-leafed lettuce, which usually was found on his offering table. The PYRAMID TEXTS refer to Min as "he Whose Arm is Raised in the East." Min's cult center was at KOPTOS, and excavations at the temple site have produced three colossal statues carved in limestone that may be the earliest sculptures of the god. They are now in the Ashmolean Museum in Oxford, England.

In the Middle Kingdom (2055–1650 B.C.), the attributes of Min and HORUS, the falcon god, were linked. Horus was seen as the god of the eastern Delta, Min was the god of the eastern desert, and the new god was called Min-Horus, the protector of mining expeditions into the Sinai.

During the pharaoh's coronation celebration in the New Kingdom (1550–1069 B.C.), an elaborate procession and feast honored Min so that his virility would be passed to the new pharaoh. The festival is recorded on the second pylon of the RAMESSEUM, the mortuary temple of Ramses II (1279–1213 B.C.), and also in Ramses III's temple at Medinet Habu in Thebes, which shows Ramses III in a palanquin (carrying chair) leaving the royal palace in a grand procession to the temple. The statue of Min sits in his shrine and is carried by priests with long poles over their shoulders that support the shrine. When they reach the public area, two priests holding a linen curtain hide the statue of Min from view while other priests chant hymns. Then the queen appears with the "White Bull," an animal sacred to Min, and they worship the king's ancestors before the coronation. Toward the end of the celebration, four sparrows are set free to fly to the four corners of the land and announce the new sovereign. In Thebes, the great god AMUN was at various times associated with Min as well.

**MNEVIS BULL**   One of the most important animal cults in the ancient world, the Mnevis bull, identified by its black hide, was one of three bulls worshipped in Egypt (see APIS and BUCHIS). Its cult center was at HELIOPOLIS, the city called "On" in the Bible, where the Mnevis bull was venerated, mummified, and buried. The Mnevis was associated with the cult of Re-Atum and, as such, it wore a gold sun disk and *uraeus* (cobra head) mounted between its horns. There was only one Mnevis Bull alive at any one time.

HESAT was the mythological mother of the Mnevis who, among other honors, was considered the earthly incarnation of the sun god. Although Heliopolis has been extensively excavated, the great necropolis of the Mnevis bulls has never been found. When a bull died, it was given full funerary rites, mummification, and burial with jewelry and USHABTIS (servant statues). Of the many Mnevis bulls that must have lived, only two burials have been discovered. Unfortunately, both tombs, which were simple pits dug in the ground and lined with polished stones, had been flooded and the bodies of the mummified bulls destroyed.

The Mnevis bull was one of the few traditional gods recognized by the heretic king, AKHENATEN. On one of the boundary stele he erected for his new city in the desert, Akhenaten states that he will prepare a tomb for the sacred bull in the cliffs east of the city. During Egypt's Late period (747–332 B.C.), when the interpretation of ORACLES became an important part of the religion, the role of the Mnevis shifted to become an intermediary in interpreting messages from the gods.

**MONTU**   The falcon-headed god of war, Montu was originally worshipped in Hermonthis, a cult center near THEBES. During the Middle Kingdom (2055–1650 B.C.), Montu grew in prominence as the warrior kings, battling for supremacy, gained victory after victory. Montu was much favored by the military, and several Eleventh Dynasty kings took the name *Montu-hotep*, meaning "Montu is pleased." Montu is shown as a man with a falcon's head wearing a solar disk and two tall feather plumes as his crown. His consorts were two local Theban goddesses, Rattawy and Tjenenyet. His sacred animal, a white bull with a black face, was later called the BUCHIS bull. Temples were dedicated to Montu at KARNAK, ARMANT, Medamud, and Tod. The sanctuary at Medamud, northeast of Thebes, was dedicated by Senwosret III (1874–1855 B.C.) and continued to be active during the Greco-Roman period. Tod, located south of Thebes, was dedicated by Senwosret I (1972–1926 B.C.) and also continued as an active temple through the Greco-Roman period, but Montu was no longer as important when AMUM became the leading deity in Thebes.

**MOON GODS**   See AAH, AAH-DJHUTY, and KHONSU.

**MUMMIFICATION**   The rituals surrounding mummification are closely tied to mythology and religion. The procedure arose from the need to preserve the body so the deceased could resurrect and become one with OSIRIS. Osiris, god of the dead, and ANUBIS, the patron of embalming, were the two most important gods associated with mummification.

Because the ancient Egyptians believed in resurrection, the physical body as well as the *BA* and the *KA*, parts of the soul, were essential for life in the next world. This was the reason for mummification—so the body would be intact when it resurrected.

In the earliest periods of Egyptian history, the deceased were simply placed in pits dug in the sand, then covered. Because the body was in contact with hot, dry sand, it dehydrated quickly, creating a natural mummy. Bacteria acting on soft tissue cause bodies

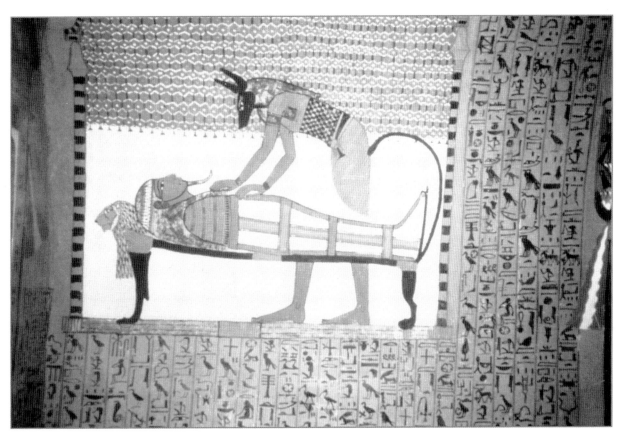

Anubis, the god of embalming, prepares a mummy. *(Photo by Pat Remler)*

to decompose, but if there is no moisture, bacteria do not attack. Because the sand quickly absorbed the moisture in the body, mummification took place naturally. Later burials were more elaborate, and bodies were placed in tombs. No longer in contact with the dehydrating hot sand, they quickly began to decay. To ensure that the body remained intact, the Egyptians developed the art of mummification.

The status of the deceased person determined what kind of mummification was performed. The most elaborate form of mummification, reserved for the king and the royal family, involved complicated surgical procedures. Because the brain is mostly water, it had to be removed with special tools. The brain was one of the few parts of the body that the embalmers discarded, as the Egyptians believed that a person thought with the heart, not the brain.

Once the brain was removed, a small incision on the left side of the abdomen was made to remove stomach, intestines, liver, spleen, and other internal organs. The heart was left in place, however, so the deceased would be able to think when he resurrected in the next world and say the magical spells necessary to bring his body back to life. The internal organs were placed in four CANOPIC JARS with lids carved in the shape of one of the FOUR SONS OF HORUS: Mesti,

the human-headed son; Duamutef, the jackal; Hapi, the baboon; Qebesenef, the hawk. After the wrapped internal organs were placed inside the canopic jars with a fluid called the "liquid of the children of Horus" (a solution of water and NATRON), the jars were sealed and the priests recited prayers to invoke the protection of the four sons. The oldest example of canopic jars was a chest with four compartments found in the tomb of Queen Hetepheres, mother of Cheops, the builder of the Great Pyramid (2580–2566 B.C.).

When the organs had been removed, the body was placed on an embalming table and covered with natron, a naturally occurring compound of sodium carbonate, sodium bicarbonate, and sodium chloride—basically baking soda and table salt. Because a body is approximately 75 percent water, it took more than 400 pounds of natron and 35 days to dehydrate the body. When dehydration was complete, the abdominal and chest cavities were washed with palm wine and aromatic spices and often packed with linen soaked in resin so the body would retain its original shape. Sometimes sawdust or onions placed in small linen bags were used as packing material. The face was padded with linen in the cheeks and under the eyelids. Just before bandages were applied, the body was anointed twice from head to toe with oils mixed with frankincense and myrrh. A priest wearing a jackal mask recited prayers as the oils were poured on the body:

> ... thou hast received the perfume, which shall make thy members perfect. Thou receivest the source (of life) and thou takest the form of the great Disk, which uniteth itself unto thee to give enduring form to thy members; thou shalt unite with Osiris in the Great hall. The unguent cometh unto thee to fashion thy members and to gladden thy heart, and thou shalt appear in the form of Ra; it shall spread abroad the smell of thee in the nomes of Aqert ... Thou receivest the oil of the cedar in Amentet, and the cedar which came forth from Osiris cometh unto thee ...

> (E. A. Wallis Budge, *Egyptian Magic*)

Once the mummy had been anointed, the bandaging followed a precise ritual. In royal burials, when the fingers and toes were wrapped, individual gold covers were placed on each finger and toe for added protection. When the arms, torso, and legs were wrapped, the priests placed magical amulets in the bandages to protect the mummy until it resurrected in the NETHERWORLD.

**MUSIC, GODS OF**  See BES, HATHOR, and IHY.

**MUT**  The goddess whose name means "mother" in ancient Egyptian. Like HATHOR and ISIS, Mut was the symbolic mother of the pharaoh. Mut is associated with both the vulture and the lioness.

As a vulture goddess she is shown with the vulture headdress with the double crown of Upper and Lower Egypt. Her brightly colored red or blue garment is a linen sheath dress, sometimes with a feather pattern, and she carries a papyrus scepter. In her role as a lioness, Mut is associated with SEKHMET, who acted as the "vengeful eye of Re." The lioness-headed goddess Mut replaced AMUNET, the first wife of AMUN, and became his chief wife when he rose to prominence in THEBES. She is the mother of KHONSU, and together Amun, Mut, and Khonsu make up the Theban triad. Mut appears prominently in all the major temples next to her husband, and her sacred precinct was joined to the Amun sanctuary by a sacred road.

**MYSTERY PLAYS**  From the Twelfth Dynasty on, mystery plays were held at ABYDOS each year to celebrate the resurrection of OSIRIS. Temple priests reenacted the events in the life and death of Osiris. The opening scenes were performed outside the temple, in the open air, and groups of pilgrims, called "Followers of Thoth," joined the festivities. The most sacred ceremonies were performed inside the temple with only the priests in attendance. Each ritual had to be performed perfectly in order to ensure the resurrection of Osiris, which was closely tied to the death and rebirth of vegetation, and the rising of the Nile to irrigate the fields. The Mystery Plays assured the resurrection of Osiris and good crops for the next year and promised the Egyptians resurrection and eternal life.

# N

**NAMES** The ancient Egyptians attached great importance to names, for they believed names held the essence of a person. To know a person's true name was to have power over him. Mythology tells us that Isis tricked Re into revealing his true name when she grew weary of life on Earth and wished to join the gods in the heavens. His secret name was unknown to both mortals and gods, but Isis was determined to learn it and gain power for herself and her son Horus. When a drop of saliva from Re's mouth fell to Earth, Isis mixed it with soil and formed it into the shape of a poisonous serpent. One day as Re walked along the path, the serpent struck and bit the great god, and its venom surged through his body. Re cried out to all the gods of heaven to come to his aid, and Isis appeared with them. None of the gods could save Re. Isis bargained with the dying god, "Tell me your name, Divine Father, for the man shall live who is called by his name." The sun god tried to avoid giving his true name by saying, "I am Khepri in the morning, Re at noon, and Atum in the evening." As the venom grew stronger and pain wracked his body, Re revealed his true name to Isis, who then magically withdrew the venom from his body. Thus, by knowing the god's true name, Isis gained power over Re and was able to enter heaven to take her place among the gods.

When a baby was named, special prayers were recited to celebrate his or her birth. A mother might keep the true name of her child a secret and give it a second name that everyone knew, for to know a person's secret name was to hold power over him or her. In the Book of the Dead, Osiris is said to have more than a hundred names.

**NAOS** A shrine carved of wood or stone to hold the statue of a god or goddess, the naos was an important part of temple furnishings. Each naos in the temple was housed in a special chapel when it was not being carried in procession. During festivals and processions, a lightweight wooden naos that held the statue of the god was placed in the divine barque (boat) of the gods. The boat rested on long carrying poles and was carried about by the priests. Most shrines were made of wood, but one stone naos remains in the chapel at the Temple of Edfu.

**NAPATA** Ancient trade route city in Nubia 600 miles south of Aswan and home of Gebel Barkal, the pure mountain where the great god Amun was believed to have lived.

**NARMER (MENES)** Probably the first king of the First Dynasty (3100 B.C.), Narmer, or Menes as he is also known, founded Memphis, the ancient administrative capital of Egypt. He is the first known king to equate himself with the gods, raising himself from a mortal to demigod.

Manetho, an Egyptian priest in the third century B.C., wrote in *Aegyptiaca*, his history of Egypt, that a man the Greeks called Menes ascended the throne of southern Egypt in primordial times. Looking north, Menes saw another kingdom with people and language like his own. A war that had separated the adjacent lands for centuries presented Menes with a great opportunity. He fought his way along the Nile, through the swampy Delta, until he conquered the north, and he married princess Neith-Hotep. Menes was then crowned ruler of both the north and the south, the first pharaoh of Egypt.

Almost no artifacts of Menes have been found except the Narmer Palette and a mace head. The principal figure on the Narmer Palette is shown wearing the crown of Lower Egypt on one side and the crown of Upper Egypt on the other side. The hieroglyphs written on the palette call him "Narmer." The Narmer Palette, which shows the king and his accomplishments, is thought to commemorate the unification of Upper and Lower Egypt. King Narmer's name is one of the first to be written in hieroglyphs. The scenes on the palette narrate Narmer's leadership of a southern confederation, with processional banners representing various communities, to its successful conquest of the north. This conquest made Narmer the first ruler of unified Egypt. Except for relatively short periods of instability, the country remained a single entity throughout its long history. The Egyptians always called their country "The Two Lands," and their ruler was called "King of Upper and Lower Egypt."

**NARMER PALETTE** One of the most important discoveries in Egypt, the Narmer Palette is the earliest historical text commemorating the unification of UPPER and LOWER EGYPT. It also has several mythological references, including the Predynastic cow goddess, BAT, and it links the king with HORUS, the falcon god, and with an early form of a bull god. A ceremonial slate palette (c. 3100 B.C.), it is believed to commemorate the unification of Upper and Lower Egypt by King NARMER/Menes. The vignettes on both sides seem to detail the events of this conquest. On the first side (recto or front), on the top register, two cows' heads represent the early cow goddess BAT, and between them is the first example of a king's name written in hieroglyphs inside a *SEREKH*, or palace facade. In the center, Narmer appears larger than life wearing the tall conical white crown of his homeland in the south (Upper Egypt) and menacing an enemy with his mace. An attendant carries Narmer's ceremonial sandals, which may indicate that he is on "holy ground" or in the presence of the gods. In front of Narmer is a hawk standing in a papyrus marsh that appears on the back of the enemy in the north. Traditionally the hawk was a symbol for the pharaoh, and this scene shows the king as Horus dominating Lower Egypt to the north. On the bottom of the palette are the vanquished enemies.

The second side (verso or back) of the palette repeats the images of Bat with Narmer's name in the *serekh* between the cow's heads. The second register shows the victorious Narmer wearing the captured crown of the north and parading four nome standards with the symbols of the gods for each nome. Most curious is the third register, in which two mythological beasts with intertwined necks are leashed and held by two attendants. (These beasts seem to be of foreign origin and do not appear in other Egyptian art.) The intertwined necks of the beasts form a circle and depression in the palette, and this is where pigment would have been ground to prepare the eye

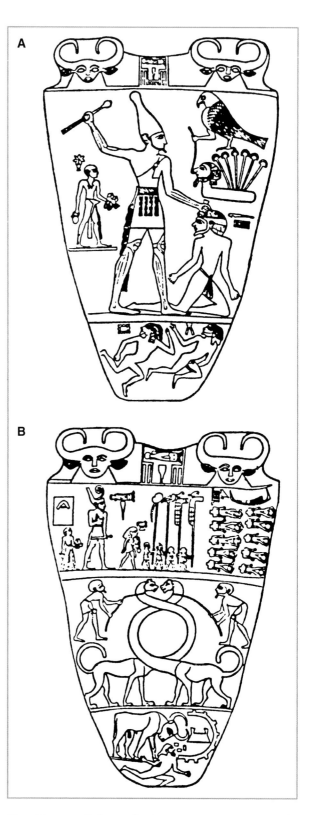

The Narmer Palette depicts King Narmer's unification of the northern and southern kingdoms of Egypt. *(Courtesy of Bob Brier)*

paint worn by the ancient Egyptians. On the bottom of the palette is the earliest representation of the king as a bull trampling his enemies. The Narmer Palette shows us the beginning of a tradition of art, religion, and mythology that was to last for ancient Egypt's 3,000-year history.

**NATRON**   Essential to the art of MUMMIFICATION, natron is a naturally occurring compound of sodium carbonate, sodium bicarbonate, and sodium chloride, or basically baking soda and table salt. But to the Egyptians it was the "stuff of the gods." A short way of writing "natron" was with the banner that stands for the gods, the small linen packet where it was kept, and the three circles representing that it came in chunks:      .

Natron was collected from the lakeshore in the Wadi Natrun, near Cairo. During mummification the internal organs were removed and placed on special dishes, then covered with natron and left to dehydrate before being placed in CANOPIC JARS. The body was placed on a wide embalming table so natron could be piled over the deceased. It was then left for 35 days, during which time the natron absorbed the body's moisture, leaving a dehydrated corpse ready for bandaging. Natron was also used as an offering to the gods, priests purified themselves with natron, and a small dish of natron was found in TUTANKHAMEN's tomb.

**NAUNET**   A principal goddess in the Hermopolis CREATION MYTH, Naunet represents water. She is part of the OGDOAD, or eight deities: four males, usually with frogs' heads, and four females with serpents' heads. The first god was NUN, the primordial ocean, and Naunet was his wife. In the Memphis creation myth, Naunet is the daughter of Nun (also PTAH), who took her as his wife, and their child is ATUM, the principal creator god of the HELIOPOLIS creation myth.

**NEFERTUM**   Nefertum was the god of the LOTUS blossom, one of the most important plants in ancient Egypt. The lotus is a water lily that closes its petals at the end of each day and forms a bud; when the Sun rises and warms the air, the lotus opens to greet the new day. Nefertum was called "the Blue Lotus Blossom from Which the Sun Rises" and "a Child of the Sun." Nefertum was also associated with the fragrance of flowers and with perfume.

Nefertum is mentioned in the PYRAMID TEXTS as the lotus blossom held before the sun god. When he appears as a child, Nefertum is sitting inside a lotus blossom; when he appears as a man, he wears the lotus blossom on his head. In the Delta (north), his mother was believed to be WADJET, a cobra goddess. In Memphis, he was believed to be the son of the lioness-headed goddess SEKHMET and her union with

the creator god PTAH. In another myth, BASTET, the cat-headed goddess, is his mother. The Greeks identified Nefertum with their god Prometheus, who brought fire to the people.

**NEGATIVE CONFESSION**   One of the steps in the "divine judgment," a ceremony to determine if the deceased was fit to enter the next world, was for the deceased to appear in the HALL OF DOUBLE TRUTH. Specific instructions in the BOOK OF THE DEAD tell the deceased how to behave when he or she enters the hall and faces the gods. He or she is to be pure, clean, dressed in fresh clothes and white sandals, eyes painted with eye paint, and body anointed with the oil of myrrh, before he or she proclaims the purity of

Nefertum, the lotus god and the son of Ptah and Sekhmet, is often shown as a child sitting on a lotus blossom. *(Drawing by Mary Jordan)*

his or her soul by reciting the negative confession as listed in the Book of the Dead. The deceased began by greeting the gods and then proceeded with his or her negative confession:

Hail to you great God, Lord of the Two Lands
I have come to you, my Lord,
I was brought to see your beauty.
I know you; I know the names of the forty-two
    gods,
Who are with you in the Hall of the Two
Truths,
Who live by warding off evildoers,
Who drink of their blood,
On the day of judging characters before
    Wennofer . . .
Lo, I come before you,
Bringing Maat to you,
Having repelled evil for you.
I have not done crimes against people,
I have not mistreated cattle,
I have not sinned in the Place of Truth.
I have not known what should not be known,
I have not done any harm.
I did not begin a day by exacting more than my
    due,
My name did not reach the bark [boat] of the
    mighty ruler.
I have not blasphemed a god.
I have not robbed the poor.
I have not done what god abhors,
I have not maligned a servant to his master.
I have not caused pain,
I have not caused tears.
I have not killed.
I have not ordered to kill.
I have not made anyone suffer.
I have not damaged the offerings in the temples.
I have not depleted the loaves of the gods.
I have not stolen the cakes of the dead.
I have not copulated or defiled myself.
I have not increased nor reduced the measure.
I have not diminished the aura.
I have not cheated in the fields.
I have not added to the weight of the balance.
I have not falsified the plummet of the scales.
I have not taken milk from the mouths of
    children.
I have not deprived cattle of their pasture.
I have not snared birds in the reeds of the gods.
I have not caught fish in their ponds.
I have not held back water in its season.

I have not dammed a flowing steam,
I have not quenched a needed fire.
I have not neglected the days of meat offerings.
I have not detained cattle belonging to the gods.
I have not stopped a god in his procession.
I am pure, I am pure, I am pure, I am pure!
I am pure as is that great heron in Henes.
I am truly the nose of the Lord of Breath,
Who sustains all the people,
On the day of completing the Eye in On,
In the second month of winter, last day,
In the presence of the lord of this land
I have seen the completion of the Eye in On!
No evil shall befall me in this land,
In this Hall of the Two Truths;
For I know the names of the gods,
The followers of the Great God!

If the 42 gods in the Hall of Double Truth accepted the negative plea, the deceased proceeded to the second part of the judgment, the WEIGHING OF THE HEART CEREMONY.

**NEHEB-KAU** A goddess associated with the ELYSIAN FIELDS, Neheb-Kau provided nourishment for the souls of the dead. She was often shown as a winged serpent with the body of a woman and carrying pots of food.

**NEHEM-AWAY** When the cow-headed goddess HATHOR was worshipped as the benefactress of the poor or deprived, she appeared as Nehem-away. Like Hathor, the SISTRUM was her symbol, and when Nehem-away shook the sistrum the sound was said to drive evil spirits away.

**NEITH** An ancient creator goddess whose cult center was in the DELTA city of Sais (modern San el-Hager in the western Delta). Like many of the goddesses of ancient Egypt, Neith had a dual nature, both fierce and gentle. She is mentioned in the PYRAMID TEXTS as a mortuary goddess, accompanying ISIS, NEPHTHYS, and SELKET when they guarded the mummy of Osiris. Neith's warlike nature was proclaimed by her symbols, two crossed arrows over a shield. Neith was the patron goddess of hunters and warriors, who asked for her blessing on their weapons. She was called "Mistress of the Bow" and "Ruler of Arrows." Neith is shown as a woman wearing the red crown of Lower Egypt. Her symbol, the crossed arrows and shield, have been linked with the early dynastic king Hor-Aha (3100 B.C.), possibly in connection with his dedicating a temple to Neith.

In her gentle nature, Neith was a patroness of weaving, and imparted her powers to Osiris through the mummy wrappings. In the New Kingdom (1550–1069 B.C.), Neith was known as "God's Mother who Bore Re Before Anything Existed," meaning that she was the first deity to give birth. On her temple wall was inscribed, "I am all that has been, that is, and that will be." She was said to be the wife of SET and the mother of SOBEK. Neith rose to prominence in the Twenty-sixth Dynasty when Sais became the capital of Egypt. HERODOTUS, the Greek traveler, in Book II of his *History*, describes a great festival honoring Neith called the "feast of lamps," in which hundreds of oil lamps were lit and burned all night in her honor.

Neith's importance as a creator goddess rose during the Roman period when an account of her part in the creation of the world was carved at Esna temple in Upper Egypt. The story goes that Neith emerged from the primordial waters, created Earth, and followed the flow of the Nile northward where she created Sais, her cult city. There are earlier references in the New Kingdom (1550–1069 B.C.) to Neith's activities as a creator goddess when she "molds the pharaoh" (Amenhotep II). A Twentieth Dynasty papyrus that relates the tale of the CONTENDINGS OF HORUS AND SET mentions Neith as one who gives good advice:

> BA-NEB-DJED urged RE to seek the advice of Neith in solving the eighty-year dispute between Set and Horus. Neith's advice is to award the throne to Horus, and to compensate Set by giving him the foreign goddesses *Astarte* and *Anat* as his wives. She threatens that if her advice is not heeded, her anger will be so great that she will cause the sky to fall to earth.

The Greeks identified Neith with their goddess Athena.

**NEKHBET**   The vulture goddess of Upper Egypt, Nekhbet was portrayed with wings spread and holding the SHEN sign of protection in her talons. Nekhbet is first mentioned in the PYRAMID TEXTS as a traditional mother goddess.

Later, Nekhbet became the vulture goddess favored by the early southern kings. Nekhbet, along with WADJET, the cobra goddess of the north, was one of the "two mighty ones," representing the unification of Egypt. The vulture and cobra heads sometimes appear side by side on the kings' crown as symbols for the unification of Upper and Lower Egypt. Nekhbet's large cult center at El Kab (modern Kom el Ahmer) today is almost completely destroyed.

**NEKHEN**   Nekhen was the ancient southern capital city called HIERAKONPOLIS by the Greeks. (Ptolemaic period 332–32 B.C.). Rich in mythology, Neheken in the south (UPPER EGYPT) and its sister city Pi in the north (LOWER EGYPT) represented the souls or BAs of the mythological kings who ruled in "the time before time began" (prerecorded history). The SOULS OF NEKHEN appear as a group of three jackal gods kneeling on one knee and with one arm raised in salute. The SOULS OF PE (the northern city) are shown with three falcon gods in the same kneeling position. It is thought that this was a gesture of praise in ancient Egypt and may have been part of a ritual dance or religious play where the priests wore jackal masks or falcon masks when they played the part of the gods.

**NEPER**   An ancient grain and vegetation god associated with OSIRIS during the Fifth Dynasty reign of Sahure (2487–2475 B.C.), the image of Neper is shown covered with grain. Neper is particularly associated with barley and emmer, a type of wheat, and his name is written with the hieroglyphic sign for grain, . After a particularly good harvest, the Twelfth Dynasty king Amenemhet I called himself "Beloved of Neper." Because grain could not grow without water, HAPI the Nile god held the title "Lord of Neper." In the COFFIN TEXTS, Neper is associated with Osiris in the inscription "[He is] living after he has died." Neper is mentioned in the second hour of the AMDUAT as piloting one of four boats that accompany the sun god Re on his journey through the second hour of the DUAT.

**NEPHTHYS**   Best known as a funerary goddess and sister of Isis, Nephthys's name means lady of the mansion. She appears in a slender sheath dress with the hieroglyphs for her name as her crown. Nephthys plays an important role in two early developments in Egyptian religion: She is part of the Heliopolitan creation myth, the ENNEAD, and she appears in the ISIS AND OSIRIS MYTH. She is the daughter of GEB and NUT and the sister of Isis, Osiris, and SET, who is also her husband. None of the evil that surrounded Set seemed to be associated with Nephthys, perhaps because all of her loyalties are with Osiris. As the wife of Set, she bore no children, and mythology tells us that she either made Osiris drunk with wine or disguised herself as Isis in order to conceive a child with him. Their son was the jackal-headed god, ANUBIS.

Nephthys, fearful of the wrath of Set, hid her child, Anubis, in the marshes. After the death of Osiris, Nephthys fled from her evil husband and joined Isis in the search for the body of Osiris. She

Nephthys, the sister and companion of Isis, helped Isis prepare the body of Osiris, the first mummy. *(Drawing by Mary Jordan)*

told her sister about Anubis, and the news of the child seems not to have caused a rift between the sisters, for Isis rushed to the Delta and found the baby.

Some myths say she adopted Anubis. From then on, Nephthys accompanied Isis in all of her trials, and Isis protected Nephthys from the wrath of Set.

Upon finding the body of Osiris, the two sisters embalmed it, changed themselves into birds and hovered over the coffin, protecting the mummified Osiris. Funerary motifs often show the sisters guarding and protecting the mummy. They became the guardians of coffins and canopic jars and are often shown with Nephthys at the head and Isis at the foot of the coffin with wings outstretched, symbolizing protection of the deceased. They kneel on the symbol for gold, a decoration on the CANOPIC SHRINE that holds the mummified organs. Nephthys is associated with the linen mummy wrappings sometimes called the "tresses of Nephthys." She appears in the PYRAMID TEXTS and in the BOOK OF THE DEAD, but perhaps because she played a subordinate role to Isis, there was no cult or temple dedicated to Nephthys.

**NETCHER** The hieroglyphic sign for god, pronounced netcher, represents a piece of cloth attached to a pole and is the emblem for divinity. The sign was often used to indicate the presence of an invisible deity, such as AMUN.

**NETHERWORLD** (NEXT WORLD, UNDERWORLD) Believed to exist beyond the confines of Earth, the Netherworld was the realm of the dead, a place not clearly defined, where the deceased would resurrect and live for eternity. For the Egyptians, the Netherworld seemed to have two parts: One part of the Netherworld was where the deceased would resurrect and spend a pleasant eternity, something like the Christian idea of heaven. The mythical FIELD OF REEDS seems to have been part of this Netherworld.

The other aspect of the Netherworld was the realm of the DUAT, the dark Underworld where the sun god and the souls of the dead journeyed for the 12 hours of the night. The AMDUAT, the guidebook for the souls of the deceased, tells us that as the sun approaches the gates of the Netherworld, they swing open and glorious light floods the entrance to the first hour. When the gates of the Netherworld swing closed, darkness prevails. A Middle Kingdom coffin text describes the Netherworld as unknown, concealed, and mysterious.

**NEW KINGDOM** One of Egypt's six historic periods (Predynastic, OLD KINGDOM, MIDDLE KINGDOM, New Kingdom, Late, and Ptolemaic), the New Kingdom (1550–1069 B.C.) is called Egypt's "golden age." During this period Egypt was prosperous, and the arts, architecture, mythology, literature and religion all flourished.

During the New Kingdom, a large group of religious texts were compiled and copied on PAPYRUS scrolls. They were called the BOOK OF THE DEAD, a series of instructions, sort of a travel guide, for how to get to the next world. Different versions of the Book of the Dead were available, and anyone who could afford one could have one in his or her tomb. During the New Kingdom, it was essential for anyone seeking RESURRECTION in the next world to have a copy of the Book of the Dead.

Many of Egypt's most famous rulers reigned during the New Kingdom, including AKHENATEN, RAMSES THE GREAT (Ramses II), and HATSHEPSUT. The cult of AMUN grew in religious power and political influence, as various kings showed gratitude for Amun's help in overthrowing the HYKSOS. The KARNAK TEMPLES were further developed in Amun's honor, along with smaller temples devoted to MUT, KHONSU, PTAH, and MONTU. The New Kingdom eventually faded, as conflict over succession to the throne added to the country's troubles with droughts, civil unrest, and corrupt officials.

**NILE** "Egypt is the gift of the Nile," proclaimed HERODOTUS, the Greek historian (485–425 B.C.), for it was the flooding of the Nile each year that allowed Egypt to thrive and prosper. HAPI, the Nile god, was believed to live in the caverns of the cataracts in the south and preside over the annual rising of the river, while KHNUM was the god of the river. Irrigation was the only means of watering crops in the bone-dry desert, and so important was irrigation to the Egyptians that they carved "nilometers" on the rocks along the riverbank to measure the height of the annual flood. Religious rituals were faithfully observed in order to ensure the rise of the Nile. One of the versions of the hymn to the Nile found on a papyrus fragment begins:

Hail, O Nile
You show yourself in the land,
Coming in peace, giving life to Egypt . . .

**NINE BOWS OF EGYPT** Representing the traditional enemies of Egypt, the nine bows evolved into an artistic device by which the pharaoh could symbolically trample and defeat his enemies. Seated statues of the king often show him with his feet upon nine bows carved into a footrest, each bow representing a different enemy.

Because Egyptian mythology put Egypt at the center of the universe, any group that was not culturally Egyptian and living in MAAT was a potential enemy. Early in Egypt's history, the enemies were most likely local warring tribes. By the MIDDLE KINGDOM, when Egypt had more exposure to the ancient world, the nine bows represented specific groups of people. Eventually they came to represent foreign nations. But these also changed from time to time. During the NEW KINGDOM reign of Amenhotep III, the nine bows of Egypt included:

1. The *Hau-nebu* (from the northeast coast of the Mediterranean)
2. The *Shat* (a Nubian group from the third cataract on the Nile)
3. The *Ta-Shema*
4. The *Sekhet-iam* (a people of the western oasis)
5. The *Ta-Mehu*
6. The *Pedjtiu-Sju* (nomadic people from the eastern desert)
7. The *Te-hennu* (the Libyans)
8. The *Iuntiu-seti* (a nomadic group, perhaps Nubian)
9. The *Mentiu nu Setet* (Asiatics living in Canaan)

Eventually the Meshwesh from Libya, the Assyrians, and the Babylonians were included among the nine bows of Egypt. While the traditional enemies were not always the same, the number nine seems to have remained constant.

**NO** (NO-AMUN) Biblical name used by prophets in the Old Testament for Egypt's ancient religious capital, THEBES.

**NOME GODS** During Egypt's Predynastic period, every settlement had its own local god or goddess. As the settlements grew and prospered, the country was divided into nomes, something like states, each with its own capital city. Some local village gods grew in importance and were elevated to the position of nome god. Each nome regarded its god as the "great god" and endowed it with many powers and attributes. Egyptian lists indicate there were 42 or 44 nomes, but the numbers seemed to change over time,

A list of nomes inscribed on the walls of Edfu Temple appears nearby.

**NORTH WIND, GOD OF** Refreshing breezes blowing across the desert were the work of Qebi, the god of the north wind, who blew from "the throat of Amun." Qebi is shown as a ram with four

# Ancient Egyptian Nomes

## Upper Egypt

| Nome | Capital | God |
|------|---------|-----|
| 1. TA-KHENT | Abu (Elephantine) | Khnemu |
| 2. THES-HERTU | Teb (Apollinopolis Magna) | Heru-Behutet |
| 3. TEN | Nekheb (Eileithyia) | |
| | Senit (Esneh) | Nekhbet |
| 4. UAST | Waset (Thebes) | Amun-Re |
| 5. HERUI | Qebti (Koptos) | Amsu, Min, or Khem |
| 6. AA-TA | Ta-en-tarert (Denderah) | Het-Heru (Hathor) |
| 7. SESHESH | Het (Diospolis Parva) | Het-Heru |
| 8. ABT | Abtu (Abydos), Thenit (This) | An-Her |
| 9. AMSU, MIN, OR KHEM | Apu (Panopolis) | Amsu, Min, or Khem |
| 10A. UATCHET | Tebut (Aphroditopolis) | Het-Heru |
| 10B. NETERUI | Tu-qat (Antaeopolis) | Heru |
| 11. SET | Shas-tetep (Hypsele) | Khnemu |
| 12. TU-F | Nut-en-bak (Antaeopolis) | Heru |
| 13. ATEF-KHENT | Saiut (Lycopolis) | Ap-uat |
| 14. ATEF-PEHU | Qesi (Cusae) | Het-Hert |
| 15. UN | Khemennu (Hermopolis) | Tehuti (Thoth) |
| 16. MEH-MAHETCH | Hebennu (Hipponon) | Heru |
| 17. ANPU | Kasa (Cynopolis) | Anpu |
| 18. SEP | Het-suten (Alabastronpolis) | Anpu |
| 19. UAB | Per-Matchet (Oxyrynchus) | Set |
| 20. ATEF-PEHU | Henensu (Herakleopolis Magna) | Her-shefi |
| 21A. ATEF-PEHU | Ermen-hert | Khnemu |
| 21B. TA-SHE | Shet (Crocodilopolis) | Sobek |
| 22. MATEN | Tep-ahet (Aphroditopolis) | Het-Hert |

## Lower Egypt

| Nome | Capital | God |
|------|---------|-----|
| 1. ANEB-HETCH | Men-nefert (Memphis) | Ptah |
| 2. KHENSU | Sekhemt | Heru-ur |
| 3. AMENT | Nut-ent-Hap | Het-Heru |
| 4. SAPI-RES | Tcheqa | Sobek, Isis, Amen |
| 5. SAP-MEH | Saut (Sais) | Net (Neith) |
| 6. KASET | Khasut (Xois) | Amun-Re |
| 7. . . . AMENT | Senti-nefert | Hu |
| 8. . . . ABT | Theket (Succoth) Per-Atem (Pithom) | Temu |
| 9. ATI | Per-Asar (Busiris) | Osiris |
| 10. KA-QEM | Het-ta-her-ab (Athribis) | Horus |
| 11. KA-HESEB | Hebes-ka (Cabasus) | Isis |
| 12. THEB-KA | Theb-neter (Sebennytus) | An-her |
| 13. HEQ-AT | Annu (Heliopolis, On) | Re |
| 14. KHENT-ABT | Tchalu (Tanis) | Heru |
| 15. TEHUT | Per-Tehuti (Hermopolis) | Tehuti (Thoth) |
| 16. KHA (?) | Per-ba-neb-Tettu (Mendes) | Ba-neb-Tattu, or Tettetet |
| 17. SAM-BEHUTET | Pa-khen-en-Amen | Amun-Re |
| 18. AM-KHENT | Per-Bast (Bubastis) | Bast |
| 19. AM-PEHU | Per-Uatchet (Buto) | Watchet |
| 20. SEPT | Qesem (Goshen?) | Sept |

heads and four wings or as a man with four heads of a ram.

NUBIA   Because of their long and tumultuous relationship, Egypt's and Nubia's mythology and religion are closely linked. Nubia has always been a geographic location, rather than a country. Nubia began just south of modern Aswan in Egypt and extended south into MEROE, part of modern Sudan. The name "Nubia" came from Strabo, the geographer, who while traveling in the area met a tribe called *Nubas* and so named the entire area "Nubia." The Egyptians called it *ta seti* (Land of the Bow), and the Bible calls it "Kush." Nubia extends over a vast desert, and in ancient times, the only way to get there was to travel up the NILE (south) and past the CATARACTS (treacherous currents formed by huge boulders in the Nile).

Nubia was home to extended families, or clans, ruled by local kings who controlled the gold mines. Egypt needed gold, and by the OLD KINGDOM (2686–2181 B.C.), her army dominated Nubia. The Egyptians built forts and opened trade routes to import exotic goods, animal skins, and ivory from deep in Africa and collected tribute in gold. Along with the military, traders, and tax collectors came an army of priests bringing Egyptian culture and religion with them. Egyptian gods and goddesses were similar to Nubian deities, and over time they merged, as the Nubians accepted Egyptian religion and mythology. Egyptian temples were built, often with a Nubian flare, and the Egyptians and Nubians worshipped their combined gods and goddesses in Nubia for 2,500 years.

The ancient Nubian capital, NAPATA, was famous for its holy site, GEBEL BARKAL, a sandstone hill that looked like a rearing cobra, or URAEUS. When Egyptian priests recognized Gebel Barkal as the mountain home of the Egyptian god AMUN, the site grew into an important religious center for both the Egyptians and Nubians.

Thutmose III (1504–1452 B.C.) erected a STELE saying Gebel Barkal was the "Home of Amun and the Throne of the Two Lands." The ancient Egyptians called Gebel Barkal *djew wab*: the "pure mountain," and it became one of Nubia's most sacred sites.

During Egypt's Twenty-fifth Dynasty, a Nubian king led his army north and gained control of Egypt. The first great Nubian king was Piye. Ancient records tell us that he swept down the Nile, "raging like a panther," and conquered Egypt "like a cloudburst" about 724 B.C. For the next 60 years, his family ruled Egypt.

Nubian kings were strong warriors and pious scholars. They revived religion, copied ancient texts,

were patrons of the arts, and restored ancient traditions in Egypt. When they died, the Nubian kings chose to be buried near Gebel Barkal and with PYRAMIDS just like the first Egyptian kings.

Four groups of pyramids were built by the Nubian kings and queens (in Nubia, queens had pyramids as large as their husbands').

1.  Pyramids of Gebel Barkal—near the holy mountain
2.  Pyramids of Nuri—across the Nile from Gebel Barkal
3.  Pyramids of El Kurru—south of Gebel Barkal
4.  Pyramid of Meroe—south of Gebel Barkal, below the third cataract

Nubian pyramids are different than those in Egypt: They are solid masonry, close together, and much smaller than Egyptian pyramids. For many years they mystified archaeologists, for there were no burial chambers inside, no treasure, and no hidden chambers. Egyptologist George Reisner, of the Harvard University and Museum of Fine Arts expedition, solved the mystery of where the kings and queens of Nubia were buried when he excavated in Nubia from 1906 to 1932. Reisner discovered that the burial chambers of Nubian royalty were separate from their pyramids. They were rock-cut chambers near (but not in) the pyramids. Instead of wooden coffins and stone sarcophagi like the Egyptians, Nubian kings were laid to rest on a stone funerary bed in the center of the burial chamber, and the walls were decorated with traditional scenes of the gods.

NUMBERS   In ancient Egypt the most important and magical number was seven. There are SEVEN HATHORS, seven *BA*s of RE, SEVEN SACRED OILS, seven orifices in the head, and the 42 judges of the HALL OF DOUBLE TRUTH are seen as a multiple of seven. The symbolism of numbers was believed to be as important as the numerical value.

Numbers were written in hieroglyphs. Seven different signs are used for writing numbers. Numbers one through nine are written with a stroke, as seen below. Numbers 10, 100, 1,000, 10,000, and 1 million each have their own hieroglyph:

1 = I, 2 = II, 3 = III, 4 = IIII, 5 = IIIII, 6 = IIIIII,
7 = IIIIIII, 8 = IIIIIIII, 9 = IIIIIIIII, 10 = ∩, 100 = ℓ,
1,000 = ⌇, 100,000 = ⌐, 1,000,000 = Ψ

The symbolism of numbers was as important as the numerical value. The following is a list of numbers and their corresponding symbols in ancient Egypt:

1 represents the beginning of time.

2 represents duality: man and woman, night and day, good and evil, and Upper and Lower Egypt.

3 represents the triad: the father, mother, and child, the family of the gods, and in particular Osiris, Isis, and Horus. Prayers were offered three times a day in the temples, and the day was divided into three parts: morning, noon, and evening.

4 represents the abstract concept of special relationships; it had to do with the four cardinal points, the four winds, and the Ogdoad whose number, 8, was reached by doubling four.

7 represents good luck.

8 represents the doubling of 4.

9 represents the pharaoh vanquishing the nine traditional enemies of Egypt, who are symbolized by "nine bows," and the nine gods of the Ennead.

During mummification, the numbers 7, 17, and 70 took on special significance; there were seven holes in the head, 17 body parts, and 70 days in which to prepare the body for burial.

**Nun**   A principal god in the Hermopolis creation myth, Nun is the god of primordial waters from which the creator god Atum emerged. He is one of the gods of the Ogdoad or eight deities: four males with frog's heads and four females with serpent's heads. Although he was referred to as "Father of the Gods," he remained a primordial god with no followers or temple. In the Memphite creation myth, Nun is associated with Ptah, and Naunet, usually his wife, is his daughter.

**Nut**   The great sky goddess Nut was part of the Heliopolitan Ennead—the first nine gods. Nut was the daughter of Shu, the air god, and sister and wife of Geb, the earth god. As the great sky goddess, Nut was represented as a woman whose body stretched across the Earth so she touched the eastern and

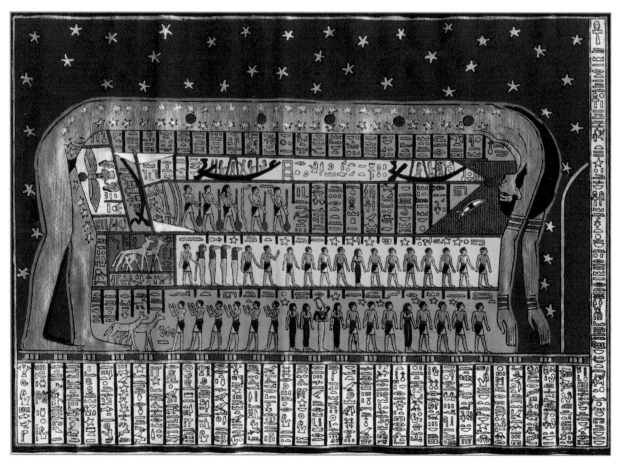

Nut, the sky goddess, swallowed the sun at night and gave birth to it in the morning. *(Courtesy of Bob Brier)*

western horizon with her hands and feet. Although paintings of Nut show her with ankles touching and her hands close together, it seems she was actually meant to touch the four cardinal points—north, south, east, and west—thus protecting all the sky.

Nut had several important associations. In the earliest texts, she was seen as having power over the gods. In some instances she is portrayed as cow goddess of the sky, but most often she is shown as a woman.

**Nut as a Sky Goddess** In the Heliopolitan Ennead mythology, Nut married her brother Geb. Their children ISIS, OSIRIS, NEPHTHYS, and SET became part of the ennead and later became the main characters in the ISIS AND OSIRIS MYTH. In one version of the myth, Nut was the wife of RE the sun god, who became angry when she slept with her brother Geb and cast a spell that prevented her from bearing children during any month of the year. With the help of THOTH, who won a bet with the moon and took some of its light to create five additional days at the end of the year, Nut was able to bear children on the five EPAGOMENAL DAYS, because they did not belong to any month. Nut is often portrayed with her body arched over Geb but separated by Shu the god of air.

**Nut and Re** As a sky goddess, Nut was closely associated with Re and the cult of sun worship, and one of her titles was "Lady of HELIOPOLIS." She was the goddess who swallowed the sun each day when it set and gave birth to the sun each morning when it appeared on the horizon; she was "Great One Who Gives Birth to the Gods." The tomb of Ramses VI in the VALLEY OF THE KINGS shows the slender body of Nut arched over the ceiling that represents the sky. The sun god sails in his solar barque (boat) along the body of the goddess during the day and disappears into her mouth at sunset for his nightly journey inside her body and is born again in the morning.

**Nut and Resurrection** Nut played an important part in the funerary beliefs of the Egyptians from the Old Kingdom PYRAMID TEXTS to the early Christian period. The Pyramid Texts tell us that the goddess enfolds the king in her soul and that she uncovers her arms for the monarch, both allusions to the funeral of the king. Further texts make reference to Nut as the king's "coffin," "sarcophagus," and "tomb." Her role as a protective goddess extends from the pharaoh to his courtiers in the Middle Kingdom (2055–1650 B.C.), when her image began to be painted on the inside of coffin lids. In the New Kingdom (1550–1069 B.C.) BOOK OF THE DEAD illustrations, Nut has risen from the NETHERWORLD and appears as a goddess rising from a sycamore tree. Nut was called "the Mistress of All Above for All Eternity" and her image, in a star-patterned dress, appeared on the second-century A.D. Christian coffin of Archon Soter from Thebes. Nut was not only a protector of the deceased; she also provided air for his or her breath and water and bread for his or her sustenance.

**OBELISKS** ⌂ ≋ ⌂ ▯ One of ancient Egypt's most impressive monuments, the obelisk is a four-sided stone pillar tapering to a PYRAMIDION (PYRAMID shape) on top. The name "obelisk" comes from the Greek word for meat skewer, and the Arabic word for obelisks, *messalah*, means needle. The ancient Egyptians called them *tekhen*.

Obelisks first appeared during the early Dynastic period (3100–2686 B.C.) in the temple of the sun god at Heliopolis, the city called On and Beit Shamsh (city of the sun) in the Bible. Obelisks were considered sacred to the sun god, because each day the first rays of the sun reflected from their pyramid-shaped tops. Obelisks seem to have evolved from a much earlier sacred stone called the BENBEN, which was associated with the BENU bird. These small obelisk shapes were a focal point of worship in the temples, but their exact purpose is not known.

Most obelisks are made of pink granite quarried near the southern city of Aswan. An unfinished obelisk found in the quarry reveals how such large stones were removed. The obelisk was pounded out with balls of hard stone called diorite, which is harder than granite. The diorite balls that have been found weigh about 12 pounds each, and they were used like hammers. The force of the blows eventually freed the sides of the obelisk, and then caverns were dug along the bottom until it was completely free. Since no chisel marks have been found on the unfinished obelisk, it is believed that most, if not all, of the work was done by pounding. A completed obelisk was placed on a barge in the Nile and towed to the spot nearest the site on which it would be erected. One of the walls of Queen HATSHEPSUT's mortuary temple at Deir el Bahari shows her twin obelisks end to end on the same barge.

It is believed that the Fifth Dynasty (2494–2345 B.C.) kings were the first to erect obelisks in front of their sun temples. The remains of one of these early obelisks, built of stone blocks, stands next to the sun temple of Niuserre, "possessor of the power of Re" at Abu Gurab (near Saqqara). It is rather squat in appearance and probably resembled the benben shape.

The oldest standing true obelisk, cut from a single block, dates from the Middle Kingdom under King Sesostris I (1965–1920 B.C.) and was erected at Heliopolis. The mate to this obelisk apparently fell during the Middle Ages, and the stone was reused in other building projects. Each side of the standing obelisk is inscribed with a single row of identical hieroglyphs that read:

> Horus, living-in-births, King of Upper and Lower Egypt, Kheperkare, Two Ladies, living in births, Son of Re, Sesostris beloved of the souls of Heliopolis, living forever, Horus of gold, living-in-births the good god Kheperkare. The first occasion of the Jubilee he made [it] to be given life forever.

Although obelisks were erected in many Egyptian cities, THEBES probably had the most and certainly the largest obelisks. The Theban obelisks were dedicated to Amun-Re, and most of them stood in KARNAK TEMPLE. Today only two are still standing: one of Thutmose I and one of Hatshepsut. Of the four obelisks Hatshepsut dedicated to "her father, Amun," the one still standing is inscribed:

> . . . She made as her monument for her father Amun, Lord of Thrones-of-the-Two-Lands two great obelisks of hard granite from the South, their upper part being of electrum, the best of all foreign lands. Seen on both sides of the river, their rays flood the Two Lands when Aten dawns between them . . .

Another has fallen, and only small pieces of the other two have been found. Hatshepsut's nephew

This nineteenth-century illustration shows the only two obelisks left standing at Karnak Temple. *(Illustrated London News)*

and successor, Thutmose III, had seven obelisks at Karnak, and the tallest surviving one is the Lateran Obelisk in Rome. Rome now has 13 obelisks, more than any other city in the world. The Romans moved many obelisks from Egypt in early Christian times but were unable to properly balance the monoliths, causing them to topple and sink into the ground. Several were excavated and erected again in the sixteenth century A.D.

Ramses II had more obelisks than any other pharaoh, but they were not the largest. Many of his obelisks stood in the Delta city, Pi-Ramses (Ramses's City) and have been lost, but fragments of at least 23 different obelisks have been found. Ramses II also erected two obelisks in front of Luxor Temple. One remains standing today, and the other was moved to Paris in 1832. The obelisk that now stands on the bank of the Thames in London belonged to Thutmose III. It is one of a pair that were dedicated to Amun-Re, erected in Heliopolis during the reign of Thutmose III (1479–1425 B.C.). In Roman times the pair was moved to Alexandria and placed in front of a temple

to Caesar. Thutmose's second obelisk was sent to New York in 1881 and now stands in Central Park. The obelisks in New York and London are sometimes referred to as Cleopatra's Needles. Another of Thutmose III's obelisks was moved to Istanbul, Turkey.

**OFFERING TABLE** At first offering tables were used only by the king, but during the New Kingdom (1550–1069 B.C.), they became an important part of the funerary equipment in private tombs. Offering tables were carved of stone and generally located in a chapel so priests or family members could easily make offerings to the deceased. Some tables were designed with channels cut in the surface so a liquid libation—water, wine, or beer—could be poured on the surface. Food and personal items were left for the *ba* of the deceased; often fine linen, cosmetic jars, and perfumed oils were included in the offerings. Images of favorite foods were often carved as a decorative border around the tabletop so they could magically become food for the *ba*. The hieroglyph for offering table was the *hotep* sign ⌓, which means "to be pleased" and represents a table with a cone of incense placed on it as an offering.

An offering table found in the Middle Kingdom pyramid of princess NeferuPtah (from the reign of Amenemhet III, 1855–1808 B.C.) bore an inscription that the king would make offerings to the gods so NeferuPtah would be well treated in the next world:

> May the king grant a wish to Anubis, Thoth, Osiris, and the great and small Enneads of the sanctuary of Upper and Lower Egypt. [May the offering be] thousands of loaves of bread, jars of beer, oxen, *r*-geese, *tcherp*-geese, *zeb*-geese, *ser*-geese, *menweb*-geese, alabaster jars, clothing, incense, and ointments, and all good things upon which the god lives for the *ka* of the king's daughter, Neferuptah, true of voice, lady of veneration.

**OGDOAD** The myth of the eight gods who inhabited the primordial waters of chaos before the world began, the Ogdoad is one of several CREATION MYTHS in ancient Egypt.

In the beginning, the Ogdoad existed only as a force of power but then took the form of frogs and serpents. Eventually they evolved into NUN and Nunet, who became water; HEK and HEKET, who became formlessness; Kek and Keket, who became darkness, and AMUN and AMUNET, who became invisibility or hiddenness.

In another version of the myth, the eight Ogdoad gods merged to become the cosmic egg that was fertilized by Amun when he was still a serpent. Yet another myth says Amun laid the cosmic egg and it hatched into the sun god.

The myth of the Ogdoad originated in Hermopolis, an important cult center for religion and magic. Because they believed the sun god was born there, the priests of Hermopolis claimed to have the first sunrise in the world.

**OLD KINGDOM** The second of six historic periods in ancient Egypt (Predynastic, Old Kingdom, MIDDLE KINGDOM, NEW KINGDOM, Late, and Ptolemaic), the Old Kingdom (2686–2181 B.C.) was a time of prosperity in Egypt because there was strong central government and a king with absolute power.

The Old Kingdom was an era of great achievement. Mythological tales arose, the notion of "divine kingship" was established, and PYRAMIDS were built—

the STEP PYRAMID at SAQQARA and the Great Pyramid complex on the Giza plateau. A new literature was born—a group of magical spells called PYRAMID TEXTS. Fifth and Sixth Dynasty kings carved magical spells on the walls of their pyramids to help them get to the next world. This was the first time an official version of life after death was recorded in ancient Egypt, though only the king was allowed to have magical texts in his pyramid.

With the death of King Pepi II, the era of the Old Kingdom was brought to a dramatic close. Pepi's advanced age (he is believed to have been around 100 when he died) made him ineffectual in his final years as ruler. This weakened government, as well as famine and drought across Egypt, caused great unrest, until the civilization finally collapsed into anarchy and chaos. The pyramids were robbed and left open, and the magical spells were no longer a secret, the consequences of which became very important in the Middle Kingdom.

**ON** The Egyptian city HELIOPOLIS, the ancient cult center of the sun god, is the biblical city On. The ancient site is about five miles northeast of modern Cairo. Two legends have grown up around a "Virgin's Tree" growing in this area. The oldest is the myth that Isis suckled the infant Horus under a tree in the Delta near the city of On. Later a "Virgin's Tree" (now located on Sharia el-Qaffasin in modern Heliopolis or ancient On) came to represent the story of Isis suckling Horus. A Christian version of the story is that the holy family rested under this tree during their flight into Egypt. Another myth set in On tells us the sun god RE bathed each day at sunrise in a sacred pool; the Christian version of the myth says in this sacred pool the Virgin Mary washed the garments of Christ.

**ONOURIS** (also ANHUR, INHERT) Primarily a god of hunting and warfare, Onouris was often associated with other gods, and most often he is associated with the struggle between Set and Horus because of the spears, ropes, and lances he carries. One of his titles is "Lord of the Lance." Onouris is portrayed as a bearded god with four tall feathers on his skullcap crown, and he carries a spear or a rope. In the Middle Kingdom (2055–1650 B.C.), his cult center was near Abydos, and later he was worshipped in the Delta town of Sebennytos, where he became the principal god of that city. During the Ptolemaic period, Onouris was viewed by the Greeks as the Egyptian equivalent of their war god, Ares.

**ONOURIS-SHU** (also ANHUR-SHU) During the Late period (747–332 B.C.), the Egyptians associated Onouris with SHU, the god of air, and he was depicted as a man wearing a long kilt and a headdress made up of four long feathers. His consort was Mehit, a lioness-headed goddess. Onouris-Shu was popular during the reign of Nectanebo II (360–343 B.C.), who built a temple for him in the Delta town of Sebennytos.

## OPENING OF THE MOUTH CEREMONY

Of all the rituals performed on the mummy, the Opening of the Mouth Ceremony was by far the most important, for it ensured that the deceased would have breath in the next world and could speak and eat again. The ceremony was held in front of the tomb on the day of burial and involved more than a dozen participants. An officiating priest held a papyrus roll that described how the rituals should proceed. Members of the family played the roles of ISIS and her sister NEPHTHYS. A central character was called "The-son-who-loved-him," and lesser characters played the guardians of HORUS.

Before the ceremony began, the ground was purified with water from four vases representing the four corners of the Earth. Incense was burned, various gods were invoked, and a calf was slaughtered to commemorate the battle in which Horus avenged the death of his father, Osiris. In the myth, Set's conspirators, in dismembering Osiris's corpse, attempted to escape Horus by changing into various animals, but Horus caught them and cut off their heads. At the Opening of the Mouth Ceremony, various other animals were ritually killed, including two bulls (one for the north and one for the south), gazelles, and ducks. When the bull of the south was slaughtered, one of the legs was cut off and, along with the heart, offered to the mummy.

The closing act of the ritual was the ceremonial opening of the mouth. A priest took an implement shaped like a miniature adze (a carpenter's tool) and touched it to the mummy's mouth. He then said the last words before placing the mummy in the tomb:

> Thy mouth was closed, but I have set in order for thee thy mouth and thy teeth. I open for thee thy mouth, I open for thee thy two eyes. I have opened thy mouth with the instrument of Anubis, with the iron implement with which the mouths of the god were opened . . . You shall walk and speak, your body shall be with the great company of the gods . . . You are young again, you live again. You are young again, you live again.

One of the last rites in ancient Egyptian funerals was the Opening of the Mouth Ceremony, performed by the high priest so the mummy would have life and breath in the next world. *(Photo by Pat Remler)*

With this prayer, the Opening of the Mouth Ceremony was concluded and the mummy was placed in its tomb to await resurrection in the NETHERWORLD.

**OPET, THE FESTIVAL OF** One of Egypt's most important religious events, the festival of Opet celebrated the journey of AMUN from KARNAK to LUXOR Temple and the symbolic sexual union of Amun and the king's mother, so that she could give birth to the king's royal *ka*. The festival of Opet took place in the second month of the season of AKHET—the three weeks in summer when the Nile flood reached it crest. The cult statues of Amun and his wife and son, MUT and KHONSU, and statues of the king and his *ka* were carried with great ceremony along an avenue of sphinxes from Karnak Temple to Luxor Temple. A distance of about three miles separates the two temples. Along the avenue of sphinxes were several resting spots called "barque stations" or kiosks, so priests carrying the ceremonial boat with the shrine and cult statue could stop and rest. It was here that the people who lined the processional way could approach the statue of Amun, which remained hidden inside the shrine unless a breeze blew aside the curtain. When the procession reached Luxor Temple it was greeted with a joyous reception by various groups of dancers, singers, and musicians. The MAMMISI, or birth house, had been prepared as a place for the king to rest and experience a symbolic rebirth and rejuvenation and where the royal *ka* magically entered his body. His emergence from the birth house signaled the renewal of royal authority and affirmed the divine nature of the king. We have a great deal of information about the

Opet Festival because the Eighteenth Dynasty king Amenhotep III (1390–1352 B.C.) commissioned the Colonnade Hall at Luxor Temple, and his grandson TUTANKHAMEN decorated the walls with scenes from the Opet Festival. The scenes carved on the west wall show the procession from Karnak to Luxor, and the scenes on the east wall show the procession sailing downstream on return to Karnak.

**ORACLES** Cult statues were used to foretell the future and to obtain divine guidance. These statues, most frequently of the god AMUN, were kept in permanent stone shrines but were also carried about in portable shrines shaped like boats and made of gilded wood, much like the sacred boats the pharaoh sailed on the Nile during festivals. The portable shrines rested on two long wooden poles, carried on the shoulders of the priests during religious ceremonies.

According to various ancient texts, oracle statues could nod their heads, and some even "talked." Since no talking oracle has ever been found, it is not certain how this was done. Perhaps the priests manipulated the statue to make the head nod or spoke for the god from a hidden chamber. We do know that oracles were consulted for all kinds of questions. There is even a record of one having solved a crime.

The story of the oracle-sleuth is told on a papyrus in the British Museum. The crime took place in Thebes, the capital of Egypt during the New Kingdom, during the festival of OPET, in which the statue of Amun was carried on the shoulders of shaven-headed priests from the Temple of Karnak to the Temple of

Papyrus fragment showing priests carrying an oracle statue in a procession *(Photo by Pat Remler)*

Luxor. Various cult statues of the districts of Thebes also were carried from the HOLY OF HOLIES for the people to see, and the British Museum papyrus records that the statue of Amun from the Theban district of Pe-Khenty solved the crime.

During the festival, a citizen named Amunemwia appeared before his local oracle and reported a theft. Amunemwia's job was to guard the storehouse of a nobleman. Apparently, while he was sleeping on the job at noon, five colored shirts were stolen from the storehouse. Amunemwia asked the statue, "My god and beloved lord, wilt thou give me back their theft?" The papyrus states, "And the god nodded very greatly." Then the guard began to read a list of all the townspeople. When he read the name of the farmer Pethauemdiamun, the god nodded and said, "It is he who stole them." The farmer was present and denied the theft before the oracle. As an appeal, he went before the oracle of his own district and asked if he were guilty. The statue of Amun of Te-Shenyt agreed with the first oracle and condemned the farmer. When he again denied the deed, the oracle of Te-Shenyt ordered that he be brought before a third oracle, Amun of Bukenen, "in the presence of many witnesses." The papyrus lists the witnesses but is incomplete from there. The farmer probably was condemned a third time. We do know that he finally appeared before the oracle of Pe-Khenty during a later festival and the farmer appealed, "Is it I who took the clothes?" The god again nodded, and the papyrus records that the oracle ". . . inflicted chastisement on him in the presence of the townsmen." This finally broke the farmer's resistance. He confessed to having stolen the shirts and said, "I have them, I will return them." He was then beaten with 100 blows of a palm-rib and made to swear that, if he went back on his word to return the clothes, he would be thrown to the crocodiles. Thus, Amun of Pe-Khenty solved a crime.

Harsiese was a priest of Amun who wished to leave the god's temple to serve at the Temple of Montu-Re-Horakhty. There is no reason given for his wish to change temples. Usually such requests were not because of religious conversion but for more practical reasons such as a wish to be closer to one's family or to earn more money. Still, the priest had to ask the god Amun-Re to relieve him of his obligation.

Twenty shaven-headed priests carried the shrine to the Hall of Review where anyone could consult the oracle. When the statue came to PEMOU, he put forth his father's request. The god nodded in agreement and released Harsiese from his service.

Oracle statues hidden inside their shrines were carried on sacred boats during festival days. This block from a temple shows the boat resting on a base. It was carried by the poles extending under the boat. *(Photograph by Pat Remler)*

Oracles were not only for the common people; there are many accounts of pharaohs having consulted oracles. Thutmose III, in one of his inscriptions, mentions that when he was a young boy attending a procession, the statue of Amun noticed him and halted, and it was then that he knew he would become pharaoh. HATSHEPSUT, the female ruler of Egypt and the aunt of Thutmose III, stated that her famed trading expedition to the land of Punt was the result of an oracle's command.

Oracle statues not only gave advice, but they could also perform miraculous cures. One of the most interesting is recorded on a stele (stone slab) in the Louvre Museum in Paris. The stele told of a cure performed by Khonsu during the reign of Ramses II, but it was recorded almost 1,000 years after the event by a priest who believed the story should be saved for posterity. According to the text, Ramses II was in the city of Naharin, where the heads of all foreign countries came with gifts of homage. The king of Bekhten brought his beautiful daughter before the pharaoh, and he married her and made her his queen. Sometime later when the royal couple were in Thebes, a messenger arrived from the king of Bekhten saying that the king's wife's sister was ill with a sickness that had affected her limbs. The king asked Ramses to send one of his wise men to cure her. Ramses sent priests in charge of secret writings in the House of Life to cure the queen's sister, but to no avail. The king of Bekhten then asked for an oracle to be sent. Ramses presented the request to Khonsu, who was one of the most powerful oracles. Ramses said, "Oh thou good lord, if thou incline thy face to Khonsu-the-Plan-Maker, the great god, smiting the evil spirits, he shall be conveyed to Bekhten." The oracle nodded vigorously, and so Khonsu-the-Plan-Maker was sent to Bekhten. According to the stele the journey took 17 months. When finally the oracle was brought before the princess, the evil spirit that possessed her left immediately and she was cured.

Upon seeing how powerful the oracle was, the king decided to keep it in his country. He retained the statue for three years and nine months, until he had a vision. In a dream he saw the oracle coming toward him in the form of a golden falcon that flew toward Egypt. The king awoke in a fright and, taking the dream as an omen, ordered the oracle to be returned with a great retinue and many gifts to Thebes.

This story demonstrates that both foreigners and Egyptians believed oracles could heal the sick, solve crimes, settle legal disputes, and send prophetic dreams. Because they had such diverse capabilities, oracles were often consulted and played an important part in an ancient Egyptian's life.

**OSIREION** A unique temple dedicated to the funerary god, OSIRIS. Built of huge granite blocks similar to those used in construction during the Old Kingdom, the Osireion is situated on a man-made island behind the temple of Seti I at ABYDOS. This may be the cenotaph, or false tomb of Osiris, "He Who Sleeps in the Water"; according to mythology, Osiris's head was buried at Abydos. The walls of the Osireion are decorated with mythological scenes from the BOOK OF THE DEAD, the BOOK OF GATES, and other religious texts. Recent scholarship suggests that the Osireion was built during the Nineteenth Dynasty in the style of the Old Kingdom by Seti's grandson, Merneptah,

when he became pharaoh. A second Osireion exists in the vicinity of the Great Sphinx.

**OSIRIS** God of the dead, husband to ISIS, and father of HORUS, Osiris is the best-known deity of the Egyptian gods. The PYRAMID TEXTS tell us that Osiris is the firstborn child of the earth god GEB and his wife, NUT, the sky goddess. Given earthly rule by his father, Osiris brought agriculture and winemaking to the people of Earth, and in that capacity Osiris was called Wennefer, "the Eternally Good Being." Because of the jealousy of his brother SET, Osiris became the central figure in the OSIRIS MYTH, a story of envy and treachery. He has more titles and associations than any other god in the Egyptian pantheon. Osiris ultimately became the god of resurrection to whom all people prayed in the hope of attaining their own resurrection in the NETHERWORLD.

In the BOOK OF THE DEAD, spell 182 accompanies the illustration of the mummy on a bier (bed), and

The Osireion is the legendary tomb of Osiris. It was built from huge granite blocks similar to those typically used in the Old Kingdom, but new studies suggest that it was built later, during the reign of Seti I. *(Photo by Pat Remler)*

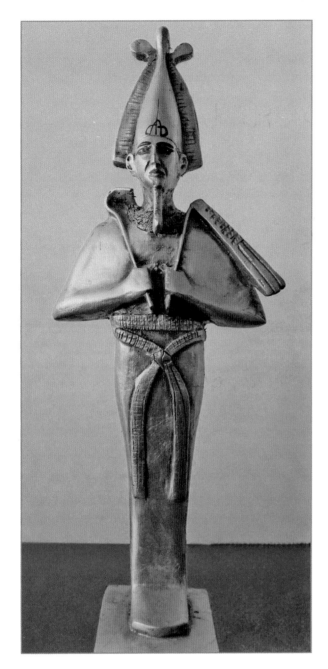

Osiris, god of the dead, is wrapped as a mummy. *(Photo by Pat Remler)*

the introduction says that reciting this spell will assist Osiris to breathe and to arise. The spell is intended to protect the deceased, who becomes associated with Osiris, who helps him resurrect in the Netherworld.

> Protection and Life surround him
> This god, guarding his *ka* soul, the king of the
>   Netherworld,
> Who rules the West, and triumphantly conquered
>   the heavens . . .
> Who shall endure for all eternity.

Osiris is shown as a bearded man wrapped like a mummy wearing an atef crown—a tall crown with a feather on each side. His hands protrude from his white mummy bandages and hold the crook and the flail, two symbols of power in ancient Egypt. His flesh is colored green when he is associated with vegetation and regeneration, black when he is associated with the Nile silt or the Underworld. Osiris was worshipped in a number of sanctuaries throughout Egypt—in the DELTA at Letopolis, Heliopolis, Memphis, Herakleopolis, and Hermopolis, but his largest and most important cult center was located at ABYDOS.

**OSIRIS BED**   A wooden frame in the shape of the silhouette of OSIRIS, the Osiris bed was a symbol of regeneration. It was filled with Nile silt and barley seed and placed in royal and private tombs during the New Kingdom (1550–1069 B.C.). When the seeds sprouted in the tomb, it was considered a symbolic resurrection of the deceased. An Osiris bed found in the tomb of Yuya and Tuya, the grandparents of AKHENATEN, was found to have produced a crop of sprouts that were eight inches tall. Osiris is mentioned in a mythological papyrus as "He Who Is in the Grain of the Gods." Osiris beds were also found in the tombs of TUTANKHAMEN and Horemheb, the last king of the Eighteenth Dynasty.

**OSIRIS MYTH**   See ISIS AND OSIRIS, MYTH OF.

**OSIRIS PILLAR**   An architectural innovation found in temples of the New Kingdom (1550–1069 B.C.), where the mummiform figure of OSIRIS, the god of the dead, is carved into one side of a four-sided pillar, to further honor the god. Osiris pillars can be seen in the mortuary temple of HATSHEPSUT at Deir el Bahri, and in the RAMESSEUM, the mortuary temple of Ramses II.

**OXYRHYNCHUS**   Characterized by its long snout, the Oxyrhynchus fish was the sacred emblem of the seventeenth Upper Egyptian nome. *Oxyrhynchus* is Greek for "long-nosed." According to the myth of ISIS AND OSIRIS, when SET hacked the body of his brother Osiris into pieces and scattered them, the phallus was thrown into the Nile and consumed by three fish. The Greek historian PLUTARCH describes the species of these fish in his book *De Iside et Osiride*, The Tale of Isis and Osiris. One is the Oxyrhynchus, and because this fish consumed the phallus of Osiris, it was considered sacred.

Priests were forbidden to eat any fish, and before entering a temple, a priest would recite the phrase, "I am clean. I have not eaten fish." In all of the offering scenes on tomb walls where tables are piled high with the finest foods, there are no fish included in the offerings—except in the tomb of Mena, in the Valley of the Nobles, where one fish appears on the table.

Although fish was a staple in the diet of ancient Egyptians, eating the Oxyrhynchus fish in the seventeenth nome was prohibited. During the Late period (747–332 B.C.), when the people of the seventeenth nome discovered that their neighbors in Cynopolis were eating the sacred fish, it caused a minor civil war.

**OZYMANDIAS** The Greek form of one of the names of RAMSES THE GREAT. In the first century B.C., the Greek historian Diodorus visited the RAMESSEUM, the mortuary temple of Ramses II, and described what he saw as the "tomb of Ozymandias." The name appears to be a corruption of one of the five names of Ramses, *usr-maat-re*. Diodorus's translation of the inscription on the colossal statues of Ramses, now toppled and broken, was the inspiration for the nineteenth-century English poem by Percy Bysshe Shelley, "Ozymandias:"

> I met a traveler from an antique land
> Who said:—Two vast and trunkless legs of stone
> Stand in the desert. Near them on the sand,
> Half sunk, a shattered visage lies, whose frown
> And wrinkled lip and sneer of cold command
> Tell that its sculptor well those passions read
> Which yet survive, stamped on these
>     lifeless things
> The hand that mocked them and the
>     heart that fed
> And on the pedestal these words appear:
> "My name is Ozymandias, king of kings:
> Look on my works, ye mighty, and despair!"
> Nothing beside remains: round the decay
> Of that colossal wreck, boundless and bare
> The lone and level sands stretch far away.

# P

**PADDLE DOLL** When discovered during excavations of MIDDLE KINGDOM tombs at Beni Hasan and THEBES (modern Luxor), paddle dolls were at first believed to be children's toys. But as more paddle dolls were discovered, Egyptologists realized they were related to mythology as fertility figures, placed in tombs to assure fertility in the next world. Linked with the popular fertility god BES, the dolls were almost always found in women's tombs.

There are many different styles, but all paddle dolls follow a basic pattern. Paddle dolls have short arms and no legs, and their bodies are elongated and paddle shaped. It has been suggested that paddle dolls resemble the MENAT, a counterpoise (a weight attached to a broad collar necklace to hold the necklace in place when it was worn) often carried by HATHOR. It is thought that the paddle doll and the menat may represent the body of Hathor.

Most paddle dolls are made from clay or wood and have long necks with tiny heads and are decorated with geometric designs and tattoos. One of the most distinctive features of the paddle doll is the elaborate hairstyle that all but dwarf its small head. Made from hundreds of clay or FAIENCE beads, the wigs are full and long and may have had some magical purpose now lost to us.

**PAKHET** (PASHT) A feline goddess whose name means "she who scratches," Pakhet is the guardian of the wadi (dry riverbed). In the COFFIN TEXTS she is called the "Night Huntress." During the NEW KINGDOM, Pakhet was worshipped at her cult center at Beni Hassan in Middle Egypt, where two rock-cut temples were dedicated to her. The larger of the two is well known as the SPEOS ARTEMIDOS, the grotto of Artemis. It was named by the Greeks, who saw Pakhet as a form of the Greek goddess Artemis. As a lion goddess, Pakhet was also worshipped with the other feline goddesses SEKHMET and BASTET. The

Eighteenth Dynasty queen HATSHEPSUT included this passage to Pakhet in her inscription on the walls of the Speos Artemidos:

> . . . Great Pakhet, who roams the wadis, resident in the eastern desert, seeking the rainstorm's paths, since there was no relevant libation-service that fetched water for her. I have made her enclosure as what this goddess intended for her Ennead, the door of acacia inlaid with bronze, in order that they might be in her register of festival-offerings . . .

**PALERMO STONE** A black basalt STELE carved on both sides, the Palermo Stone is the earliest known king's list. The Palermo Stone was seven feet wide and two feet high when it was carved in the Fifth Dynasty (2494–2345 B.C.). Unlike most Egyptian stelae, the Palermo Stone stands on its long side, so it is longer than it is tall. It includes names of mythical rulers before Egypt's historic period and continues to the middle of the Fifth Dynasty. The text is mythological in the sense that it lists rulers for thousands of years before HORUS, who (see CONTENDINGS OF HORUS AND SET) chose Menes to be the first mortal king of Egypt. The stele lists each king, the years of his reign, and notable events that occurred, such as the year of the Battle and Smiting of the Northerners, the year of the Second Occurrence of the Numbering of all Large and Small Cattle of the North and South, the year of the Seventh Occurrence of Numbering Gold and Land. The stele also chronicles the carving and dedication of statues of the gods, festivals celebrated, and the height of the inundation, the annual Nile flood.

Now fragmented, pieces of the Palermo Stone are in various museums: the Palermo Museum in Sicily, the Egyptian Museum in Cairo, and the Petrie Museum in London.

**PALETTE**  An important part of ceremonial and magical equipment in ancient Egypt, there were two different kinds of palettes: one for grinding minerals to make COSMETICS, and the other for holding a scribe's brushes and ink. Cosmetic or ceremonial palettes like the NARMER PALETTE were usually carved from greywacke, a dark slatelike stone, and were made during the Predynastic period (5500–3100 B.C.). Cosmetic palettes were usually in the shape of animals, often a turtle, but some represented MIN the fertility god. Whether magical or ceremonial, their primary use was to grind pigments such as malachite for green and galena for black, to make the eye paint worn by Egyptians and applied to the cult statues.

The scribe's palette became the hieroglyph for writing: 𓏞. The rectangle with two circles is the palette that contains the ink. The loop is a PAPYRUS cord that holds the reed brush or writing tool to the palette. Some scribe's palettes were purely ceremonial, used in temple rituals or as offerings to THOTH, the god of writing. Scribes used palettes carved from wood that was about 12 inches long and three inches wide. Each had a shallow groove to hold the reed pens and brushes and small circular depressions at one end to hold the red and black ink.

**PAN**  Ancient Greek god from the mountains of Arcadia, Pan was a playful god with a lusty nature who could become sinister if provoked. He was a god of the shepherds and their flocks, a fertility god, and a god of the woods. He was shown as half man, half goat, holding a seven-reed flute. When the Greek Ptolemies ruled Egypt, the Greek god Pan was associated with the Egyptian god, BA-NEB-DJED, a fertility god who is shown as a ram and is known as the RAM OF MENDES.

**PANTHEISTIC DEITY**  (Pan = all, theistic = gods)  A composite god or goddess that embodies all the divine power of the deities it represents. MAGIC played an important part in Egyptian religion, and it was by magic that the powers of individual gods could be combined to form a pantheistic deity. For example, when ISIS is shown with wings, she has all of her power and magic combined with the strength and power of her son HORUS, the FALCON god.

It was not so much that pantheistic deities were new gods joining the cosmos but that by using their existing powers, a new and stronger magic could be employed against a specific enemy. Because poisonous snakes and scorpions were so dangerous in ancient Egypt, a pantheistic deity was often called upon for protection from their bites.

**PANTHEON**  See GODS OF ANCIENT EGYPT.

**PAPYRUS**  Much of what Egyptologists know about Egyptian mythology, magic, religion, and medicine has come from ancient papyri. Many papyri are named for the person who found or owned them. All of the most famous papyri have been translated, and the following is a list of some of the best known:

**Abusir Papyri**  Three sets of fragmentary papyri written in hieratic (a cursive form of HIERO-GLYPHS), the Abusir Papyri were found in the mortuary temple of the Fifth Dynasty King Neferirkare at Abusir. Divided into various categories, the papyri give us a glimpse into the daily life of the priests who attended the mortuary temple. Priests were grouped into seven *phyles* or categories, each with different duties, and were called the "servants of the gods" and "the pure."

Listed on the papyri was a schedule of priestly duties showing which tasks were to be carried out at the king's mortuary temple. Some were scheduled for every day, some for every month, and additional rituals were scheduled during important festivals. Some of the duties included making offerings to the KA of the deceased, making sacrifices to the gods, and guarding various parts of the mortuary temple. Special rituals were performed on the specific festival days, such as the Festivals of SOKAR, god of the dead; the Festival of the Night of the god RE; the Festival of the Goddess HATHOR; and the Festival of the fertility god, MIN.

Along with the duties of the priests, there were jobs in the mortuary temple for scribes, physicians, hairdressers, and flute players.

Large tracts of land or estates were allocated to support the pharaoh's mortuary cult. An estate provided grain, fruit, vegetables, milk, wine, beer, fats, poultry, and meat offerings to the *ka* of the deceased pharaoh and the gods, and they were then used to feed the temple staff. The papyri also give accounts of furniture, funerary equipment, and financial transactions showing the flow of goods from the royal estates to the various temples.

**Papyrus Chester Beatty**  A mythological papyrus in the British Museum, one part of which relates the tale of the CONTENDINGS OF HORUS AND SET.

**Papyrus Ebers** Written about 1500 B.C., this medical papyrus is the longest and most famous of the medical papyri. A collection of bits of medical wisdom and magic, many sections are believed to have been copied from much older documents. The papyrus was discovered with another medical papyrus (the Edwin Smith Surgical Papyrus) in a tomb on the west bank in Luxor in 1862 and is named for the German Egyptologist George Ebers, who found it. The papyrus is now at the University of Leipzig in Germany.

**Edwin Smith Surgical Papyrus** Named for the first American Egyptologist, the Edwin Smith Surgical Papyrus is a compilation of medical advice and magical spells for dealing with trauma injuries. The surgical portion of the papyrus contains 48 cases dealing with injuries from the head to the spinal column. The front of the papyrus records the scientific approach to medicine, and on the reverse is an almost purely magical set of cures. The papyrus is almost 15 feet long and is a New Kingdom copy of an Old Kingdom text. It was purchased from an antiquities dealer in Luxor and given to the New York Historical Society when Smith died.

**Harris Papyrus** A mythological papyrus in the British Museum that relates the Myth of the Doomed Prince, a tale about love and loyalty when a prince goes in search of his destiny.

**Leiden-London Papyrus** A magical and medical papyrus listing complex rituals, the Leiden-London Papyrus was purchased in the early part of the nineteenth century in Alexandria. Today, half the papyrus is in the British Museum and half is in the museum in Leiden, Holland. Written in demotic, a late Egyptian script, in the third century A.D., the spells are a mixture of Greek and Egyptian mythology and medical advice.

**Papyrus Westcar** A mythological text chronicling tales of magic in the Old Kingdom. It tells the tale of Sneferu (Fourth Dynasty

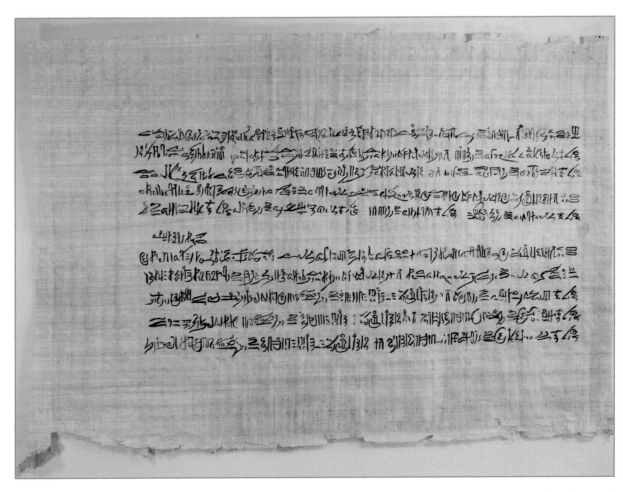

Papyrus was used like paper in ancient Egypt and was made from thin slices of the papyrus stalk. Sheets of papyrus were glued together to make long scrolls. *(Photo by Pat Remler)*

2552–2528 B.C.) and how he summoned his magician to part the waters when one of the palace maidens lost her turquoise amulet while rowing on the pleasure lake. Papyrus Westcar is in the Egyptian (Agyptisches) Museum in Berlin.

**Rhind Mathematical Papyrus** Discovered in Luxor on the west bank in a small chapel near the Ramesseum (the mortuary temple of Ramses II), the Rhind Mathematical Papyrus was purchased by A. Henry Rhind in 1858. The papyrus was written in about 1650 B.C. by a scribe named Ahmose, who notes that he is copying from an older text. Written in hieratic, a cursive form of hieroglyphs, the papyrus is divided into three sections: mathematics, geometry, and a collection of mathematical problems. Originally the papyrus was 18 feet long and about 13 inches wide. When it arrived at the British Museum, however, it was fragmented, and several pieces were missing. These were later discovered among the property of the New-York Historical Society.

**Turin Papyrus** Known as the Royal Canon of Turin, the Turin Papyrus dates from about 1200 B.C. and is a list of more than 300 king's names, starting with Menes and ending with Ramses II. The papyrus was written in the hieratic script and was the most complete chronicle of Egypt's monarchs through the Nineteenth Dynasty, including the length of each king's reign in years, months, and days. The papyrus was badly damaged during transportation to the Turin Museum, and scholars are still trying to piece together the fragments. It is, however, the most complete kings' list yet discovered.

**PAPYRUS PLANT** The papyrus plant was one of the symbols for Lower (northern) Egypt, and it grew in profusion in the swampy marshes of the Delta. Many of the most ancient mythological texts have been preserved on papyri. The plant not only provided fibers for ropes, baskets, and papyrus paper; it also represented the vigor, growth, and renewal of the country. As important as papyrus was to the Egyptians, there is no particular deity associated with papyrus other than Thoth, the god of writing.

The papyrus plant became scarce in Egypt for hundreds of years, and only in modern times has it

The papyrus plant grew wild along the banks of the Nile and in the marshy northern Delta. Papyrus stalks were used for making papyrus scrolls, ancient Egyptian writing paper. *(Photo by Forest and Kim Starr/Used under a Creative Commons license)*

been reintroduced and cultivated commercially in Egypt. Papyrus has tall, slender stalks with feathery green tufts on top and grows best in marshy areas around the Nile. When papyrus is harvested, it is cut just above the water level. The lower portion of the stalk makes the best paper. The stalk is peeled and the inner pith is sliced into strips from one quarter to one eighth of an inch thick, then placed on an absorbent surface with the edges overlapping. The strips are pounded with wooden mallets for an hour or two and placed in a press. The sap from the papyrus provides an adhesive necessary to glue the strips into sheets of papyrus paper. After the papyrus is burnished, or rubbed, it is ready for use.

**PERSEA TREE (***MINUSOPS LAURIFOLIA***)** A tree sacred to the Egyptians. The Benu bird was said to have come into being from the fire that burned on top of the Persea tree of Heliopolis. In the coronation scenes of the kings, the gods are shown inscribing the

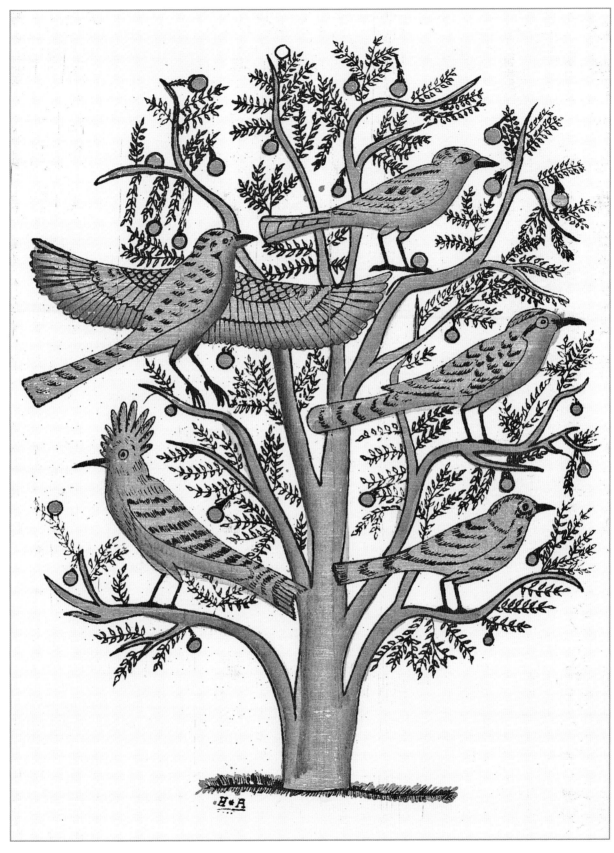

Mythology tells us that the flames of a burning Persea tree caused the sacred Benu bird to come into existence. *(Courtesy of Bob Brier)*

king's name on the leaves of the tree so that he may rule for millions of years.

The antechamber of TUTANKHAMEN's tomb contained a bouquet of Persea branches, and baskets of Persea fruit have been found in several tombs. The tree has dark green, leathery leaves; small, yellowish flowers; and small yellow fruit that the Greek botanist Theophrastus proclaimed "sweet and delicious."

**PERSEPHONE**   When the Greeks ruled Egypt, they associated their goddess of the Underworld, Persephone, with Isis, the Egyptian mother goddess.

**PHARAOH**   The supreme ruler of Egypt, the pharaoh was believed to be the living manifestation of the god HORUS. The word *pharaoh* is not Egyptian. Pharaoh is a title used in the Bible and was not commonly used in Egypt until the NEW KINGDOM (1550–1069 B.C.). In ancient Egyptian language, *per ah* simply meant "The Great House," a term the Israelites applied to the person who lived in the palace, and from the New Kingdom on, the word was sometimes used to refer to the ruler of Egypt.

From the beginning of Egyptian mythology, the pharaoh was identified with the gods—especially with Horus, the falcon god. According to one myth, when the goddess SEKHMET became angry and was sent to destroy humankind, RE saved the people and continued to rule in Egypt until he grew weak. In his place he sent his son Horus to rule and protect the people of Egypt. Mythology tells us that when Horus no longer ruled on Earth, he helped Menes unite UPPER and LOWER EGYPT and become the first king of Egypt.

**PHILAE TEMPLES**   Cult center of the great mother goddess ISIS, the Temples of Philae stand on an island that must have appeared as a green oasis among the boulders of the first cataract, south of modern Aswan. Philae emerged as a religious center during the reign of Nectanebo I (Thirtieth Dynasty, 380–343 B.C.). As Isis rose to prominence on the island, construction of temples and shrines continued through the Ptolemaic and Roman periods until the second century A.D., when Ptolemy II (285–246 B.C.) built a grand temple dedicated to Isis that became the focal point of the island. For the next 500 years, Philae remained one of the most important religious centers in the ancient world.

Although Christianity came to Egypt in the first century A.D., the Temple of Isis at Philae was one of the last places where the ancient gods continued to be worshipped. Graffiti from as late as A.D. 473 tell us that Nubian pilgrims visiting the temple were still making offerings to the old gods. Other notable buildings on the island are the Temple of HATHOR, the Gateway of Hadrian, the Temple of Augustus, the Kiosk of Trajan, and the Gate of Diocletian. Today the Isis Temple at Philae is among the best preserved in Egypt.

The Isis Temple was designed with 12 rooms: the Hall of the King's Purification, Hall of Offerings, Hall of the ENNEAD, the HOLY OF HOLIES (sanctuary), and several rooms for storage and for the priest's regalia. The walls of the temple are decorated with scenes of Isis, HATHOR and the Ptolemaic queens and inscribed with the LAMENTATIONS OF ISIS, a series of prayers and rituals performed in the temple during the celebration of the story of ISIS AND OSIRIS.

When the Aswan dam was opened in 1902, it flooded Philae Island and made it inaccessible for much of the year. In the 1960s, when the new high dam was built, the temples were dismantled and 40,000 blocks were reassembled on a nearby island. The moving and rebuilding of the temple was completed in 1980, and the temples now stand above the Nile, 43 feet higher than before.

**PIGS**   Centuries before the religious taboos of the Hebrews and the Moslems, the pig was censured in ancient Egypt. The evil god SET could appear in many different forms, and one of his manifestations was a pig. Scenes from the Festival of Victory carved on the wall of Edfu Temple show Set as a hippopotamus and as a pig. Curiously, at one time the pig represented one of the nomes (states) in the Delta (north), but it was generally viewed as a lowly animal and was raised and eaten only by the lower classes. If a pig was offered as a sacrifice to the gods, it was viewed as a lowly or poor man's sacrifice.

When Egypt was first united under king NARMER, the pig was deemed an unacceptable sacrifice to the falcon god, HORUS. In the myth the CONTENDINGS OF HORUS AND SET, the evil Set kills Horus's father, OSIRIS. Because of this, the pig, forever associated with Set, became an unworthy sacrifice.

Herodotus, the Greek historian, tells us that swineherds, because of their association with the pigs they tended, were not allowed to attend important religious festivals in the Delta.

**PLANETS, GODS OF THE**   The Egyptians recognized five planets and called them the "stars that knew no rest." Their movement across the heavens reminded the Egyptians of the five gods sailing across the sky in their solar barque (boat). The planet now known as Jupiter was called "Horus Who Limits the Two Lands"; Mars was "Horus of the Horizon"; Mercury was "Sebegu," associated with Set; Saturn was "Horus the Bull of the Sky"; and Venus was "the God of the Morning."

**PLUTARCH** (A.D. 46–120)  Greek historian, biographer, and philosopher who recorded the myth of ISIS AND OSIRIS and cult practices surrounding the myth in his account of *De Iside et Osirde*, The Tale of Isis and Osiris. Modern scholars have debated the veracity of Plutarch's account, but it is the only comprehensive narrative of the myth that exists from the ancient world.

Plutarch is best known for his *Parallel Lives*, a series of 80 biographies of famous Greeks and Romans, including ALEXANDER THE GREAT and Julius Caesar. He was educated in Athens and was initiated into the priesthood of the temple at Delphi in Greece.

**PRIAPUS**  When the Greeks ruled Egypt, they associated their fertility god Priapus with the Egyptian ram-headed god BA-NEB-DJED, also a fertility god.

**PRIESTS**  Egyptian priests were called *hem-netjer*, "servant of god," and every temple had various classes of priests. At the top of the hierarchy was the high priest, the "First Prophet of the God." He was well educated, an elder of the temple, and a skilled administrator and politician. As overseer of the temple and all of its land holdings, the high priest was very powerful. Usually a man would rise to this position through the ranks of the priesthood, but sometimes the pharaoh chose his son as the high priest.

In the early days of Egypt's nationhood, the pharaoh was undoubtedly the high priest, but later a designated high priest acted as a substitute for the pharaoh during temple ceremonies. As the number of temples and ceremonies grew, each temple needed a high priest and many lesser priests.

Beneath the high priest was a whole cadre of priests in different groups, each with specialized training. Among these was the "second prophet," an administrator to oversee the offerings that were made in the temple each day. One important group was the "horologers," or "priests of the hours of the day and night." They were crucial to the functioning of the temple, since rituals pleasing to the gods had to begin at the correct time. By watching the progress

When performing funerary rituals at the time of mummification, a priest wore an Anubis mask. *(Photo by Pat Remler)*

of the sun or stars across the sky, the priests correctly determined the beginning and end of each season.

Equally important to the horologers were the astrologer-priests. Unlike modern astrologers, they did not watch the procession of the stars and planets in order to predict what would happen on Earth. They were the keepers of the mythological calendar of lucky and unlucky days, and they determined which were the best days for any given activity. For example, they might consult the position of the stars and determine that during the season of inundation, the first day of the month, Akhet was the birthday of the god Re-Horakhty. On that day the Nile began to rise, and the people celebrated. Day one of Akhet was, therefore, a very favorable day.

Lector or *sem* priests composed the prayers and incantations to the gods, and during the rituals, they chanted to the accompaniment of temple musicians. The priesthood of the goddess Sekhmet provided the best physicians in Egypt, for despite her ferocious nature, Sekhmet was an important goddess of healing. *Wab* priests were administrators and attended to the daily running of the temple. *KA* priests made daily offerings and recited prayers for the *ka* of the deceased. When a mortuary temple was completed, an annuity or allowance was set aside to support the *ka* priest, and sometimes a portion of land was set aside to grow food for the offerings.

Herodotus, the Greek historian, writes in his *Histories, Book II* that he found the Egyptians religious to excess and fanatical about cleanliness. He wrote that priests bathed in cold water four times a day, shaved their entire bodies daily to avoid body lice, and were required to be circumcised. Priests were forbidden to wear clothing not made from the finest linen, and their sandals were made only from papyrus. In spite of this rigorous routine, Herodotus says the priests had a good life, for they were provided with fine clothing and excellent food and wine during the time they served in the temple.

**PRIMEVAL MOUND** (HILL)  A key concept in the creation myths of ancient Egypt, the primeval mound is the hill of Earth that emerged from NUN, the primordial waters of chaos. In the CREATION MYTH popular at the religious center at HELIOPOLIS, the creator god ATUM emerged from the waters of Nun onto the primeval mound itself, where he created the ENNEAD, the nine gods.

At the religious center in Memphis, the primeval mound served as the symbol of creation, and the obscure god Tatenen ("He Who Raises the Land") was the primeval mound. In the PYRAMID TEXTS, the primeval mound is called the "hill," and the BENBEN, the religious symbol from Heliopolis, may have been derived from the primeval mound. The Egyptians must have been reminded of the primeval mound each year after the annual flooding of the Nile when the water receded and the first bit of land emerged.

**PTAH** 𓊹𓏏𓎛  As the creator god of MEMPHIS, Ptah is shown in a tight-fitting garment and looks as if he is wrapped as a mummy. His close-fitting skullcap shows only his face and ears, and his hands protrude from the wrappings and he holds a staff that combines the following symbols: 𓌀, the *was* scepter of authority; 𓊽, the *djed* column of stability; and 𓋹, the ANKH, the sign of life. Throughout ancient Egypt's long history, Ptah was easily recognized because his costume and shape barely changed. Although his cult center was in Memphis, Ptah was worshipped in all the major temples in Egypt and Nubia.

Ptah may have originated as a local patron god of craftspeople, for the invention of the arts was

Ptah, the creator god, wears a tight-fitting cloak and a skullcap and holds a scepter with a *djed* pillar, the sign of stability, on top. *(Photo by Pat Remler)*

attributed to him. Although he is rarely mentioned in the Pyramid Texts, Ptah was an important god who created the universe from his heart and tongue; he spoke the word and fashioned the world. The following is inscribed on the Shabaka Stone, translated by Miriam Lichtheim in *Ancient Egyptian Literature*.

> Thus: it is said of Ptah: "he who made all and created the gods." And he is Tatenen, who gave birth to the gods, and from whom every thing came forth, foods, provisions, divine offerings, all good things. Thus it is recognized and understood that he is the mightiest of the gods. Thus Ptah was satisfied after he made all things and all divine words.

> He gave birth to the gods,
> He made the towns,
> He established the nomes,
> He placed the gods in their shines,
> He settled their offerings,
> He made their bodies according to their wishes,
> Thus the gods entered into their bodies . . .

Ptah was known as the "the ancient one" who combined his being with that of Nun and Naunet (gods of the Ogdoad creation myth). He is the principal god of the Memphite Triad, which includes the lioness goddess Sekhmet and Nefertum, the god of the lotus blossom.

Ptah held numerous titles and associations with other gods. Some of the most important associations were:

**Ptah, "Lord of Ankh Tawy"**  "Life of the two lands" refers to the unification of Upper and Lower Egypt.

**Ptah, "Res Inebef"**  "Ptah who is south of his wall" refers to the boundary wall that enclosed the temple precinct of Ptah at Memphis, known as White Walls in ancient times.

**Ptah, "Nefer Her"**  "Ptah of the beautiful face" refers to the belief that his flesh was of gold.

**Ptah-Hapi**  The union of the attributes of Ptah with the elements of the Nile god Hapi.

**Ptah-Osiris**  Ptah's association with Osiris is demonstrated in the Book of the Dead, where he assists the deceased.

**Ptah-Sokar**  Ptah's association with the hawk-headed god of death, Sokar, links the primeval creative power of Ptah with Sokar's powers in the Underworld.

**Ptah-Sokar-Osiris**  Combined attributes of the gods became popular in the Late period (737–332 b.c.), and this composite deity helped the deceased in his or her journey to the next world. Funerary goods included a carved wooden statue of the composite god that was placed inside the tomb with the mummy.

**Ptah-Sokar-Tem**  Ptah's association with Atum, the creator god from Heliopolis, and Sokar, a god of the dead, with many of the attributes of Osiris.

**Ptah-Tatenen**  Ptah's most important link with the world of the dead is his relationship with Tatenen, a primeval god of barren earth. The association of Ptah and Tatenen is chronicled on the Shabaka Stone, a stele erected at the Temple of Ptah in Memphis.

As a funerary god, Ptah plays an active part in the Book of the Dead and is associated with minor as well as major gods. In Chapter 11 the deceased proclaims he will, "stand up like Horus, I shall sit down like Ptah, I shall be mighty like Thoth, and I shall be strong like Tem." Chapter 23 describes that Ptah officiates with Shu at the Opening of the Mouth Ceremony, with an instrument of iron.

So popular was Ptah among the people that his name was often included as part of a king's or noble's name, such as King MernePtah, "beloved of Ptah," or the nobleman Ptahotep, "Ptah is pleased."

**Ptolemy**  Founder of the Ptolemaic Dynasty, Ptolemy I (323–282 b.c.) was a general in the army of Alexander the Great. When Alexander died in Babylon in 323 b.c., Ptolemy claimed Egypt for himself. He knew it was the most prosperous land in Alexander's empire and that it would be the easiest to defend against foreign invasion. To ensure his control of Egypt, Ptolemy ambushed Alexander's funeral procession, which was on its way to Greece, and instead escorted Alexander's body to Memphis. A later Ptolemaic king moved Alexander's body to the port city of Alexandria, where it was displayed in a great mausoleum.

Ptolemy I proved to be a good ruler. Much to the relief of the priests, he supported Egypt's traditional religion and maintained the temples and the priesthood. In keeping with the tradition of Egyptian kings, Ptolemy I and his successors were all declared to be gods, and in temples throughout Egypt, they were worshipped along with the traditional Egyptian gods. Also known for their commercial interests, one of the early Ptolemies built the famed Pharos

Lighthouse, reputed to be the first lighthouse in history. It was situated less than a mile off the coast and cast a beacon by reflecting the light of a fire with huge mirrors. Today virtually nothing is left of the original lighthouse, and the fortress of Qait Bey now stands on the Pharos peninsula.

Under the Ptolemies, Alexandria became a center for learning and ideas. The Ptolemies built one of the marvels of the ancient world, the great library at Alexandria. It was said that when ships sailed into the harbor, they were detained and searched for books. If a volume was found that was not in the library, it was borrowed, copied, and returned to the ship. In spite of their personal excesses and family feuds, for which the Ptolemies were known, they maintained a tradition of scholarship and learning in Alexandria. The love of learning extended to Cleopatra VII, the last Ptolemy to rule Egypt, who was known for her literary interests and language skills. With the death of Cleopatra in 30 B.C., the Ptolemaic dynasty ended, and Egypt became part of the Roman Empire.

**PYRAMIDION**  Derived from the ancient BENBEN Stone in the court of the sun god at HELIOPOLIS, the pyramidion is the small pyramid shape that rests on the top of an OBELISK. King Amenemhet III (1855–1808 B.C.) capped his mud brick pyramid with a black granite pyramidion that was inscribed with his name. It has been suggested that the Great PYRAMID, when it was completed, was capped with a pyramidion of gold that was looted in antiquity.

**PYRAMIDS**  Of the Seven Wonders of the Ancient World, the Great Pyramid is the only one left standing. An old proverb says, "All things

Imitating the burials of kings, private people often placed a pyramidion, a small pyramid like this one, on top of their tombs. *(Photo by Pat Remler)*

dread time, but time dreads the pyramids." When Napoleon was about to lead his men into battle, he pointed to the pyramids and shouted, "From the summit of these monuments, 40 centuries look down upon us!" And he wasn't far wrong.

Pyramids were magical structures built for the OLD KINGDOM PHARAOHS and were meant to house the king's mummy until the time of his RESURRECTION in the NETHERWORLD. Much has been written about the pyramids, but perhaps the most amazing fact is that the Great Pyramid was built at the beginning of ancient Egypt's long history, and all the largest and most famous pyramids were built over a period of about 200 years. When TUTANKHAMEN was alive, the pyramids were already ancient.

The pyramid shape has no particular significance. It began as a MASTABA, a low rectangular structure over a tomb, and when one was placed on top of another it became a Step Pyramid. When the sides were filled in, it became a true pyramid. Pyramids were the first large stone buildings in Egypt, and there are about 100 of them left, although today many are ruined and look like large piles of stone.

The Step Pyramid, built by King ZOSER, at SAQQARA, was the first attempt at pyramid building. It is a series of mastabas, placed one on the other, creating six successively smaller steps. As each pharaoh tried to build bigger and better, his architect learned the art of pyramid building by trial and error. Sneferu, the greatest pyramid builder, had three built under his supervision. Two were unstable—the Pyramid of Meidum and the Bent Pyramid—and could not be used. His third attempt, the so-called Red Pyramid, at Dashur, was his burial place. It is the first true pyramid.

HERODOTUS (c. 485–424 B.C.), the Greek traveler to Egypt, wrote that the pyramids were built by 100,000 slaves, who erected a mud brick ramp on which to drag the stone blocks, and that it took 20 years to build the Great Pyramid of Khufu (or Cheops, as he was called by the Greeks). Egyptologists now believe that the pyramid builders were Egyptian farmers and laborers who worked on pyramid construction during the season of inundation, when the NILE overflowed its banks and their fields were flooded. Ancient papyri show that the workers were paid in food, lentils, onions, leeks, and BEER for the three months that they worked.

There are competing theories as to how the stones were raised. Herodotus said the Egyptians used machines (perhaps a crane) to raise the blocks. Modern thought suggests that a long mud brick ramp was built on one side of the pyramid, on which to pull the blocks into place. As the ramp was made longer and higher, the pyramid grew taller. Another idea is that a mud brick ramp corkscrewed around the outside of the pyramid in order to move the blocks higher. Many people disagree with each of these three ideas. A new and more promising theory by a French architect suggests that an internal ramp for moving blocks was built on the inside of the pyramid. When this theory is tested, it may prove to be the correct one.

## Major Pyramids Standing Today

| Name of Pyramid | Location | Owner of Pyramid |
|---|---|---|
| Step Pyramid | Saqqara<br>Third Dynasty<br>2667–2648 B.C. | King Zoser |
| Meidum Pyramid | Meidum<br>Fourth Dynasty<br>2613–2589 B.C. | King Sneferu |
| Bent Pyramid | Dashur<br>Fourth Dynasty<br>2613–2589 B.C. | King Sneferu |
| Red Pyramid | Dashur<br>Fourth Dynasty<br>2613–2589 B.C. | King Sneferu |
| Great Pyramid | Giza<br>(Cheops)<br>Fourth Dynasty<br>2589–2566 B.C. | King Khufu |
| Khephren Pyramid | Giza<br>(Chephren)<br>Fourth Dynasty<br>2558–2532 B.C. | King Khafre |
| Mycerinus | Giza<br>(Mycerinus)<br>Fourth Dynasty<br>2532–2503 B.C. | King Menkaure |

Over the centuries, the pyramids of Egypt have been the focus of wild speculations about their purpose and power. Various myths have suggested that the pyramids held the secrets of the universe, were filled with GOLD and treasure, contained life-restoring energy, were the repository of all ancient knowledge, and were constructed by aliens or the inhabitants of the fabled island of Atlantis.

Several years ago, the remains of a workmen's village and cemetery were discovered near the site of the Great Pyramid. Excavators found bakeries, breweries, and everything needed for a city that supported the workmen who built the pyramids. The workers' cemeteries show that many of the men buried there carried heavy blocks all their lives. X-rays reveal that

The Great Pyramid at Giza is the last of the Seven Wonders of the Ancient World still left standing today. *(Photo by Pat Remler)*

their vertebrae were compressed from years of hard labor. As the excavations continue, Egyptologists are discovering what life was like for the men who built the pyramids.

**PYRAMIDS AND MYTHOLOGY**  Ancient Egyptian CREATION MYTHS tell us that when the first mound of earth emerged from the waters of chaos, the sun god was born on this patch of dry land. The Egyptians may have believed that the PYRAMID shape represented the primordial mound of creation called a BENBEN. Thus, the pyramid, designed to hold the mummy of the dead king, is a reminder and celebration of the creation of life.

Architecturally, the pyramid shape evolved from the first mound of sand heaped over a Predynastic burial. Then a mud brick structure—the MASTABA—was created to mark the burial of early dynastic kings. As mastaba was stacked upon mastaba, the STEP PYRAMID of ZOSER arose at SAQQARA. Royal architects experimented and filled in the sides of a stepped pyramid, creating the first true pyramid. Today we can see the results of their early (Third Dynasty) miscalculations in the pyramid at Meidum—it collapsed because the sides were too steep. The Bent Pyramid of Dashur had to be changed halfway up, because the burial chamber inside was collapsing. Eventually the ancient architects got it right, and the first true pyramid was the Red Pyramid at Dashur.

The golden age of pyramid building was the Fourth Dynasty, with the building on the Giza Plateau of the Great Pyramid, the Pyramid of Khephren, and the Pyramid of Mycerinus. With the rising importance of the sun cult and worship of RE, Fifth Dynasty kings built small pyramids and big SUN TEMPLES at Abusir—squat structures on a platform with a PYRAMIDION shape on top. During the NEW

KINGDOM, pyramid shapes emerged again, appearing on the top of elegant obelisks as small pyramidions. A thousand years after Egypt built pyramids, the flame was rekindled in NUBIA, and today there are more pyramids in Nubia than in Egypt.

**PYRAMID TEXTS** A collection of the earliest funerary texts, carved on the walls of the Fifth Dynasty (2375–2345 B.C.) pyramid of King UNAS and Sixth Dynasty (2345–2181 B.C.) pyramids of Teti, Pepi I, and Pepi II at SAQQARA (and in some queens' pyramids). All the texts from all the pyramids total roughly 800 spells, but the 280 "utterances" or spells in Unas's pyramid are the oldest. The pyramids of his successors in the Sixth Dynasty are also covered with texts, but no two have exactly the same spells.

The Pyramid Texts give us the first official version of life after death, which at the time of their writing applied only to the pharaoh. Unas's pyramid, built at Saqqara, is part of the largest cemetery in the world. When it was discovered, the pyramid looked like those of earlier kings of the Fifth Dynasty, but inside, the walls were covered with hundreds of magical inscriptions. The hieroglyphs are painted blue and stand out clearly against the white limestone walls. Long vertical lines running from the ceiling to the floor separate each column of hieroglyphs. When the hieroglyphs were translated, scholars found that they contained five kinds of spells: dramatic texts, hymns, litanies, glorifications, and magical incantations. Taken together these spells formed the Pyramid Texts. The spells deal primarily with three stages in the king's transition from this world to the next: (1) his awakening in the pyramid; (2) his ascending through the sky to the Netherworld; and (3) his admittance into the company of the gods. The magical principle behind all these spells is the same: The word is the deed. Saying something, or having it inscribed on the pyramid wall, made it so.

So important was the magic in these spells that one of the first spells on the entrance to the antechamber of Unas's pyramid says, "Unas does not give you his magical power." The spells tell us that in the second stage of the king's resurrection, he ascends to heaven in a variety of ways: He flies ("The opener of the ways has let Unas fly toward heaven amongst his brothers the gods . . ."); he rises on incense (". . . and he rises on the smoke of a great fumigation"); he ascends on a ladder, assisted by RE and HORUS ("The ladder is secured by Re before OSIRIS. The ladder is secured by Horus before his father Osiris when he goes to his spirit . . .").

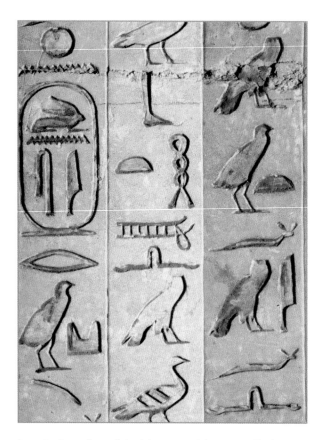

Inscriptions found inside pyramids are called Pyramid Texts and consist of collections of prayers and spells to help the deceased king resurrect in the next world. *(Photo by Pat Remler)*

The spell explains that in case Unas's wings tire, or the incense does not reach the heavens, or the ladder breaks, then he will be ferried across to heaven by the ferryman who transports the god. Once Unas reaches the next world, there are spells to assure that he is welcomed into the company of the gods: "Thou standest [there as a king], ruling over them [the gods] as Geb rules over his Ennead. . . . Thy name comes into being with the gods."

The pyramid texts tell us what the Egyptians thought life after death would be. First, the king's body would rest in the burial chamber of the pyramid until it was time for it to travel through the sky to the next world, in the west. The west was associated with the dead because each day the sun set there. Osiris, god of the Netherworld, was called "Lord of the West," and the dead were called "Westerners." Once the pharaoh completed his journey west, he would be welcomed by Osiris and begin his eternal life. Life would continue in the west much as it had in this world, and the pharaoh would be provided with everything he needed.

# Q

**QADESH** (QEDESHET, QUDSHU)  Syrian goddess of ecstasy worshipped in Egypt during the New Kingdom (1550–1069 B.C.). Qadesh was identified with HATHOR, the Egyptian goddess of love, pleasure,

Qadesh, the Syrian goddess of pleasure, was adopted by the Egyptians. *(Photo by Rama/Used under a Creative Commons license)*

and music, and with ASTARTE and ANAT, two other Syrian goddesses with a popular following in Egypt. Qadesh, breaking with the established artistic tradition in Egypt, is shown facing front, in the nude, and standing on the back of a striding lion. She often holds flowers and snakes in her upraised hands, symbols that may originate in Syrian mythology.

**QASR IBRIM** (CASTLE OF ABRAHAM)  One of the last outposts of Egyptian religion in NUBIA, Qasr Ibrim was built around 1500 B.C. and over the centuries was used by just about everyone—the Egyptians, Nubians, Greeks, Romans, Turks, Mamelukes, and Arabs. During the NEW KINGDOM, chapels were dedicated to HORUS of Mian (a Nubian form of the god Horus), KHNUM, SATIS, and HATHOR. The shrines were cut into the rock cliffs on the west side of the NILE, and each one held a statue of a king accompanied by two gods. The rising water behind the Aswan Dam has completely covered the shrines, so they are no longer visible. The Nubian king Taharka built a mud brick temple around 680 B.C. and dedicated it to several Egyptian and local gods. Centuries later it was converted into a church.

When the Ptolemaic kings (332–32 B.C.) fortified Qasr Ibrim, it became both a religious center and a military stronghold for the Ptolemies and later the Romans. Situated just north of ABU SIMBEL, the settlement was so remote that it was one of the last Egyptian temples to worship the ancient gods after the spread of Christianity in Egypt. Eventually the fort became a center for Christianity and remained a place of worship for almost 2,000 years.

**QEBESENEF**  One of the FOUR SONS OF HORUS, Qebesenef is represented with a hawk's head and acts as the guardian of the intestines during mummification. He is represented on one of the lids of the CANOPIC JARS.

**QEBUI**   God of the north wind (see also WINDS, GODS OF THE FOUR).

**QERHET**   A local nome goddess in the Delta (north), Qerhet is most often shown as a serpent. When Egyptologists excavated the Delta site called Pithom in the Bible (modern Tel al-Maskhutah), they found inscriptions for the "Holy Serpent," and a portion of the temple was called "the house of the snake goddess, Qerhet." Qerhet is also associated with the creator god ATUM of HELIOPOLIS.

**QUEEN**   There was no word for queen in ancient Egypt. What is translated as "queen" really means "King's Great Wife," the most prestigious title a woman could hold in ancient Egypt. There were several legal relationships that women in the palace could have with the pharaoh. Concubines were the lowest rank, for they were not wives, but they did have legal status in the palace and could inherit, and in some instances their sons became kings. Above the concubines in social standing were the "wives," who often had royal blood or were the daughters of foreign kings married to the pharaoh to seal a political treaty. Among the wives there was only one "King's Great Wife," who almost always carried royal bloodlines from some branch of the reigning royal family. During the New Kingdom, the "Great Wife" accompanied her husband on state occasions and performed important religious functions in the Temple of Amun. "Chantress of Amun" and "God's Wife" (wife of Amun) were two of the most important titles that the queen or "Great Wife" could hold. They assured the queen a powerful position and entrée into the inner workings of the temple and gave the king a means of supervising the priests.

**RAMESSEUM** The mortuary temple of Ramses II, the Ramesseum was dedicated to AMUN, the great god of THEBES. The huge temple complex was the center of Ramses's funerary cult, where offerings were made for the soul of the deceased pharaoh. It also included a school that trained scribes and painters, an administrative center, a palace, storerooms, stables, granaries, and houses for the priests of Amun and the servants. Constructed on the west bank of the Nile, the Temple of Amun in the Ramesseum has a large entrance pylon leading into the first courtyard, and the reliefs on the inside of the pylon tell the story of RAMSES II's famous victory over the Hittites in the Battle of Kadesh. When Ramses visited the complex he stayed in the small palace just west of the entrance.

In the first century B.C. the Greek historian Diodorus visited the Ramesseum and described what he saw as the "tomb of OZYMANDIAS." The name appears to be a corruption of one of the five names of Ramses, *usr-maat-re*. Diodorus's translation of the inscription on the colossal statues of Ramses, now toppled and broken, was the inspiration for the 19th-century English poem by Percy Bysshe Shelley, "Ozymandias."

**RAM OF MENDES** A sacred ram that, like the APIS BULL, was chosen to replace the previous ram only after an exhaustive search to ensure that the markings on the animal were auspicious. When the previous ram died, it was believed that its soul entered the new Ram of Mendes at the time it was installed in the temple with all the necessary ceremonies and rituals. The ram would then live the rest of its natural life in the temple precinct as a pampered and sacred animal. The Ram of Mendes was associated with the ram god BA-NEB-DJED, who was believed to house the soul of OSIRIS.

**RAMSES THE GREAT** (RAMSES II) (NINETEENTH DYNASTY, 1279–1213 B.C.) One of the greatest warrior kings and builders in Egypt's history, Ramses II, was known as Ramses the Great. He possessed a great ego and declared himself the equal of the gods. In the HOLY OF HOLIES at his temple at ABU SIMBEL, Ramses carved statues of himself boldly sitting among the gods.

Ramses was the only surviving son and heir to Seti I, and he was raised to accomplish great things. When Ramses was in his teens, he was proclaimed successor to the throne and was presented with his own palace and harem. Little is known about his beautiful wife, Nefertari, except that she was his "Great Wife," and that he was devoted to her. When he built a temple for her at Abu Simbel, Ramses inscribed over the door the epithet "she for whom the very sun doth shine."

Throughout his long life (he lived to be about 86 and fathered more than 100 children), Ramses distinguished himself with military expeditions and building programs. His name can be found in almost every major temple, for what he did not build or remodel, he usurped by inscribing his name on other kings' monuments. Soon after he was crowned pharaoh, he chose a new site in the Delta for his capital city. Traditionally Egypt had two capitals—the administrative center in MEMPHIS and the religious center in THEBES—but Ramses preferred to live in the Delta, north of Memphis. It is here that he built his "store city," Pi-Ramses, which is mentioned in the Bible. He called his city "Domain of Ramses, Great of Victories." It was the ideal location from which to launch military expeditions into Syria and Libya, and some scholars believe Ramses the Great was the pharaoh mentioned in the biblical book of Exodus.

The biblical story of the exodus of the Hebrews from Egypt is one of the greatest archaeological mysteries of our time. There is no mention of the exodus

Known as the Ramesseum, the funerary temple of Ramses II was dedicated to the god Amun. After Ramses died, it was here that worshippers would make offerings to honor him in his new status as deified former king. *(Photo by Pat Remler)*

in ancient Egyptian records, and the Bible is the only written account of the event that exists today. It is found in the Pentateuch, the first five books of the Old Testament, which tradition attributes to Moses; the second book of Moses is the account of the Israelites' departure from Egypt.

The earliest connection between Israel and Egypt is the story of Joseph. According to the Bible, Joseph's jealous brothers sold Joseph into slavery. Taken to Egypt, his talent for interpreting dreams brought him great success, and eventually he became vizier of Egypt, a position equal to that of prime minister. Through his ability to interpret prophetic dreams, Joseph was able to save Egypt from starvation during seven years of famine, gaining the eternal gratitude of the pharaoh. Centuries later, when a new pharaoh came to power, he feared an uprising from the growing number of Israelites in Egypt and called for the death of their newborn male children.

> There came to power in Egypt a new king who knew nothing of Joseph. "Look," he said to his subjects, "these people, the sons of Israel, have become so numerous and strong that they are a threat to us. We must be prudent and take steps

against their increasing any further, or if war should break out, they might add to the number of our enemies. They might take arms against us and so escape out of the country." (Exodus 1:8–11)

According to the biblical account, when the pharaoh's daughter found an Israelite baby in the reeds on the banks of the Nile, she took the baby and named him Moses, which means "born" or "born of" in ancient Egyptian. It was a common name, often linked with another, such as Ramses, which is *Ra-messes*: "Re is Born." When Moses was grown, God appeared to him and commanded him to lead the Israelites out of Egypt. But the pharaoh refused to release them, because by then they were building huge storehouses in his cities in the Delta. The Bible tells us that the Lord was angry and sent 10 plagues to Egypt. The first nine (blood, frogs, gnats, flies, death to the livestock, boils, hail, locusts, and windstorms) can be attributed to natural causes that sometimes occurred in Egypt. The 10th plague killed the firsborn son (and male animal) in every house. When the pharaoh's firstborn son was struck by this plague and died, the pharaoh agreed to let the Israelites leave

Egypt. Some scholars estimate that the firstborn son of Ramses the Great (Amun-Her-Khepshef) died around the postulated date of the exodus.

The name of the pharaoh of the exodus is never mentioned in the Bible. The best clue to his identity is in the cities the Israelites were forced to build.

> Accordingly they put slave drivers over the Israelites to wear them down under heavy loads. In this way they built the store-cities of Pithom and Rameses for Pharaoh ... The Egyptians forced the sons of Israel into slavery and made their lives unbearable with hard labor ... (Exodus 1:11–14)

The town name Ramses is the primary reason Ramses the Great has been identified as the pharaoh of the exodus.

**RE (RA)** The manifestation of the power of the sun, Re was the great creator god of HELIOPOLIS. Re ruled the sky, the Earth, and the NETHERWORLD. To strengthen the position of the cult gods they represented, priests associated their gods with the great sun god: AMUN-RE, RE-HORAKHTY, Khnum-Re, and Sobek-Re, to mention a few. In Heliopolis (called ON in the Bible), it was believed that Re emerged from the primordial waters on to the mound of Earth called the BENBEN. Re is also said to have arisen from the first lotus blossom. The BOOK OF THE DEAD tells of Re's self-mutilation (perhaps the first circumcision): He cuts his phallus and from the drops of blood creates *Hu*, the god of authority, and *Sia*, the god of the mind.

Re is most often characterized by the falcon with a sun disk on his head, encircled with a cobra head (URAEUS), symbolizing the power of the god. In the realm of the dead, Re appears as a ram-headed god, and his title is "Sacred Ram of the West." In the DESTRUCTION OF MANKIND myth, Re is described as elderly with flesh of gold, bones of silver, and hair of lapis lazuli. The PYRAMID TEXTS describe the deceased king as ascending to the sky to join his father, Re. The LITANY OF RE describes how Re becomes lord of the Netherworld, where he makes his nightly journey in his solar barque (boat).

Re was joined with AMUN to become Amun-Re, the great god of Thebes in the NEW KINGDOM (1550–1069 B.C.). During the MIDDLE KINGDOM, the warrior kings associated Re with MONTU, the god of war, and he was called Montu-Re. When Re was joined with Horus, he became Re-Horakhty. Under the reign of AKHENATEN, the New Kingdom pharaoh who changed the religion of Egypt, the sun god Re became the universal deity in the form of the ATEN (the sun disk), who enveloped all other gods.

**RE-ATUM-KHEPRI** One of the forms of the sun god, this combination of Re, ATUM the creator god, and KHEPRI the scarab represented Re in the early morning.

**RED CROWN** A royal crown that symbolized Northern Egypt, the red crown originated in the Delta, and although there are many representations of the crown on statues and in tomb paintings, an actual crown has never been found. Scholars have suggested that only one crown existed at any time, and because of its magical powers, it was not buried with the deceased king but instead passed to his successor. The cylindrical crown with a peak at the back and a curled feather in the front may have been made of leather or reeds and perhaps disintegrated over the centuries. It remains a mystery as to what happened to the royal crowns of Egypt.

**RE-HORAKHTY** A composite god, Re-Horakhty resulted from the merging of two gods, Re and Horus. The name Horakhty means "Horus who is on the horizon." He is shown as a hawk-headed man with a solar disk.

**RELIGION** Ancient Egyptians believed in many gods (polytheism). Over Egypt's long history, the gods in her pantheon were born, died, changed their characters, and combined with one another and with foreign deities.

The official state religion was concerned with a divine order, or *MAAT*, that kept Egypt safe from invaders and natural disaster. It was the duty of the PHARAOH, the "living god on Earth," to make sure that divine order was not disturbed. Building temples for a god, and filling each temple with a hierarchy of priests to serve the god, helped ensure that divine order was preserved. Priests performed daily rituals for the temple's cult statues, which served as dwelling places for the essence of the deity. Aside from national gods and goddesses, there were local NOME GODS who sometimes rose to prominence and foreign deities who resembled Egyptian gods and who were also worshipped. Household gods were honored with small shrines in Egyptian homes. Since MAGIC played such an important role in Egyptians' daily lives, the statues of favorite gods were viewed much like good luck charms to help a family avoid disasters.

Although there were more than 2,000 gods in the Egyptian pantheon, when it came to the realm of the dead, the Egyptians were united in their worship of OSIRIS. From the pharaoh to the common man, the greatest desire of all Egyptians was to resurrect and live again in the NETHERWORLD. No civilization ever put more faith, energy, and resources into its belief in life after death. Because of that, most of what we know about ancient Egypt comes from the Egyptians idea that life did not end with this world. Funerary rituals, from MUMMIFICATION to the OPENING OF THE MOUTH CEREMONY were rigidly controlled, because any change in the ritual or ceremonies could mean disaster for the deceased. However, the Egyptian view of the universe was rather flexible. CREATION MYTHS emerged in several different religious centers, with no apparent conflicts, for one god was easily associated with another. In the ancient world, Egyptian religion was viewed as a powerful force. HERODOTUS, the Greek traveler in Egypt, wrote that the Egyptians "are religious to a higher degree than any other people." Half a century later, the legendary Greek Hermes Trismegistos suggested that Egypt "was like the image of heaven."

**RELIGION AND MAGIC** The Egyptians were famous in the ancient world for their knowledge of MAGIC. In the early second century A.D., Egypt was called "the mother of magicians" by Clement of Alexandria, an early Greek theologian who lived and wrote in Alexandria. His sentiments were echoed by much of the rest of the ancient world. In the Old Testament, Exodus 7:8–23, Pharaoh summons his magicians, who match Moses and Aaron in performing "the snake trick," changing their staves into serpents and water into blood.

Even before Moses, Egypt had a long history of magic and MAGICIANS, many of whom appear in ancient writings (see EUCRATES). Over the centuries, magic and religion became intertwined—so much so that it is often difficult to separate the two.

Both magic and religion involve a belief in the supernatural and the realm of the unseen. Two characteristics, however, separate magic from religion and magicians from priests. First, magic has a quality of immediacy that is lacking in religion. When a magician recites a spell, it is *he* who brings about the desired effect. When a priest prays for something, it is *the god* who is expected to answer the prayer, not the priest. The priest is an intermediary between this world and the supernatural or next world. That points to the second difference

between religion and magic. In a religious ritual, such as reciting a prayer, there is often a goal—the hope that the prayer will be answered. But it is also possible to pray without asking for anything special; one could be giving thanks to the god through prayer. A magician, on the other hand, never recites a spell for its own sake. Magic is never an end in itself; it is always the means to an end. Magic is a direct attempt by a person to control supernatural forces to achieve a specific goal. In ancient Egypt, magic and religion were practiced without apparent conflict, and it often happened that they were used together to gain the desired end.

**RENENUTET** Serpent-headed fertility goddess, particularly of the harvest, Renenutet was also associated with ISIS. Her nurturing and supportive nature is like that of Isis, and like Isis, Renenutet was a guardian of the pharaoh. As the embodiment of the "divine mother," Renenutet is often shown suckling the children of the gods, the king, or the royal children, and it was said that her fierce gaze vanquished all of their enemies. As a goddess of the harvest, Renenutet was called the "Lady of the Granary," and shrines were erected in the fields during the annual harvest to honor her. As a protector of the crops, Renenutet is shown as a cobra nurturing the crops in the fields and presiding over the harvest.

**RENPET** Goddess of the New Year, represented as a young woman with a palm frond.

**RESHEF** (RESHEP, RESHPU) A Syrian war god adopted by the Egyptians during the New Kingdom (1550–1069 B.C.), Reshef was especially appealing to the warrior kings of Egypt because of his bold and warlike nature. He is mentioned on the stele of Amenhotep II (1427–1400 B.C.) erected near the Great Sphinx on the Giza Plateau. Reshef, along with the foreign goddess, Ashtoreth/ASTARTE, celebrates Amenhotep II's prowess and skill in horsemanship, and they "rejoice in the crown prince's diligence in caring for his horses."

During the early Eighteenth Dynasty, when Egypt was expanding its territory into Syria, the Egyptians must have recognized the foreign god who so closely resembled their own war gods. It is not surprising that Reshef is associated with SET and the Theban wargod MONTU with whom he has the most in common. Interestingly, Reshef's deadly force in battle could also be used in peacetime. Reshef's power could be a source of help for the common people,

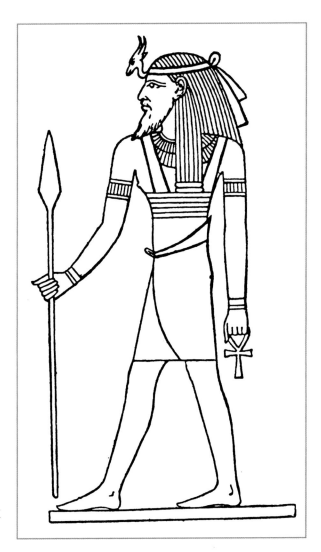

Reshef, a war god from Syria, was worshipped in Egypt during the New Kingdom. He is often depicted carrying a mace or an ax. *(Courtesy of Bob Brier)*

and they appealed to him for deliverance from their ills and diseases. He was particularly sought out to relieve stomach pains, and Reshef and his wife, Itum, were frequently called upon to "consume the demon causing the ailment."

So assimilated into the Egyptian pantheon was Reshef that he is shown in Egyptian garb, wearing the white crown of Upper Egypt, but with a gazelle's head, which associated him with Set, rather than the traditional cobra head, URAEUS. He is often shown wielding a club and wearing a Syrian-style beard. The only known carved stone statue of Reshef in Egyptian costume is in the Metropolitan Museum of Art in New York. A stele with the image of Reshef stands in the garden of the Egyptian Museum in Cairo.

**RESURRECTION** Ancient Egyptian religion was based on the idea of resurrection—the belief that the physical body would literally get up and go again in the NETHERWORLD. Unlike reincarnation, where it is believed that a person will come back to this world again, but in a completely different body, resurrection means that a person's body will be needed in the next world, and so it was necessary to preserve the body by MUMMIFICATION.

The MYTH OF ISIS AND OSIRIS tells the story of the first mummification and resurrection. ISIS went to extraordinary lengths to retrieve the body of her dead husband, OSIRIS, from Byblos (modern Lebanon) and return it to Egypt for proper burial. When her evil brother SET discovered the burial place of Osiris, he hacked the body into 13 pieces and scattered them across Egypt. For Osiris to live again in the Netherworld, it was crucial that Isis find all the pieces of Osiris's body and reassemble them so he could resurrect. Using her MAGIC, Isis restored Osiris's life force, and he arose to become the god of the Netherworld.

During the MIDDLE KINGDOM (2055–1650 B.C.), the priesthood introduced the idea that when a person died, he or she could become one with Osiris, and it became the dream of every Egyptian to resurrect with Osiris in the Netherworld. The concept of resurrection was one of the most powerful ideas in Egyptian religion, and when the Greeks and Romans ruled Egypt, they practiced mummification and hoped for immortality as well.

**ROSETTA STONE** A large inscribed stone discovered during Napoleon Bonaparte's Egyptian Campaign (1798–1799), the Rosetta stone was one of the most important archaeological finds in Egypt because it was the key to deciphering hieroglyphs. The Rosetta stone enabled early linguists to translate and read the myths of ancient Egypt.

When Napoleon sailed for Egypt, he took with him a group of scholars whose job it was to record everything they could about Egyptian civilization. The most significant discovery of the expedition was an accidental one. In the summer of 1799, the French army was fortifying the northern coast of Egypt. While digging a few miles from the town of Rosetta, they discovered a large black stone that was covered with writing in three different scripts. The scientists recognized that the top script was hieroglyphs and the bottom script was Greek. Later they realized that the middle script was DEMOTIC, a late form of Egyptian writing, and that the stone contained the same

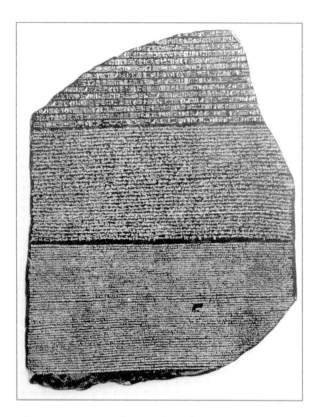

The Rosetta stone, key to deciphering ancient Egyptian hieroglyphs, was found by Napoleon's troops as they repaired a wall at Fort Rosetta. *(Photo by Pat Remler)*

The stone was taken to Cairo, where Napoleon had established an institute to study ancient Egyptian civilization. Copies of the stone were made and sent to France before the original went to the house of General de Menou in Alexandria for safekeeping.

In 1801, when the French army surrendered to the British, all Egyptian antiquities collected by Napoleon's expedition were confiscated, and the Rosetta stone went to the British Museum, where it remains today. In 1808, Jean-François CHAMPOLLION, who was then a teenager, obtained a copy of the Rosetta stone and began his life's work deciphering Egyptian hieroglyphs.

One of the most important decipherers of the stone was the brilliant English physicist Thomas Young. A physician and scientist by training, Young had made the study of ancient languages his avocation, and the Rosetta stone was just the kind of challenge he loved. By decoding it, he hoped to open the door to discovering the sciences of the ancient Egyptians. He decided to work on the demotic text first.

Young quickly realized that groupings of signs in the demotic inscription corresponded to names of the pharaoh in the Greek text. Soon he deduced that the demotic signs were basically phonetic. But more important, he began to see similarities between the demotic-sign groups and groups of signs in the hieroglyphic text. This meant that the hieroglyphs were phonetic, and by 1818, he had determined with some accuracy the hieroglyphic alphabet. After this start at deciphering the Rosetta stone, Young lost interest in the project and left it for Jean-François Champollion to complete.

message written in Greek and two Egyptian scripts. By translating the Greek, the scholars could tell that the Rosetta stone was a kind of "thank-you note" from the priests of Memphis to Ptolemy V for the gifts that the pharaoh had donated to the temple.

**SACRED LAKE** The Egyptians created artificial lakes, pools, and ponds to fulfill the needs of the various gods, and each temple usually had a sacred body of water within its precinct. The sacred lake at Karnak Temple was called the "divine pool," created for the sacred barque (boat) of Amun to sail on during his festivals. The temples of Armant, Dendera, Edfu, Medinet Habu, and Tanis all had sacred lakes that were used for the sacred barque of the gods and filled with ibises, geese, or crocodiles—the animals considered sacred to the temple.

**SACRED TREES** Because of the scarcity of trees in Egypt, the few varieties that thrived in the hot, dry land were associated with the gods. The Sycamore tree is linked with Hathor—as the "Lady of the Sycamore"—and with Nut and Isis. Sacred trees were often shown in funerary scenes on tomb walls, offering food and water to the deceased. In the burial chamber of Thutmose III, the sycamore tree has breasts and suckles the king.

The Persea tree is associated with the god Thoth and goddess Seshat, who are shown inscribing the

Every day at sunrise, the priests of Amun gathered at the sacred lake, where they set a goose free on the water to commemorate Amun's link with the Great Cackler who laid the cosmic egg. On festival days, the sacred boat of Amun sailed in a procession with other boats on the sacred lake. *(Photo by Pat Remler)*

**167**

The goddess Nut pours water from the sycamore tree to refresh the deceased on their journey to the Netherworld. *(Courtesy of Bob Brier)*

name of the king and the number of years of his reign on its leaves.

The date palm branch is the hieroglyphic symbol for year and is often linked with HEH, the god of eternity, and with Seshat when she records the king's *HEB-SED* FESTIVAL. HORUS is associated with the acacia tree, and the tamarisk tree is sacred to WEPWAWET.

The willow tree is associated with OSIRIS because in Byblos it was a willow that grew around the coffin that held the slain god. The various towns that claimed to have parts of his dismembered body all planted willow groves to honor the god.

## SAITE RECENSION

A revision of the BOOK OF THE DEAD that occurred during the Twenty-sixth Dynasty, when the Delta city of Sais was the capital of Egypt. When priests of the Saite period (664–525 B.C.) standardized the Book of the Dead, they organized the prayers, incantations, and spells into 192 chapters and eliminated all duplications that existed in previous versions of the Book of the Dead.

## SAQQARA

The sprawling necropolis for the city of MEMPHIS takes its name from SOKAR, a god associated with Osiris. The cemetery at Saqqara was used from the Predynastic to the Christian period (A.D. 395–540) and covers roughly four and one half square miles. It is one of the most densely populated cemeteries in all of Egypt. Because it was considered a sacred site, the tombs were reused over the centuries. During the Third Dynasty (2686–2613 B.C.), the architects began building in stone, and IMHOTEP designed the first large stone building, the STEP PYRAMID, over the tomb of ZOSER. Part of a large funerary complex, the Step Pyramid was built on a plateau overlooking ancient Memphis. Successive kings erected smaller pyramids, many of which are still standing. The Pyramid of Unas, the last king of the Fifth Dynasty (2375–2345 B.C.), was the first to be inscribed with magical spells, known as the PYRAMID TEXTS, that served as a guide to help the deceased king ascend safely to the heavens. Among the many tombs is the sacred burial place of the APIS BULL, the SERAPEUM. A series of underground chambers, the Serapeum housed the mummified bulls in huge granite sarcophagi. An avenue of sphinxes ran from the tomb to the mortuary temple some distance away. During the Ptolemaic period, the god SERAPIS was worshipped in a semicircular shrine that was built for statues of Greek poets and philosophers. Although nothing remains of the superstructure today, this shrine still stands near the entrance to the Serapeum.

## SARCOPHAGUS (Greek for "flesh eater")

Intended to preserve and protect the body, a sarcophagus is the

The sprawling necropolis Saqqara is best known as the site of the first pyramid (the Step Pyramid), built for King Zoser. *(Photo by Pat Remler)*

outer stone coffin that holds the inner anthropoid, or body-shaped, coffin. A sarcophagus can be either rectangular, anthropoid, or oval. It was usually carved from hard stone, typically granite or basalt, and was often decorated with scenes of funerary goddesses protecting the deceased. Mummies were sometimes placed in "nesting coffins" (TUTANKHAMEN had three) inside the sarcophagus. Although the sarcophagus is distinct from the coffin, they both served the same purpose—to protect the body of the deceased.

**SA SIGN** Representing the HIEROGLYPH for protection, the *sa* sign is enigmatic. It may represent a rolled-up herdsman's shelter or a PAPYRUS life preserver used by boatmen on the NILE. Whatever its origin, the *sa* was so popular in ancient Egypt that it was widely used in jewelry designs and decorative motifs. Often combined with the ANKH in a repeating motif, they formed a decorative border—giving life and protection. MAGIC WANDS from the MIDDLE KINGDOM (2055–1650 B.C.) were decorated with the *sa* sign to increase their potency. Many New Kingdom (1550–1069 B.C.) and later coffins had the *sa* sign inscribed on the head and the foot to give additional protection to the mummy. BES, the lion-headed household god, and TAURET, the hippopotamus goddess of childbirth, both carry the *sa* sign as their symbol, to bring added protection to those who honored them.

**SATIS** A member of the Elephantine Triad, Satis was either the daughter or the wife of Khnum the ram-headed god, depending on the period in Egyptian history (see FAMILY OF GODS). She was a goddess of the cataracts (boulders in the Nile) and a water goddess, with the Nile part of her domain. As guardian of Egypt's southern frontier, Satis was believed to fend off Egypt's invaders with her arrows. As a fertility goddess, Satis was worshipped in all of Nubia. She is shown as a woman wearing the tall white crown of Upper Egypt decorated with antelope horns on either side. Elephantine Island at Aswan in southern Egypt was the main cult center for Satis, although her name is mentioned in the PYRAMID TEXTS as a goddess of purification of disease.

**SCARAB BEETLE** For the ancient Egyptians, the common scarab beetle, *Scarabaeus sacer*, was a daily reminder of KHEPRI, the manifestation of the sun god RE in the early morning. Khepri's job was to help the rising sun journey across the sky each day, and he is often portrayed as a beetle rolling the sun in front of him. The Egyptians noticed that the scarab beetles rolled balls of dung along the ground, and they saw this as an analogy for the sun moving across the sky. When they observed young beetles emerging from the ball of dung, it gave rise to the idea that the scarab reproduced without benefit of a mate. Actually, after fertilization, the female deposited her eggs in a bit of dung and rolled it into a ball so that when they hatched, the newborns had food. Since the emergence from the dung ball was the only part of this cycle that the Egyptians saw, they assumed the beetle was somewhat like the god ATUM, who begot children without a partner.

The Greeks were fascinated with the Egyptian culture and often wrote about their observations. The fifth-century Greek philosopher Horapollo from Alexandria gave an account of how the scarab beetle reproduces:

> To denote an *only begotten, or generation*, or a *generation*, or a *father*, or a *world* or a *man*, they delineate Scarabaeus. And they symbolize by this an *only begotten*, because the Scarabaeus is a creature self-produced, being unconceived by a female; for the propagation of it is unique after this manner:—when the male is desirous of procreating he takes dung of an ox, and shapes it into a spherical form like the world; he then rolls it from the hinder parts from east to west, looking himself toward the east, that he may impart to it the figure of the world (for that is borne from east to west); then, having dug a hole, the Scarabaeus deposits this ball in the earth for the space of twenty-eight days (for in so many days the moon passes through twelve signs of the zodiac). By thus remaining under the moon, the race of scarabaei is imbued with life; and upon the ninth and twentieth day after having opened the ball, it casts it into the water, for it is aware that upon that day the conjunction of the moon and sun takes place, as well as the generation of the world.

> Horapollo, Book 1, X

For thousands of years, scarab AMULETS were carved in Egypt. It was believed that wearing a scarab amulet brought protection and a long life. It was actually a pun, for the word *kheper* in hieroglyphs means both "scarab" and "to exist." Egyptians wore scarabs as protection from harm and evil, and they sometimes carved the name of a pharaoh because the pharaoh was under the protection of all the gods. A scarab with the name of Thutmose III was a favorite.

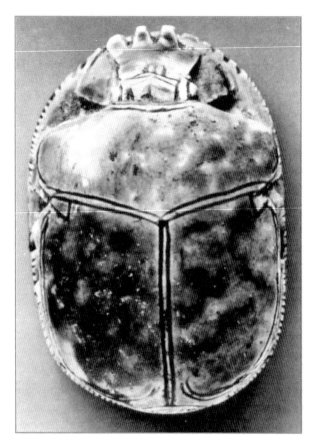

The scarab was associated with long life, and scarabs were often placed on the mummy to give new life after death. The hieroglyph for scarab means "to exist." *(Photo by Pat Remler)*

One of the five names of the pharaoh (see KINGSHIP AND THE GODS), ⌂⚮⊙ (Men-Kheper-Re), as Thutmose was also called, was so popular that scarabs with the name Men-Kheper-Re were being produced a thousand years after Thutmose's death. Sometimes scarabs had popular inscriptions such as "Amun-Re is behind you, there is no fear," or "A mother is a truly good thing." There is even an inscription that reads "Have a good day." Whatever the message, it was meant to bring protection to the wearer.

Not all scarab amulets were protective. Royal commemorative scarabs were issued to celebrate events and to send messages about the power of the pharaoh. Usually large, sometimes nine inches long, they were carved on the bottom with details of the event. These scarabs were sent like proclamations to rulers of foreign countries and to high Egyptian court officials. The most famous commemorative scarabs are those of Amenhotep III (1479–1425 B.C.). These scarabs celebrated five major events: a wild bull hunt; a lion hunt; the arrival of one of his minor wives, a

princess from the land of Mitanni; the construction of a pleasure lake for Queen Tiye; and the marriage of Amenhotep III and Tiye.

The scarab was also crucial in Egyptian funerary rites. Starting in the Middle Kingdom and continuing into the Ptolemaic period, scarabs were used to protect the heart of the mummy. When the deceased entered the Netherworld, he or she was judged and his or her heart was weighed against the feather of truth. Heart scarabs, usually carved in stone and about four inches long, were inscribed with a magical spell on the bottom designed to keep the heart quiet during judgment. It was feared that the heart might speak out against its owner and testify against him or her. This is why part of the spell reads:

> O heart of my mother, O heart of my mother. Do not stand against me as a witness. Do not outweigh me before the keeper of the balance.

> Book of the Dead, spell 30B

The heart scarab of the Middle Kingdom mummy of Wah was solid silver. On the top, Wah's name and titles were inlaid with gold. On the bottom was an ankh sign with a few other hieroglyphs. Before the heart scarab was buried with Wah, the eyes and mouth of the scarab were destroyed so that if the scarab magically came to life, it could not harm its owner.

Scarab beetles were an essential ingredient in various magical potions. One spell in the Leiden-London magical PAPYRUS includes a complex set of instructions to make a woman fall in love with the magician. In part, the instructions read: When the sun rises, the magician dressed in a magic cape, with palm fibers masking his face, catches a "fish-face" scarab, and as the sun rose in the sky, he recited the following magical spell seven times:

> Thou are this scarab of real lapis-lazuli, I have taken thee out of the door of my temple thou carriest [?] . . . of bronze to thy nose [?], that can eat [?] the herbage that is trampled [?], the field-plants [?] that are injured for the great images of the men of Egypt. I dispatch thee to N. born of N. to strike her from her heart to her belly, to her entrails, to her womb; for she it is hath wept [?] before the Sun in the morning, she saying to the Sun, 'Come not forth,' to the Moon, 'Rise not,' to the water, 'Come not to the men of Egypt,' to the fields, 'Grow not green,' and to the great trees of the men of Egypt, 'Flourish not,' I dispatch thee to N. born of N. to injure her from her heart

unto her belly, unto her entrails, unto her womb, and she shall put herself on the road [?] after N. born of N. at every time [?]

The scarab beetle then was drowned in the milk of a black cow and left until evening, when more spells were chanted. This was followed by several complicated rituals that ended when the resulting potion containing the dead scarab was dropped into a beaker of wine and given to the person whom the magician hoped would fall in love.

Sometimes scarab beetles were mummified, so it is almost certain that they were sacred to the Egyptians. Their magical powers can be assumed from several of their uses: parts of the body and the wings were used to make an ointment for stiff joints; the wing cases were used in an unguent to facilitate childbirth; and evil spells were undone when a large beetle was beheaded, its wings removed, and body burned.

**SCORPION GODDESS**  See SELKET.

**SEKHMET**  The lioness-headed goddess, Sekhmet was called the "Powerful One," a name that fit the destructive side of her personality. Mythology tells us that Sekhmet was the "destructive eye" of RE, and with the fire-spitting cobra (the URAEUS), they were protectors of the king. The hot desert wind was called the "breath of Sekhmet," and it was said that she belched fire upon her enemies. So great was her fury that the evil SET and the terrible serpent APOPHIS gave way to her.

The BOOK OF THE DIVINE COW says that HATHOR becomes Sekhmet when the sun god Re sends her to destroy humankind. Sekhmet rampaged on a blood lust across the land. Only the gods' trickery stopped Sekhmet's fury, and humankind was saved.

In the capital city of MEMPHIS, Sekhmet was the wife of PTAH and mother to NEFERTUM (see FAMILY OF GODS). In the Delta, she was associated with the cat goddess, BASTET. Sekhmet is shown as a lioness or as a woman with a feline head, wearing the solar disk and a uraeus. Her garment is a long sheath dress with rosettes over her breasts.

When the Theban Triad—AMUN, and his wife, MUT, and their son KHONSU—rose to prominence in THEBES, Mut became associated with Sekhmet and assumed many of her attributes. Numerous statues of Mut-Sekhmet were erected in the Precinct of Mut at Karnak Temple.

If a plague swept through Egypt, it was said to be carried by a "messenger of Sekhmet," and the Egyptians believed that if Sekhmet could bring

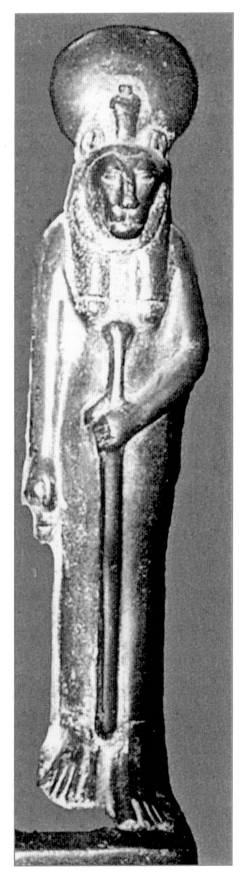

Sekhmet, the lioness-headed goddess, was known for her violent nature. *(Photo by Pat Remler)*

pestilence, then she could also ward off illness. So Sekhmet became a goddess of healing as well as of destruction.

**SELKET** (also SERKET or SELKIS)  A scorpion goddess, Selket is usually shown as a woman with a scorpion on her head, and her name is derived from a term that means "she who causes the throat to breathe." Perhaps the rest of the phrase might have been "for the last time," as a scorpion sting is extremely dangerous and can cause death. Selket is one of the most ancient goddesses in Egypt, having been associated with the Predynastic King Scorpion. In the Old Kingdom, she appears as a protector of the throne and the king, but her most important role is with the funerary cult and the deceased. She is called "Lady of the Beautiful House," a reference to her assistance in the embalmer's tent during mummification. In the BOOK OF TWO WAYS, she watches over the "dangerous winding path," a reference to moving the mummy to its tomb. She is one of four guardians of the canopic chest and assists Isis as she performs the funerary rites over OSIRIS. In the myth of the SEVEN SCORPIONS, the seven appear as a manifestation of Selket when they accompany Isis to the Delta.

**SEPT**  A NOME GOD, Sept was worshipped at Per-Sept (house of Sept), the capital of his home. He is a warrior god, and his titles include "Lord of the East," "the Bull That Tramples Menti," and "Sept, the Smiter of Menti," a tribe from the Eastern Desert. When he is portrayed as a man, Sept can wear different attributes as his crown: the sun disk, the double plume, or the tall triangle symbol △, meaning "to give." Sometimes he wears a MENAT on his back. He can also appear as a mummified hawk with plumes on his head and with a menat. As the "lord of battle," he appears as a hawk-headed lion holding a bow and a club in his human hands. Sept is mentioned in the BOOK OF THE DEAD as the one who "drives away the crocodiles of the south," among other epithets, and appears on the walls of Edfu Temple as "the hidden sign of Sept."

**SERAPEUM**  There were two serapeums in ancient Egypt, one at SAQQARA and the other in Alexandria. The name "serapeum" comes from a corruption of the names of Osiris and Apis, Osir-Ap. The older of the two is at Saqqara, near modern Cairo, and is the best preserved. The Saqqara Serapeum served as the tomb of the sacred APIS BULLS from the Eighteenth Dynasty (1550–1295 B.C.) through

the rule of the Greek Ptolemies (332–32 B.C.). The huge underground chambers held massive granite sarcophagi of the mummified Apis bulls. One of Ramses the Great's sons, Prince Khaemwaset, took an interest in preserving the serapeum, and his own tomb, as yet undiscovered, is believed to be nearby. The Greek writer Strabo (63 B.C.–A.D. 21) mentioned the serapeum and the sphinxes.

The serapeum in Alexandria was a temple serving as the cult center for the composite Greek and Egyptian god SERAPIS. When the Christian emperor Theodosius II (A.D. 379–395) ordered the destruction of all ancient religious monuments, the serapeum in Alexandria was destroyed. Ancient writers frequently praised the beauty of the Alexandria Serapeum, which was built in two stages. The first part was built during the reign of Ptolemy III, when worship of Serapis became popular, and a large enclosure wall was built around the temple of Serapis. The second part was built during the reign of the Roman emperor Hadrian. Like all Ptolemaic temples, the walls and foundations were set in trenches cut into the rock, but the most unusual features of this temple were the two fireplaces used to heat the air that was circulated through pottery ducts. Because of the destruction of the temple, it is difficult to tell what the rooms were used for. Undoubtedly, some were used as storage rooms for the priests' garments and cult objects. Scholars have suggested that some rooms held the volumes of the "Daughter Library," the annex to the great library of Alexandria, which was established in the serapeum by Ptolemy III. When the "Mother Library" (the famed Library of Alexandria) burned in 48 B.C., Antony gave Cleopatra VII 200,000 volumes from the library in Pergamum (in modern Turkey), and it is believed that some of these volumes were housed in the serapeum. It has been suggested that the fireplaces may have been used to heat the air and keep the books dry in Alexandria's damp climate.

Cleopatra had a special interest in the serapeum, for it was in this temple that she dressed as Isis, assumed the role of the "living goddess," and presided over religious rituals and festivals. It was also where Antony presented her with the captive royal family after his conquest of Armenia.

Rufinus, one of the ancient sources of information on the serapeum, mentions that the upper floors of the temple contained lecture halls and that there was a window through which the sun's rays bathed a statue of Serapis.

**SERAPIS** The cult of Serapis was introduced by the Ptolemies and was the result of merging the Egyptian gods Osiris and Apis. When Ptolemy I became ruler of Egypt after the death of Alexander the Great, he embraced Serapis, the new composite god, and gave him a Hellenized or Greek appearance, making Serapis a more appealing god to the Greek population in Alexandria. Serapis was shown wearing a chiton, a Greek garment, and long hair and a beard. He carries a basket on his head as a symbol of Egypt's bountiful harvests. Because Serapis was a combination of the names Apis and Osiris, and because Osiris's wife was Isis, the goddess also became the wife of Serapis. Isis and Serapis were often shown together with their new "Hellenistic" look.

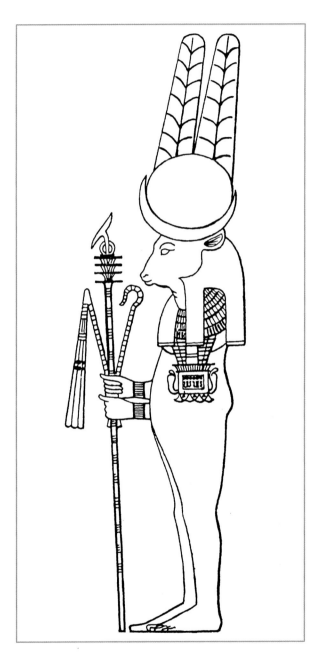

The Egyptian name for Serapis is *usr ap*, a combination of the gods Osiris and Apis. Shown with the body of a man and the head of a bull, Serapis has a sun disk between his horns and an atef feather headdress, and he holds the crook and flail of the king. *(Courtesy of Bob Brier)*

**SERDAB** (*PER-TWT*) The Arabic word for "cellar," the serdabs of the Old Kingdom (2686–2181 b.c.) were rooms in the early mastaba tombs that held *KA* statues of the deceased. The serdab was an enclosed chamber with no doors or windows and was next to, or part of, the offering chapel in the funerary complex. Inside was a life-size stone statue of the deceased intended to provide a resting place for the *ka* if the mummy were destroyed. The serdab had two small holes in one wall so the statue could gaze out for all eternity and the *ka* could move in and out and receive offerings of food and incense.

**SEREKH** One of the earliest symbols in hieroglyphs, in Egyptian mythology the *serekh* represents protection of the king by the gods. The *serekh* sometimes has the king's name inside the rectangular shape that is said to represent a palace façade, and often on top of the *serekh* is Horus, the protector of the king. Even after the king's name was customarily written in a cartouche, his Horus name continued to be placed in the *serekh*. The *serekh* shape often adorned coffins and sarcophagi, associating the deceased with the protection of Horus.

**SERPENT GODS** In Egyptian mythology, the many serpent gods tend to merge together into one cosmic serpent, making it difficult to tell them apart. They often represented chaos and possessed demonic powers. Serpent gods were frequently shown with beards to identify their gender and sometimes with many heads or legs and feet to help them move through the Underworld.

The first serpent god was the primeval serpent who arose in darkness from the primordial waters before anything was created and who proclaimed in the Pyramid Texts:

> I extended everywhere, in accordance with what
>     was to come into existence . . .
> I bent around myself, I was encircled in my
> coils,
>     one who made a place for himself in the midst of
>     his coils.

The primeval serpent is a symbol for creation. In a sense, the primeval serpent is an aspect of ATUM the creator. Once the creator god, Atum, was manifest, the primeval serpent returned to the days of chaos. There was a belief that when the world came to an end, it would fall into a state of chaos, and Atum would once again become the serpent. This prophecy is mentioned in Chapter 175 of the Book of the Dead. It was common for leaders in the First Intermediate period (2181–2055 B.C.), a time filled with turmoil, to equate themselves with "the great surviving serpent [who remains] when all mankind has reverted to slime."

The cosmic serpent played many parts in Egyptian mythology. Not only was he the ancient being who existed before the world was created, the cosmic serpent also was the archetype of evil who had to be vanquished each day to keep order in the world. In the Book of the Dead, the serpent serves both as a guardian of the Underworld and as APOPHIS, who represents darkness and is the archenemy of the sun. He became Sito, the serpent whose coils encircled the Earth and who stretched around the Earth until his tail met his mouth. He claimed he would exist for all time: "I am Sito, with many years, I die and am reborn every day. I am Sito who dwells in the farthest regions of the world." The cosmic serpent was associated with the Nile and its hidden caverns that were thought to produce the annual flood and with fertility and the corn god, Neheb-kau.

Judging by the number of curses to ward them off, venomous snakes were abundant in ancient Egypt. Snakes were to be feared and avoided, but from the Pyramid Texts it is clear that, because of their association with the gods, they were also respected:

If you are harmful to me, I will step on you,
But if you recognize me I will not tread on you,
For you are the mysterious and shapeless thing, of whom
The gods foretold that you should have neither arms nor legs
On which to go following your brother gods.

**SESHAT** The goddess of measurement and writing, Seshat presided over the STRETCHING OF THE CORD CEREMONY, particularly when the foundations of the pyramids were aligned with true north, south, east, and west. She was the patron goddess of builders, and in her capacity as goddess of measurement and writing, Seshat is often shown wearing a panther skin and a headband with a seven-pointed star and bow. In the Eighteenth Dynasty (1550–1069

B.C.), she became associated with the king's royal jubilee. Her most important task was to record the years that each king reigned and she symbolically attended the king during his *Heb-Sed* Festival, a ceremony to renew the king's vigor. One inscription reads, "Thou shalt renew thy youth; thou shalt flourish again like Aah-Thoth when he is a child."

During this time, her attribute changed and she carried a notched palm frond that marked the passing of time. Seshat was sometimes shown writing the name of the king on the leaves of the PERSEA TREE, following the tradition of THOTH, the god of wisdom, who was her male counterpart or consort.

**SET (SETH)** The god of evil, chaos, and darkness, Set began with a peaceful and benign nature. He was the son of GEB and NUT, husband and brother of NEPHTHYS, and brother of OSIRIS and ISIS. Images of Set appear in the Early Dynastic period (c. 4000–3500 B.C.) on an ivory fragment and on the mace head of King Scorpion (c. 3150 B.C.). He was favored by the Second Dynasty kings Peribsen and Khasekhemwy, who adopted Set as their benefactor. The Set animal adorns the top of their *SEREKHS* (rectangular shapes symbolizing the king). The *serekhs* also included the image of HORUS, the traditional protector of the king.

Set is mentioned in the PYRAMID TEXTS as ruling the sky with Horus, the falcon god. Early mythology refers to a platform of iron resting on four pillars that formed the floor of heaven and declares that Set and Horus worked together to help Osiris reach the floor of heaven. But a rivalry soon occurred. Horus was the god of the sky by day, and Set was the god of the night sky, but he was not satisfied. Their conflict was viewed as the battle between good and evil. The opposition of day and night was manifested in a battle called the CONTENDINGS OF HORUS AND SET. In one version of the myth, Set wished to stop the sun from appearing in the sky each morning, and he changed into various forms, one of which was Apep, the evil serpent of the Underworld, in order to stop the sun. Set also had an association with SOBEK, the crocodile god, who had an evil side to his nature as well.

The Set animal has never been identified, but scholars have suggested that it is a mythical creature. It has a canine body, with a long nose resembling that of an anteater; the ears are tall and squared off; the tail is long and forked. The Set animal was associated with the color red, the color of the desert, and animals with red fur, even men with red hair, were believed to be followers of Set.

As god of chaotic forces, Set was both respected and reviled. The Set animal has never been identified and may be a composite or mythical animal. *(Drawing by Mary Jordan)*

One of the most popular Egyptian tales, the ISIS AND OSIRIS myth, relates how Set, the archetype of the devil, killed his brother Osiris, dismembered the body, and scattered the pieces. To avenge his father's death, Horus battled with Set for 70 years, and finally the gods settled the dispute, making Set ruler of the desert, foreign lands and the night sky.

Each year the Festival of Victory was held at Edfu Temple, the cult center for Horus, to celebrate Horus's victory over Set. In the drama that was enacted each year, Set took the form of a hippopotamus or a pig. The temple wall shows scenes of Horus harpooning Set. An allegory for good triumphing over evil, the triumph of Horus is complete when he inflicts 10 wounds on the body of the hippopotamus: the snout, forehead, neck, back of the head, ribs, back, testicles, haunches, legs, and hocks.

In spite of his evil nature, a cult of Set existed that seems to have developed early in Egypt's history. It was sometimes considered auspicious to make sacrifices to Set during certain seasons of the year when his influence was considered the greatest. An antelope was sacrificed to stop Set from attacking the full moon. Sometimes birds and fish associated with Set were caught and hacked to pieces while priests chanted, "Ye shall be cut to pieces, and your members shall be hacked asunder, and each of you shall consume the other; thus doth he triumph over all his enemies."

It has been suggested that in killing Osiris, Set contributed to the idea of resurrection, which became the basis of Egyptian religion and, as such, it appears that followers of Set were not discriminated against in ancient Egypt. In fact, the father of Ramses the Great, Seti I, was named for the god: His name means follower of Set.

**SETI I, TEMPLE OF** Built by Seti I, the father of Ramses the Great, the temple of Seti I is at ABYDOS, next to the OSIREION, the symbolic burial place of OSIRIS. Seti built his temple to emphasize his piety and his support of the traditional gods of Egypt. Inside the temple the seven chapels are dedicated to Seti as a god, Ptah, Re-Horakhty, Amun-Re, Osiris, Isis, and Horus. Each chapel is decorated with scenes of offerings and the daily life of the gods. In a corridor known as the Gallery of Kings, Seti I and his son Ramses II are reading the names of the previous kings of Egypt, their ancestors, to ensure that they will have food and drink for the coming year in their continued existence in the NETHERWORLD.

**SEVEN ARROWS OF SEKHMET** In the myth of the DESTRUCTION OF MANKIND, HATHOR and SEKHMET represent the dual of good and evil. When the sun god RE asks Hathor to destroy humankind, she becomes Sekhmet, a bloodthirsty lioness. The Seven Arrows of Sekhmet symbolize the evil or corrupt nature of the goddess, while the SEVEN HATHORS represent the warm and loving aspect of her nature.

**SEVEN GODDESSES OF CHILDBIRTH** BES, HATHOR, HEKET, MESKHENET, ISIS, NEKHBET, and TAURET all assisted in childbirth in some way. Since ancient Egyptians were free to worship as many gods or goddesses as they wished, when it came to childbirth, several goddesses could be involved. Different goddesses were responsible for different aspects of the process, so a woman might wear the amulet of the pregnant hippopotamus called Tauret, "the great one," around her neck throughout the term of her pregnancy. After the child was born, she might wear a Bes amulet and place one on the baby as well.

One of the myths written on the PAPYRUS Westcar is called the "Birth of Kings" and tells how the goddesses assist in childbirth:

> "... They entered into the presence of Reddedet ... Isis placed herself in front of her, Nephthys behind her, and Heket hastened the childbirth. Isis then said: Do not be strong in her womb in this your name of Wo-sr-ef. This child slipped forth upon her hands as a child, one cubit long, whose bones were firm, and covering of whose limbs was of gold, and whose headdress was of real lapis lazuli. They washed him, his umbilical cord was cut, and he was placed upon a cushion on bricks. Then Meskhenet approached him, and she said: A king who will exercise the kingship in this entire land! Khnum caused his limbs to move.
>
> Next Isis placed herself in front of her [Reddedet], Nephthys behind her, and Heket hastened the childbirth. Isis said: Do not kick in her womb in this your name of Sa-hu-re. And this child slipped out on her hands as a child, one cubit long, whose bones were firm, and covering of whose limbs was of gold, and whose headdress was of real lapis lazuli. They washed him, his umbilical cord was cut, and he was placed upon a cushion on bricks. Then Meskhenet approached him, and she said: A king who will exercise the kingship in this entire land! Khnum caused his limbs to move.
>
> Then Isis placed herself before her, Nephthys behind her, and Heket hastened the childbirth. Isis said: Do not be dark in her womb in this your name of Keku. And the child slipped forth upon her hands as a child, one cubit long, whose bones were firm, and covering of whose limbs was of gold, and whose headdress was of real lapis lazuli. They washed him, his umbilical cord was cut, and he was placed upon a cushion on bricks. Then Meskhenet approached him, and she said: A king who will exercise the kingship in this entire land! Khnum caused his limbs to move.
>
> Now the goddesses came forth after having delivered Reddedet of the three sons and they said: May you be pleased, Rewosre [the father] for there have been born to you three children ..."

Here we see the importance of repetition in ancient literature—to say it is to make it happen for each of the three births. Each goddess had a specific magical function to perform, and with all the goddesses participating, healthy children would be born.

**SEVEN HATHORS** A list of the goddess HATHOR's most important titles that were viewed as seven goddesses, sometimes called "the Seven Celestial Kine" (cows). The names of the Seven Hathors varied from temple to temple. Representations of the Seven Hathors appear in the tomb of Nefertari, the wife of Ramses II.

**SEVEN SACRED OILS** Magical unguents used in embalming and preserving mummies were the same seven sacred oils the Egyptians used in their daily lives. Traditionally the seven sacred oils were: festival perfume, *Hekenu* oil, Syrian balsam, *Nechenem* salve, anointing oil, best cedar oil, and best Libyan oil. The importance of sacred oil is evident from the OLD KINGDOM. Utterance 72 of the PYRAMID TEXTS ensures that UNAS has a supply of sacred oil for the next world:

> Osiris Unas, I make full thy eye (for thee) with ointment—festival perfume
> Osiris Unas take the outflow of his face— *Hekenu-oil*
> Osiris Unas, take the Eye of Horus, on account of which he fought—*Sefeth oil*
> Osiris Unas, take the Eye of Horus of which he took possession—*Neshenem Oil*
> Osiris Unas take the Eye of Horus, which brought the gods to him through it—*Tuat-oil*
> Oh ointment, O ointment, arise, hurry!
> Thou who art on the brow of Horus, arise! First quality Cedar oil ...
> Osiris Unas, I bring thee the Eye of Horus which he takes, which is on thy brow,
> First quality Libyan oil ...

Unas is called OSIRIS UNAS because he is being associated with Osiris, god of the dead, who will help Unas resurrect in the next world.

The seven sacred oils were kept in small jars, many of which were carved from alabaster. COSMETIC chests were often fitted with seven small pots to hold the oils. Besides being used in MUMMIFICATION, sacred oil was used to anoint cult statues in temples and as perfume and unguents in the home.

**SEVEN SCORPIONS** Manifestations of the scorpion goddess, SELKET, the seven scorpions were the companions of ISIS when she fled into the Delta to hide from her evil brother SET.

**SHABAKA STONE** A black basalt stone slab inscribed in the Twenty-fifth Dynasty by the Nubian king Shabaka, the slab describes the creation of the world. It proclaims that the god PTAH created the world and everything in it.

The introduction on the Shabaka Stone says it was copied from the original document (probably written on PAPYRUS), which was damaged with worm holes:

> ... This writing was copied new ... for his majesty found it to be a writing of the ancestors that was eaten by worms [and] could not be understood from beginning to end ...

The text is archaic (an early form of the language), perhaps dating from the time of the PYRAMID TEXTS. It talks about what is today called the "Philosophy of a Memphite Priest," or The Memphite Theology—one of the three main CREATION MYTHS in ancient Egypt. Most important in the Memphite Theology are the ideas that Ptah was unifier of the country and king of Egypt; Memphis is the capital of Egypt and oversees UPPER and LOWER EGYPT; and Ptah created the world and everything in it. Part of the inscription reads:

> The gods who came into being in Ptah ... they took shape in his heart, they took shape on his tongue ... for the very great one is Ptah, who gave life to all the gods and their *ka*s through his heart and through his tongue ...

In other words, Ptah created the world and everything in it by thinking (the Egyptians believed a person thought with the heart) the thing and speaking the name.

The text is badly damaged because in the nineteenth century, Egyptian farmers recut the stone to use as a grindstone. Also, the scribes left blank spaces on the stone where the original papyrus copy was damaged. Religious texts are usually read from right to left, and at first the script did not make sense to Egyptologists until they realized that the columns of text were retrograde—written backward—left to right. Although the Shabaka stone is terribly damaged, it remains one of the most interesting documents in ancient Egypt's 3,000-year history, for it suggests an earlier version of the creation story found in the New Testament.

**SHEHBUI** God of the west wind (see WINDS, GODS OF THE FOUR).

**SHEN** ☥ A circle without beginning or end, the shen symbolizes eternity, protection, and infinity. The shen hieroglyph represents a length of rope looped into a circle, folded and tied at the bottom. The shen sign is used in funerary decorations to symbolize eternal life for the deceased and on royal jewelry as amuletic protection to the wearer. The shen is associated with the sun disk and is called the first round CARTOUCHE, the magical oval that encircles the name of the pharaoh. In many royal ritual scenes, NEKHBET, the vulture goddess, appears with wings outstretched and grasping the shen sign in her claws.

**SHESMU** (SHEZMU, SESMU) ▭ 𓄿 𓄿 or ▽ Best known as the god of the wine press, Shesmu has a complex personality. From the PYRAMID TEXTS of UNAS, we learn of his generous nature—he offers grape juice to Unas with which to make wine in the next world, and he ferociously attacks the enemies of Unas: "... He casts wickedness on him that is wicked and truth upon he who follows truth. ..." Shesmu directs the pressing of grapes and oils of all kinds, including olive, pine, castor, almond, and oil from the seeds of the moringa tree, which grows in the desert and is quite rare. Oil from the moringa tree was used for making perfume, and Shesmu also became a god of perfume and SACRED OILS used in temple rituals and embalming.

Egyptian mythology interchanges the idea of red wine and blood. It was the color, rather than the actual substance, that was important to the Egyptians. When Shesmu is portrayed as a friend of the dead, he offers them WINE to ease their journey to the NETHERWORLD. At the same time, he is linked with Apep, a terrible demon of the Underworld, and is shown tossing the heads of enemies into his wine press to extract the blood as if it were grape juice. For the Egyptians, red wine was synonymous with blood. In the CANNIBAL HYMN, Shesmu helps Unas gain power in the next world:

> ... Behold, Shesmu has cut them up for Unas, he has boiled pieces of them in his blazing cauldrons. Unas has eaten their words of power, he has eaten their spirits.

The BOOK OF THE DEAD tells us that one of Shesmu's titles is "Lord of the Blood," and in Chapter 175, Osiris commands that Shesmu dismember the evil ones and place their heads in a wine press to be pressed like grapes and create wine.

Most often Shesmu appears as a lion-headed or a hawk-headed man with a URAEUS on his head. His main cult center was in the Fayoum, but he was also worshipped at Edfu and Dendera, where he is shown on the temple walls traveling in a solar boat wearing a uraeus and two stars on his head. Shesmu is linked with RE (as the setting sun for the red color), Apep (the evil god of the Underworld and enemy of Re), HERISHEF (who shares his title, "Lord of the Blood"), HORUS (when he assumes the head of a falcon), THOTH (as a god of wisdom), and Nefertum (as a god of perfume).

**SHIPWRECKED SAILOR, MYTH OF THE** The tale of the shipwrecked sailor was written in the Twelfth Dynasty (1985–1795 B.C.) and is seemingly part of a series of myths. The single surviving version is in the Hermitage Museum in St. Petersburg, Russia. The story begins during the reign of Amenemhet I, the king who had restored peace and prosperity to Egypt after years of civil war and strife. One day an Egyptian sailor wandering in the courtyard of the great palace at Thebes spied the king's vizier and rushed to his side to ask for a favor. The vizier, or prime minister, was not accustomed to such requests and spoke sharply to the sailor. But the sailor continued to beg for an audience with the pharaoh so that he could delight the king with his strange tale. Finally the vizier agreed to hear the tale himself and judge whether the tale would please the pharaoh. So the sailor began his tale.

> We set off for the mines of the pharaoh, in a fine ship rowed by a hundred and fifty of the pharaoh's heartiest sailors. . . . The captain watched the skies for storm clouds, but the weather was clear and the sea was calm. Then suddenly a storm was upon us, and a gale wind drove our boat toward land. As we neared the shore the waves were 8 cubits high (the cubit is an Egyptian measurement that equals about 2 feet) and they broke over our ship, and dashed us on the rocks. I held fast to a piece of wood and made a great leap into the sea as the rocks smashed our boat. At that moment a huge wave carried me high over the rocks and onto a sandy beach. The boat was destroyed and every man perished. I crawled into a sheltering thicket away from the storm. When the sun rose the next morning, I gave thanks to the gods for my safe delivery, when all my companions had perished. The island was uninhabited and I was alone, but it was a beautiful island, like no man has ever

seen. When I was hungry there were fruits and vegetables of every variety and birds and fish of every kind. I ate from all the fruits around me, and on the third day I kindled a fire and made a burnt offering to the gods, and then I prepared meat and fish. After my fine meal I sat resting comfortably, when suddenly there was a terrifying noise as loud as thunder and the trees were bending under the terrible wind. I was frightened and thought a gigantic wave was upon me. When no wave washed over me, I lifted my head to look around, and saw a most frightening sight. Slowly making its way toward me was a gigantic serpent, 30 cubits long, its scales were made of gold and its eyes were of lapis lazuli. The serpent stopped and coiled itself in front of me where I lay with my face on the ground. He reared his head high and demanded, "What has brought you here? What has brought you here, little one? Say what has brought you to my island! Tell me at once or I will burn you with fire. Speak! I am waiting to hear what I have not heard before, something new!" Then the serpent lowered his head and grasped me in his huge jaws and carried me to his cave. He placed me on the ground without hurting me. Again he said, "What has brought you, what has brought you, little one? Say what has brought you to this island in the midst of the sea with waves breaking all around it?" So terrified was I, that I prostrated myself before him as if I were in front of the pharaoh himself. "I sailed by command of Amen-em-het, Pharaoh of Egypt, in a great ship one hundred and fifty cubits long to bring the treasure from the mines in the south. But a great tempest dashed the ship upon the rocks, and all were lost except for me. I held fast to a piece of wood and a wave carried me over the rocks to the shore. I have been here for three days. So I am your servant brought here by the waves."

> The serpent assured me that I was in no danger and urged me not to be sad over my fate. The gods must have sent you he said, since I alone survived the storm. And he said he would predict my future: After four months have passed, a ship from Egypt will come to the island and carry me home safely into the arms of my wife and children. When I was reassured the great serpent said, "Let me tell you of the island, for it is pleasant to hear of strange things, and you will have a tale to tell when you return to your home and kneel before the Pharaoh. I dwell on this island with my family and my children,

seventy-five serpents in all, and only one stranger has come among us, a lovely girl who appeared strangely and on whom the fire of heaven fell and who was turned into ashes. As for you, I do not think that heaven holds any thunderbolts for one who has lived through such dangers." I bowed before him and thanked him saying, "All that I have said is the truth, and if what you have told me is true, I will go before the pharaoh and tell him of your greatness when I return to Egypt. And I will return with offerings of sacred oils and perfumes in incense that is of the quality offered to the gods in their temples. I will tell him of the wonders of this island, and sacrifice an ass to you, and Pharaoh shall send out a ship filled with the riches of Egypt as presents to your majesty." The great serpent laughed at my words, saying: "I am the prince of Punt; myrrh belongs to me!" and he told me that his island had more perfume than Punt (a land known for its perfume and incense) and they only lacked for sacred oils. But he said I would never return with them because as soon as I left the island it would disappear and never be seen until the gods decided to reveal it again to some wanderer like myself.

I lived happily on the enchanted island and the four months passed all too quickly, and one day I saw a ship sailing toward me. I sought the serpent king, but he knew of the ship already, and he bid me farewell, and gave me many precious gifts. When I boarded the ship, the island seemed to float away. Eventually we landed on the shores of the Red Sea in Egypt, and I have hurried across the desert to Thebes to tell my story to the pharaoh. The vizier was greatly impressed and said, "Whether or not I believe your adventures, you have told a great tale such as to delight the heart of the pharaoh. Therefore come with me at once and be sure of a rich reward . . ."

**SHU** The god of air, Shu separates the Earth and the sky, which are also his children GEB and NUT. Shu's sister-wife is TEFNUT, the goddess of moisture, and they are all part of the HELIOPOLITAN ENNEAD, the creation myth that originated in HELIOPOLIS.

**SISTRUM** A musical instrument used in religious ceremonies, the sistrum is a kind of rattle shaken to honor the gods and to ward off evil spirits. The sistrum was particularly sacred to HATHOR and ISIS but was also carried by AMUN, the great god of THEBES, BASTET, the cat goddess, and, on some occa-

Carving of a sistra, a musical instrument carried by the followers of Hathor and shaken during religious festivals.

sions, by many of the other gods of Egypt. During the Greek and Roman periods, the sistrum was a popular and powerful symbol of the cult of Isis. The Roman writer JUVENAL mentions that sinners could be struck blind by the power of Isis's sistrum. In the Temple of Dendera is a sistrum player's epithet that reads, "I drive away the enemy of the Mistress of Heaven." The ceremony of presenting sistra to Isis is shown on the walls of the Isis Temple at Philae, and the text says, "I play the sistra before thy fair countenance, O Isis, Eye of Re, who has no peers."

The sistrum came in two basic styles: the NAOS, shaped like a shrine, and the "hoop" type. The naos style is the earliest, dating from the Old Kingdom (2686–2181 B.C.). The top of the handle (of the naos style) is a Hathor head, and on top of that is the naos, or shrine shape. Three or four wire rods with loose rattles (similar to those on a tambourine) extend horizontally through the naos. The hoop sistrum has a tall loop on top of the handle, in place of the naos, but the wires and rattles are similar. The decorations on either style varied over time, but the favored motifs were Hathor and Isis heads, serpents, and cats. A sistrum could be made of bronze, FAIENCE (ceramic), wood, gold, or silver, although faience and bronze seem to have been favored. The sistrum may have been derived from bunches of papyrus flowers, which were a favorite offering to Hathor. When the bouquets were presented to Hathor, they were shaken so the papyrus stalks made a swishing sound.

**SITULA** A sacred vessel used for religious ceremonies, the situla is a very small round-bottomed bucket or pail, usually cast from bronze and decorated with mythological motifs. During the Ptolemaic and Roman periods, the situla was carried by the priests of Isis and used in rituals and processions. The situla held holy water from the Nile or milk as a symbol of Isis in her form as a mother goddess.

**SKY GODDESS** See NUT.

**SOBEK** (also SEBEK or SUCHOS) The crocodile god, Sobek was worshipped in two cult centers: Crocodilopolis in the Fayoum, a marshy area southwest of Cairo, and Kom Ombo, south of Luxor. There were also numerous shrines and smaller temples dedicated to Sobek throughout Egypt. According to HERODOTUS, the Greek writer, crocodiles were sacred in some parts of Egypt but in other areas were hunted and killed. In the precincts where they were sacred, they were kept in sacred pools in the temple complex, adorned with gold and crystal earrings and jeweled bracelets on their front legs.

When the Twelfth Dynasty kings built their capital in the Fayoum, Sobek rose from a minor god to become the patron god of the kings. Sobek is the son of NEITH, the warrior goddess, and is shown as a man with a crocodile's head or a crocodile resting on a shrine; he wears animal horns and the sun disk as his crown. Sobek was closely associated with the sun god RE and was often referred to as Sobek-Re.

Sobek was generally viewed as a gentle god, in spite of his vicious nature, but mythology tells us that at one time the gods became angry with him. It is said that the gods ate sparingly, often dining only on bread and cool water, and although roasted meat was eaten from time to time, eating large quantities was frowned upon.

(One day) Sobek, the crocodile, surprised a band of enemies and massacred them. A victim of his natural inclinations, he unhesitatingly devoured them all; but he carried their heads back home with him as proof of his exploit. The gods rushed toward him, shouting, "Prevent him from eating them (the heads), give him bread!"

Sobek could not control his desire for meaty dishes and was sometimes overwhelmed by sudden cravings. When the dismembered Osiris was cast into the Nile, Sobek yielded to temptation and gulped down part of the body. He was punished for this lapse, due to his boundless hunger more than to a desire to harm the body of his fellow god: He had his tongue cut out. In Egyptian mythology, this is why crocodiles have no tongues.

**SOKAR** The necropolis or cemetery for Egypt's ancient capital city, MEMPHIS is called SAQQARA after the mortuary god Sokar. He was closely associated with OSIRIS, the most important funerary god in Egypt, and with PTAH, the leading god of Memphis. Sokar appears in the Old Kingdom (2686–2613 B.C.) and in the PYRAMID TEXTS is called the creator of "royal bones." The BOOK OF THE DEAD says he fashions a "foot-basin of silver," the material of the bones of the gods. The AMDUAT, a guidebook for the dead, calls him "He Who Is Upon His Sand." Sokar is usually shown as a man with a hawk's head. One of the most impressive images of Sokar is from the silver coffin of the Twenty-second Dynasty king Sheshonq II (c. 890 B.C.), discovered at TANIS.

**SOLAR BARQUE** The sacred boat of the sun god RE, the solar barque was actually two boats: Mandet, which sailed across the sky during the day, and Mesektet, the boat that sails through the NETHERWORLD, the land of the dead, each night. Mythology tells us that Mesektet, the boat of the "west," became the right eye of the sun, and Mandet, the boat on the eastern horizon, became the left eye of the sun. Frequently mentioned in the BOOK OF THE DEAD, the solar barque ferries the souls of the dead on their way to the Netherworld.

**SOPDU** (SOPDET) An Egyptian star god identified with ISIS, Sopdu was known to the Greeks as Sothis, the Dog Star. Signaling the annual rise of the Nile, the season of Akhet or inundation, and the celebration of the new year, the appearance of Sopdu was cause for great rejoicing in Egypt.

**SOULS OF NEKHEN** It was believed that PHARAOHS in ancient Egypt were protected by the souls, or BAs, of mythological kings who lived before time began. When the mythological kings died, they became celestial beings, or stars, who were called the souls of Nekhen, and were associated with the JACKAL. (The SOULS OF PE were associated with the FALCON.) NEKHEN, modern HIERAKONPOLIS in UPPER EGYPT in the south, was the cult center and the ancestral home of the souls of Nekhen. They are shown as three jackal-headed men in a ritual pose on one knee, with one arm held to their chest and the other arm raised. This posture resembles the hieroglyphic sign *henu* (🧎) meaning "jubilation" or "praise." It has been suggested that the posture, kneeling on one knee, is a final pose in a ritual dance called the "Recitation of the Glorifications."

Decorations on temple walls show the souls of Nekhen carrying the shrines of the gods. One of the scenes carved on the wall of the Hypostyle Hall at KARNAK TEMPLE depicts the souls of Nekhen carrying the sacred boat of AMUN in a coronation procession. The souls protect Ramses I on his tomb wall, and in Edfu Temple they shield the falcon god from harm. The souls of Nekhen and the souls of Pe served as protectors of Upper and LOWER EGYPT. Egyptians believed that the souls were very powerful and could protect both deceased and living kings from danger.

**SOULS OF PE** The souls of Pe appear as three men with FALCON heads. Their domain is the city of Buto (ancient Pe), the capital of the DELTA (in the north). The Egyptians believed that the PHARAOHS were protected by the souls, or BAs, of mythological kings who lived before time began and who in death became celestial beings, or stars, called the SOULS OF NEKHEN and the souls of Pe. The souls of Pe are sometimes seen as stars themselves, forming a ladder upon which the deceased king can ascend to the heavens where he will become an AKH, a "radiant light"—a star.

In the PYRAMID TEXTS, the souls of Pe are angered over the murder of OSIRIS, the symbolic father of the king, and mourn by tearing at their flesh and pulling their hair and urging HORUS to seek revenge for their father's murder.

In the ISIS AND OSIRIS MYTH, their evil brother SET tricks Osiris and murders him. When Osiris's son, Horus, grows up, he seeks revenge for the murder of his father, and he fights Set. When Horus's eye is torn out by his evil uncle Set, Horus is given the town of Pe as compensation by the gods, thus creating a close bond between the souls of Pe and

The souls of Nekhen have the head of a jackal and body of a man and were believed to be an embodiment of Predynastic rulers who protect the living king. *(Photo by Pat Remler)*

The souls of Pe have the head of a falcon and the body of a man and were believed to be an embodiment of Predynastic rulers who protect the living king. *(Drawing by Mary Jordan)*

Horus. Decorations on temple walls show the souls of Pe and Nekhen carrying the shrines of the gods. In funerary scenes on temple walls, the souls of Pe and Nekhen kneel on one knee, with one arm to their chest and the other arm raised in the air, ready to smite the enemies of the deceased. Because this depiction resembles the hieroglyphic sign *henu* (𓀠), meaning "jubilation" or "praise," it may be that the kneeling position is a final pose in the ritual dance called the "Recitation of the Glorifications."

**SPELLS** See MAGICAL SPELLS.

**SPEOS ARTEMIDOS** One of two small MIDDLE KINGDOM temples cut into the living rock at Beni Hassan. The Speos Artemidos is located on the east side of the NILE and dedicated to the lion goddess PAKHET, whose titles include "She Who Scratches" and "She Who Guards the Entrance of the Wadi."

When the Greeks ruled Egypt (Ptolemaic period, 332–30 B.C.), they identified Pakhet with their goddess Artemis and renamed Pakhet's temple the Speos Artemidos, or the "Grotto of Artemis." Inscriptions dedicated to various gods covered the walls of the temple, and during the NEW KINGDOM, when the temple had fallen into disrepair, HATSHEPSUT, the

queen who crowned herself king, ordered repairs to be made and added her own inscription. In one segment she takes credit for having expelled the HYKSOS from Egypt almost 100 years before her reign:

> . . . So listen, all you elite and multitude of commoners: I have done this by the plan of my mind. I do not sleep forgetting, [but] have made from what was ruined. For I have raised up what was dismembered, beginning from the time when the Asiatics were in the midst of the Delta, [in] Avaris, with vagrants in their midst, toppling what had been made. They ruled without the Sun, and he did not act by god's decree down to my [own] uraeus-incarnation. [Now] I am set on the Sun's thrones, having been foretold from ages of years as one born to take possession. I am come as Horus, the sole uraeus spitting fire at my enemies. I have banished the gods' abomination, the earth removing their footprints . . .

**SPHINX** One of the icons of Egypt, the sphinx is a mythical beast usually with the head of a king (occasionally a queen or the head of a ram) and the body of a lion. The most famous is the great sphinx

The embodiment of royal power, the sphinx on the Giza Plateau was carved for the pharaoh Chephren from a large outcropping of rock. *(Photo by Pat Remler)*

at Giza, which is carved from an outcropping of rock in the funerary complex of King Chephren (Khafre) (2558–2532 B.C.). The great sphinx represents "Horus of the Horizons," the sun god when he rises in the east. It is believed that the face of the great sphinx is a likeness of Chephren.

While a sphinx is not a god, it is the embodiment of royal power, and in the case of the ram-headed sphinxes at KARNAK TEMPLE, the power of the king is closely associated with the god AMUN. The Egyptian sphinx is viewed as male and benevolent, although it sometimes represents the king smiting his enemies. The Greek sphinx, in contrast, is shown as female and malevolent. In fact, in ancient Greek the word sphinx meant "strangler."

**STELE** (STELA, plural: STELAE)  A round-topped slab of wood or stone often erected in front of a temple as an offering to the gods, a stele might commemorate a special event or serve as a funerary monument. The earliest stelae are of the funerary type and show the deceased making or receiving offerings. Commemorative and votive stelae are associated with temple offerings and have been found in great quantities at ABYDOS and near the SERAPEUM. Our tombstones are derived from ancient Egyptian stelae.

**STEP PYRAMID**  Built for the pharaoh Horus Net-jer-ik-het, better known as ZOSER, the Step Pyramid was a sacred site for centuries after Zoser's mummy was sealed in the burial chamber. The Step Pyramid represents a milestone of achievement in ancient architecture. It was the first time stone was used in a large-scale building project. A NEW KINGDOM inscription found at south SAQQARA calls the

PYRAMID builders "openers of stone." Situated on a plateau overlooking the ancient Egyptian capital city, MEMPHIS, the pyramid began as a simple MASTABA, and as the pyramid neared completion, the architect IMHOTEP added five more stepped-in platforms, thus creating the Step Pyramid. Because it was the first building in stone, the architects did not know that it was important to square the blocks with smooth, even sides, and the pyramid became unstable. Visitors can still see cedar logs imported from Lebanon that were used to shore up the sides during construction.

Surrounded by a stone enclosure wall, carved to imitate the mud brick walls of earlier mortuary complexes, the space inside the walls is the TEMENOS, or sacred space. This is where the king's HEB-SED FESTIVAL, or "jubilee," took place at least every 30 years. Recognized as a holy site after Zoser died, the magnificent funerary complex that grew up around the Step Pyramid became a pilgrimage destination, and for centuries the faithful came to the Step Pyramid to pray, to be healed, and to be buried. In the Eighteenth Dynasty, Imhotep, the architect of the Step Pyramid, was deified, declared to be a god of healing and medicine. Egyptologists have recently found the tomb of Qar, a physician, near the Step Pyramid, and inside they found the most ancient copper medical instruments ever discovered. This is an indication that the area was associated with Imhotep.

Zoser's mummy was never found in his burial chamber, but in the 1920s and 1930s, Egyptologists excavated parts of the burial chamber and discovered six vertebrae and part of the right hip of a man and, later, rib fragments and a left foot. Egyptologists question whether the findings belong to Zoser.

**STRETCHING OF THE CORD CEREMONY**  A measurement to decide where the foundation of a building should be dug by determining the four cardinal points: north, south, east, and west. Officiating at the Stretching of the Cord Ceremony was SESHAT, the goddess of measurement and writing. The ceremony, recorded on a granite block during the reign of the Second Dynasty king Khasekhemwy (c. 2686 B.C.), tells how ancient architects aligned the four sides of the temples with the four cardinal points. Egyptian astronomers took sightings from the stars called the Great Bear and Orion using an instrument something like an astrolabe, which measures the position and altitude of the stars. With great accuracy they oriented pyramids and sun temples to true east, west, north, and south.

**SUN GOD** See RE, HORUS, KHEPRI, and ATEN.

**SUN TEMPLE** From Egypt's most ancient history the sun was worshipped as a life-giving force, and solar gods played an important role throughout ancient Egypt's 3,000-year civilization. The first sun temple was dedicated to the sun god RE in HELIOPOLIS (today a modern suburb of Cairo). Nothing but fragments have survived from the first sun temple, but the solar temples of the Fifth Dynasty (2560–2420 B.C.) at Abu Ghurab and Abu Sir must have been based on the original Heliopolis temple.

As the solar cult (worship of the sun god) became an important aspect of Egyptian religion, Fifth Dynasty kings moved away from traditional burial sites at SAQQARA and the Giza Plateau. They built small pyramids and impressive sun temples at their new mortuary sites, Abu Sir and Abu Ghurab (just north of Saqqara). This break with tradition seems to have been predicted in the PAPYRUS Westcar. As the story goes, a magician was brought to King Khufu (Dynasty IV) to predict the future, and what the magician saw was the beginning of a new dynasty. The Papyrus Westcar says a new dynasty will begin with the birth of triplets, who will become the first kings of the Fifth Dynasty. We do not know if triplets were born to the royal family, but Dynasty V began with a lot of changes. The new kings were called solar kings, or *re nes-sut*, and six of them built sun temples.

Userkaf, the first king of Dynasty V, started the sun temple trend. He remained loyal to Saqqara and built his small pyramid in the shadow of the STEP PYRAMID, but then he built the first sun temple at the new site, Abu Sir. His son, Sahure, is the first of five kings whose names end in "Re"—all of them so-named to honor the sun gods, and they all built sun temples dedicated to Re in addition to their funerary complexes. Sahure built the first complete mortuary complex at Abu Sir, which includes a pyramid, a mortuary chapel, a valley temple, and a sun temple.

Like pyramids, the new sun temples had restricted access (only one way in and out). They were built on the west bank of the NILE, the believed "domain of the dead," so there must have been a connection between solar temples and the next world.

Only two of the six sun temples have been excavated, but from the ruins it appears that the sun god was worshipped in the open air rather than in an enclosed sanctuary. Ne-user-ra's sun temple had a large TEMENOS wall with an entrance on the east side. Opposite the entrance stood a sacred BENBEN, a short obelisk resting on a limestone podium with granite base. The sacred benben (whose exact meaning is not known) was the focus of religious rituals and prayers directed to the sun god Re. In front of the obelisk was an alabaster altar for making offerings, and on all four sides was the *hetep*-HIEROGLYPH, meaning "to offer" or "to give." Situated around the courtyard were storerooms and an animal enclosure. Inscriptions tell us that at U-ser-kaf's sun temple, two oxen and two geese were sacrificed on the altar every day.

Covered corridors (large hallways) leading out of the sun temple and to other mortuary buildings were decorated with scenes from daily life and with scenes from the king's HEB-SED FESTIVAL and the seasons of the year. Scenes of netting birds, fishing, making papyrus boats, and working in the fields all celebrated the bounty of nature and the benevolence of the sun god.

Almost a thousand years later, sun temples reappeared in the NEW KINGDOM when AKHENATEN, the heretic king (1352–1336 B.C.), denounced the traditional gods of Egypt in favor of one god, the ATEN. In his first sun temple complex, erected in the huge sprawling KARNAK TEMPLE in THEBES, Akhenaten employed an innovative construction technique. Using *talatat* blocks (a small block that could be carried by one man), the construction time of his new temples was cut perhaps by one-third. In the 1960s, the Akhenaten Temple Project, undertaken by a group of archaeologists, painstakingly sorted the blocks of the dismantled temples, photographed them, and made a computer record of each one. They could not rebuild the temple, but they managed to match photos of the blocks to re-create scenes carved on the walls.

At Karnak Temple, the ruins of four Aten temples have been identified. *Gem-pa-aten* ("The Aten Is Found") is the largest of the newer sun temples, with several open-air courtyards for making offerings to the Aten. Instructions for the priests were inscribed on the walls of the temples. One inscription lists the offerings to be made to the Aten each day: "the gods offering which His Majesty laid down for his father [the Aten] as an offering list for every day on the altar of Re . . ."

The list included 40 loaves each of *bit*-bread and *pisn*-bread, 87 loaves of other bread, 33 jugs of BEER, a quantity of pigeons, incense, vegetables, and milk.

The smaller temples presumably had similar instructions for daily offerings. They were named *Rudmenu* ("Enduring in Monuments"), *Tenimenu* ("Exalted in Monuments"), and *Hutbenben* ("Mansions of the Benben Stone").

After a few years, Akhenaten moved his court from the capital city Thebes (modern Luxor) to a desolate spot in the desert, some 200 miles to the north. There, Akhenaten established his city, Akhet-Aten (modern AMARNA), and built open-air sun temples for the worship of the Aten. The Great Aten Temple, *Gem-pa-aten*, was the center of all official ceremonies pertaining to the Aten. There was a smaller chapel for family use near the palace. The Great Temple was surrounded by a rectangular temenos wall and was one of the only buildings in the city to be faced with white limestone—everything else was built of mud brick and covered with plaster. Inside the temple courtyard were mud brick altars—365 for offerings from UPPER EGYPT and 365 for offerings from LOWER EGYPT. Each day vegetables, fruits, breads, ducks, geese, and beef—products from the north and the south—were piled on the altars and offered to the Aten. After a time the food was removed and distributed among the priests and workmen.

One curious change occurred at the Great Aten Temple. The age-old sacred benben stone, associated with the sun god Re at Heliopolis, was replaced with round-topped stelae resting on a base. Carved on the stele are scenes of the royal family bowing down to the Aten. Scenes on an Amarna tomb wall show the benben having been destroyed and replaced with a tall, round-topped stele. It seems that the stele became a focus of devotion in the great Aten temple after the benben was discarded.

**SYCAMORE TREE** (*FICUS SYCOMORUS*) Symbolizing the goddesses HATHOR and NUT, the sycamore tree is important in both mythology and religion. Trees are rare in Egypt, and the sycamore offered a cool resting spot in the desert. A large tree with dense foliage and a small, sweet fruit, the sycamore was considered magical and was sacred to the goddesses.

An ancient tree cult thrived in the capital city of MEMPHIS, where Hathor's title is "Lady of the Sycamore." Mythology tells us that the tree magically becomes a source of water, and the goddess quenches the thirst of newly deceased souls as they pass into the next world. Tomb paintings show Hathor emerging from the branches of the sacred sycamore pouring water and offering food to weary souls.

In this painting from the tomb of Senedjem, the sycamore tree, a symbol of Hathor, offers refreshment to the souls of Senedjem and his wife. *(Photo by Pat Remler)*

The sycamore tree of Nut grew in the ancient HELIOPOLIS. The BOOK OF THE DEAD shows the sun god's rays shining between two turquoise-colored sycamore trees as he rises to cross the sky. One of these trees was the sycamore of Nut. It was under this tree that the evil snake god Apep was killed by the sun god RE, who changed himself into a cat. To commemorate this victory over evil, branches of the sacred sycamore tree drooped down to form a shelter for the souls of the dead when they journeyed to the NETHERWORLD. Nut offered them food and water while they rested in the shade of the holy tree.

Today a sycamore tree in Heliopolis at Matariya is believed by many to have been the resting place of the holy family during their flight into Egypt. The Bible says the holy family took shelter under a sycamore in Egypt during their journey and that Jesus created a well and blessed it so they could drink from it.

**TANIS** A northern cult center for AMUN, Tanis was the royal residence and burial place of the Twenty-first and Twenty-second Dynasty kings (1069–747 B.C.), surrounded by a large enclosure wall that also included a sacred pool and a temple to Horus.

Because of the large number of statue pieces and material inscribed for Ramses II found at Tanis, some early Egyptologists thought this was the site of Pi-Ramses, the ancient capital city mentioned in the Bible. Modern excavations have so far found nothing to indicate that Tanis was the ancient Pi-Ramses. Scholars believe the statues of Ramses II were moved to Tanis by the Twenty-first and Twenty-second Dynasty kings to decorate their temples.

**TAURET** (ALSO TAWERET, THOERIS) A household deity, Tauret the pregnant hippopotamus goddess was the patron of pregnant women. She assisted in childbirth and watched over young children. Because of her calm nature and kindly disposition, she was a favorite household goddess. AMULETS in the shape of the goddess were produced by the hundreds and worn by pregnant women. Small figurines of Tauret were frequently kept in household shrines. It was thought that her fierce appearance—the head of a hippopotamus, the arms and legs of a feline, the tail of a crocodile, and long pendulous breasts—would ward off any evil spirits and keep the women and children of the house safe. Stone vases were carved in her image with a perforation at one of her nipples so that milk could be poured from the vase while magical spells were recited to cure children stung by scorpions. Her name means "the great one" and her attribute is the *SA* SIGN, a protective sign in the shape of a papyrus life preserver used by sailors, held in her left paw. The Greek writer PLUTARCH says she was the concubine of the evil god SET but that she eventually deserted him for HORUS the falcon god.

Tauret, the pregnant hippopotamus, was the goddess of childbirth. *(Drawing by Mary Jordan)*

**TAYET** The goddess of weaving and patroness of weavers, Tayet is associated with bandages and especially with bandaging of mummies. Utterance 81 in the PYRAMID TEXTS calls to her: "Thou awakest in peace, The goddess Tayet awakes in peace, Tayet awakes—two rolls of linen—in peace."

When Tayet was shown with OSIRIS, she was called ISIS-Tayet and prepared bandages for the mummy. In the myth of Sinuhe, the pharaoh invites Sinuhe, an Egyptian living abroad, to come home to Egypt. He reminds Sinuhe of the importance of a proper funeral on Egyptian soil, saying that after Sinuhe's death there will be a night of unguents and "wrappings from the hand of Tayet," referring to her skill at bandaging.

Tayet was the goddess of the Akmin NOME in UPPER EGYPT (south).

**TEFNUT**  The personification of life-giving dew, Tefnut was the goddess of moisture. Her tears, when they fell to Earth, caused incense plants to thrive and grow. In the HELIOPOLITAN ENNEAD, Tefnut and her brother-husband, SHU, were the children of ATUM, the primeval god who created himself. They were born of his semen or his spittle and were so close that they shared one soul. They were the parents of GEB the earth god and NUT the sky goddess. As the mother of Nut, Tefnut helped her support the sky, and together they greeted the sun as it rose each day in the east. In the MEMPHIS creation myth, Tefnut is called the "tongue of Ptah," who created the universe by speaking it into existence. In other myths Tefnut is associated with the left eye of Horus and the Eye of Re. In later myths she is said to have married THOTH.

**TELL EL AMARNA**  Modern name for the remote desert site of the ancient city Akhet-Aten, "the horizon of the Aten." The pharaoh AKHENATEN built the new capital city when he changed the religion of ancient Egypt from the worship of many gods to the worship of one, the Aten. Akhenaten selected virgin territory for his new capital, unsullied by shrines and temples for other gods. Initially, perhaps a thousand people followed him into the desert, and they camped along the Nile while the city was being built. The plan of the city was dictated by the geography; the Nile was on the west and the cliffs were on the east. The land between was a crescent about three miles wide and six miles long, and a royal road ran through the center. The royal residence and several temples dedicated to the Aten dominated the city. A private temple, the "Castle of the Aten," situated near the palace provided a sanctuary where the royal family worshipped privately and were rejuvenated by the rays of the Aten. Unlike traditional Egyptian temples, in which an open courtyard led to a succession of small, dark rooms, the Great Aten Temple was a large rectangle about the length of two football fields with four walls and no roof. Inside were rows of offering tables, one for each day of the year, at which the Aten received daily food offerings. The new "open-air" temple did have one similarity to the old Theban temples: massive entrance pylons like those in front of KARNAK and LUXOR temples. The other temples to the Aten varied only slightly in design, and some were smaller. Akhenaten vowed never to leave his city and remained there until his death in about year 17 of his reign.

One of the most important archaeological discoveries of Tell el Amarna was the new art style that Akhenaten initiated in his city. In 1824, John Gardiner Wilkinson, an early British archaeologist, traveled to Tell el Amarna and found the remains of the ancient city. Among the ruins, he discovered that the art, the paintings, wall carvings, and sculpture were different from any other in Egypt. The royal family appeared to be deformed, with wide hips, sagging bellies, drooping breasts, long and spindly arms and legs, and elongated heads. It was also at Tell el Amarna that one of the most beautiful portraits in the world was discovered, the famous bust of Nefertiti, Akhenaten's queen.

**TEM**  See ATUM.

**TEMENOS**  An ancient Greek word meaning "sacred space," the temenos is the area that encloses a temple and adjacent buildings associated with the temple. It separates the sacred precinct of the gods from the mundane world.

Excavations of Egypt's earliest temples revealed a temenos wall surrounding the space belonging to the gods. As Egyptian religion became more complex, auxiliary buildings like the MAMMISI, SACRED LAKE, and purification kiosks were added to the temple complex in order to perform the new rituals honoring the gods. Priests purified themselves with NILE water in the sacred lake or in a purification kiosk before entering the temple, and the elaborate processions honoring the gods assembled in the temenos. Archaeological excavations of First Dynasty temples at ABYDOS have shown that early temenos walls were not substantial and were built with unbaked mud bricks. Later additions to the temple reveal mud brick walls up to 30 feet thick, with entrances to the temenos made of fine stone. Temenos walls were often decorated with battle scenes, mythological stories, and hieroglyphic inscriptions.

**TEMPLES**  Ancient Egyptian temples were dedicated to a particular god, with chapels dedicated to other gods in the same temple. Temples were, for the most part, dark and mysterious places that were closed to the public. Each temple had three main sections, one leading into another. The first was an open courtyard where commoners could come and pay their respects to the gods on feast days. The second room was usually roofed and was reserved for the nobility when they came to make offerings at the temple. The inner room was called the HOLY OF HOLIES and was reserved for the priests. Inside each holy of holies was a sacred statue of the god of that temple, usually cast in bronze and covered or inlaid with gold or silver.

Between the open court and the enclosed court was a ramp or stairway. As the priests proceeded deeper into the temple and approached the domain of the gods, the space became smaller and more enclosed. Besides the temple proper there was a temple complex that included chapels to other gods and goddesses. An enclosure wall that helped to control who came in and out of the temple surrounded auxiliary buildings.

When a new temple was built, precise ancient rituals determined each step. The goddess of measurement, SESHAT, presided over the STRETCHING OF THE CORD ceremony: At night a cord was stretched between two poles, and the four corners of the temple were determined by the location of four stars in the sky. This was done with the king's help, and the king also oversaw the digging of the four corner foundations. When the four ceremonial bricks had been molded from mud and straw, the king placed them in the ground and covered them with sand. This represented the primordial soil that was the base for every temple. HA, the god of the western desert, presided over the difficult task of transporting the virgin sand. Foundation deposits—small, magical objects made of clay, FAIENCE, gold, silver, copper, iron, and stone, including small plaques inscribed with the name of the king—were placed in the foundations. Once these rituals had been faithfully performed, the construction of the temple could proceed. When the temple was completed, it was purified with burning incense and natron so as to be a fit dwelling place for the god. Images of the god and his divine family filled the temple, awaiting the moment when the divine presence would enter. A version of the OPENING OF THE MOUTH ceremony was reenacted as each statue was "opened" by the priests so the spirit of each god could enter it. When this ceremony was complete, the statues were regarded as "living."

The temple complex of Medinet Habu was built by the pharaoh Ramses III as his mortuary temple. The sprawling complex also served as a royal palace and a fortress. *(Photo by Pat Remler)*

**TENEN** (ALSO TATENEN)  An ancient earth god personifying the primeval mound, Tenen was the symbol for the rich NILE silt that emerged when the river receded after the inundation. His name means "illustrious Earth." He is represented as a man with two plumes and rams' horns on his head. Sometimes his skin is painted green, symbolizing his connection with vegetation. Originating in MEMPHIS, Tenen was soon associated with PTAH in his manifestation as a creator god.

**TET**  See KNOT OF ISIS.

**THEBAN RECENSION**  Copies of the BOOK OF THE DEAD written when Thebes was the religious capital of Egypt are called the Theban Recension. During the New Kingdom (1550–1069 B.C.), when all of the prayers, rituals, and incantations that make up the Book of the Dead were compiled, there was little attempt to organize the material. When scribes made copies of the Book of the Dead, they repeated some chapters and skipped others. Eventually, several versions, called the Theban Recension, included more than 200 spells. Not every version contained every spell, but each copy had the most important spells. Copies of the Book of the Dead written later, after the Saite period (664–525 B.C.), are called the SAITE RECENSION.

**THEBES** (WASET) (modern Luxor)  Symbolized by the *was* scepter, Thebes, as the Greeks called it, was the religious capital and principal city of Upper Egypt.

The city of Thebes sprawled across the east bank of the NILE; on the west bank was a city of the dead, the site of mortuary temples and tombs of the pharaohs and their families and officials. Thebes was a city of great prosperity during the Eighteenth Dynasty (1550–1069 B.C.). Homer, the Greek poet, called it "hundred-gated Thebes," probably for the countless huge pylons that formed the entrances to the many temples. The patron god of the city was AMUN-RE, the "hidden one," to whom the Egyptians attributed their wealth and success. They gave thanks to him for their deliverance from anarchy and foreign invasions and for maintaining divine order in their land.

**THOTH** (DJEHUTY) God of writing and knowledge, Thoth's most ancient association is as the moon god, symbolized by the IBIS or the BABOON. Both symbols are well known in Egypt's early history. Thoth appears in the image of an ibis on slate PALETTES and on totems or standards from the Predynastic period (5500–3100 B.C.). In the First Dynasty (3100–2890 B.C.), figurines from ABYDOS represented Thoth as a squatting baboon with a full moon resting on a crescent moon.

Some myths cast Thoth as the actual moon, and in others he is the moon's guardian. When he is the actual moon, Thoth is frequently called "Lunar-Thoth." A passage in the Turin Papyrus associating him with the DUAT, the Underworld, reads: "Hail O Lunar-Thoth who enlightenest the Duat in the necropolis! Hail to thee Lunar-Thoth, thou self-engendered, the unknown!" Thoth often acts with AAH, another ancient moon god. In the New Kingdom (1550–1069 B.C.), Thoth was associated with KHONSU, a moon god who was the son of AMUN and MUT.

When Thoth was not viewed as the moon itself, he was a protector of the moon. In this case the mythology tells us that Thoth is the left eye of god or the heavens, and the sun is the right eye. The left eye, represented by the waxing and waning of the moon, is called the healthy or sound eye. In one version of the myth of the CONTENDINGS OF HORUS AND SET, Thoth heals the damaged EYE OF HORUS.

Thoth accompanies RE in his solar barque as a protector, but mythology tells us that he rendered a far greater service to the sun god when he recovered the EYE OF RE from NUBIA after it had escaped in the form of TEFNUT. In gratitude, Re created the moon as a reward for Thoth, and he made Thoth his representative in the night sky.

Because of the waxing and waning of the Moon, one of Thoth's many titles was the "Measurer of Time," symbolized by the frond of notched palm

Thoth, the god of writing, draws the hieroglyph for truth. *(Photograph by Pat Remler)*

branches { he sometimes held. In this capacity Thoth was called the bringer of mathematics, astronomy, and magic. Thoth was the great lord of magic, and his spells allowed Isis to bring her husband back to life. It was from Thoth that Isis learned her magic, and it was Thoth's magical spell that brought the infant HORUS back to life when he had been bitten by a scorpion.

Thoth was known as the scribe of the gods and was the patron of all scribes. As "lord of the sacred word," Thoth represented the embodiment of all knowledge, scientific and literary. He was the patron of the *per ankh*, "the house of life," where the sacred papyri were kept. Books of Divine Words or the Book of Thoth are mentioned in ancient inscriptions, and it is believed that they are a collection of "sacred spells" compiled by Thoth. The most important cult center for Thoth was in Hermopolis, although he was worshipped throughout Egypt and in Nubia.

**THOTH, THE BOOK OF** The Greeks attributed a group of 42 papyri to the Egyptian god of writing, THOTH. According to Clement of Alexandria, a Greek theologian (A.D. 150–215), the Book of Thoth included:

Two papyri with HYMN TO THOTH,
Four papyri on astrology and astronomy,

Ten religious papyri that include rituals and festivals,

Ten papyri concerning the priesthood and the administration of the temples,

Ten papyri concerning philosophy and general knowledge, and

Six papyri devoted to medicine

The Greeks identified Thoth with their god HERMES, and the books became known as the Hermetic Texts. While there are ancient references to the Book of Thoth, the manuscript has never been discovered and may have existed only as a myth.

**TOMB** A place of burial. Because the Egyptians believed in resurrection, it was necessary to preserve the body of the deceased by mummification and to place the mummy in a tomb until it would resurrect in the next world. Sometimes called the "MANSION OF THE *KA*" or the "eternal house," the tomb was also home to the *KA*, or double of the deceased. It was believed that as long as the mummy remained in the tomb the *ka* would remain there too, although it was free to move in and out of the tomb. Egyptian tombs started out as simple pit burials in the sand and evolved into MASTABAS and then tombs within pyramids for the king's burial. Pyramids proved costly to build and were obvious targets for tomb robbers, so eventually the pharaohs were buried in rock-cut tombs in secluded or hidden spots (see VALLEY OF THE KINGS).

The tomb of King Tutankhamen was the first intact royal burial to be discovered, and it was filled with all the objects the king would need in the next world: guardian statues, magical objects, USHABTIS, a small golden shrine, furniture, jewelry, clothing, cosmetic boxes, games, musical instruments, writing materials, keepsakes from his family, chariots, weapons, fans, beds, headrests, chairs, thrones, boxes, lamps, tools, vessels, FAIENCE, wine, baskets, and food.

**TREES, SACRED** See SACRED TREES.

**TRIADS** See FAMILIES OF GODS.

Wealthy Egyptians often painted the gods on walls of their tombs for protection. In this painting from the tomb of Senedjem, the deceased and his wife pray before a row of seated gods. *(Photo by Pat Remler)*

When Tutankhamen's tomb was opened in 1922, it was the only undisturbed tomb of a pharaoh ever found in the Valley of the Kings.

**TUTANKHAMEN** (1334–1325 B.C.) Although a relatively minor king of the Eighteenth Dynasty, Tutankhamnen is perhaps the most famous. His intact tomb was discovered in the Valley of the Kings by Howard Carter in 1922. The opening of his tomb gave the world a glimpse of the treasure buried with Egyptian kings, and sparked a world-wide interest in the boy king. Tutankhamen is believed to be the son of AKHENATEN the "heretic king" and a minor wife, Kiya. When Akhenaten died, the nine-year-old "Tutankhaten" was crowned king and married to his young sister "Ankesenpaten," the last remaining royal princess. The royal court was moved back to Thebes, the religion reverted to the worship of AMUN, and the royal names were changed to Tutankhamen and Ankhesenamen.

The contents of the the young king's tomb give us insights into the pharoah's relationship with the gods of Egypt. Four wooden shrines, nested one inside the other, surrounded the SARCOPHAGUS, each inscribed with magical and mythological texts. On the inside surface of the largest (outermost) shrine were spells from the BOOK OF THE DEAD and also part of the BOOK OF THE DIVINE COW, which contains the myth of the DESTRUCTION OF MANKIND.

The second outermost shrine showed the deceased Tutankhamen before OSIRIS. At the head of the shrine the sisters ISIS and NEPHTHYS spread their protective wings to guard the mummy of the king. Chapters from the Book of the Dead are also inscribed on this shrine.

The third-smallest shrine is decorated with inscriptions from the AMDUAT, the book of the NETHERWORLD. The inner walls of the shrine are covered with a procession of gods.

The last shrine, the one next to the sarcophagus, is covered with the story of the CREATION MYTHS and the myth of ISIS AND OSIRIS. On the roof are Isis, Nephthys, SELKET, NEITH, and ANUBIS. The FOUR SONS OF HORUS adorn the sides of the shrine along with a group of gods including GEB and HAPI, all protecting the mummy of Tutankhamen. Inside the shrine, for additional protection, the walls are inscribed with spells from the Book of the Dead.

The sarcophagus is carved with figures of Isis, Nephthys, Selket, and Neith at the four corners. Tutankhamen's mummy was wrapped with 150 items of jewelry, most with magical significance to give added protection to the mummy. Of all the things included in the tomb, perhaps most surprising is what was not there. There was no papyrus version of the Book of the Dead—the text on the four shrines was intended to take its place. Also missing were the royal CROWNS. The pharaoh had a crown for UPPER EGYPT and for LOWER EGYPT, a double crown, an ATEF CROWN, and a blue "war" crown, as well as a nemes headdress, and none were found in the tomb. Scholars have suggested that the crowns were believed to have magical properties and only one of each type existed at any time. When a pharaoh died, he did not take his crowns to the next world. They were inherited.

**TUTU** An Egyptian protector god, Tutu is a late form of the god SHU. He is often shown as a man wearing the tall ATEF CROWN with a URAEUS and sun disks, and he sometimes holds his finger to his mouth, similar to Harpocrates, HORUS THE CHILD. He is also shown in the form of a striding sphinx who tramples small demons under his feet. A large temple dedicated to Tutu was built in the town of Kellis in Egypt's Dakhla Oasis.

**TYPHON** Greek god of turmoil and evil, the hundred-headed Typhon was associated with the Egyptian god of evil, SET. The name seems to have been interchangeable during the Greek and Roman periods in Egypt. PLUTARCH's *De Iside Et Osiride* refers to Isis's and Osiris's evil brother Set as Typhon.

**TYPHONEAN ANIMAL** A mythological creature associated with the god SET, the animal resembles a jackal with an anteater's snout, square ears, and a forked tail. The Typhonean animal was associated with the Greek god of chaos, TYPHON.

# U

*UCH*  A symbol belonging to the cult of Hathor, the uch was a fetish in the shape of a papyrus stalk surmounted by two feathers. The exact meaning of the uch is not known.

**Udjat Eye**  See Eye of Horus.

**Unas**  The last king of the Fifth Dynasty (2375–2345 b.c.), Unas was the first king to have inscriptions carved on the walls of the chambers inside his pyramid at Saqqara. These magical inscriptions, called the Pyramid Texts, were also written in the burial chambers of the Sixth Dynasty pharaohs Teti, Pepi I, Mernere, and Pepi II and their queens. The original 228 texts inscribed in Unas's pyramid were copied, with a few changes in the Sixth Dynasty Pyramid Texts. The texts in Unas's pyramid are prayers, spells, and incantations to help the deceased king ascend to his place among the gods in the sky and to resurrect. Unas takes a forceful tone with the gods as he prepares for resurrection:

> Re-Atum, this Unas comes to you,
> A spirit indestructible, who lays claim to the place
>    of the four pillars!
> Your son comes to you, this Unas comes to you,
> May you cross the sky united in dark
> May you rise in lightland, the place in which you
>    shine!
> Set, Nephthys, go proclaim to Upper Egypt's
>    gods and their spirits:
> "This Unas comes, a spirit indestructible,
> If he wishes you to die, you will die,
> If he wishes you to live, you will live."

**Upper Egypt**  The southern portion of Egypt is called Upper Egypt because the Nile flows from south to north. The "upper" part of the Nile is in the south, and the lower part of the Nile is in the north.

Hence the south of Egypt is Upper Egypt, and the north is Lower Egypt. During Egypt's Predynastic period, upper and lower Egypt were two separate kingdoms. The Narmer Palette commemorates the victory of the southern king, King Narmer, over Lower Egypt and subsequent unification of the two lands. The crown of Upper Egypt is the tall conical white crown, its flower is the lotus, and its protective goddess is Nekhbet.

**URAEUS** (plural: *URAEI*)  A Greek word meaning "serpent," the uraeus is a symbol of kingship in ancient Egypt, and it signifies the power and protection of the pharaoh. It is also a symbol of the cobra goddess Wadjet, a fierce protector of the king.

The uraeus takes the form of a rearing cobra with its hood extended. The origin of the uraeus is Egypt's Predynastic period, where images of a serpent were carved in stone and ivory. Images of the cobra goddess Wadjet appear throughout Egypt's history and into Roman times. A small ivory plaque in the British Museum is the first-known example of a king depicted under the protection of the cobra goddess. King Den of Dynasty I (2915–2865 b.c.) wears a rearing cobra on his forehead as he smites an enemy of Egypt.

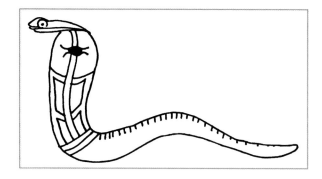

The cobra was the protector of the pharaoh and appears on the royal crown. *(Drawing by Mary Jordan)*

The uraeus appears in different contexts over ancient Egypt's long history. In the Predynastic period, it is shown with other animals or with a sun disk (the symbol for RE the sun god). In Dynasty I (3,000–2,970 B.C.), the uraeus becomes a HIEROGLYPH for the letter "dj" and is written in a king's name, *djer*. It also appears on two-dimensional carvings on the headdresses of kings and deities and on the standards of NOME GODS. In Dynasty III (2655–2635 B.C.), the uraeus is featured as an architectural decoration. You can still see the frieze of cobra heads at the top of the SAQQARA chapel wall in ZOSER's STEP PYRAMID complex. Uraei appear on the statues of Fifth and Sixth Dynasty kings, and King Pepi II of Dynasty VI (2276–2193 B.C.) is shown with a double uraei on his royal kilt.

Mythology tells us that the cobra goddess played many roles in Egyptian beliefs, and inscriptions on tomb walls and coffins tell us that she, like many Egyptian goddesses, had a dual personality—both sweet and fierce. A gentle prayer to waken the goddess each morning is found on the wall of the Fifth Dynasty Pyramid of UNAS (2375–2345 B.C.):

> Awake in peace! Great Queen, awake in peace;
>   Thine awakening is peaceful.
> Awake in peace! Snake that is on the brow of
>   [the king] awake in peace; thine awakening is
>   peaceful.
> Awake in peace! Upper Egyptian snake, awake
>   in peace; thine awakening is peaceful . . .

Two kinds of cobras are indigenous to Egypt: the Egyptian cobra and the Egyptian desert cobra. They thrive mostly in the arid desert areas but are often still found in temples and tombs. When frightened or angry, cobras rear up and expand their hoods. Ancient Egyptian craftsmen were careful observers of nature, and they accurately recorded the look and aggressive character of the cobra, often giving their work the character of the serpent.

The serpent or snake plays a major part in much of the world's ancient mythology and religion. In the Bible, Moses's staff becomes a serpent, and there was a serpent in the Garden of Eden. The Greek *caduceus*, a rod with two intertwined snakes—originally the magic wand of the Greek god Hermes (Roman/Mercury)—is today a symbol for medical organizations.

**USHABTI** (SHAWBTI, SHAWABTI) Servant statues that were to magically come alive and serve the deceased in the NETHERWORLD, ushabtis were small figurines placed in the tomb with the deceased.

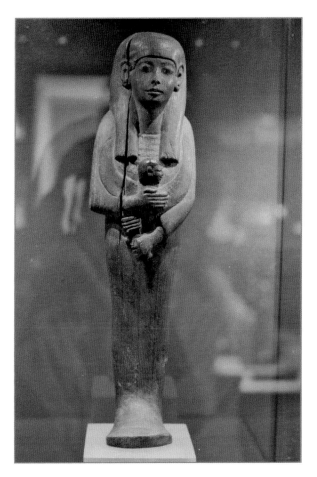

The ushabti, or servant statue, was supposed to magically come to life and serve the deceased in the next world. *(Photo by Einsamer Schütze/Used under a Creative Commons license)*

Because the daily life of ancient Egyptians centered on agriculture, they viewed the next world as agrarian, so they believed they might be called forth to labor in the FIELD OF REEDS. Ushabtis were intended to do this work. They are mummiform in shape so as to be identified with Osiris, the god of the dead, but their hands protrude from the bandages so they can work, and in their hands they hold farming tools, often a hoe. At first, these statuettes were inscribed with only the name of the deceased, but soon magical spells were added as well, to ensure that they would come alive and do their chores. A common spell was:

> O shawbti, if the deceased is called upon to do work in the next world, answer, "Here I am!" Plough the fields, fill the canals with water, and carry the sand of the east to the west.

The word *shawabti* apparently referred to the PERSEA TREE from which these little figures were occasionally made. Another word for them is *ushabti*, which means, "answerer." They are called by both names.

Because they were servants, it was desirable to have many. During the New Kingdom, it was common to have hundreds. Because the number found in tombs often totals nearly 365, it has been said that there was one for each day of the year. There is no evidence for this theory, and, in fact, the number is rarely exactly 365. The figures varied considerably in size and material. The least expensive were made of terra cotta, only two inches tall, and were mass-produced in molds with no inscriptions. More elaborate terra cotta ushabtis were up to nine inches tall and were painted with facial details, wigs, and inscriptions. These usually had the name of the deceased painted on the front as well. One of the most commonly used materials was FAIENCE, and these ushabtis varied considerably in size and quality. The color ranged from green to turquoise to blue. Some of the larger faience ushabtis are exquisite works of art with beautiful detailing. The most elaborate ushabtis were carved from wood or stone (limestone or serpentine).

These were reserved for royalty and high-ranking nobility. Each was an individually carved statue, usually with the magical spell around the torso. When the Egyptians began burying ushabtis in tombs in large numbers, they thought the ushabtis might become unruly and unable to organize themselves, so for about every 10 ushabtis in a tomb, there was one overseer ushabti who held a flail or some sign of authority and wore a starched kilt (a kind of apron), a sign that he did not perform physical labor.

**UTTERANCE**  An ancient Egyptian spell meant to be read aloud or chanted during a ceremony. Numerous spells and utterances are recorded in the PYRAMID TEXTS, COFFIN TEXTS, BOOK OF THE DEAD, and other ancient Egyptian literature. The terms *utterance* and *spell* are often used interchangeably, since Egyptologists do not know exactly which ones were meant to be read aloud or chanted by chorus. From paintings and inscriptions on tomb walls it appears that Egyptians recited or chanted most utterances and spells in the belief that it made the magic all the more powerful.

**VALLEY OF THE KINGS**  The cemetery for pharaohs of the New Kingdom (1550–1069 B.C.), the Valley of the Kings is located on the west bank of the Nile across from modern Luxor. For a period of almost 500 years, the most talented artists and craftsmen worked on the tombs of the pharaohs in the Valley of the Kings, decorating the walls of the royal tombs with elaborate scenes from Egypt's religion and mythology. The Valley of the Kings has an eastern and western spur, and of the 62 tombs discovered thus far, only four are in the more remote Western Valley. The following chart identifies the tombs as KV for King's Valley and WV for the Western Valley. Each is numbered in the order in which it was discovered. Two tombs in the Western Valley have been identified, the tomb of Amenhotep III, the grandfather of TUTANKHAMEN (WV 22), and the tomb of Aye, vizier and possible murderer of Tutankhamen (WV 23). There are two unfinished tombs with no inscriptions (WV 24 and 25). Unfinished tombs in the Eastern Valley are not listed.

On February 6, 2006, the discovery of a new tomb in the Valley of the Kings was announced by the Supreme Council of Antiquities. Designated KV 63, the tomb is located near that of Tutankhamen (KV 62) and was discovered when archaeologists were excavating nearby workmen's huts.

A 20-foot shaft leads to a single chamber that appears to have been entered and resealed several times. Inside the chamber are seven wooden coffins, two of them for children. Some coffins were badly damaged by termites, and no names or inscriptions have been found. When the coffins were conserved and opened, they revealed not mummies but pieces of pottery, linen, and natron—all materials used in mummification. In addition to the coffins, 28 large storage jars were found, and they, too, contained bits of linen, natron, and pottery—leading Egyptologists to speculate that KV 63 was the burial of an embalmer's cache and not an actual tomb.

| KV Tomb Number and King | King Mythological Decoration |
| --- | --- |
| KV 1 Ramses VII | Book of Gates, Book of Caverns, Book of Earth |
| KV 2 Ramses IV | Litany of Re, Book of Gates, Book of the Dead, Book of Caverns |
| KV 5 Sons of Ramses II | Damaged |
| KV 6 Ramses IX | Amduat, Litany of Re, Book of Gates, Book of the Dead |
| KV 7 Ramses II | Damaged |
| KV 8 MernePtah | Litany of Re, Amduat, Book of Gates, Book of the Dead |
| KV 9 Ramses VI | Book of Gates, Amduat, Litany of Re, Book of Caverns, Book of Heavens, Book of the Earth |
| KV 10 Amenmesse | Litany of Re |
| KV 11 Ramses III | Amduat, Litany of Re, Book of Gates, Book of the Dead |
| KV 14 Tausret/ Setnakht | Book of the Dead, Book of Gates |
| KV 15 Seti II | Litany of Re, Amduat, Book of Gates |
| KV 16 Ramses I | Book of Gates |
| KV 17 Seti I | Litany of Re, Amduat, Book of Gates |
| KV 18 Ramses X | Incomplete |
| KV 20 Hatshepsut | Amduat, fragmented |
| KV 34 Thutmose III | Amduat, Litany of Re |
| KV 35 Amenhotep II | Amduat |
| KV 38 Thutmose I | Undecorated |
| KV 42 Thutmose II | Undecorated |
| KV 43 Thutmose IV | Unfinished decoration |
| KV 47 Siptah | Amduat, Litany of Re |

KV 55 Tiye/Smenkare   Undecorated
KV 57 Horemheb   Book of Gates
KV 62 Tutankhamen   Book of Gates, Amduat
WV 22 Amenhotep III   Amduat
WV 23 Aye   Amduat

**VALLEY OF THE QUEENS** The Valley of the Queens, a necropolis for the royal wives and their children, mainly from the Nineteenth and Twentieth Dynasties, is located on the west bank of the Nile across from modern Luxor. Most of the 75 or so rock-cut tombs have an antechamber, a corridor, and a burial chamber. Many are decorated with scenes from the BOOK OF THE DEAD and the BOOK OF GATES. The most beautiful tomb in the Valley of the Queens is that of Queen Nefertari, wife of RAMSES II. The tomb is brilliantly painted with scenes of Nefertari in the company of the gods, and the queen is also shown relaxing with a board game. Two of the sons of Ramses III, Amen-her-Khepshef and Khaemwaset, are buried in the Valley of the Queens.

**VIZIER** A position of authority similar to a prime minister, the vizier was second in command to the pharaoh and was often of royal or noble birth and picked by the pharaoh. He was the chief administrator of the land in charge of Egypt's legal, economic, and foreign policy. If the pharaoh was a child, as sometimes happened, the vizier ruled in his name until the young king came of age. A record of a vizier appears in the Second Dynasty (2890–2686 B.C.), although Egyptologists now believe a figure on the NARMER PALETTE is an earlier figure. The duties of the vizier are recorded on the walls of the tomb chapel of Rekhmire on the west bank of the Nile. The vizier is shown administering the land and presiding over meetings with foreign ambassadors.

**VULTURE** Sacred to NEKHBET and MUT, the vulture appears in many forms, often with outstretched wings in a gesture of protection. As a decorative motif the vulture appears on the ceilings of temples and in royal jewelry design. The URAEUS on TUTANKHAMEN's golden mask has Nekhbet, the vulture goddess of UPPER EGYPT, and WADJET, the cobra goddess of LOWER EGYPT, as the royal insignia.

**WADJET** (Buto, Edjo, Udjat, Wadjyt) The cobra goddess of Lower Egypt (north), Wadjet protected the Delta and was the patron goddess of the town of Buto, which also was the mythological location where Isis gave birth to her son, Horus. Mythology tells us that Wadjet wove stalks of papyrus into a screen in order to hide Isis and her child from the evil god Set. In the Book of the Dead, Wadjet protects the souls of the deceased by destroying their enemies in the Underworld. Nekhbet, the vulture goddess, was Wadjet's twin sister and guardian of Upper Egypt in the south.

*WADJ WER* An Egyptian phrase meaning "the great green," the *wadj wer* refers to the abundance or fecundity of the Nile god Hapi. The *wadj wer* is the mythological site, mentioned in the papyrus Ramesseum VI, as an area to be crossed on foot rather than by boat. It is perhaps a reference to the swampy marshland of the Delta. The Mediterranean Sea was also called the *wadj wer*.

**WAR GODS** See Anhur, Baal, Montu, and Reshef.

*WAS* SCEPTER A sign of authority, the *was* scepter had a long wooden shaft with the head of a canine animal said to represent Set. The scepter is most often associated with Ptah but frequently is an emblem of the gods in funerary scenes where it symbolized the well-being of the mummy. During the Middle Kingdom, a *was* scepter was sometimes placed next to the mummy in the tomb. The *was* scepter was also an emblem for the city of Thebes (Waset).

**WATERS, PRIMORDIAL** (Waret) See Nun and primeval mound.

**WEAVING** In the Isis and Osiris myth, when Osiris brings farming to humankind, Isis teaches the people the art of weaving. Another myth says that Neith, the goddess of war, was the inventor of weaving and that she oversaw the preparation of mummy bandages made from strips of linen. Tayet, the goddess of weaving, was also associated with funerary rites and mummy bandages.

**WEIGHING OF THE HEART CEREMONY** Chapter 125 in the Book of the Dead describes one of the most dramatic encounters for the deceased on his or her quest to enter the Netherworld. The Weighing of the Heart Ceremony is a second judging that occurs after the deceased has passed through the Hall of Double Truth. Illustrations show a balance scale with one side holding the heart of the deceased and the other side holding *maat*, the "feather of truth." Thoth presides over the ceremony, and Anubis, the jackal-headed god, acts as the "guardian of the scale": He steadies the side holding the heart while he watches the plumb bob to make sure it is properly balanced.

The heart on the balance scale represented the deceased person's thoughts or emotions, and the feather represented *maat* or "truth and justice." If a

In the Weighing of the Heart Ceremony, the deceased's heart (right) is weighed against the feather of truth (left). Thoth, the Ibis-headed god of writing, records the results. If the scales balanced, the deceased would be admitted to the next world. *(Photo by Pat Remler)*

person had led a good life in accordance with *maat*, the scale would balance and the deceased could enter the Netherworld. If the deceased's heart was heavy with evil deeds and outweighed the feather of truth, it fell from the balance scale into the jaws of AMMUT. A mythical creature with the body of a hippopotamus and the head of a crocodile, the devourer Ammut would consume the heart, and the deceased would go out of existence.

## WEPWAWET

A JACKAL-headed god of UPPER EGYPT, Wepwawet was one of several canine deities associated with funerary traditions in ancient Egypt (see also ANUBIS). His name means "opener of the ways," and he protects the PHARAOH both in life and after death. Wepwawet's titles are "Lord of Abydos," "Lord of the Necropolis," and, as the local NOME GOD for the thirteenth nome in Upper Egypt, he was called "Lord of Zauty."

Wepwawet is often shown on a standard, and during the MIDDLE KINGDOM, a standard of Wepwawet was carried in procession before the king. A STELE in the Sinai (eastern desert) calls Wepwawet the "Opener of the Way for King Sekhemkhet's Victory," and the PYRAMID TEXTS say he is as "Re who has gone up from the horizon" as the opener of the sky. Wepwawet is shown in the temple of Seti I at ABYDOS, where he is often confused with Anubis. In a funerary context, Wepwawet assists at the OPENING OF THE MOUTH CEREMONY, and he helps guide the deceased into the NETHERWORLD.

The Pyramid Texts say Wepwawet was born in the *pernu*, a shrine of the northern goddess WADJET. Another myth says he sprang from a tamarisk bush, and yet a third tradition calls him the son of ISIS.

## WERES

The magical headrest AMULET, the *weres* represents the pillow or headrest placed under the head of the mummy. It was often inscribed with a spell to protect the mummy's head: "Their enemies have no power to cut off the heads of the deceased. The deceased shall cut off the heads of their enemies." *Weres* amulets were sometimes placed in the mummy wrappings to magically protect and lift the head. Chapter 125 of the BOOK OF THE DEAD refers to the headrest:

> Thou art lifted up, O sick one that liest prostrate. They lift up thy head to the horizon, thou art raised up, and triumphs because of what has been done for thee. Thou art Horus son of Hathor, . . . who givest back the head after slaughter. Thy head shall not be carried away from thee. Thy head shall never, never be carried away from thee . . .

**WHITE CROWN**   See CROWNS.

## WINDS, GODS OF THE FOUR

Each of the four winds was viewed as a minor god, although SHU was the god of air "who saved all things" in his "form as the pleasant north wind." The COFFIN TEXTS mention Shu and his power over the four winds of heaven. The north wind was called Qebui and was shown either as a ram or a man with four rams' heads and two pairs of wings. When shown as a man, Qebui held an ANKH in each hand and had a four-feather crown on his rams' horns. When he was shown as a ram, he had a single feather on his rams' horns.

The south wind was Shehbui, who had the body of a man with the head of a lion. He held an ankh in each hand and had two sets of wings. On his head was a crown of rams' horns and four feathers.

The east wind was Henkhisesui and had either the body of a scarab beetle with one set of wings or the body of a man with two sets of wings. When he was shown with the body of a man, he held an ankh in each hand. When Henkhisesui had the head of a ram, a single feather sat on his rams' horns, or he had four feathers if he was shown with the body of a man.

The west wind, called Hutchaiui, was shown with the body of a man and the head of a serpent.

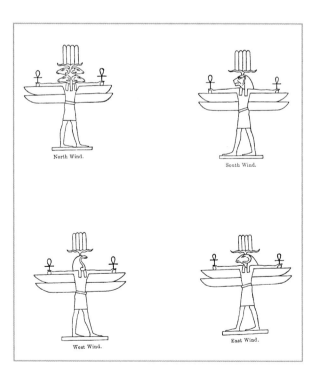

North Wind.

South Wind.

West Wind.

East Wind.

The gods of the four winds are relatively minor gods, but they play an important part in Middle Kingdom Coffin Texts. *(Courtesy of Bob Brier)*

He had two pairs of wings and he held an ankh in each hand.

WINE ⌢▯ In ancient Egypt, wine was reserved for the king's court and the wealthy. Because it was so costly, jars of wine were a worthy offering to the gods. The goddess HATHOR was known for her love of wine, and on her festival days everyone who could drank wine. The PYRAMID TEXTS of UNAS tell us that SHESMU, god of the wine press, gave Unas a vat of grape juice with which to make wine in the next world. The BOOK OF THE DIVINE COW tells us that when SEKHMET was called upon to become the "fiery eye" of the god RE to punish the people on Earth, she overzealously rampaged across the land in search of blood. Becoming alarmed over her thirst for blood, the gods flooded the land with red wine to trick Sekhmet. She consumed so much wine that she fell asleep and her rage was over.

A prayer to OSIRIS, god of the dead, asks that the deceased be looked after by the great god and given wine to enjoy: "May he [Osiris] give water, a cool breeze and wine to thy spirit."

Vivid tomb paintings show the harvest and pressing of grapes. Egyptians used the age-old method of trampling the grapes with bare feet in large vats to extract the juice. A large beam placed across the top of the vat was fitted with several ropes hanging down. Up to six men could work in the vat, hanging onto the ropes so they would not slip and fall into the crushed grapes. Children often encouraged the workers by singing and drumming a rhythm with sticks. As the juice began to flow, it ran out of a spout at the bottom of the vat and into a large container. Since grapes have a natural yeast on their skin, it was easy to ferment the juice by pouring it into clay wine jars about two feet tall and leaving them in the warm sun. When fermentation was complete, the jars were covered with a plug made from mud and straw. While the mud was still damp, Egyptians stamped it with a seal showing the name of the vineyard, the year, and the quality of the wine, from "good" to "very good" to "very very good!"

When TUTANKHAMEN's tomb was discovered in 1922, along with his gold and treasure were 26 jars of wine. Labels on the jars tell us they came from the DELTA's finest vineyards. When the jars were examined it was found that only four of the jars were labeled "sweet." It seems that Tutankhamen preferred dry wine. Some of the wine appeared to be imported from Syria, for some wine jars were a different shape than traditional Egyptian jars, and another batch of wine had the seal of Tutankhamen's grandfather, Amenhotep III. Although tomb paintings show vineyards with grapes varying in color from red to pale rose, we cannot tell today if Egyptian wine was red or white.

Egypt's vineyards were famous throughout the ancient world, with their best wine produced in the Delta (Lower Egypt) and in the oasis in the western desert.

Athenæus, a writer living in Naucratis (an Egyptian city in the Delta whose population was mainly Greek), tells us that one of his favorites, Mareotic wine, was "white, its quality excellent, and it is sweet and light with a fragrant bouquet; it is by no means astringent, nor does it affect the head."

The Greek writer Strabo mentions that "the wine was also known for its long shelf life."

In Egypt, wine was not only made from grapes but also from the juice of pressed figs, dates, and pomegranates. The best wine was reserved for the king and for the gods and appeared on offering tables with the choicest cuts of meat, freshest fruits and vegetables, and loaves of bread. Rarely was wine used to pay the PYRAMID work gangs, but they were often given beer, along with bread and onions. The Egyptian word for "wine" is onomatopoetic and is pronounced "urp"—like the sound associated with a burp.

**XOIS** (SAIS)  The capital city of the Kaset nome (state), whose chief god was AMUN-RE. The goddess HATHOR rose to prominence in Xois when she became associated with the local goddess Urt-Apset. In the myth the CONTENDINGS OF HORUS AND SET, Hathor sent a letter to Osiris in the NETHERWORLD asking him to mediate the dispute on Earth between his son Horus and his brother Set. Osiris's answering letter was sent to the tribunal of gods where they sat in a mythical place called the White Fields at Xois.

**YAMM**  A foreign sea god, Yamm was defeated by BAAL, the Syrian storm god who was master of the sky. Yamm's tyrannical nature and terrible temper are chronicled in a story told by ASTARTE, a warrior goddess of Canaan. Yamm was an unreasonable god and demanded tribute from all other gods, threatening to imprison them if they did not pay. Astarte apparently interceded on their behalf, but the papyrus that records this myth is damaged and the end of the story is lost.

**YEAR, GODDESS OF THE NEW**  Renpet, the goddess of the New Year, was associated with spring, the season that Egyptians called emergence. Her attribute was a long palm frond curving over her head. She was venerated in the city of Crocodilopolis, where she was also worshipped as an aspect of the goddess ISIS.

**YUNI**  One of the most ancient sanctuaries in ancient Egypt, Yuni was the early cult center for the worship of the sun god at Heliopolis (suburb of modern Cairo). It was here that the Heliopolis CREATION MYTH began.

**ZEUS**  A sky god identified with AMUN, Zeus was the principal god in the Greek pantheon. He had power over the weather and controlled the wind, rain, thunder, lightning, and clouds. Like Amun-Re, his powers were immense and he was worshipped as the god of war, the father of games, the god of agriculture, and the protector of the country. Unlike Amun-Re, who could appear as a ram, Zeus was always shown as a man, sometimes with an eagle next to him.

**ZEUS-AMUN**  When ALEXANDER THE GREAT was told by the oracle at Siwa Oasis that he was the son of the Egyptian god AMUN, the symbolic father of Egypt's kings, the Greeks translated the name Amun as ZEUS. Before Alexander's visit to Siwa Oasis, the oracle, or god in residence who answered important questions, was called Amun-Re. After Alexander's visit, Amun along with many other Egyptian gods, became associated with Greek gods, and they were known by both Egyptian and Greek names. The association of Zeus and Amun was an important one, for it assured the Egyptian people that Alexander would honor their gods as well as his own. For his part, Alexander paid special homage to the god that legitimized his claim to the Egyptian throne, and in times of crisis he made special offerings to Zeus-Amun. In Roman mythology Zeus was known as Jupiter, and during the Roman period, the oracle was known as JUPITER-AMUN.

**ZODIAC, SIGNS OF**  Although the signs of the zodiac did not originate in Egypt, the Egyptians were well acquainted with the constellations. Around 2000 B.C., dedicated Babylonian priests studying the night sky recorded the movement of the heavenly bodies. The signs of the zodiac form an imaginary belt in the sky, which was believed to be the path of the sun, moon, and planets as they moved through the sky. In ancient times the Earth was thought to be stationary. By studying the position of the sun, moon, and planets at a specific time, especially at the exact time of a person's birth, a map or horoscope could be drawn that would give clues to the newborn's personality.

SIGNS OF THE ZODIAC

1. Aries.
2. Taurus.
3. Gemini.
4. Cancer.
5. Leo.
6. Virgo.
7. Libra.
8. Scorpio.
9. Sagittarius.
10. Capricornus.
11. Aquarius.
12. Pisces.

The signs of the zodiac form an imaginary line in the sky that the ancients believed was the path of the sun. *(Courtesy of Bob Brier)*

Each of the 12 aspects of the zodiac occupied and ruled a portion of the imaginary belt, and these were known as houses or signs of the zodiac. Each of the signs had specific mythological characteristics, and it was believed that an astrologer, by studying the position of the planets and their relationship to the signs of the zodiac, could predict events in the future.

The belief that the Babylonians could predict the future was a very valuable asset, and word of the zodiac traveled fast in the ancient world. It seems to have arrived in Egypt during the Eighteenth Dynasty by way of the Greek settlers who learned about the zodiac from the Babylonians.

### The Twelve Signs of the Zodiac in Egypt

| | |
|---|---|
| Aries | The Ram |
| Taurus | The Bull |
| Gemini | The Twins |
| Cancer | The Crab |
| Leo | The Lion |
| Virgo | The Virgin |
| Libra | The Balance |
| Scorpio | The Scorpion |
| Sagittarius | The Archer |
| Capricorn | The Goat |
| Aquarius | The Water Bearer |
| Pisces | The Fishes |

In the private tomb of Senenmut, the powerful adviser to Queen HATSHEPSUT, the signs of the zodiac were sketched on the ceiling but never completed. This celestial diagram painted on the ceiling of the first chamber in the tomb is the oldest large astronomical diagram in the world.

Today visitors can see the Nineteenth Dynasty zodiac ceiling in the tomb of Seti I in the Valley of the Kings. The large vaulted ceiling is painted blue, the color of the night sky, and decorated with all the constellations, the stars that form the zodiac, including the North Star and the Big Dipper.

The Dendera Zodiac is the best known of the Egyptian zodiac ceilings. Dendera is a late Ptolemaic temple near the modern town of Qena, and it had an impressive round zodiac ceiling in the Osiris Chapel on the roof of the temple. In the center of the zodiac one can see the front leg of a bull, which represents the constellation Ursa Major, and a hippopotamus, which represents Draco. Forming a circle around them are the constellations Aquarius, Pisces, Capricorn, Sagittarius, Scorpio, and Libra. Virgo, a woman holding a shaft of wheat, is across from Pisces and next to Leo and Cancer (the Egyptian scarab beetle). Gemini is represented as a man and woman holding hands and is followed by Taurus, Aries, and many other constellations that are not part of the zodiac. ISIS and HORUS form the outermost circle and support the constellations with their upraised arms. Bands of hieroglyphs separate the figures and complete the circle.

In 1820, Jean-Baptiste Lelorrain, a Frenchman touring Egypt, was so impressed with this zodiac that he decided to remove the ceiling and ship the large blocks to France. The zodiac ceiling was in the center of three small rooms of a chapel, on the roof of Dendera Temple. Removing the ceiling was a difficult task, for it was carved on two huge blocks, and each one was three feet thick. The local workmen Lelorrain hired had only chisels and saws, and the work progressed

The Egyptians sometimes decorated the ceilings of their temples and tombs with the 12 signs of the zodiac arranged in a circle. One of the most complete zodiac ceilings was found in one of the rooms on the roof of Dendera Temple. *(Courtesy of Bob Brier)*

very slowly. Lelorrain decided to blast holes in the stone with gunpowder so the workmen could insert their tools in the holes left after each blast. Luckily the entire ceiling did not fall to the floor. Still, it was tedious work and took three weeks to remove the blocks that were then placed on rollers and dragged four miles to the river. A boat was moored on the Nile awaiting its precious cargo. At the river bank the heavy blocks slipped off the rollers and the zodiac slipped into the mud. It was only by the heroic efforts of the workmen that the stone slabs were recovered

and placed on the boat. By that time the boat was leaking badly and had to be caulked to prevent it from sinking. At last the boat was seaworthy, and Lelorrain was anxious to be underway. Sensing his advantage, the captain refused to cast off until he had been paid a large bribe. Once the money was paid, the boat set sail downstream for Cairo, only to be set upon by the British, who wanted to take the valuable cargo for England. Lelorrain boldly stood up to his challengers and kept the zodiac ceiling. The treasure eventually arrived in Paris, where it was sold to King Louis XVIII for 150,000 francs. The Dendera Zodiac ceiling was moved to the Louvre Museum in Paris in 1919, and a plaster copy of the ceiling has been installed in the ceiling of the chapel at Dendera Temple.

**ZOOLATRY** The worship of animals. In ancient Egypt, some animals were revered because of their power, like the bull or crocodile. Other animals were thought to be sacred to a particular god, like the cat to the goddess BASTET or the ibis to the god Thoth. When the Egyptians wished to honor the god, they would bring a mummified cat or ibis to the temple as an offering.

During the Late period (747–332 B.C.), Egypt had a religious revival and the people wanted to go back to the old way of doing things. Not fully understanding the relationship of animals and religion during the Old Kingdom, the later Egyptians followed *their* idea of the religion. They held all kinds of animals sacred—beetles, birds, bulls, cats, crocodiles, rams, snakes, and more—and they performed ceremonies, rituals, and mummification for thousands of animals.

When the Greek rulers, the Ptolemies, came to power, they glorified the Egyptian animal cults and fused Egyptian gods with their own Greek gods. The APIS BULL became associated with the new Ptolemaic god, SERAPIS, and they continued to mummify animals by the thousands.

When the Romans ruled Egypt, they carried on the tradition and combined the Egyptian gods with their own. Some Romans misunderstood animal worship in Egyptian religion and viewed the practice with disdain, as is described in the fifteenth satire of the Roman writer Juvenal (c. A.D. 65–128), *On the Atrocities of Egypt.*

**ZOSER** (DJOSER) The second king of Dynasty III, Zoser is best known for his funerary monument, the STEP PYRAMID at SAQQARA. Zoser was considered a living god and was worshipped as the incarnation of HORUS the sun god. Stonemasons mastered the art of quarrying and moving stone by trial and error but soon had the technology to build a grand funerary monument worthy of their king. Zoser's Step Pyramid was the first large stone building in the world and the prototype for all other pyramids. Beneath the

The Step Pyramid was designed for use as Zoser's funerary monument. This statue of Zoser was discovered in the small room on the north side of the pyramid. *(Photograph by Pat Remler)*

pyramid are a maze of shafts and tunnels that lead to the burial chamber, but Zoser's mummy was never found. On the north side of the Step Pyramid is a SERDAB (Arabic for cellar), a small room that contains a statue of Zoser. The inlaid eyes, now missing, were made from rock crystal, alabaster, and obsidian and gave the statue a surprisingly lifelike appearance. Two small holes are carved in the north wall to allow the statue to gaze out on his pyramid complex for all eternity. The original statue of Zoser can be seen at the Egyptian Museum in Cairo, and a replica statue is now in the Serdab.

Zoser extended Egypt's southern border to Aswan and east into the Sinai Peninsula in the search for turquoise, a semiprecious stone highly prized in the OLD KINGDOM. Turquoise was popular throughout Egypt's history, but the only examples we have today are the Old Kingdom butterfly bracelets from Queen Hetepheres's tomb, now in the Egyptian Museum in Cairo. An inscription at Sehel Island (south of Aswan) from the Ptolemaic period, carved by priests of KHNUM, claims that Zoser gave them land south of Aswan. Interestingly, the priests of Isis at the PHILAE TEMPLES claim that Zoser gave the land to them.

# SELECTED BIBLIOGRAPHY

Baines, John, and Jaromir Malek. *Atlas of Ancient Egypt*. New York: Facts On File, 1980.

Barret, Clive. *The Egyptian Gods and Goddesses*. London: Diamond Books, 1996.

Bonnefoy, Yves. *Greek and Egyptian Mythologies*. Chicago: University of Chicago Press, 1992.

Boylan, Patrick. *Thoth, the Hermes of Egypt*. Reprint. Oxford: Oxford University Press, 1999.

Brier, Bob. *Ancient Egyptian Magic*. New York: William Morrow, 1980.

———. *Egyptian Mummies*. New York: William Morrow, 1994.

Budge, E. A. Wallis. *The Gods of the Egyptians*. 2 vols. Reprint. New York: Dover Publications, 1969.

———. *The Egyptian Book of the Dead*. Reprint. New York: Dover Publications, 1967.

———. *Egyptian Magic*. London: Kegan Paul, Trench Trübner & Co., 1899.

———. *Osiris and the Egyptian Resurrection*. Reprint. New York: Dover Publications, 1968.

Bunson, Margaret. *The Encyclopedia of Ancient Egypt*. New York: Facts On File, 1991.

Cooke, M. A. *Osiris: A Study in Myths, Mysteries, and Religion*. Chicago: Ares Publishers, 1931.

Edwards, I. E. S. *The Pyramids of Egypt*. Revised. London: Penguin Group, 1993.

Faulkner, R. O. *Book of the Dead*. Revised. New York: Macmillan, 1985.

Goodenough, Simon. *Egyptian Mythology* (Mythology Series). Todtri Productions, 1998.

Harris, Geraldine. *Gods and Pharaohs from Egyptian Mythology*. New York: Peter Bedrick Books, 1981.

Hart, George. *A Dictionary of Gods and Goddesses*. London: Routledge & Kegan Paul, 1986.

———. *Egyptian Myths*. Austin: University of Texas Press in cooperation with British Museum Publications, 1990.

Hornung, Eric. *The Valley of the Kings*. New York: Timkin Publishers, 1990.

———. *The Ancient Egyptian Books of the Afterlife*. Ithaca, N.Y.: Cornell University Press, 1999.

Johnson, Sally B. *The Cobra Goddess of Ancient Egypt*. London and New York: Kegan Paul International, 1990.

Lichtheim, Miriam. *Ancient Egyptian Literature*. Vol. 1, *The Old and Middle Kingdom*. Berkeley, Los Angeles, and London: University of California Press, 1975.

———. *Ancient Egyptian Literature*. Vol. 2. *The New Kingdom*. Berkeley, Los Angeles, and London: University of California Press, 1976.

———. *Ancient Egyptian Literature*. Vol. 3. *The Late Period*. Berkeley: University of California Press, 1975.

Long, Charles H. *Egyptian Mythology*. http://www.reshafim.org.il/ad/egypt/egyptian_mythology.htm. Accessed August 28, 2009.

Lurker, Manfred. *The Gods and Symbols of Ancient Egypt*. London: Thames & Hudson, 1980.

McDevitt, April. *Ancient Egypt: The Mythology*. www.egyptianmyths.net. Updated March 25, 2008. Accessed August 28, 2009.

Meeks, Dimitri, and Christine Favard-Meeks. *Daily Life of the Egyptian Gods*. Ithaca, N.Y.: Cornell University Press, 1996.

Mercante, Anthony S. *Who's Who in Egyptian Mythology*. Edited and revised by Robert Steven Bianchi. New York: Barnes & Noble Books, 1995.

Millmore, Mark. *Discovering Ancient Egypt*. www.discoveringegypt.com/index.htm. Accessed August 28, 2009.

PBS Online. *Pyramids: The Inside Story*. www.pbs.org/wgbh/nova/pyramid. Accessed August 28, 2009.

Pinch, Geraldine. *Egyptian Mythology: A Guide to the Gods, Goddesses, and Traditions of Ancient Egypt*. Oxford: Oxford University Press, 2004.

———. *Magic in Ancient Egypt*. Austin: University of Texas Press, 1994.

Shaw, Ian, and Paul Nicholson. *The Dictionary of Ancient Egypt*. New York: Harry N. Abrams, 1995.

Shorter, Alan W. *The Egyptian Gods*. Reprint. Thetford, Norfolk: Lowe & Brydone, Ltd., 1978.

Spence, Lewis. *Ancient Egypt Myths and Legends*. Reprint. Canada: General Publishing Company, Ltd., 1990.

Thomas, Angela P. *Egyptian Gods and Myths*. Aylesbury, England: Shire House Publications, 1986.

Vernus, Pascal. *The Gods of Ancient Egypt*. London: Tauris Parke Books, 1998.

Wilkinson, Richard H. *The Complete Gods and Goddesses and Traditions of Ancient Egypt*. New York: Thames and Hudson, 2003.

Witt, R. E. *Isis in the Ancient World*. Baltimore, Md.: Johns Hopkins University Press, 1971.

Zabkar, Louis V. *Hymns to Isis in Her Temple at Philae*. Hanover, N.H.: Brandeis University Press by University Press of New England, 1988.

# INDEX

Boldface page numbers indicate main entries. Page numbers followed by *f* indicate figures.